G000138435

Food and Judaism

A Special Issue of
Studies in Jewish Civilization

Volume 15

Proceedings
of the Fifteenth Annual Symposium
of the Klutznick Chair in Jewish Civilization-
Harris Center for Judaic Studies
October 27-28, 2002

Food and Judaism

A Special Issue of
Studies in Jewish Civilization
Volume 15

Editors

Leonard J. Greenspoon
Ronald A. Simkins
Gerald Shapiro

The Klutznick Chair in Jewish Civilization
The Harris Center for Judaic Studies
The Center for the Study of Religion and Society

Creighton
UNIVERSITY
PRESS

Distributed by the University of Nebraska Press

Library of Congress Cataloguing-in-Publication Data

Food and Judaism/Studies in Jewish Civilization, Volume 15/
    Leonard J. Greenspoon, Ronald A. Simkins, and Gerald Shapiro,
        editors.
    p. c.m—(Studies in Jewish civilization, ISSN 1070-8510; 15)
    "Proceedings of the fifteenth annual Symposium of the Klutznick Chair in Jewish Civilization-Harris Center for Judaic Studies, October 27-28, 2002"
    Half t.p.
    ISBN 1-881871-46-0 (paper)
    1. Food, Jewish—History, criticism, theology, interpretation, etc.
    Congresses. I. Greenspoon, Leonard J. (Leonard Jay), Simkins, Ronald A., Shapiro, Gerald.
    II. Klutznick Chair in Jewish Civilization-Harris Center for Judaic Studies (15th : 2002: Creighton University)
    III. Series

EDITORIAL
Creighton University Press
2500 California Plaza
Omaha, NE 68178

MARKETING & DISTRIBUTION
University of Nebraska Press
233 North 8th Street
Lincoln, NE 68588-0255

Printed in the United States of America

Dedicated to

Rabbi Myer S. Kripke
Dorothy Kripke

Table of Contents

Acknowledgments

"Too many cooks spoil the broth" may indeed be the case in many kitchens. But as we concocted the Fifteenth Annual Klutznick-Harris Symposium— "Food and Judaism," held on Sunday, October 27, and Monday, October 28, 2002—we were fortunate to have the advice and generous support of so many individuals and groups without whom our broth would not only have been spoiled, but would not have made it on to the table in the first place.

We were, first of all, beneficiaries of a tried-and-true recipe, formulated by the original holder of the Klutznick Chair, Menachem Mor, who devised the general format for fruitfully combining the expertise of the specialist with the interests of the general public. Our ingredients, the participants and presenters, could not have been better. To extend the metaphor—I hope not too far!—each was superb in his or her own right, adding a distinctive flavor to the unique mixture that is our Symposium.

But it is the cooks or, better, chefs themselves to whom principal appreciation is due. We are especially grateful that, in the face of changes in personnel at both the Jewish Federation of Omaha and the Harris Center for Judaic Studies at the University of Nebraska-Lincoln, our close, mutually rewarding working relationships with both entities persevered and were strengthened. In a period of considerable transition, staff members of the Federation's Jewish Educational and Library Services (JELS) helped make Oct. 27th, our day at the "J," a great success.

Because food was the topic of the Symposium, we decided to expand our traditional Sunday night dinner to include a wider range of Jewish foods, based largely on recipes compiled by Joan Nathan, and in consideration of a larger number of guests (nearly two hundred sat down to a marvelous meal of some of the most incredible h'ors d'hoeuvres, tapas, and other finger foods imaginable). This accomplishment could not have been made except through the extra efforts of community volunteers Eunice Denenberg and Susanne Richards. Following the dinner, Sunday night's equally delicious keynote address by Joan Nathan was in part underwritten by Eve and Fred Simon through Omaha Steaks International. In addition, many of our guests brought canned goods later distributed to local food banks by Omaha Jewish Family Services.

The leadership of the Harris Center for Judaic Studies at UNL passed from our good friend Jean Axelrad Cahan to Gerald Shapiro, a nationally-known short story writer and gifted professor of creative writing. Gerry's advice was sought and received at every point in the preparation and execution of this Symposium. We also thank former Harris Center administrative assistant Doreen Wagenaar, whose professionalism we greatly relied on and whose friendship we miss.

The steadying hand of several experienced colleagues ensured smooth progress from concept to presentation to the preparation and publication of this volume. Special thanks go to senior editorial specialist and program coordinator Adrian Koesters. As her titles correctly indicate, she plays a crucial and leading role in every aspect of the Chair's activities, and in the preparation of this Symposium and volume we especially relied on her organizational and creative talents. Ronald Simkins, director of Creighton University's Center for the Study of Religion and Society, is, for the fifth time, co-editor of our Symposium volume. We also rely on Ron's calming influence amid even the most difficult of circumstances. Finally, we thank Susan and David Davies, owners of Omaha's Soul Desires bookstore, who provided an exceptionally appealing array of books at all Symposium sessions as well as a gracious presence to our guests.

For the most part, the articles contained in this volume represent presentations at the Symposium itself. Jonathan Brumberg-Kraus substituted his very useful chapter, "Meals as Midrash," for one of his Symposium presentations, and Ori Z. Soltes contributed a chapter on Jewish food and Jewish art.

We are grateful to our benefactors, whose ongoing generosity and support make possible the Klutznick-Harris Symposium:

Dorothy and Henry Riekes
The Ike and Roz Friedman Foundation
Omaha Steaks International
Dr. Jerome Bleicher
The Eve and Louis Wintroub Endowment
Jewish Educational and Library Services (JELS)
The Henry Monsky Lodge of B'nai Brith
The Creighton College of Arts and Sciences
The Creighton Committee on Lectures, Films, and Concerts

This volume is dedicated to Rabbi Myer S. Kripke and his late wife, Dorothy Kripke. Through their example of tireless support for the Jewish community, we are all immeasurably enriched.

For the attentive guest, the best-planned meal contains unexpected treats along with anticipated pleasures. We wish you, our readers, an equally surprising and delightful experience as you begin this volume. And now, "let's dig in."

Leonard J. Greenspoon

Editor's Introduction

I believe I can pinpoint, more or less exactly, the moment when we first considered "Food and Judaism" as the topic for the Fifteenth Annual Klutznick-Harris Symposium. Appropriately enough, it occurred at a meal, specifically a Shabbat dinner, at the home of Mary Fellman, an Omaha resident whose Friday nights combine traditional cooking with an ever-changing, always interesting array of guests, from members of her large extended family to relative new-comers, like my wife Ellie and myself.

After this particular dinner, our hostess and her guests, including Oliver and Karen Pollak (Oliver's essay on cookbooks is included in this volume), began to consider an appropriate focus for the next Symposium, which was to be held in October 2002. Since we had no agenda or preconceived notion of what might make a good topic, the discussion was far-reaching and, if you will forgive the food metaphor, ultimately fruitful. Ellie recalls that she was the first to suggest food and Judaism as the topic. Although, as is often the case when parentage or etiology is at stake, there is some dispute about origins, I am happy to acknowledge Ellie's pivotal role. Not only is she a great cook, the daughter of a great cook and, I presume, one of an even longer line of great cooks, she is also unfailingly creative and perceptive.

Very soon after, other Symposium sponsors gave their assent to this topic. The sheer arsenal of positive puns at our disposal—has a good taste to it, it's something people can sink their teeth into, it's pretty meaty, among others—was often heard early on, with no signs of diminishing as the planning process continued. We did not know then that independent conferences on Food and Judaism have rarely occurred in either the scholarly or the popular realm. Since our Symposia are consciously crafted to bridge the gulf that all too often separates scholars and their scholarship from the general public and its interests, we took special satisfaction in providing a forum for interchange and interaction on the rich and often richly-documented story that links Jews and Judaism with food.

Among the insights our presenters highlighted is the centrality of food within the Jewish tradition. What one eats, when one eats, how one eats, with whom one eats are questions that are at one and the same time simple to answer and amazingly complex to analyze. How was the food gathered or harvested? How, and by whom, has it been prepared? What special provisions, if any, have been taken to ensure separation of milk products from meat, or unkosher items from kosher? Further, what prayers, if any, began and concluded the meal? To what extent does a given meal reflect solidarity with the tradition, including special foods on certain holidays and distinctive rituals to accompany the meal? How much attention is given to regional or local practices and to family customs? What does it mean when a given family or community unconsciously falls away from the food traditions of Judaism or consciously chooses to abandon them—or, more painfully, cannot, because of circumstances, retain them?

Because Judaism maintains a textual basis at its heart, our presenters examined a wide array of written materials, almost all reflecting lived realities. We are brought into close contact with the Hebrew Bible; some of its passages suggest that eating meat is a concession to human nature, with vegetarianism the biblical ideal. We analyze a number of rabbinic texts that deal with vegetarianism, as well as looking at mystical texts that open up to us levels upon levels of meaning and significance in even the most mundane of activities, such as the daily meal or weekly Shabbat dinner.

But it is not only in documents of an avowedly religious nature that we seek guidance. More than five centuries of memoirs, from central Europe to the southern United States, are systematically and profitably mined for narratives and other accounts that show how it really was, in distinction from (and often in opposition to) how traditional sources intended the system to operate. Literary sources, including works of short fiction, add to this tapestry. Menus and cookbooks play a prominent role in filling out the picture of the many interrelations between Jews and food. It soon becomes apparent that "Jewish" cooking is not always identical to kosher cooking. Either through ignorance, lack of concern, or confusion, many "Jewish" cookbooks have included recipes that incorporate unkosher items or mix milk and meat products.

The papers in this volume demonstrate that our presenters have indeed searched out rare morsels of knowledge, many of which are presented here for the first time; they are as well chroniclers of people and events, some well known, others relatively obscure prior to publication of this volume. The scholars we present here have adopted, adapted, and devised many interpretive schema and have proffered a wealth of judgments about their findings. Readers of this volume will find that its editors have made no effort to impose any "party line" or yardstick in the presentation of these materials.

Like the courses in a good meal, each chapter in this volume deserves to be savored in its own right and in its own way. Not every dish is to everyone's taste, but each is worthy of at least a sampling. If a good meal leaves one satisfyingly full, but nonetheless ready for more in due course, then this volume should, at the very least, whet one's appetite and encourage more "consumption"—as a reader and as a gourmet—of what is sampled here.

A word on the organization of this volume: we begin with an essay by Joan Nathan, the well-known food historian, cookbook author, and television personality. She presented the Symposium keynote address on Sunday evening, which also serves as the perfect introduction to the volume. The last essay by Jenna Weisman Joselit is based on her Monday luncheon keynote presentation. A gracious, lucid, and informative account of kashrut in modern America, it provides the ideal conclusion to this collection. The remaining fifteen essays are organized in chronological order, from the most recent to those dealing with antiquity. This order is not exact, inasmuch as several essays cover more than one era. Ordering the chapters (more or less) chronologically is fairly standard in volumes of this sort; nonetheless, it may strike some as odd to make use of reverse chronology. I have no deep theoretical or theological imperative for making this choice. Rather, it reflects one of my most pleasant childhood food memories; namely, the day when, at overnight camp, our first meal began with dessert from dinner and our last meal ended with breakfast cereal. The lesson learned: no matter how it comes to you, it's all good (or, in the case of camp food, not so good), but varying the order of presentation and eating cannot help but provide novel and even noteworthy insights and experiences.

Leonard J. Greenspoon
Omaha, Nebraska
July 2004
ljgrn@creighton.edu

Contributors

Ruth Abusch-Magder

Maplewood, NJ
rutham@comcast.net

S. Daniel Breslauer

Department of Religious Studies
University of Kansas-Lawrence
Lawrence, KS 66045
barsela@ku.edu

Jonathan D. Brumberg-Kraus

Department of Religion
Wheaton College
Norton, MA 02766
jkraus@wheatonma.edu

Marcie Cohen Ferris

Curriculum in American Studies
University of North Carolina Chapel Hill
Chapel Hill, NC 27599
marcieferris@nc.rr.com

Cara De Silva

New York, NY
cara_cara@earthlink.com

Maria Diemling

School of Hebrew, Biblical, & Theological Studies
Trinity College Dublin
Republic of Ireland
m_diemling@mac.com

Joel Hecker

Reconstructionist Rabbinical College
Wyncote, PA 19095
joelhecker@comcast.net

Eve Jochnowitz

New York, NY
eqj9203@nyu.edu

Jenna Weissman Joselit

New York, NY
joselit@princeton.edu

David Kraemer

Jewish Theological Seminary
3080 Broadway
New York, NY 10027
dakraemer@JTSA.edu

Allan Nadler

Drew University
Drew, NJ 07940
anadler@drew.edu

Alice Stone Nakhimovsky

Department of Russian
Colgate University
Hamilton, NY 13346
Anakhimovsky@mail.colgate.edu

Joan Nathan

c/o Royce Carlton, Inc.
New York, NY 10017
Nathan4221@aol.com

Oliver B. Pollak

Department of History
University of Nebraska at Omaha
Omaha, NE 68182
obpomni@aol.com

Gary A. Rendsburg

Department of Jewish Studies
Rutgers University
New Brunswick, NJ 08901
grends@rci.rutgers.edu

Ori Z. Soltes

Washington, DC 20036
orisoltes@aol.com

Brannon Wheeler

Near Eastern Languages and Civilization
University of Washington
Seattle, WA 98195
wheelerb@u.washington.edu

Food and Judaism

Studies in Jewish Civilization,
Volume 15

Proceedings
of the Fifteenth Annual Symposium
of the Klutznick Chair in Jewish Civilization-
Harris Center for Judaic Studies
October 27-28, 2002

A Social History of Jewish Food in America

Joan Nathan

With nearly six million Jews, the United States is the major cultural center of the Jewish Diaspora. In many ways, it is also the culinary center of the Diaspora. Not only has America welcomed Jewish immigrants from all over the world, but it has also incorporated their foods into the American diet. Because this country's culinary traditions are always evolving, Americans are equally at home with Italian pizza, Chinese wontons, and Jewish bagels.

Throughout their wandering history, Jews have adapted their lifestyles to the local culture. Food is no exception. But because they have lived in so many places, there is no single "Jewish" food, other than matzo, haroset [the Passover spread], and cholent and *chamin* [the Sabbath stews that surface in different forms in every land where Jews have lived]. Instead, Jews have relied on local ingredients, developing regional dishes in accordance with their dietary laws.

In the same ways that they adapted other aspects of their lives to the culture of their new home, immigrants to America adapted most of their foods. In so doing, it is fair to assert that they also enriched their adopted homeland. Sweet challah, overstuffed deli sandwiches of pastrami and corned beef, large bagels filled with cream cheese and lox, New York cheesecakes, and even bagel sushi (rice wrapping wasabi, lox, and cream cheese) are today as American as apple pie. Once in America, most Jewish colonists observed the laws of kashrut in their homes. Some of their dishes, like cod or haddock fried "Jewish style" (in olive oil, not lard), soon became popular among non-Jews.

But not all foods that Americans consider Jewish are Jewish in origin. More than two-thirds of the six million Jews in America today can trace their roots to greater Poland, which includes parts of Austria and Hungary (Galicia), the Ukraine, and Lithuania. Russian Jewish food as it came into its own with the arrival of these immigrants. These Jews brought with them many dishes from these countries; for example, herring in sour cream, rye bread, gefilte fish, borscht, and bagels. Despite being identified here as Jewish, none of these dishes would be labeled "Jewish food" in European countries, since everybody ate them. But because Jewish immigrants introduced them to America, they have been labeled Jewish.

Like other immigrants to this country, Jews went through several stages in the preservation and adaptation of their culinary culture. The first generation brought the traditions of the past with them. Depending upon how they felt about their Jewishness and the degree to which they wanted to assimilate, they cherished, rejected, or modified the cooking and cuisine from home as well as their dietary laws. For second- and third-generation American Jews, what was once daily subsistence became a special occasion food. For example, in Europe, knishes, like kugels and latkes, provided the poor with a way to vary the daily monotony of potatoes. Here, during the sweatshop era in New York's Lower East Side at the turn of the century, knishes, a portable food like pasties—the small lunch-time potato- and meat-filled pies of Welsh ironworkers—were eaten for lunch every day. Thereafter, these foods disappeared as daily fare. Now they are in vogue again, reappearing in miniature form as hors d'oeuvres at weddings and other ceremonial events and as fast-food snacks.

As "scientific" foods like vegetable shortenings and shortcut foods like phyllo dough became available to the Jewish housewife and, currently, as "healthy" has replaced "heftiness," some traditions, like rendering *schmaltz* [chicken fat] or stretching strudel dough by hand, have become obsolete even within the Orthodox community. Yet the members of later generations often want to return to their roots, leading them to question their elderly relatives or track down cookbooks in search of original recipes. In the 1990s, for example, many *baalei tshuvah,* or returnees to the faith, began to transform Jewish food. These Jews, often from nonobservant homes, study orthodoxy and are creating a new kosher cuisine mindful of new health guidelines.

The story of Jewish food in America begins three hundred and fifty years ago, in 1654, when twenty-three Sephardic Jews arrived in New Amsterdam (what is now New York City). After being expelled from the Iberian Peninsula in 1492, Sephardic Jews fled to Greece, the Middle East, England, the Netherlands, and the Americas. This small New Amsterdam band first sought haven from the Spanish Inquisition in Recife, Brazil. While there, they discovered and adopted exotic and unfamiliar foods, such as sugar, molasses, rum, vanilla, turkeys, chocolate, peppers, corn, and tomatoes, as well as kidney and string beans.

Sephardic cuisine set the tone for Jewish food in America during colonial America's early history. Because many of the colonial Jews' foods were holiday foods, bound for centuries to tradition, they were the last to change during cultural and culinary assimilation in America. Allspice or hot pepper might have been added to a fish or meat stew by Jews in Brazil or in the West Indies, but the basic recipes of stew and fish fried in olive oil, beef and bean stews, almond puddings, and egg custards come directly from the Iberian peninsula and represent the most authentic Sephardic foods we know in the U.S. Esther Levy's *Jewish Cookery,* the first kosher cookbook in America, appeared in Philadelphia in 1871 and included many of these old recipes.

At the same time that Sephardic Jews were setting the tone for Jewish cuisine on the East Coast, the descendants of crypto, or hidden, Jews who had fled the Inquisition were settling in the Southwest. They had come from Mexico in the sixteenth century, even before the New Amsterdam group. Anthropologists are now discovering that crypto Jews retained many of their three-centuries-old cultural and culinary traditions, which they continued to practice in secret. Many of their present-day descendants have no idea of the origin of these customs.

Before Jewish communities developed, most Jewish men learned how to slaughter meat according to the dietary laws. My favorite story of this period centers on Mordecai Sheftel, a prominent Jew during the Revolutionary period in Georgia. His friend George Wereat wrote him a letter, telling him to visit, but to bring his knife because he was fattening a sheep and wanted him to partake of it. If they did not learn, they went without meat. As opportunities arose, some of these kosher butchers who lived on the Atlantic seacoast expanded their businesses and became merchants.

Between 1830 and 1880, many Jews from Germanic lands arrived in the United States. While early American Jewry settled along the Atlantic Coast, after 1830 the second wave of immigrants forged westward, crossing the mountains to the Ohio and Mississippi rivers. Many, like Levi Strauss, strapped packs on their backs and traveled all the way across the continent to San Francisco, peddling as they went. Jews have always been peddlers, selling wares that could easily be packed up when they were expelled from a country. In America, they became a familiar sight in the countryside before mail order catalogues, like the Jewish Sears Roebuck, put them out of business.

Food, especially kosher food, posed a problem for them when they were traveling. Peddlers would often roast herrings, wrapped in newspaper over an open fire, or subsist on preserved or hard-boiled eggs and kosher sausage for as long as those supplies lasted. As a result, they came to be called egg-eaters by non-Jews. On Saturdays the men created Sabbath communities in little towns where they met to pray. Often, as they made a little money peddling, they would buy a wagon and eventually settle in these communities, sending for their families in Europe or back in New York. Of the ten million immigrants to this country between the years 1830 and 1880, three million were Germans and 200,000 were Jews from German-speaking lands. The most important German-Jewish center of commerce, culture, and cuisine was Cincinnati, Ohio. By 1872 Cincinnati had nine schochetin [kosher slaughterers], five Jewish restaurants, sixteen abattoirs for kosher meat, and three matzo bakeries.

Until World War I, German immigrants-Jews and non-Jews alike-thought of their native culture as superior to that of America. By the end of the nineteenth century, these Jews had become American-German-Jewish. This tri-ethnicity played itself out in both culture and cuisine. In Jewish homes, foods like chicken noodle or vegetable soup, roast chicken, and goose graced the tables for Friday night dinner or Sunday lunch when the entire family gathered together. Because baking had reached a more sophisticated level in Germany than it had in the United States at that time, these immigrants brought with them marvelous kuchen, breads, and tortes. In addition, as whole Jewish communities from Bavaria emigrated, they carried their own German regional recipes such as *lebkuchen* or *dampfnudeln*, a wonderful brioche-like cake soaked in caramel and served with a vanilla sauce. Surely it was no coincidence that Cincinnati became the home of Fleischmann's yeast and Crisco, a vegetable-based shortening for which, according to Procter and Gamble's advertisements, the Jews had waited four thousand years.

However, in nineteenth-century America, both traditional Jews and those wanting a more "enlightened American Judaism" were having a hard time. Since laws prohibited shops from being open on Sunday, Jews usually had to keep their shops open on Saturday and often either postponed their Sabbath meals to Sunday dinner or had a Friday evening get-together. As a result of these and other accommodations with which

American Jews were faced, Isaac Mayer Wise, the leader of the reform movement of Judaism, called for many changes in the old order of Orthodoxy: for women to come down from the balcony, for hats to come off in the synagogue, and for many people to realize that the dietary laws were an archaic relic of the past. He himself started eating oysters.

Wise's ambivalence toward the laws of kashrut and the growing gap within the Jewish community with regard to dietary laws contributed to an event that has become known as the "Trefa Banquet," which led to the final schism between traditional and American Reform Jews. On July 11, 1883, the graduation of the first class of American rabbis was celebrated with an eight-course dinner for two hundred people at the Highland House in Cincinnati. Terrific excitement ensued when two rabbis rushed from the room: littleneck clams had been placed before them as the first course.

While Reform Jews tasted American produce, their own family recipes were becoming regionalized. In Mississippi and Alabama, pecans replaced almonds in tortes and cookies; in Ohio, molasses or brown sugar replaced honey in schnecken; in the state of Washington, salmon appeared instead of carp in gefilte fish on Northwest Sabbath tables; and in Louisiana, hot pepper and scallions were used instead of mild ginger in matzo balls. Crossover foods were already beginning to affect the non-Jewish public as well, appearing with greater frequency in mainstream nineteenth-century American cookbooks. The introduction to *Smiley's Cook Book and Universal Household Guide,* published in 1901, notes: "Jewish cookery is becoming much like that of their Christian neighbors, as, except among the more denominationally strict, the old restrictions are melting away."

Between 1881 and 1921, approximately 2,500,000 Jewish immigrants from Eastern Europe entered the United States. With European pogroms, forced military conscription, lack of civil rights, periodic expulsion from towns and villages, and displacements due to the industrialization of the 1870s, millions of Jews sought a freer life in America. Not surprisingly, even on the journey over, food became a major issue for the Orthodox immigrants. Not all passengers of course observed the dietary laws. Many were radicals who rebelled against this Orthodoxy.

During this period, entire Jewish communities were often transplanted together, including the rabbi and the schochet. They crowded into New York's Lower East Side, Chicago's West Side, Boston's North End, and south Philadelphia. At one time there were almost four thousand kosher butcher shops in New York City alone. The immigrants were successful at finding work and housing and became a part of a network of familiar social and cultural institutions, such as *Landsmanshaftn*, the Jewish mutual aid societies that were formed by immigrants originating from the same villages, towns, and cities in Eastern Europe.

As the immigrants adjusted to new food habits, they quickly forgot some of the foods that symbolized their poverty, like *krupnick*, a cereal soup made from oatmeal, sometimes barley, potatoes, and fat. If a family could afford it, milk would be added to the *krupnick*. If not, it was called soupr mit nisht [supper with nothing]. Today, *krupnick* is considered a health food. Bagels, knishes, or herring in a newspaper were taken to the sweatshop, providing a poor substitute for the large midday lunch the immigrants were used to having in Europe, where, then as now, the midday meal was the largest of the day.

Orthodox Jews, sometimes with some difficulty, clung to their old traditions, including kashrut, in the spirit of combating these changes as well as the rise of Reform Judaism in America, where, as we have seen, in most cases kashrut was abandoned. Because most of these newer Eastern European immigrants were so concerned with kashrut, the United States gave them great opportunities in the food business. The butchers, bakers, and pushcart peddlers of herring and pickles soon became small-scale independent grocers, wine merchants, and wholesale meat, produce, and fruit providers. Furthermore, not only did these immigrants go into the business of food, but they also adapted their Eastern European foodways to the new environment. Sunday, for example, as a second day of rest, provided them with new gastronomic opportunities like the dairy brunch, an embellishment of their simple dairy dinners in Europe.

Cooking and women's roles in the kitchen changed dramatically from the 1880s to the 1930s. Not only did women gain the right to vote, but the first national Jewish women's organization, the National Council of Jewish Women, was founded in the fall of 1893 as an outgrowth of a national Jewish women's congress. By 1900, the 7,080 members in fifty-five cities helped support the rights of women, mission and industrial schools for poor Jewish children, free baths in Kansas City and Denver, and of course cooking classes in the settlement houses.

Council cookbooks, like The Settlement Cook Book, were promoted nationwide, with proceeds of sales going to help support these projects. As with The Settlement Cook Book, most of these books had a German slant and included many goose recipes as well as other American dishes such as chicken chow mein, often made from leftover chicken soup, and Saratoga chips, a turn-of-the-century potato chip. Other organizations followed suit. In September 1905, for example, the Montefiore Lodge Ladies of the Hebrew Benevolent Association of Providence, RI, published the following in its newsletter: "It was voted that 'this lodge publish and sell a cookbook of favorite recipes.' Two separate committees were appointed, one for the cooking recipes and the other to solicit advertising."

While the women's organizations were working to help the less fortunate, another revolution was taking place: that of food technology and scientific discovery. Slowly the kitchen was transformed, liberating women from time-consuming, labor-intensive chores. Not only was Heinz producing its bottled ketchups and other fledgling companies making their kosher canned foods, but many food companies were also manufacturing that white vegetable substance resembling lard that came to be known as shortening, an ingredient that would change forever the way Jews cooked. The invention of cream cheese, rennet, gelatin, junket, Jell-O, pasteurized milk, Coca-Cola, nondairy creamer, phyllo dough, and frozen foods would all affect the amount of time spent in the kitchen and thus the way Jews cooked in America.

With the growth of food companies, delicatessens, school lunch programs, and restaurants, both American food generally and American Jewish food in particular became more processed and more innovative. In 1925, the average American housewife made all her food at home. By 1965, 75 to 90 per cent of the food she prepared had undergone some sort of factory processing. Today, Jewish consumers can buy almost everything prepared.

As the latest wave of Eastern European Jews became more Americanized, their food choices began to reflect this emerging phenomenon. They tried new dishes like macaroni and cheese and canned tuna fish casseroles. Jewish cookbooks included recipes for Creole dishes, chicken fricassee using canned tomatoes, and shortcut kuchen using baking powder. In terms of kashrut, many Jews cared little about the import of scientific discoveries on it, but others cared deeply. At the turn of the century, the Union of Orthodox Jewish Congregations, the umbrella organization for Orthodox Jews, was established as a means of bringing cohesion to the fragmented immigrant Jewish populations. In 1923, the year it created its women's branch, four years after women won the right to vote, the Union's official kashrut supervision and certification program was introduced.

At about that time, a New York advertising genius named Joseph Jacobs encouraged big companies to advertise their mainstream packaged products in the Yiddish press. Jacobs' mission was to change the way Americans thought about Jewish dietary practices. Up to this point, that had been a problem, since the chains and the big food companies who employed no Jews did not know how to attract the Yiddish-speaking population. Jacobs decided to approach Joel Cheek, the founder of Maxwell House Coffee. Cheek, who had started selling his coffee from saddlebags off a horse in Tennessee, was searching for ways to expand his East Coast market. Jacobs suggested to him the Jewish Passover clientele. For some reason, Eastern European Jews thought that coffee beans, like other beans, were forbidden during Passover. Jacobs consulted a rabbi who told him that coffee beans were technically berries and, therefore, kosher for Passover. After the rabbi approved Maxwell House, Jacobs hired men to go into independent stores with the coffee. The merchants were delighted to sell the coffee, which became such a success that in 1934 the company started producing Maxwell House Haggadahs for Passover, another Jacobs idea.

When canned products like H.J. Heinz Company's baked beans and pork came on the market, an inventive advertising man named Joshua C. Epstein, an Orthodox Jew, thought it would be useful and lucrative if Heinz made kosher vegetarian baked beans. Company officials liked Epstein's suggestions but they balked at the idea of writing the word "kosher" in Hebrew or English on the package. "Heinz wanted something identifiable, but not too Jewish: they didn't want to antagonize the non-Jewish population," recalls Abraham Butler, the son of the late Frank Butler, Heinz's first mashgiach [kashrut supervisor]. Thus was born the Orthodox Union "U" symbol, today the best-recognized trademark of the some 120 symbols for kosher certification.

Jews themselves entered the packaged food industry, and some food merchants struck it rich. One Jewish food manufacturer, faced with a bumper crop of oranges, invented concentrated frozen orange juice. A Chicago baker named Charley Lubin made a luscious cheesecake; in the spirit of the new age of frozen food, he tried freezing his cake. The experiment was a success, and Lubin named the product "Sara Lee" after his daughter, giving birth to one of the most extraordinary triumphs of food marketing to date. The fast-growing influence of radio and television also affected how Americans saw each other and how products were sold. "The Goldbergs," a program about a fictional Bronx family, reached a radio audience of ten million people in the 1930s, and at least forty million two decades later on television. Just as the film I Remember Mama taught the country about Scandinavians, "The Goldbergs" familiarized non-Jews with a simple, everyday Jewish family. Sometimes Molly Goldberg just cooked throughout the whole program, cutting up a chicken, chopping fish or herring, as the problems of her family paraded through her kitchen.

After World War II another "cooking lady" stepped onto television. Her name was Edith Green, whose popular "Your Home Kitchen" ruled the airwaves in the San Francisco Bay area from 1949 to 1954. Although this "queen of the range" was Jewish, her cooking was "American" and it was "gourmet." A week's recipes might include veal scallopini, coffee chocolate icebox cake, coconut pudding, or frozen tuna mold. She showed her viewers how to use new gadgets, such as electric mixers and electric can openers, all products of the post-war period of affluence.

As Jews became more Americanized, notions of "Jewish food" changed with the availability of regional ingredients. Taste buds adjusted to local spices and new dietary guidelines. While Jews in Burlington, Vermont, ate potato latkes with maple syrup, Californians preferred theirs with local goat cheese. Gefilte fish was made with whitefish in the Midwest, salmon in the far west, and haddock in Maine. Matzo balls, gefilte fish, and even the Passover desserts American Jews eat today are certainly very different from those eaten in Europe or in this country a century ago.

More recent Jewish immigrants to the United States from places other than Eastern Europe have also helped shape Jewish food in America. When Sephardic Jews from Syria and Turkey came to the U.S. at the beginning of the twentieth century, most American Jews already knew about knishes and pirogi. But as new immigrants came, they taught the old immigrants about other "Jewish" finger-food pastries. Syrian Jews brought cheese *sambousek* [small fried savory pastries] and date *adjwah* [butter cookies], and Turkish Jews brought eggplant *burek* [another filled pastry using phyllo or yeasted dough].

We sometimes forget that food in the old country was evolving just as it was in the United States. Many older Eastern European immigrant recipes have a culinary lag in this country. Because they were handed down, brought out only for special occasions, they were not changed. In the old country these dishes were constantly evolving. Thus, for example, with the rise of Hitler, refugees from Germany and Eastern Europe fled to America; they brought with them updated version of recipes that had come to this country one or two generations before.

Most of the Hasidim arrived after the war, following their leaders. In 1940, the story goes, the U. S. State Department intervened with the Nazis to allow the Lubavitcher Rabbi Joseph Schneerson and his followers to leave on a train from Germany to Switzerland. Other Hasidim came by harder routes, carrying their belongings in kerchiefs and cardboard boxes. In Brooklyn they resettled their own shtetls, U.S.-style. Now, a generation later, their numbers are expanding, reaching out to assimilated second- and third-generation American Jewish youth, with religious centers in cities coast to coast. Their influence has increased in many areas and with it a newly-increased demand for strict adherence to kosher foods.

Political and economic upheavals brought more Jews who were persecuted in other countries by regimes unfriendly to them in the decades following World War II. In a sense, the creation of Israel itself inspired a worldwide awareness of Jewish food. Now, some of the children of immigrants to Israel are immigrating to the United States. These Mediterranean Jews have enriched the tapestry of Jewish cuisine here. They have contributed new "Jewish" dishes with such treats as Syrian tamarind-flavored meat pies, fresh cumin-accented carrot salads from Morocco, and Israeli falafel. Americans are attracted to their cuisines because of the many vegetable-based dishes they find there, the kind of cooking that is in keeping with American's new dietary trends.

While masses of Jews came to the shores of the United States during pogroms and the Holocaust, others went to Mexico, to Cuba, to China, to Australia, and to Argentina. As political problems swept through these lands, many Jews moved from there to America, or, as they visited relatives here, they stayed on. And they brought still more new dishes with them. With upheavals in the former Soviet Union, a new kind of Russian Jew arrived, one who knew very little about the religion and customs of Judaism, which had been outlawed in 1917. Settling in large cities, converting places like Brighton Beach, Brooklyn, into a new kind of ghetto, they are learning quickly about Jewish foods.

Since the 1980s, kosher food has had an astonishing revival from coast to coast. People responded to an advertisement from Hebrew National Brand's kosher hot dog, which "answers to a higher authority." Many can identify with the fact that "you don't have to be Jewish to like Levy's." To many Americans the word "kosher" has become synonymous with "better" and "safer." But ninety percent of Americans do not even know (nor, seemingly, do they care) that they are buying "kosher" when they pick up a box of Pepperidge Farm cookies or a bottle of Heinz ketchup, only two of the thousands of kosher products that are on the market today.

As mentioned earlier, a modern-day shot in the arm for kosher food has been the increased number of the *baalei tshuvah*, formerly non-observant Jews who, returning to their Jewish roots, observe the laws of kashrut. *Baal tshuvah* restaurateur Sol Kirschenbaum, of New York's Levana restaurant, has introduced his kosher clientele to rare beef and kosher bison. Many of them are also eager to try new, lighter tastes and dishes that they enjoyed before they became kosher. They have welcomed new look-alike products such as mock shrimp and lobster made of pollock, and they prefer radicchio with shitake mushrooms but without the prosciutto. Likewise, the days of preparing heavy, time-consuming traditional Jewish foods are gone. First-class kosher wines are being produced in California and Israel, kosher meals are prepared for all airlines and cruise lines, and the kosher product market continues to expand rapidly.

Although Jews have long been in the food business, only recently did they start to become chefs. Today many second- and third-generation American Jews are cooking professionally. Some cooks, although not observant Jews, swear by kosher chickens. Many non-Jewish chefs have become intrigued with Jewish customs, preparing Roman Jewish menus and even seders in their restaurants. Not only are there many Jewish chefs and Jewish cookbooks today, but whole chapters in professional cookbooks are devoted to cooking for the kosher market.

There are also many kosher restaurants where the word is taken seriously-not just metaphorically, as in kosher-style delis, a term coined in the fifties. You can eat kosher Hunan, Indian, Italian, Moroccan, French—whatever you want—in New York, Los Angeles, and many cities in between. The latest trend in Jewish cooking in America, as in

American food generally, is that cooks are watching chefs for new recipes as opposed to the chefs watching home cooks.

The question for our post-9/11 world is where Jewish cooking will be a hundred years from now. I suspect that if traditions linger, they will manifest themselves on Sabbath and holiday tables. We have a wonderful history of welcome in this country. I hope that this next generation of newcomers will remember their heritage and try to continue it in the foods they cook, bringing out well-worn recipes to show in our increasingly homogenous world that they have a Jewish distinctiveness. Along with good taste, new recipes tell the rich stories of families and cultures that should not be lost.

Works by Joan Nathan:

An American Folklife Cookbook. New York: Random House. 1984.

The Children's Jewish Holiday Kitchen: 70 Ways to Have Fun with Your Kids and Make Your Family's Celebrations Special. Brooke Scudder, illus. New York: Schocken Books. 1995.

The Flavor of Jerusalem. New York: Little, Brown. 1975.

The Foods of Israel Today. New York: Knopf. 2001.

Jewish Cooking in America. New York: Knopf. 1994.

The Jewish Holiday Baker. Emma Celia Gardner, illus. New York: Schocken Books. 1997.

The Jewish Holiday Kitchen: 250 Recipes from Around the World to Make Your Celebrations Special. New York: Schocken Books. 1998.

Joan Nathan's Jewish Holiday Cookbook: Revised and Updated on the Occasion of the Twenty-Fifth Anniversary of the Publication of The Jewish Holiday Kitchen. New York: Schocken Books. August, 2004.

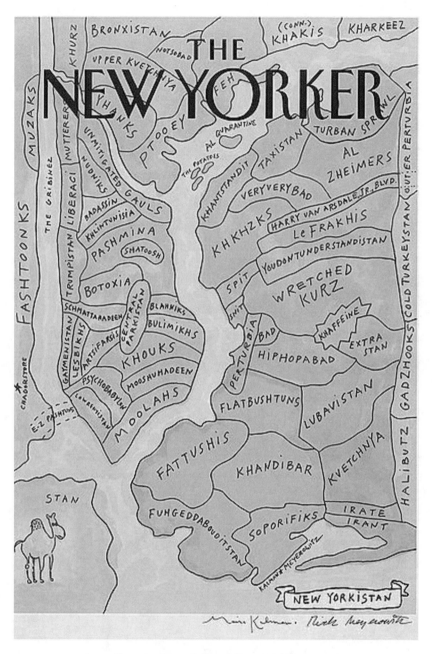

fig. 1: *"New Yorkistan"* illustration in *The New Yorker*
Original artwork by Maira Kalman and Rick Meyerowitz.
Copyright © 2001 Conde Nast Publications, Inc.
Reprinted by permission. All rights reserved.

Smoked Salmon Sushi and Sturgeon Stomachs: The Russian Jewish Foodscapes of New York

Eve Jochnowitz

Since the beginning of the 1990s, a new wave of immigration from the former Soviet Union has dramatically reshaped the gastronomic landscapes of many New York neighborhoods, most notably Brighton Beach, Rego Park, Washington Heights, the Diamond District, and Ocean Parkway. A new culinary infrastructure has sprouted up to provide the ingredients for traditional Russian Jewish cooking in the home as well as in restaurants, bars, coffee shops, nightclubs, and catering halls.[1]

A culinary landscape, or foodscape, is not just the foods alone. It also includes the traditions of display and performance associated with the food. I define a foodscape as consisting of five separate and partly nested personal sites: the mouth, the body, the kitchen, the table, and the street. This chapter will examine each of these culinary landscapes in relation to food venues, anomalous foods, the geography of Russophonic Jewish New York, and the ritual calendar. Stemming from Eastern Europe, Georgia, the Caucasus, and Central Asia, these Jewish communities use food to articulate an intense and intimate connection with place, both the place left behind and the new place created through sensory and social practices. The cuisines of uprooted and rearticulated Jewish communities selectively retain traditions and innovate at each point in the food system. Name, décor, menu, and styles of sociability are among the ways that public eating places negotiate memory, taste, and identity in relation to kashrut and economics.

Hybridization is crucial, but it is also crucial to note that a hybrid does not necessarily fall somewhere between the two parent cuisines. I cannot draw a straight line with Russian or Jewish or Russian Jewish foodways on one end and American foodways on the other, and then point to a spot in the middle and predict or anticipate that Russian

15

Jewish food practices in New York will fall there. Timothy Lloyd studied a case of hybridization in immigrant cuisines in which a traditional Greek meat sauce with some resemblance to Southwestern chili con carne has become a component of a dish associated not with Greece or Texas, but with Cincinnati, Ohio.[2] Similarly, Russian sushi, such as smoked salmon with cream cheese, is a delicacy equally unknown in Russia and Japan. Krishnendu Ray shows ways in which cuisines of the Old World and New converge in the course of a day.[3] Ray has observed that among Bengali Americans, breakfasts are frequently more Western, while the evening meal is more likely to be traditional. I have found in Russian restaurants in New York that frequently the main course is Russian, but dessert is Western.

THE MOUTH

While I am not suggesting that there is any difference between a Russian mouth and a mouth belonging to a person from anywhere else, I believe I can safely make a case that communities of the former Soviet Union use and view their mouths differently than people from other places speaking other languages. Tasting and smelling,[4] chewing and swallowing, speaking, smoking, and spitting, all are performances that distinguish the "mouthscapes," if we may so call them, of a culture. Within the community of recent Russian immigrants, for example, smoking is widely considered acceptable among males. Almost no restaurants enforce the city's smoking prohibitions, and it is common that men will smoke even when food is being served.

THE BODY

The body represents the precise ways in which people see their bodies as needing nourishment (good food) and protection from harm (bad food). Historian Mark Swislocki has noted that a new eating system involves a new concept of what the body is and how it works.[5] He describes those people who participate in two eating systems as "bi-corporal." "In Russian there is no cholesterol," one restaurateur told me. He was partly joking, of course, but in fact it is no joke. There is a very different Russian body, which requires what it requires according to an internally consistent system.

THE KITCHEN

While perhaps not as intimate as the landscape of one's own body, for many cooks a kitchen is a crucially personal place. For Russian Jewish immigrant women, the kitchen is the seat of their power and a safe venue to play out their enthusiasm for innovation while also choosing at times to resist change. As one young woman observed, "We try new things we find here and then we make it in our Russian way."

THE TABLE

Within Jewish tradition the table is a stage for eating and meal-related ritual. For example, different traditions dictate sitting or standing and the proper way of handling salt. At religious or quasi-religious ceremonies in the Russophonic Ashkenazic community, the Hebrew liturgy might be missing, but a variation of the Yiddish wedding song, "*Lomir ale in eynem khosn-kale mekabel ponim zayn, lomir ale in eynem trinken a gleyzele vayn*" [Let us all greet the bride and groom together; let us all drink a little glass of wine together], appears without the reference to the wedding as "*lomir ale in eynem trinken a gleyzele vayn.*" This song has become an almost liturgical fixture as a secular kiddush.[6]

THE STREET

Street food, fast food, cafes, restaurants, and grocery stores comprise a culinary "streetscape." When architect Louis Kahn famously noted, "A street is a room by agreement," he had in mind the synergy created by buildings, businesses, pedestrians, other travelers, and their means of communication. In any urban context the street is a significant theater, and particularly in the Jewish context the street is where observers can most clearly discern the patterns and communications of a neighborhood. The phrase "*di yidishe gas*" [the Jewish street] means not just the street itself, but also what is going on inside the homes and even inside the minds of a Jewish community. In Brighton Beach, as in New York's Hasidic neighborhoods, handbills, posters, and flyers cover the unused walls and fill the windows of retail businesses, informing neighbors about upcoming events and opportunities.

MANHATTAN'S DIAMOND DISTRICT

Manhattan's Diamond district covers West 47th Street between Fifth and Seventh Avenues. No exterior signage marking an office building on West 47th indicates that one of the city's best restaurants is to be found upstairs. No sign displays the restaurant's name, and indeed the restaurant does not seem to have a name. People who know it call it "The Kosher Restaurant," as the legend states on an otherwise unmarked door at the top of the third flight of stairs. The small but sunny space has eight tables. A hand-washing station and laminated copies of the Grace after Meals indicate that the restaurant accommodates strictly observant clients, but many of the men (and the clientele here is overwhelmingly male) are sitting with uncovered heads, indicating that guests follow a diverse range of practices. Almost all the clients are diamond merchants on their lunch breaks; sometimes, a large group will reserve a table for a big meeting. Sometimes non-Russophonic, non-Bukharan, and even non-Jewish colleagues attend, but the spot is not visited by tourists, and, as mentioned, does not sport an exotic-sounding name to engage tourist trade.

The space is pleasant, but clearly one is dining in an office building. The white lace tablecloths are covered with plastic. The dishware is colorfully painted china. The short menu is in English and Russian, featuring salads, soups, and meat dishes. Freshly baked hot flatbread, also called "Turkish bread," appears on the table. The menu is overwhelmingly dominated by meat, but also offers assorted salads, including *baba ganoush* made with mayonnaise instead of sesame. *Kharcho*, a broth with vegetables and cilantro, can be ordered with or without lamb.

WASHINGTON HEIGHTS
The Washington Heights neighborhood is unique in Manhattan in that it is isolated from adjacent neighborhoods by the sharp elevations from which it takes its name. Manhattanites drawing cognitive maps of their island frequently leave Washington Heights out altogether. In this sense, topography is destiny. On 181st Street, Russian markets alternate with Hispanic and East Asian businesses. The stores feature a variety of smoked fish and meats, and packaged foods from Europe. "It doesn't matter if you are here or in Russia," explained the proprietor of one such grocery store, "If you have money, you can get everything."

REGO PARK AND "QUEENSISTAN"
Rego Park is a neighborhood in the triangular area formed by Queens Boulevard, Yellowstone Boulevard, and Woodhaven Boulevard in central Queens, just south of Flushing Meadow Park, the site of the two New

York World's Fairs. It was in fact the 1939 World's Fair that spurred development in this area that had been farmland up until the 1920s.

Rego Park, named for the Real Good Construction Company that began developing the area and its immediately adjacent neighborhoods of Forest Hills and Kew Gardens, forms the region affectionately called "Queensistan"[7] after the names of the central Asian republics of Uzbekistan, Kyrgyzstan, Kazakhstan, Turkmenistan, and Tajikistan [fig. 4]. The Jews from this part of central Asia all identify themselves as Bukharan Jews, after the Bukharan Emirate that controlled the area until 1868. The capital of the emirate was the city Bukhara in what is now western Uzbekistan. Queensistan is home to fifty thousand Central Asian Jews.

OCEAN PARKWAY

Ocean Parkway is neighborhood on both sides of the boulevard from which it takes its name. The Ocean Parkway Boulevard runs five and a half miles from the Parade Grounds at the southern tip of Prospect Park, south to the Boardwalk between Brighton Beach and Coney Island. The two-hundred-ten foot wide parkway has two tree-lined pedestrian malls with benches, gardens, and New York's first and longest bicycle path. It is unusual to refer to an area so long and skinny as a "neighborhood," but the five-mile expanse, which runs through many Brooklyn neighborhoods, is united by the malls and sidewalks along the boulevard, filled with neighbors strolling, sitting, chatting, eating and drinking, reading the paper, or playing cards. Ocean Parkway is an example of a Jewish street which really is a *yidishe gas*.

Many recent immigrants have brought foods and food practices unfamiliar to earlier generations of American Jewish immigrants with roots in these same places. In a butcher shop I visited on Ocean Parkway, meat was displayed in the open on a waist-high table rather than behind glass in a high counter, as is customary at most western butchers. A lady from the "Mountain Jewish" Kavkasi community with whom I went shopping casually patted and palpated the cuts of raw meat lying on the butcher's counter, using her bare hands. A companion who joined us in the store picked up a knife and began trimming fat off the meat as a way of using up nervous energy. These food behaviors are not odd or out of place within the foodscape of Kavkasi Ocean Parkway. This lady's performance is an example of behaving appropriately with regard to food in this particular context. Later, when I asked the butcher for a receipt, he tore off a piece of butchers' paper from the table and scribbled down the amount I paid. "This is an Ocean Parkway receipt" he chuckled, dropping the blood-stained note into the plastic bag I held open with trembling fingers. The butcher's comment, his laughter, and his obvious amusement at my discomfort show that he is not unacquainted with western food behaviors, but that he feels free to reject them in the context of his own shop. Had I been shopping in Baku, or in a store owned and run by a more recent immigrant, my discomfort with handling the bloody paper would not have been as funny because there would be no context for it.

BRIGHTON BEACH

This neighborhood never achieved more than middle class affluence, but the stately loopiness of the art deco apartment buildings that line the blocks between Brighton Beach Avenue and the boardwalk speaks to a kind of aristocracy. The neighborhood was named after an elegant English seaside resort by nineteenth century developers, who hoped to profitably reproduce it in Brooklyn. The boardwalk, forming the southern boundary of Brighton Beach, is one of the neighborhood's main thoroughfares. It is lined with restaurants that offer ample outdoor seating for those who wish to enjoy the seaside and the spectacle of neighbors strolling by. The stretch of the boardwalk from Coney Island Avenue to Ocean Parkway is an utterly urban boulevard, heavily strolled by residents and visitors of every age and background. Brighton Beach Avenue, the main drag of Brighton beach, runs parallel to the boardwalk one block inland. The elevated Q train thunders above a vibrant business street lined with shops, restaurants, and clubs. Factories such as the Golden Chocolate Company make delicacies that could once only be found in the old country or imported.

Primorski

Brighton Beach Avenue is famous for its restaurants. The National, Arbat, and Best Pearl Café all offer quiet intimate lunches by day and music and dancing in the evening. The most famous restaurant on Brighton Beach Avenue, however, is the Primorski. By day one can take advantage of the $3.99 lunch special. In the evening, a night of food, dancing, and vodka can easily exceed one hundred dollars per person. The highlights of the menu are the Georgian specialties such as *Khatchapuri*, a flaky pastry filled with cheese, spinach, or red beans scented with cloves, and *Loubia*, a soup made of red beans, garlic, and walnuts, and Georgian mineral water. Gestures are also made to a kind of pan-Jewish cuisine with the inclusion of gefilte fish and Israeli salad.

Odessa Gastronome and I&M International

Brighton Beach Avenue has countless shops and delis offering delicacies of the former Soviet Union. The two largest and most important are I&M International at the west end of the avenue and Odessa Gastronome on the east. Both of these stores are owned by members of the Georgian community, but offer a range of foods that cover all of Russian and Russian-Jewish cuisine, including some preparations that seem entirely anomalous. Mayonnaise, for example, is a preparation of French origin, but it has been enthusiastically embraced by all Russophonic communities. Many traditional salads are prepared with mayonnaise instead of the oils, sesame, or sour cream that would be called for in traditional Russian or Jewish cooking, where mayonnaise would not have been found before the nineteenth century.

At Russian groceries and delis *baba ganoush* invariably refers to a salad of eggplant with mayonnaise rather than tahini, the traditional sesame paste. These places prepare red cabbage salad and mushroom salads with mayonnaise as well. It is possible, as some claim that one reason for the popularity of mayonnaise as a substitute for dairy-based lubricants is that it complies more readily with the laws of kashrut, which require separation of meat and dairy. I find this unconvincing for a number of reasons. The Ashkenazic community has adopted countless dishes that violate the laws of kashrut, such as the ubiquitous, mayonnaise-swathed *Salat Olivier*, and this still does not explain why mayonnaise should replace oil or sesame paste in non-dairy preparations.

In the context of Russian cuisine, vinaigrette (usually spelled "vinegret" when romanized by Russians into English) is a salad of boiled potatoes and beets. It may also contain carrots, pickles, and oil or mayonnaise. It does not ever contain vinegar. In French the term "vinaigrette" refers to any salad or preparation made with *sauce vinaigrette*, a sauce named for its main ingredient, vinegar. In the Russian food world, "vinegret" means this particular salad only.

Salat Olivier, or *salat stolichnii* [table salad], is a salad made of boiled potatoes, other boiled vegetables (including peas and/or green beans), and meat (boiled chicken, beef or ham), lavishly dressed with mayonnaise. It seems by its name to claim French lineage, and indeed Escoffier and the *Larousse Gastronomique* list a very similar recipe as part of the canon of French cuisine. They call it *Salade Russe*. Escoffier's recipe calls for truffles, lobster, and anchovy filets, not commonly used in *Salat Olivier*, but both versions involve potatoes, peas, green beans, meat, and lavish amounts of mayonnaise. This salad has also appeared in Iranian cuisine, where is called salad *Olivieh*.

Rasputin
The largest and best known of the Russian nightclubs in Brooklyn is Rasputin at Avenue X and Coney Island Avenue in Sheepshead Bay, adjacent to and slightly inland from Brighton Beach, away from the bustle of Brighton Beach Avenue. "A true supper club on the grand scale," as it self-proclaims, Rasputin has advertising and some narration in English, but the clientele is overwhelmingly Russophonic.

FIELD REPORT, NOVEMBER 24, 2000
To conclude, I would like to provide a field report of the actual experiences, ambiance, and protocols of a typical restaurant experience at Rasputin. The venue is enormous, with a circular dining room surrounding a spacious round dance floor. Lights are low, but not so low that it is too dark to see. Most guests have come in large parties, but there are also a few tables for two.

The dance floor displays two elaborately decorated birthday cakes. One, "Happy Sweet Sixteen, Julia," is decorated with a white Cinderella-style slipper, dark and white chocolate, and red roses. Julia's table is also decorated with orange roses and African daisies. The other, "Happy 50th, Piter," is all chocolate and has a chocolate champagne bottle and red and white roses. I cannot think of any venue within the Anglophonic community where a girl of sixteen and a man of fifty would both choose to celebrate their birthdays.

When we arrive at about 8:30, some people are already seated and eating. Our table is already laid with a rich array of *zakuski*, or appetizers: zucchini in tomato sauce, beet salad, boiled potatoes with dill, cucumber, tomato and radish salad, assorted pickles (cucumber, cabbage, carrot, pepper, tomato), grapes, pickled mushrooms, white cheese, chicken breast in sauce, five kinds of cold cuts, and *baba ganoush à la Russe*. An ice bucket holds our bottle of Vodka Kremlyovskaya. As soon as we are seated and begin eating, the procession of hot dishes starts to arrive.

Flaky cheese pastries and *blini* with sour cream and salmon caviar join the cold appetizers.

At 9:30, after most of the guests have been appeased with abundant appetizers and vodka, a bilingual message welcomes us to Rasputin. An electric band begins playing on a raised platform behind a scrim. A female singer dressed in a sparkly metallic dress sings in Russian, and a few couples drift to the dance floor. The next singer, also a woman, sings in heavily accented English and wears a black leather camisole. The waiters bring rice and stuffed chicken breasts with dill, and a male singer in a black leather blazer and sunglasses takes the stage. A trio of women wearing camouflage-patterned uniforms sings an Andrews Sisters' song of the 1940s. A constantly changing parade of costumed singers performs songs in Russian and English, interspersing a few in French and Spanish. Towards the end of the evening, after the floor show, a woman in a skin-tight shimmering black leotard sings *Tum Balalayke* in Yiddish, provoking the most enthusiastic response from the crowd all night.

At 10:30, a PA announcement warns us that we have four minutes to return to our seats for the floor show. The restaurant is plunged into total darkness. Steam fills the room as colored laser lights play across the space. The steam clears and the lights lift to reveal sixteen young women, in clown-face and clown costumes, dancing to a Hip-Hop number played on an accordion. The next dance is a techno piece performed by women in cellophane costumes dressed as robots. A tango number with dancers in fedoras follows, and then, during a brief intermission, we see a speeded-up film of the dancers changing their costumes backstage.

In the second half, girls dressed in yellow and black matador costumes dance to a Spanish song, and a French song is danced by girls in red cob-webby suits reminiscent of the costumes of Jewish silent film vamp Alla Nazimova. The next act, danced by men in cowboy suits, is a bluegrass tune with Russian words. A trio of women, in costumes made of glow-in-the-dark string, dances to Aretha Franklin's "Natural Woman," and the show closes with another hiphop number danced by women wearing neon bungee cords. After the show, credits for the singers, dancers, designers, and lighting roll in English on an enormous video screen.

At 11:30, the main courses arrive at our table: chicken Kiev and chicken and beef kabobs on French fries. The dance floor is packed as the band continues to play and the singers continue their costume changes. At 12:30, we are brought nested coffee cups, carafes of coffee and tea, melon, berries, and apple strudel with chocolate sauce. At 1:00 a.m., a voluptuous woman brings down the house with another rendering of *Tum Balalayke*. The singing and dancing continue late into the night.

The evening at Rasputin is a *gesamtkunstwerk* designed to produce sensory saturation. The lavish overabundance of food and liquor is overwhelming both in its quantity and in its variety. Broadcast flow is jarring, including as it does such an anomalous mix of music, dance styles, and theater. Other than the performance of *Tum Balalayke*, nothing in the program explicitly signifies Jewishness, and the menu is exuberantly *treyf* [non-kosher], but the very weirdness of the combination of styles and genres implicitly signifies Jewishness. The privileged position that the Yiddish song occupies at the peak of the evening and the appreciative response of the audience indicate that it is more than just another element in the multilingual mix of the program. As Anna Sternshis has noted, *Tum Balalayke* has almost liturgical significance for Jews from the former Soviet Union.[8]

ACKNOWLEDGMENTS

Grateful acknowledgment is made to *New Yorker* magazine for kind permission in reprinting this image. Original artwork by Maira Kalman and Rick Meyerowitz Copyright (c) 2001 Condé Nast Publications Inc. Reprinted by permission. All rights reserved.

NOTES

[1] The cartoon map of "New Yorkistan" is funny, but in a way it also is a perfect illustration for this chapter about how the virtual geography of one place maps itself onto a new home.

[2] See Timothy Lloyd, "The Cincinnati Chili Culinary Complex," *Western Folklore* 40:1 (1981).

[3] Krishnendu Ray, "Meals, Migration and Modernity: Domestic Cooking and Bengali Indian Ethnicity in the United States," *Amerasia* 24:1 (1998): 105-27.

[4] Most of the ability to smell occurs via mechanisms inside the mouth. See Linda Bartoshuk, "The Biological Basis of Food Perception and Acceptance," *Food Quality and Preference* 4 (1993): 21-32.

⁵ Mark S. Swislocki, "Feast and Famine in Republican Shanghai: Urban Food Culture, Nutrition, and the State (China)" (Palo Alto: Stanford University Press: 2002).
⁶ See, for instance, "Dust" by Amelia Glasser.
⁷ The term "Queensistan" became widespread after appearing in Sandee Brawarsky's November 16, 2001, article in the *New York Times*, titled, "Central Asian Jews Create 'Queensistan.'" The December, 2001, cover of the *New Yorker* illustrated by Mayra Kalman and Rick Meyerowits, titled "New Yorkistan" [fig 1], mapped the virtual landscape of central Asia onto the five boroughs of New York City.
⁸ See Anna Shternis, "Kosher and Soviet: Jewish Cultural Identity in the Soviet Union, 1917-41" (Oxford: Oxford University Press: 2001).

The Art of Jewish Food

Ori Z. Soltes

THE LAYERS OF JEWISH HISTORY AND CULTURE

Consider the varied ranges of Jewish history. In one sense it begins with Abraham, whom we credit with engendering the spiritual revolution that directs humankind toward one God. But Abraham is called a Hebrew, and obviously many of the details of what we call Judaism—our prayer book, our life cycle and festival cycle celebrations, the Bible we read—did not exist for him and his belief system. He passes a very personal covenantal relationship on to his son, Isaac (as well as to his son Ishmael), who passes it on to his son Jacob—who is transformed, nominally and conceptually, into Israel.

Israel's descendants, the children of Israel, enslaved in and liberated from Egypt, come to accept the written statement of the covenant at Sinai under the leadership of Moses. These Israelites (they are not yet called Jews), define themselves as a unity, both by the idea of descent from a common pair of ancestors and by that common spiritual covenant accepted at the foot of the mountain. Their descendants are formed into a kingdom that breaks into two after three generations; a fragment, two tribes of the original twelve, remain by the time the Babylonians destroy the Temple in 586 BCE.

Indeed, it is in the exile that accompanies this destruction that the Judaeans (as they by then call themselves) begin to reshape their faith. From a focus on the Temple and its sacrifices, they begin to shift toward focus on the Torah and prayer. Even as they return from exile and rebuild the Temple, they continue to hold to the idea that God is accessible in all places where Judaeans gather to address Him. The idea of a *Bet Knesset* [house of gathering], roughly rendered as *synagoge* in Greek and as *congregatus* in Latin, begins to evolve. Not only the general concept, but also the specific architecture of structures in which gathering for prayer and study of the Torah might take place dates from this Second Temple period.

27

Over the centuries which follow the return from Babylonian exile, the Torah also takes the full shape that we would come to recognize; the other biblical books, one by one, gain acceptance as part of divine writ. With them, the contours of celebrating the Sabbath and the festivals evolve further. By the time the Romans destroy the Second Temple in 70 CE, much of what is familiar to us as Judaism has been fitted into place, including the mechanisms of discussion and debate that are the basis for the rabbinical literature that flows out of the centuries which follow. Such mechanisms give to Jewish culture and customs the rich range of variations that one encounters in following its history across time and space.

Between the period of the Roman destruction and our own time, Judaism has been a vibrant, breathing being in large part due to the dynamic tensions between its urge to cling to tradition and its willingness to adapt to new conditions, as also between its continuous apartness from what is around it and its hunger to adopt elements from the civilizations among which Jews have moved and lived. We see the evidence of this in every aspect of Jewish life, from gastronomy to liturgy, from the style and materials of ritual objects to the internal and external shape of the synagogue.

Jewish life, then, has centered on the Torah, and the circles around it have included the biblical, rabbinic, and post-rabbinic literatures that have grown out of it: the Sabbath, the holidays and life cycle events, and the particular aspects of marking them that have evolved in different places and different times.

THE SACREDNESS OF JEWISH GASTRONOMY

If Aristotle, the 4th century BCE Greek philosopher, is credited with making the observation that "you are what you eat," then surely no group has taken that dictum to heart more profoundly than the Jews.[1] The concern for what we ingest is imbedded in the notion of kashrut [from the word *kasher*, found in Esth 8:5 and Eccl 11:6, which means "good" and "proper," eventually applied to objects fit for ritual use and to witnesses fit to testify in a court of law]; as with other aspects of Jewish culture and religion, this concern began to take shape as the foundations for the edifice of Judaism were being laid. To this day, it continues to be formed across the centuries and miles of Jewish history.

Kashrut, as it applies to Jewish eating habits, is established both in principle and in extraordinary detail in the Torah. Indeed, its basis—to whatever extent it may be construed as hygienic or health-related, or a matter of what is available or convenient—is above all a matter of priestly discipline. To be a people apart, one defined by an emphatic spiritual mission spelled out at Sinai, is to accept, among other things, a highly specific set of gastronomic parameters that affects not only the conduct of Sabbaths and festivals, but of everyday life, not only for a spiritual upper class, but for every Israelite.

The precise shaping of so banal an act as that of eating—not only in terms of what may and may not be eaten, and in terms of how, in some cases, what may be eaten must be prepared, but also in terms of ritual and the blessings that frame the beginning and ending of a meal—transforms the dinner table into an altar. As the synagogue is a sacred space that, through most of Jewish history stands for the Temple (to serve, as some believe, the awaiting of the Messiah, the return from exile, and the rebuilding of the Temple), the home becomes a sacred space that may stand for the synagogue, in the sense that it offers its own sacred rituals, the spiritual weight of which can equal the importance of what is celebrated in the synagogue.

But the foundations upon which the edifice of kashrut is built are laid even before the Temple stood, while Israel was still wandering in the wilderness between Egypt and the Promised Land. From the beginning of the Torah, humanity is connected to the land and its produce, through Adam, in senses both positive ("I give you every seed-bearing plant that is upon all the earth" [Gen 1:29]) and negative, after disobeying God's commandment regarding the fruit of the Tree of Knowledge: "Cursed be the ground because of you; by toil shall you eat of it" (Gen 3:17-18). As the Torah narrows its focus on that slice of humanity that accepts the covenant at Sinai, Israel is viewed as "a kingdom of priests, and a holy nation" (Exod 19:6), to whom rain is granted in due season, who will therefore "gather in [your] new grain and wine and oil... [and have provided] grass in the fields for [your] cattle" (Deut 11:13-17).

The Torah, in connecting the people Israel to the land of promise, in sweeping them to the land with Abraham, away from it with Jacob, and back to it with Moses and Joshua, describes it in gastronomic terms. It is both a "land flowing with milk and honey" (Ex 3:8), "with streams and springs and fountains issuing from plain and hill" (Deut 8:7), and "a land of wheat and barley, of vines, figs and pomegranates, a land of olive trees and honey" (Deut 8:8-9). The text thus spells out seven species and not only as symbols of the abiding connection to the land from whatever myriad lands into which Jews have been dispersed. Their very "seven-ness" underscores the promise and responsibility of the covenant, which we celebrate every seventh day and which was accepted at Sinai as our ancestors left Egypt and servitude to seek the Promised Land and freedom.

If the seven-ness of the species of the land carries a redemptive, messianic connotation across Jewish experience, that connotation is reinforced by the expanding regulations pertinent to food that are also set forth in the Torah, forming part of the foundations for the edifice of our sacred relationship to food.

WHAT AND HOW TO EAT?

The foundations of this relationship are in part broadly gastronomic, including a repetition of reminders of what species will be found in the Promised Land and the marvelous and peculiar "bread from Heaven" that tastes like "wafers made with honey" (Exod 16) and is called manna (elsewhere, in Num 11, described as "like coriander seed, and in appearance... like bdellium [a myrrh-like substance]... It tasted like rich cream."). They also describe specific instructions about what may and may not be consumed and how certain substances may and may not be used.

Thus, for example, in Exod 30:37, spices used for religious purposes, especially as incense, are forbidden with regard to other uses, and in Lev 2:13 we are told that meal offerings are to be sprinkled with salt. Above all, we are reminded: "You shall be a holy people to Me: you must not eat flesh torn by beasts in the field" (Exod 22:30), and "you shall not make yourselves unclean through any swarming thing that moves upon the earth (Lev 11:44 — yet, interestingly, some insects are kosher: "the locust after its kinds, and the bald locust after its kinds, and the cricket after its kinds, and the grasshopper after its kinds" [Lev 11:20-23]). Finally, in any case "you shall not eat anything that has died a natural death... for you are a people consecrated unto the Lord your God" (Exod 22:30 and again Deut 14:21).

If nearly all manner of fruit and vegetable are permissible for consumption by people of the covenant, not all fish are: "Anything in water, whether in the seas or in the streams, that has fins and scales, these you may eat" (Lev 11:10-12). As for "land animals: any animal that has true hoofs, with a cleft through the hoofs, and that chews the cud, such you may eat" (Lev 11:1-8). In the case of these animals, how we prepare them for eating is also prescribed: "No person among you shall partake of blood...of any flesh, for the life of all flesh is its blood" (Lev 17:12-14). Thus the manner of slaughter and preparation is implied, in order to assure conformance with the "blood" clause.

Yet we might note that this is implied, not clearly stated. Both the food that we consume as defined by the Torah and the manner of its preparation are elaborated into evolving legislation through the rabbinic discussions and interpretations that follow us down the centuries. Thus, for example, not only the prescriptions of *sh'heeta* [kosher slaughtering] are laid out in those discussions, but the *shohet* [trained butcher] prepares a special knife, the *hallaf*, that is razor-sharp. The animal's gullet and windpipe must be cut in one quick stroke, yielding a quick death. All residual blood is drained off through soaking and salting, and a final inspection determines that the animal was neither diseased nor injured.

The notion of rabbinic interpretation follows in other directions, as well. For example, based on that moment in Jacob's night-long wrestling match when he strained his thigh, it is written that "therefore the children of Israel eat not the sinew of the thigh vein" (Gen 32:33). Thus hind quarter cuts of meat are deemed non-kosher, although technically, if one applies the expensive process of *taybering* [by which the sciatic nerve is removed], some would consider such meat acceptable. In the case of the now-famous Jewish community that once flourished in Kai Fung Fu, China, this gastronomic feature was regarded as so distinct that the Chinese expression meaning "Jews" was "those who do not eat the sinew" [*tiao-chin chiao*].[2]

Nowhere is the matter of interpreting the Torah's gastronomic prescriptions more fascinatingly apparent than in the matter of mixing milk with meat. Exodus 23:19 enjoins us not to "seethe a calf in its mother's milk," an action not many moderns are ever likely to have the opportunity to commit. Presumably, though, the custom of not doing so distinguished the Israelites from their neighbors, for whom the custom was part of their tribes' cult and possibly a highly-favored delicacy.

Rabbinic and post-rabbinic interpretation carries in two directions, one conceptual, the other practical. Conceptually we are first led to understand that such a delicacy represents an act of cruelty inappropriate to the covenantal people. Second, since the process of digestion may be likened to the aforementioned seething process, and since, as the Diaspora expanded, Jews lived in increasingly urbanized settings (where one cannot know from which cow our milk comes and from which calf our meat), and since we are enjoined to "build a fence around the Torah," and since that injunction is often interpreted to mean going beyond the straightforward and narrow meaning of the commandment, as a practical matter we are therefore told to separate meat from milk as we eat.

In turn, this comes to mean separating all meat and milk products, neither cooking them together nor eating them at the same time; in other words, no cheeseburgers! It yields a discussion, based on the determination of how long the digestive process takes, about how much time must elapse between the hamburger we eat and the ice cream we later want to have for dessert: one hour? four hours? six hours? It comes to mean providing separate cooking and eating utensils for milk and meat products, as well as yielding a discussion as to what utensils may be cleansed and shifted from milk use to meat use or vice versa, and which cannot (clay pots, for example, due to their perceived porousness).

All of this is derived from one small thrice-stated passage (Exod 23:19, 34:34-26, and Deut 14:21) and from the seriousness attached to the notion that God's word must not be abrogated at any cost by those who would be a priestly people. Moreover, we are reminded that gastronomic prescriptions are part of the larger picture of priestly discipline and sacredness when we recall that, based on Deut 22:9-12, a range of issues of separating species (not simply milk and meat, and not simply gastronomic) is set forth, including seeds, different kinds of trees and vegetables, domestic and wild animals, wool and linen. The most important factor regarding these proscriptions is that their basis appears to be irrational. As with milk and meat and, ultimately, nearly all gastronomic and many other kinds of legislation, we must interpret so as to find logical reasons for it. In the end we are reduced to the realization that the real reason is simply that it is God's commandment and part of God's unique covenant with his people.

FOOD AND JEWISH LIFE

Over the course of Jewish history and geography, as Jews have dispersed among myriad peoples and as the Jewish literature of interpretation has proliferated through both the time and the space of the Diaspora, the gastronomy that one might term "Jewish" has continuously expanded its range. Wine, for example, is mentioned periodically in not just the Torah, but in the Hebrew Bible at large, from the story of Noah's drunkenness (Gen 9) to Hosea and the Song of Songs. Often the context is one that warns against intemperance, but grapes are one of the marvelous natural products of the land brought back by the spies to Moses, as described in Num 13. A container of wine is later specified as a *neset* [libation] on the altar. As a reminder of the blood-sacrifices in the Temple, red wine has been a centerpiece of ritual throughout the subsequent Jewish Diaspora.

The kiddush [sanctification] is the instrument with which we make sacred our entrance into and exit from the Sabbath, as well as into nearly every festival and joyous life cycle event. Similarly, as we use sweet spices during the havdalah ceremony of Sabbath exit, in an attempt to sensuo-symbolically extend the sweetness of that sacred day into the week, the spices also echo the incense and spices that were part of the Temple ritual. Of course, as the Torah is the beginning and the center of the Jewish discussion of all aspects of covenantal life and as the Tabernacle (and later the Temple) was once the center of (and remains a constant reference point for) the ongoing development of Jewish ritual, the Sabbath is the center of the seasonal applications of that discussion and those rituals. We enter the Sabbath not only with light (recalling the beginning of the order of divine creation through light, inviting us into a day of Eden-like rest) and with wine, but, as with all Jewish meals, with bread. The Sabbath loaf is special. Recalling the twelve shewbreads baked and brought weekly as an offering by the priests, as well as the weekly offering of bread set aside by the people for them, it is called challah, meaning "offering" (Num 15:19-20).

Made of white flour and water, yeast, sugar, and salt, enriched with eggs and shortening, shaped to recall the shewbread, challah has evolved along varied physical lines across Jewish time and space. The twisted, braided style dates, perhaps, from the fifteenth century and echoes the twisted white breads in central and eastern Europe, particularly Poland and the Ukraine. From northwest Africa to the Near East, it is plain and round, ranging from puffy to flat. Elaborate arrangements of twelve rolls developed in eighteenth-century Ukraine, and some Syrian Jews also place twelve small rolls on the table, to symbolize the twelve shewbreads. Indeed the number of challot varies from community to community, but two (to suggest the double portion of manna; or one "to remember the Sabbath day" and one "to keep it holy") is the minimum that one is likely to find.[3]

The Sabbath afternoon meal is special; it is also a special challenge, for, even as it should carry us above the gastronomy of the rest of the week, the prohibition against working on the Sabbath has come to include a fairly universal prohibition against cooking on that day. This echoes both prescription ("You shall kindle no fire throughout your settlements on the Sabbath day" [Exod 35:3]) and narrative action: the Israelites gathered a double portion of *manna* before the Sabbath, so that they would not be gathering it on that sacred day (Exod 16). Variations are thus found across the Jewish world on the theme of a meal in a pot that cooks slowly on its own, to be consumed as the main Sabbath meal: of vegetables and legumes, grains, spices, and sometimes meat or eggs. Not only do the particular additives change from Poland to Turkey, from Tunisia to Italy, but the names vary: *cholent, t'fina, dfina, hamin, scheena, hameen.*

So, too, every Jewish holiday and life cycle event has its own gastronomic specialties and variations. If crown-shaped challot remind us that Rosh Hashanah is the crowned head of the year and any number of variously sweet foods seek to promise us a sweet new year, the Ukrainian bird challot remind us that "as birds hovering, so will the Lord of Hosts protect Jerusalem" (Isa 31:5) as we move through the days of awe and judgment. This may be eaten on the eve of Rosh Hashanah or at the meal preceding the Yom Kippur fast. So, too, a key-shaped challah baked for the Sabbath following Passover offers the hope that the gates of heaven will remain open for the righteous toward the feast of Shavuot and even until the next Passover.

Indeed, Passover, or Pesach, celebrating the deliverance of the Israelites from Egyptian bondage, offers the ultimate exercise in gastronomy as a symbol of culture, history, and spirituality. The central gastronomic aspect of the festival is the exclusion of leavening [*hometz*] suggested by means of interpreting Exod 12:39, where the historical connection is set forth: "They baked unleavened cakes...because they were forced out of Egypt, and could not linger, nor had they prepared themselves any food." Indeed, our consumption not only of matzo [unleavened bread], but also of other Pesach foods, is designed to create a bond between us and our ancestors, whereby the line between past and present is blurred, and a sense of never-ending empathy, reinforcing the covenantal continuum, is defined.

The ritual sensibility that elevates the Passover meal to a sacred act is also underscored by the fact that the meal is referred to as a Seder [an Order] in which everything has its precise place. Not just the ordinary wine of celebration is present, but four cups consumed at four junctures with four conceptual purposes, with a special goblet set out for Elijah, who has emerged over the centuries as the patron of redemption and harbinger of the messiah. Conversely, ten drops of wine ritually removed from our goblets lessen our joy (wine, among other things, symbolizes joy) in a manner that numerologically corresponds to the number of plagues that the Egyptians had to suffer so that our ancestors might go free.

Not just two matzot corresponding to the two Sabbath challot, but a third, both to transform this into something unusual and for a number of other interpretively possible reasons (for example, they correspond to *kohayn, levi,* and *yisrael,* the division of the Jewish people for honorific ritual purposes, that represents the descendants of the high priestly family, the priestly tribe, and everyone else). In the 1970s, a fourth matzo was added in some communities, lest we forgot the Jews still "enslaved" in the Soviet Union. Other foods on the Seder table suggest the bitterness of slavery, the sweetness of freedom, the offerings at the Temple.

Beyond those ritual foods shared across the world, special Passover menus have emerged in different Jewish communities. In the case of Morocco, there is an entire special meal, *maimouna*, celebrated on the eve of the last day of the holiday, in which Jews' Muslim neighbors often participate (and that may be inspired by the special meal that ends the Muslim fast-month of Ramadan). On the other hand, major distinctions exist between the Ashkenazi and Sephardic communities at large: Ashkenazim consider rice to be *hometz* [inedible during the holiday], whereas for Sephardim it is a staple all week long.

OTHER FESTIVALS AND THEIR FOODS

In many parts of the Jewish world, Shavuot, commemorating the receiving of the Torah at Sinai, has come to be celebrated by eating dairy. There have been diverse interpretations for this, from the simplicity of seasonal availability to the arcane connections between the giving of the Torah, the cycle of the agricultural year and the Temple offerings, and the dietary injunctions (especially that of separating milk from meat). Among the particularly noteworthy locale-specific Shavuot foods is the "Seven Heavens Cake" baked in Italian Jewish households, designed to recall Mount Sinai itself.

Sukkot, or the Festival of Booths, celebrates the ingathering of the harvest as it also commemorates the Israelites' forty years of wandering in the wilderness, when their housing was limited to the kind of temporary structures that are built next to Jewish homes for this holiday. The primary foods of this festival are actually not consumed: the sweet-smelling, special citron [etrog] is used, together with palm, myrtle, and willow branches [the combination is called a lulav], as a symbol waved in the four directions from which rain is sought in its due season. The booth [sukkah], in which the family dines all week long, is hung with fruits and vegetables, but they are not eaten. The primary gastronomic language is that of recognizing the bounty with which God has endowed us; while a secondary vocabulary of foods that have become typical in different communities is as true of Sukkot as it is of other holidays, it is perhaps more noteworthy that, surrounded by physical sustenance, we focus primarily on the historical and the spiritual symbolism and not the physical practicality of that sustenance.

This, in turn, leads the discussion in two obvious directions. One is the logic with which Sukkot has come to be immediately followed by Simhat Torah [Rejoicing in the Torah]. It further underscores the idea that the ultimate bounty for which we are grateful to God is the spiritual, even as the tying of the two festivals together reminds us that Judaism never seeks to deny the physical; it never aspires to be ascetic. Thus, for example, the rabbinic phrase, "*eyn kemah eyn Torah*" [Where there is no flour there is no Torah], reminds us that we cannot and should not exclude the physical gifts of the Lord in appreciating the spiritual ones; a reasonably (not excessively) filled belly makes the study and understanding of the Torah more feasible than an empty one.

Secondly, where both Passover and Sukkot are concerned, it is not enough to celebrate alone or even with one's family. It is a desideratum to extend hospitality, to share both food and fellowship with guests. This is wonderfully stressed with the custom of inviting into the sukkah, and acting as if they are present, the Hebrew patriarchs and their spouses (adding another layer of emphasis to the trans-historical sensibility of Judaism). The custom is called *ushpizin* and has a particular reflection in the opening words of the Passover Seder, which, rather than being a prayer, are an invitation to "all (strangers and not just family members and friends) who are hungry to enter and eat."

Thus, the range of communal social services that had already evolved by late Second Temple times has its beginnings in the down-to-earth recognition of the importance of feeding those who cannot as easily provide for themselves, like beggars, orphans, widows, and strangers—those generally disenfranchised in ancient communities. This recognition shares equal honor as an obligation with that of having the most august of guests at one's table.

Indeed, when Lev 11:13-19 specifies which birds are not kosher (including, for example, magpies and vultures, who consume garbage as well as the flesh of dead animals) the list also includes the *hassida* bird. Again it is the Talmud that interprets and explains that the bird is so named because it performs acts of *hesed* [righteousness, kindness] by giving food to its friends. Only to its friends, as a nineteenth-century commentator, HaRim, founder of the Ger Hasidim, observes, explaining that the bird excludes others, thereby failing to fulfill the Torah's commandments to practice acts of *hesed* universally.[4] Once again, gastronomical prescriptions are connected to the larger commandment to be "holy, as the Lord your God is Holy."

And so, as the Jewish calendar proliferates together with other aspects of Jewish culture and celebration, this principle continues to be underlined, together with the principle of remembering the past as if it were the present, so that covenantal continuity is never lost. From the making of potato pancakes [*latkes* or *l'vivot*] on Hanukkah, because the oil in which they are boiled recalls the miracle of the oil that burned for eight days, to the myriad variations on three-cornered *hamantaschen* that we devour on Purim [named for the villain Haman, who is described in the book of Esther that is celebrated on this day], and the obligation on Purim to send gifts [*mishloah manot*] of food and other goodies not only to friends but to others; to the dates and nuts and figs and raisins that are associated with *Tu b'Shvat* to commemorate the tithe of the first fruits once brought to the Temple, and the noodle dishes said to resemble the waves of the Red Sea, in which the raisins or pieces of meat are like the Egyptians drowning (since the parting of the Red Sea is described in the Torah passage read on the Sabbath preceding *Tu b'Shvat*). Again and again the devouring of food is associated with the condition of one's soul as much as or more than one's body.

LIFE CYCLE CELEBRATIONS AND GASTRONOMIES

The same applies to the life cycle events celebrated by Jews. While wine is part of the *brit milah* [circumcision] everywhere, special foods have come to be associated with the celebration in some communities. Unique to the Bene Israel of India is the *Malida* ceremony, in which sweet foods, consisting of grains of rice mixed with raisins, almonds, coconut flakes, pistachio nuts, sugar, cardamom, and nutmeg; five kinds of whole fruit; and roasted livers of chicken or goat are served on enormous round plates. These foods symbolize meal offerings in the Temple (and the hope for a sweet, strong life).[5]

The *Malida* ceremony usually takes place with any life cycle celebration, not only circumcision. Thus it will be part of the Bar Mitzvah feast, just as other Jewish communities have other, similar customs to mark the arrival of a Jewish child to a position of spiritual adulthood, where she or he becomes responsible for fulfilling the Torah's commandments without parental supervision.

So, too, different communities have different gastronomic (and other) customs associated with the wedding ceremony: for example, in Morocco, at the end of seven days of festivities, the "meal of the fish" is served as a symbol of fertility. Similarly, honey, milk, and doughnuts are placed outside the newlyweds' room on the morning after the wedding ceremony, to suggest a sweet and clear life. In Djerba, Tunisia, the bride breaks eggs against the doorposts of her new home to suggest fertility; and in Daghestan and the Republic of Georgia the doorposts are smeared with butter and honey. In the latter locale, the groom sets free a white fowl from the roof and drops rice and raisins on his bride's head to assure a sweet and fertile marriage.

At the opposite end of the spectrum of life experience, Georgian Jewish mourners returning from the cemetery are traditionally received by their neighbors, who provide the meal of condolence [*Se'udat Havra'a*], including wine, offered in a "cup of consolation," and hard-boiled eggs. In the spherical shape of their yokes, without beginning and end, these offer the consoling hope of continuity.

As one follows the course of Jewish history across the geography of Jewish experience, one encounters an endless proliferation of foods, not only for special celebrations and commemorations, but for everyday life. One associates specific foods with the Jews of Morocco, which are not identical, but are similar, to those found in Algeria or Tunisia. Within the community of Jews in India are several distinct communities, each with distinct foods. As Greece was for so long under Turkish control, (and, in any case, they are geographically near each other), there is a strong similarity, although not identity, between what one finds in Istanbul and Salonika (for example, the Turkish Jews tend to spice their foods more strongly). Roman Jews and non-Jews alike associate Italian-Jewish cooking above all with a particular preparation of artichokes (in fact called *carciofi alla giudea* or "artichokes in the Jewish style"), which some consider an older part of Italian cuisine than any other Italian dish, including pasta (which probably didn't emerge until it arrived, as noodles from China, in the fourteenth-century pockets of Marco Polo).

The various countries of northwestern and eastern Europe have contributed foods and their style of preparation to the Jewish palate. Foods have remained unchanged, but changed their names (wontons become *pelmeni*—which become ravioli, which become kreplach—and smoked salmon becomes lox), or kept their names, but changed the details of their substance. All of this has managed to find its way to America or been carried to Israel, where it has been met by, opposed by, or synthesized with menus from Ethiopia to Yemen to Iran. In some instances, what began as Jewish enters the non-Jewish mainstream: for instance, the Jewish-style cheesecake that became part of the American, particularly New York, celebration of Shavuot has become known as New York-style cheesecake. If the first specifically Jewish cookbooks appeared in the mid-nineteenth century in the United States and England, dozens have appeared in recent decades focused on the particular gastronomies of particular communities.[6]

THE ART OF JEWISH FOOD

One of the many realizations in considering Jewish food is that its definition is as elusive as that of nearly anything else to which we attach the adjective "Jewish." With music, dance, theatre, literature, visual art, it is nearly impossible to isolate precisely what makes this motif or theme or that genre or gesture Jewish — both because Judaism is too long-historied and because Judaism has been too far-flung geographically, and has thereby absorbed too much from too far afield for us to be able to isolate simply and purely defined elements as incontrovertibly "Jewish." We encounter the same sort of difficulty when trying to answer the question: What is Jewish food? An endlessly rich compendium of flavors and forms may be derived from the endlessly delightful and delicious interweave of Jews within the tapestry of humanity. To isolate what is absolutely and specifically Jewish in the bagels and lox that derive from central and Scandinavian Europe, or the gefilte fish that comes from Poland, or even the twisted loaves of challot that connect to Eastern European culture is difficult, to say the very least. What Jews have adopted and adapted, and what has come to be thought of as uniquely "Jewish," represents Judaism in the sense that Jewish culture as a whole has been so dispersed and diverse, rather than offering specific elements that we might globally term "Jewish."

On the other hand, there is a kind of distinctness to Jewish food that derives from how it has been adapted, what has not been adopted, and in the way in which Jews engage what they consume and impose an intentional sacredness on that process. Ritual engages every morsel we ingest, whether it is a general blessing recited before eating, to cover diverse foods, or a specific blessing over specific foods, such as bread or vegetables or wine; whether it is an extensive blessing after the meal recited as a group or a similar, more limited blessing recited when dining alone.

Further, the issue of commonality and variation that defines so much of Jewish life across time and space, including food and art, also includes the ways in which Jewish (and non-Jewish) artists have through the ages, but particularly in this century, visually addressed the subject of food. We see this in the array of ritual objects devoted to food, from kiddush goblets to havdalah spice boxes to Passover plates with their divisions for all of the special Passover foods and the three matzot. Interestingly, until the twentieth century, most such objects in the Christian world were made by non-Jews,

thereby raising the question of how we define even "Judaica" as Jewish art.
We do so by its purpose, how it is used for Jewish ritual, rather than by the
identity of the artist or by particular elements of style or symbol. But recently,
with expanding volume in the past few decades, Jews have exploded into
productivity regarding such objects, which, as it were, connect the issues of
art and gastronomy to that of identity.[7]

As such, Jewish artists have reentered the dialogue between God and
humanity by restoring to Jews the role of creation that both emulates God's
aboriginal act and yields instruments to serve the rituals that articulate the
patterns of intermediating between God and ourselves. The ceremonies,
the objects that center them, and, where those with a gastronomic or quasi-
gastronomic context are concerned, the substances that they contain offer a
co-joined means of connection between heaven and earth. Not only ethereal
candlelight, but sweet-tasting wine and sweet-smelling spices, bitter and
sweet herbs and the flat matzo of Passover; all contribute to the sensual
engagement that makes the abstraction of the covenant and its history
somehow more concrete and more current. There is also a specific aliveness
for the artist who engages the traditions by way of the objects that she or he
fashions to accompany ritual and ceremony.

Among the food-specific range of newly-conceived objects for Jewish
ritual created by Jewish artists one might note an Elijah's Goblet by Cynthia
Eid [fig.1]. Strong, simple lines that offer a dialogue between pewter and
brass hark back to the principles of style adumbrated in the fin-de-siècle
Vienna *Werkstatt*: utility and unadorned aesthetics come together at this
conceptual and visual meeting point between realms. Its style could not be
more opposite to that of Robert Lipnick, whose Elijah's Goblet [fig. 2] is,
like all of Lipnick's work, brightly colored, intricately painted ceramic overrun
with personal and national symbols. Lipnick's Elijah Goblet has a top with
a miniature chair seated upon it, and the chair is left empty for the hoped-
for advent of the biblical prophet who is traditionally viewed as the harbinger
of the messiah. But all the artist's ritual objects, be they Passover seder
plates, Sabbath candle sticks, or *Hanukkiyyot* [eight-branched Menorahs],
include among their images pyramids and other visual elements associated
with Egypt and thus with Passover, the quintessential trans-historical Jewish
festival—and the most American celebration, one might also say, since its
theme of freedom accords so well with the American sense of what the
United States is all about. Other symbols of other portions of the Jewish
historical narrative are also part of the decorative vocabulary of Lipnick's
work. This vocabulary includes a small white house with a red roof, an

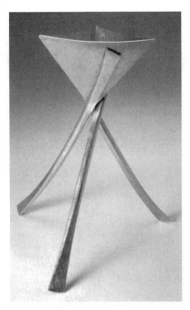

fig. 1 Eid, *Elijah's Goblet*

fig. 2 Lipnick, *Elijah's Goblet*

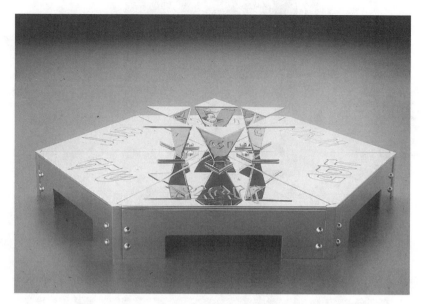

fig. 3a *Passover Plate*

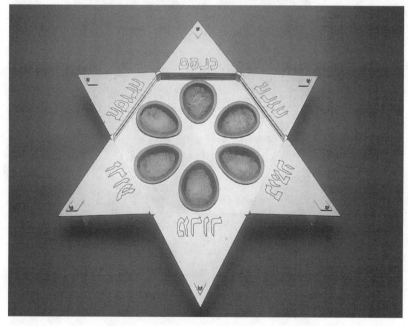

fig. 3b *Passover Plate*

allusion to the house of his own childhood, where he first heard portions of that narrative around the dinner table. Growing up there, he heard of the most egregious chapter in the Jewish story, the Holocaust, which helped to form his determination to be a ceramic artist who specialized in Judaica: part of his impulse is to fill part of the hole left by the destruction of so much Jewish material culture at the hands of the Nazis.

Among the artists who have created splendid new versions of the Passover Seder plate in materials and style much different from Lipnick is the Israeli-born sculptor in metals, Dalya Luttwak. Her hexagonal Passover plate, for example, is dominated by a strong Bauhaus sense of exposed utility [fig.3a]. Each corner is emphasized by the highly polished bolts that hold it together, and each of its six triangular leaves is echoed by a sharp triangular handle. Its sharp edges and straight lines contrast with the fluid Hebrew writing on each leaf. Together, the handles present the form of a six-pointed star, a Star of David, the geometric form that has emerged in the last few centuries (and particularly the twentieth century) as the quintessential Jewish visual symbol. But this is a folding plate, perhaps wedding form to content. One thinks of that characteristic as an allusion to the Israelites, packing up their belongings into the smallest possible forms as they hurried out of Egypt. When one opens the triangular "doors" of Luttwak's Seder plate, the handles now serve as supplementary legs for them. We are confronted by two surprises. First, the large, tear-drop-shaped ("the tears of affliction" is a key phrase within the Passover text) recessions for the Seder foods are a deep copper color. Second, the entire plate now assumes the form of a Star of David that, closed as a hexagon, had characterized the interior handles [fig.3b].[8]

Chava Wolpert Richard also works in metals and is part of a continuing family tradition begun by her father, Ludwig Wolpert, one of the early twentieth-century pioneers of the movement toward new Judaica created by Jewish artists. One might note not only her Seder plates (in one she combines silver with acrylic and glass to provide a dynamic series of color and texture contrasts that might be seen to symbolize the strong contrasts between slavery and freedom that are offered in the foods placed on the Seder plate), but, among other objects, an aluminum combination tray and candleholder, silver and anodized to a deep, gleaming blue, to be used for *Biur Hametz* [removal of leavening] [fig. 4]. Such an object (hers is inscribed in Hebrew with the word *Hametz* and shaped, in part, as a flower, to symbolize the spring season of rebirth of which Pesach partakes) is part of a growing variety of ritual objects assuming concentrated visual focus and with it beautification: the feather, pan, and candle used to seek out all traces of leavening that might have taken refuge in corners of the house as the home is prepared for Passover has moved from mere utility object to work of art.

No category has more emphatically reflected new conceptual and visual directions within the context of Jewish ritual and its objects than the Miriam's Cup. A recent outgrowth of the re-examination of Judaism from within, specifically with regard to its traditions as they relate (or do not relate) to women, the Miriam's Cup is an altogether new object, offering a female counterpart to the Elijah's Goblet on the Passover table. Its purpose is to restore Miriam to the narrative of Passover, from which she has been too often omitted in its retelling; this restoration begins the next phase in the long process of shaping and reshaping Judaism, a phase that one hopes will offer a contemporary Judaism with more profound gender parity than its traditional forms offer. The cup, filled with wine (as the Elijah's Goblet is), is thus filled with joy (of which wine is the symbol). This symbol of joy is very appropriate, since it is Miriam, Moses' sister, who leads the women of Israel in the culminating joyous song and dance of thanksgiving to the Lord after the Israelites have arrived at the far shore of the Red Sea and thus been saved from the Egyptian armies swallowed up by the Sea's swirling waters (Exod 15: 21).

Luttwak's *Miriam's Cup* [fig. 5] offers a goblet rising from a contrastively colored, anodized aluminum stand or base formed to suggest the surging waters of the Red Sea, over and out of which the Israelites emerged into safety. The perfectly formed silver vessel bearing Miriam's name suggests her carefully-wrought song. A second example of the Miriam's Cup, in a very different style and medium, is that by Linda Gissen [fig. 6]. She titles the work "Miriam's Dance," which offers an attenuated, Giacometti-like bronze figure rising from the pool of its own base and holding in her outstretched hands the glass goblet, in turn decorated in lively enamel with the hora-like image of swirling dancers, who celebrate the safe passage of the Israelites through the Red Sea.[9]

ILLUSTRATION AND ILUMINATION
With its supreme emphasis on the actualization of the potential for the sacred symbolism of food, Passover, not surprisingly, offers a particularly dynamic range of works of art that center around the Seder table. Thus the two-dimensional counterpart to the kind of three-dimensional objects noted above is the Passover Haggadah, which tells the story and often illustrates

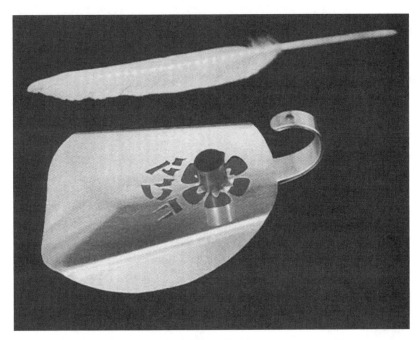

fig. 4 *Biur Hametz*

fig. 5 Luttwak, *Miriam's Cup*

fig 6 Gissen, *Miriam's Cup*

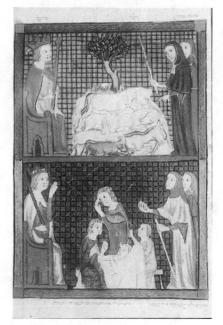

fig. 7a *Sarajevo Haggadah*

key elements in the narrative with careful line and sometimes brilliant color. This is one area where Jewish hands are at work fairly early on.[10] Perhaps the most famous of Jewish-made medieval Haggadot is the *Sarajevo Haggadah*, with its profusion of splendid illustrations and illuminations, made around 1400 in northeastern Spain [fig. 7a]. The attenuated gothic style of the figures, the patterned backgrounds of events, and the doubling of some of them within the same register help underscore the notion of the narrative as transcending normative time and space. The sense of the connection between the present and not only the Passover story, but the entire sweep of God-governed history, is further implied by how the introductory illustrations carry from the creation of the world to the family leaving the synagogue to come home and begin the celebration of the seder [fig. 7b].

Among other well-known medieval works, the *Bird's Head Haggadah* from Germany from around the same time period is nearly as famous as the *Sarajevo Haggadah*. In it, the discomfort with representing the human form in a straightforward manner (since creating humans is God's province, to do the same could be considered an act of sacrilege) is expressed (and the problem solved) by presenting human figures with the heads of birds; hence its popular name [fig. 8]. Further, to mention a group of works for which we know the name of the illuminator, stunning manuscripts in the mid-fifteenth century were written and illuminated by Joel Ben Simeon, also called Feibusch Ashkenazi. In turn, the *Breslau Haggadah* of 1768 carries both the architecture and the clothing of its characters—for example, the wise son—into a rich and contemporary visual context [fig. 9].

As one follows Jewish art into the twentieth century, the range and variety of Haggadot proliferate, from the work earlier in the century of Saul Raskin [fig. 10] and Ben Shahn [fig. 11], with their social realist overtones, to more recent efforts. These include the fabulously lush woodcuts and papercut and gold-leaf and micrography by artists like David Moss, Bernard Solomon, and Joyce Ellen Weinstein [fig. 12].[11] Haggadot, such as the water-color-illustrated Haggadah in "the original Tradition of the Jews of Yemen" published by the Association of Jewish Yemenites in the United States, or the *Australian Haggadah*, in which Victor and Andrew Majzner have, among other things, added micrographic illustrations of Australian wildflowers, further the notion of gastronomic appurtenances that are simultaneously part of Jewish commonality and distinctive to distinct time and location [fig. 13].

On the other hand, non-Jewish artists like Bernard Picart [1673-1733] produced fairly early engraved illustrations of Jewish life (he was drawn to

fig. 7b *Sarajevo Haggadah*

fig. 8 *Bird's Head Haggadah*

fig. 9 *Breslau Haggadah*

fig. 10 Raskin, *Haggadah*

fig. 11 Shahn, *Haggadah*

fig. 12 *Women's Haggadah*

what for him and his audience was the exotic quality of that life), including the food-centered celebrations that have occupied much of our discussion [fig. 14]. Conversely, the "Jewish" cookbooks that began to appear in the nineteenth century frequently offered gastronomically-related artistic efforts, including illustrations of Jewish life. Lavishly illustrated Jewish cookbooks often focus on location-specific menus. There is a growing genre of "Jewish" food-related art. For example, handsome pen-and-ink line drawings were created by Nikos Stavroulakis for his illustrated *Cookbook of the Jews of Greece*, printed several years ago. More recently, his compendium of 150 recipes from the *Salonika Donme* community (that "show strong Ottoman influences," as the author points out) includes chapter headings that have been illuminated with details from extant Donme buildings in Salonika. These include both the Mosque and one of the better-known nineteenth-century private homes, the Kapanci mansion, further illustrated with photographs dating from the 1860s.[12]

In a different direction, but within the book genre, are works like *Good Yontif: A Picture Book of the Jewish Year*, a volume by Rose Blue that centers on lush illustrations by Lynne Feldman.[13] With strong primary colors that themselves stir the palate, Feldman not only offers non-gastronomic scenes like the blowing of the shofar, but sets her family around the festively food-laden Sabbath table. The artist also transforms line and shape and hue into the sounds and smells and unerring tastes of Jewish celebration, within a handsomely decorated sukkah [fig. 15], raising the goblet of Havdalah kiddush wine before the gleaming of three bright stars and the approving smiles of ancestors, their pictures on the wall as reminders of continuity. From the deliciously set *Pesaḥ* table [fig. 16] to the kitchen where Hanukkah latkes are being prepared [fig. 17], the artist works in a folk-art style intended to be enjoyed by young eyes; it will entrance older eyes as well, inviting a sense of connection between the generations both inside and outside the book's pages.

If, on the one hand, works like these are apart from recent studies that are not illustrated by original work, such as John Cooper's *Eat and Be Satisfied: A Social History of Jewish Food*, or Ruth Fredman Cernea's *The Passover Seder: An Anthropological Perspective on Jewish Culture*,[14] they are also separate from works of lush and serious/humorous art like Ita Aber's sukkah decorations. Aber has made a series of gigantic textile fruits and fishes [fig. 18], encompassing even the *s'ḥaḥ* [the greens that are arranged on the sukkah roof so that the sky may be seen through them]. Combining fiber, shells, beads, buttons, and silver paper, the artist has given us not only

fig. 13 *Australian Haggadah*

fig. 14 *Passover in Portuguese Home*

fig. 15 *Sukkah*

fig. 16 *Pesach Table*

fig. 17 *Hanukkah Latkes*

fig. 18 *Sukkah Decorations*

pears and pomegranates, apples and bananas, berries and citrons; in addition, she has whimsically decorated some of them to look like Israeli or American flags. And she has given us fabulous fish, that ubiquitous gastronomic symbol of good luck, fertility, and general well-being. Indeed, she derives the idea of giant foods from a medieval illumination that includes a gigantic etrog as a symbolic statement of hope that in the messianic era there will be food enough for everyone.

Like Feldman's book paintings, Aber's "Sukkah Decorations" pull us gently over the line from ritual objects and art, which are directly related to ceremonial objects or constructions, toward art that has no function but happens to offer a connection to food that is specifically Jewish. Thus, for example, in the works of Jane Logemann, the artist repeats and repeats a word so that it becomes a visual pattern as much as a read or spoken word [fig. 19]. Among these is a 1991 piece called "*Manna*—Hebrew Calligraphy," in which the repeated "*man*" (for she herself does not read Hebrew and thus repeats "*man*" as if it were "*manna*") becomes an infinitizing rhythmic reference to the ongoing patterns of the universe. The style at once recalls the recitative patterning and deconstruction of words associated with Jewish mysticism, the infinitizing patterns of Arabo-Islamic art, the modernist visual sensibilities of Sol Lewitt, and the musical sensibilities of Philip Glass. Hers is a synthesis of sensibilities, but the perspective most relevant to this discussion is that of Jewish mysticism. By means of the mindless, senseless repetitions that elevate one beyond sense and mind, Logemann has taken a word that refers to God's physical sustaining of the Israelites in the wilderness and transformed it into an aspect of the mystical goal of union with God in its most deeply and hidden spiritual interior. One might argue that such painting carries to an extreme the principle of elevating the physical-gastronomic to a different, spiritually symbolic level, thus transforming the Jewish dining room table to an altar.[15]

In contrast, the work of Adam Rolston is typical of a pop style that is a combination of painting, sculpture, photography, video, and installation work; in the last twenty years or so this combination genre has found matzo as a particularly significant symbol of Jewish American life in its most reduced form, one that might be called Passover by synecdoche, a brief annual gastronomic experience disconnected from most or all of its traditional significances.[16] This is the ironic opposite of the way in which Passover as a celebration has offered such a wide array of gastronomic, art, and art-related-to-gastronomy issues across Jewish time and space. It is the dark underside of the brightly-hued sensibility offered in Lipnick's Judaica. Rolston's 1993

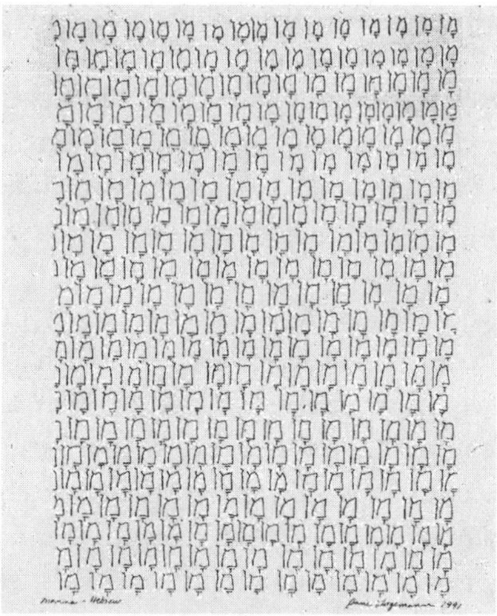

fig. 19 *Manna*

fig. 20 *The History of Matzah*

rendition of a box of matzot—"Untitled (Manishewitz American Matzos)"—large, flat, and schematic on the canvas, simultaneously does two things. It plays on the Warholian transformation of commercial imagery designed to attract the eye to a given container on the supermarket shelf into a work of art recognized for the aesthetic elements that draw the eye to the gallery wall. It also turns the transformation of that center piece of the Passover experience into two things. It is a pop icon in the way the post-Warhol Campbell's soup can became an icon; it is also a commentary on the lack of spirituality that has become attached to that icon. The entire point in the relationship between food and thought has been lost, in the same way that it has been lost in the relationship between food as physical and food as connected to the spiritual, central to so much of the Jewish gastronomic experience, particularly to the Passover experience.

Larry Rivers turns the issue of matzo upside down again and reclaims for Judaism what Rolston finds lost in the American Judaism he knows. When Rivers arrived at the point of seriously considering his Jewish identity, he shaped a fabulous series of mural-like paintings across a background painted to resemble matzo; in fact, he called his epic coverage of Jewish history "The History of Matzah" [fig. 20]. In this sweeping work, Rivers combines carefully finished with roughly sketched details and turns icons of Western art into Jewish re-visions. Thus, for example, his uncle's face sits on the body of Christ in Leonardo's "Last Supper." The artist's question— "Where do I as a Jew fit into all of this art?"—is underscored by the very structure and nature of the work: the structure is in the form of a triptych, that very traditional form of Christian visual self-expression, symbolizing the triune God that is the basis and focus of Christianity; its nature is revealed as a soaring pageant that resembles Baroque-era reviews of the accomplishments of a family or city-state.[17]

Mel Alexemberg relates to Rolston in his often schematically flat, postmodern images, to Logemann in his sometime use of rhythmic patterns of repetition, and to Rivers in his concern for the issues that encircle the question of where Jewish artists fit into art history. From the perspective of one well versed in both the intricacies of Jewish texts and the history of art, he wrestles with the relationship between the spiritual and the physical. He has used food as a motif in his work for years. Alexemberg's inspiration comes from a secure and ongoing sense of Jewish identity, honed along traditional modern Orthodox, albeit lavishly literate and intellectual, lines. His images are textually based at a double level. First, he consistently includes quotations from the Bible, rabbinic literature, and others of his own with his images [fig. 21]. Second, he explicates the word play between the Hebrew words for food and art: they are made up of the same letters ['a-ch-l], thus reminding us that there is a relationship between what we eat and what we create. Further, as the artist, priest, or prophet functions as a divinely-inspired intermediary between heaven and earth, so the line between the physical and the spiritual is sometimes a blurry one made clearer by art. This connection is reinforced by the artist's added play with those same letters, which, when scrambled, can also be construed as the root of the Hebrew word for angel, the ultimate traditional intermediary between heaven and earth, bringing messages from one realm to the other.

In Alexemberg's work, angels are computer-generated versions of those rising from Rembrandt's version of Jacob's dream; they rise from a street in Brooklyn with its inviting delicatessen and from subway poster advertisements for coffee and bagels. Out of the depths of banality and the underground world rise these images of digitalized connectors between divinity and humanity, intermediated by the circular/helical technology of the computer—and not by mere happenstance, since the latter is a Jewish kind of technology, according to the artist, constructed not linearly in the Greek-based western style, but along the lines of the doubly-scrolled Torah and stylistically circular thought lines of Talmud and midrash [fig. 22].[18]

EPILOGUE: THE SACRED, FROM DINING TABLE TO *TEVAH* AND BACK

In keeping with the circularity that is endemic to Jewish thought, we have come some distance from our starting point to arrive back where we began. Jewish history and culture are edifices built upon the Hebrew-Israelite-Judaean foundations essential to it but not identical with it. What we recognize as Judaism per se is recognizably shaped in the aftermath of the destruction of the Second Temple by the Romans and has continued to evolve over the centuries.

Indeed, between the period of the Roman destruction and our own time, Judaism has been a vibrant, breathing being, in large part because of the dynamic tensions between its urge to cling to tradition and its willingness to adapt to new conditions and because of its continuous apartness from what is around it and its hunger to adopt elements from the civilizations among which Jews have moved and lived. We see the evidence of this in every aspect of Jewish life, from gastronomy to liturgy, from the style and materials of ritual objects to the internal and external shape of the synagogue.

fig. 21 *Famous Angel*

fig. 22 *Divine Angel*

The lines of Jewish history and all aspects of Jewish life seem in retrospect to have converged in particular and peculiar ways toward the middle third of the twentieth century as a result of two events. The creation of the State of Israel is the second of these, and with it new celebrations have come into existence, with their varied shares of diverse gastronomy and diverse art. More troubling in the past half century has been the first, the Holocaust. Among the myriad ways in which that trauma has been reconsidered and reviewed, in every conceivable medium, are the visual arts.

One might ask what the Holocaust, and art pertaining to the Holocaust, could possibly have to do with the subject of "The Art of Jewish Food," particularly given the fact that Jews were systematically starved by the Nazis as part of their program of extermination.[19] Indeed, a healthy adult male could be expected, all things being equal, to perish after eight months in any given concentration camp, the number of calories he was served daily having been calibrated to yield that exact result.[20] Yet that irony is precisely the point of the video installation by Julie Dermansky and Georg Steinboeck, "Auschwitz Museum Cafeteria."[21] Eight monitors disturb us with images of people stuffing their mouths, accompanied by the sounds of eating, cutlery scraping against cutlery, and not quite discernible small talk, in the café that has been established at Auschwitz in what had once been a room where incoming inmates waited to learn what fate awaited them. The images stuff our eyes and ears. Dermansky writes:

> An Australian woman caught me taking a photo of her and her children eating lunch. She asked me, "We seem rather gauche eating here?" answering her own question by asking it. She hadn't thought about what it meant to be eating lunch at Auschwitz, where people were systematically starved to death and then placed in ovens.[22]

The banalization and profanation of memory itself, that most sacred and extraordinary of human qualities, the transgression of the sharp edge between different forms of horror, confront us. And the medium within the medium of exploration is food itself, but differently viewed, one might say.

Synthesizing the issue of the Holocaust with its conceptual antipode, Passover—the latter seeks to turn the pasts of Jewish experience into an eternal present; the former sought to turn present and future into a finalized past—Jay Zeiger's "Seder Table" installation bursts with everything but food [fig.23]. Yet, what it bursts with is what the foods of Passover traditionally burst with: continuity. Birch boughs thrust through it, from floor to ceiling. The table is covered with diverse candlesticks, their wispy flames symbolic of souls now gone; crockery, together with myriad other evocative objects: the flotsam and jetsam of diasporatic existence, most of it broken, as the table itself is broken. But the table is broken by the trees; they are sawed truncated trees, but trees nonetheless, which suggest the pushing up of trees from the earth toward the heavens. They particularly suggest the spring, the season of Passover, with all of its connotations of freedom and rebirth. Light blue cloth (the color of the sky, of the tallit, of the stripes and star of Israel's flag; in short, the color of Jewish hope) flutters from the wall beyond the table, illuminated by bulbs framed by blunted Stars of David made of old tennis racket presses. The installation is a splendid study in the tension between wholeness and breakage, between continuity and interruption.

In seeing Zeiger's "Seder Table" displayed as it habitually is, with a second piece called "Resistance," we see it as part of one larger idea. We are confronted with the preeminent role of the Holocaust in the historical efforts to destroy Judaism and the double effort to defy destruction. One of the latter includes the specifics of resistance to the Nazis, risking certain death. The other is the general context of Passover as a festival that rejoices in the overwhelming of would-be destroyers and, through the yearly remembering and retelling around the food-laden table mandated by the Torah, in making the past live in a continuous and eternal as well as vital present.[23]

Jewish life, then, has been like a series of concentric circles in time and space—except that the circles move in a three-dimensional, volumetric fashion, as if around a series of concentric spheres. The center has been the Torah, and the circles around it include the biblical, rabbinic, and post-rabbinic literature that has grown out of it; the Sabbath, the holidays, and life cycle events; and the particular aspects of marking them that have evolved in different places and different times. These aspects clearly include the gastronomy that has marked Jews as similar to and dissimilar from their neighbors and to and from each other, across time and space. This issue of similarity and dissimilarity, centered, tongue-in-cheek, on food, defines Alan Wexler's "Do It Yourself Charity Box" installation [fig. 24]. In it, *tzedakah* and *zakat* and *caritas* and charity are contrasted and compared, as it were, by means of different types of foods, such as *Rokeach* versus *Campbell's* tomato soup, implying the alleged differences among cultures, ethnicities,

fig. 23 *Seder Table*

fig. 24 *Do It Yourself Charity Box*

and religions that, in spite of differences, share the sense of obligation to help those with less than we have. Jewish life includes the various arts that assist the Jewish tradition in plotting a connective course between ourselves and others and between God and ourselves. Among the more interesting of these arts is that which weds gastronomy and visual expression to offer an art of Jewish food and Jewish experience across time and space.

NOTES

[1] This notion is part of the sense of *De Anima* II, Chapter 4; 416a19-416b31.

[2] There are a number of interesting books on the Kai Fung Fu Jewish community. Four that might be noted, for further information, are: Pan Guang, compiler & ed., *The Jews in China*, (Guang Dong: China Intercontinental Press, 2001); Michael Pollak, *Mandarins, Jews, and Missionaries: The Jewish* Exod*perience in the Chinese Empire*, (Philadelphia: The Jewish Publication Society, 1980); Sidney Shapiro, ed., *Jews in Old China*, (New York: Hippocrene Books, 1984); and William Charles White, *Chinese Jews*, (Toronto: University of Toronto Press, 1942). The first-named is bilingual, largely a picture book on the history of the past century (by which time the Kai Fung Fu Jewish community was all but extinct); the volume by White is still probably the most definitive and detailed history overall.

[3] See Louis Ginzberg, "The Sabbath in Ancient Times," in *United Synagogue Record*, 1:1, and A. Berliner, "Die Juedische Speisetafel," in *Jahrbuch fuer Juedische Geschichte und Literatur*, 1910. Among other challah-related customs, of course, is the particularly eastern European "taking of challah," by which is meant the pinching off a piece of the challah dough and tossing it into the stove's fire as a remembrance and fulfillment of the precept of setting aside the first piece of challah dough as a gift for the High Priest in the Temple in Jerusalem (Num 15:19-21). Since among others, Muslims practice the same custom, it may not be a post-Temple substitution for a Temple-related custom, but perhaps the other way around: the Temple-related custom was put into place to drive out that shared with their pagan neighbors, of throwing an offering into the fire to appease evil spirits ("giving the devil his due," in our later terms). The old custom renewed after the destruction of the Temple would have been recast, as so many other customs have been, into a new conceptual form, treated as if a Jewish post-Temple invention.

[4] Rabbi Yitzhak Meir Rothenberg (1799-1866), known as the *Hidushei HaRim*, was the first Gerer rabbi. His emphasis on intense study of the Torah is continued by the Ger Hasidim today. His comment on the *hassida* bird is found in his tractate, *Chullin and Teshuvot HaRim* (a collection of his responsa on the *Shulhan Arukh*), published in Warsaw in 1892.

[5] See Suzon Fuks, *Keeping the Light: A Diary of South India*, (exhibition catalogue; published jointly by the B'nai B'rith Klutznick National Jewish Museum, Washington, DC; The Memorial Foundation for Jewish Culture, New York; and Commonwealth

Jewish Council, London), 1997; and Nathan Katz and Ellen S. Goldberg, *The Last Jews of Cochin: Jewish Life in Hindu India*, Columbia: University of South Carolina Press, 1983).

[6] The first published ones were that of Esther Jacobs Levy in 1871, in America, and still earlier, that of Judith Montefiore (wife of Sir Moses) in England, in 1846.

[7] For further discussion on the issue of defining Judaica as Jewish, see Ori Z Soltes, *Tradition and Transformation: A Vivid history of Jewish Art and Architecture* (a twenty-six part video course), Cleveland Ohio: Electric shadows Corporation, 1984-90, parts 2B, 3B and 13B; and Soltes, *Realm Between Realms; Histories Between History* (exhibition catalogue; B'nai B'rith Klutznick National Jewish Museum, Washington, DC, 1997), especially 4-8 and 22.

[8] For more on Luttwak's work, see the exhibition catalogue *Dalya Luttwak: Twenty Years of Metal Work*, published by the artist in conjunction with a retrospective at Gallery A, Washington, DC in 2001.

[9] An entire and very excellent exhibition of Miriam's Cups was offered in 1996 at the Joseph Gallery of Hebrew Union College in New York City.

[10] The Purim Megillah is the other most obvious medium of lush and light-hearted Jewish ceremonial visual self-expression that carries back to the medieval period. See Soltes, "Images and the Book of Esther: From Manuscript Illumination to Midrash," in *The Book of Esther in Modern Research* (London and New York: T&T Clark International: Continuum Press, 2003) 137-75.

[11] Weinstein has produced a number of handmade, single-edition *Haggadot*. The one pictured here is the *Women's Haggadah*, but she has also produced, for example, a modernist version of the *Bird's Head Haggadah*. For more in formation see her website: http://www.joyceellenweinstein.com/

[12] See Nikos Stavrolakis, *Cookbook of the Jews of Greece* (Athens: Takos Press, 1995) and Nikos Stavrolakis, *Salonica: A Family Cookbook*, (Athens: Takos Press, 1997). See also the articles in this volume: Joan Nathan, "A Social History of Jewish Food in America" and Oliver Pollak, "Nebraska Jewish Charitable Cookbooks, 1901-2002," in *Food and Judaism* (vol. 15; Studies in Jewish Civilization; ed. L. J. Greenspoon et al.; Omaha: Creighton University Press, 2005).

[13] Rose Blue, *Good Yontiff: A Picture Book of the Jewish Year*, with illustrations by Lynne Feldman (Brookville: Millbrook Press, 1997). The book is now out of print; for further information regarding the art, see <artistlf@Rochester.rr.com> or <http://www.lynnefeldman.com>.

[14] John Cooper, *Eat and Be Satisfied: A Social History of Jewish Food* (Northvale: Jason Aronson, 1998). Ruth Fredman Cernea, *The Passover Seder: An Anthropological Perspective on Jewish Culture* (Lanham: University Press of America, 1995).

[15] For more on Logemann's work in the context of Jewish mysticism, see Soltes: "Spirituality into a New Millennium: Mysticism in Jewish Art" in *Studies in Jewish Civilization 13: Spiritual Dimensions of Judaism* (eds. L. J. Greenspoon et al.; Omaha: Creighton University Press, 2003), 105-160.

[16] While Rolston's work may be seen in any number of places, I am thinking in particular of the image described below that appeared in the exhibition *Too Jewish? Challenging Traditional Identities*, New York: The Jewish Museum, 1996.

[17] For more detail on Rivers' "History of Matzah: The Story of the Jews," see Norman Kleeblatt's exhibition catalogue pertaining to that work as it was shown at the Jewish Museum in New York, 1984. See also Soltes, *Fixing the World*, 85-89. Rolston's work is also discussed in both *Fixing the World* and in the exhibition catalogue, *Too Jewish? Challenging Traditional Identities* (ed. Kleeblatt; New York: The Jewish Museum, 1996); it may be seen in the Kleeblatt catalogue (149) but was unfortunately not available for reproduction here or in *Fixing the World*. One might also note a matzo-backed work by Neil Goldberg titled *Shecky*, illustrated in *Too Jewish?*, 136.

[18] For further discussion of Alexemberg's thoughts on the relationship between Jewish thinking and the sort of art he creates, see Soltes, *Tradition and Transformation*, part 13B.

[19] See also the article in this volume, Cara De Silva, "*In Memory's Kitchen*: Reflections on a Recently Discovered Form of Holocaust Literature," in Greenspoon, *Food and Judaism*.

[20] See Richard Rubenstein, *The Cunning of History: The Holocaust and the American Future* (New York: Harper Torchbooks, 1975), especially 24-27, 46, 58-60, and the sources from which he quotes.

[21] Unfortunately no images are available.

[22] The quotation comes from the artists' statement for the exhibition, *Jewish Artists: On the Edge*, curated by Ori Z Soltes, at The Marion Center and The Gallery of the College of Santa Fe, 2000 and Yeshiva University Museum, New York, 2001. For more on the Dermansky-Steinboeck installation, see the exhibition catalogue of the same name, edited by Soltes, 42, 81. One of the additional interesting wrinkles to this discussion (bringing us obliquely back to the gastronomic problem of defining what might be called "Jewish" food, as opposed to foods adopted and/or adapted from other cultures and habitually consumed by this or that group within the Jewish Diaspora) is the fact that the video installation is a collaboration between a wife who is an American Jew and a husband who is an Austrian Christian. They approach the same subject from simultaneously consonant and opposite sides of the historical and conceptual fence.

[23] For more on Zeiger, see Soltes, *Jewish Artists: On the Edge*, 64, 79-80.

Exploring Southern Jewish Foodways

Marcie Cohen Ferris

Jews who live in the Northeast and other centers of Jewish population find it hard to believe that Jews actually live in the American South, and some believe that "if they were really Jewish, they wouldn't live there." Yet southern Jews are comfortable with their synagogues, religious schools, rabbis, holidays, and organizational activities. They enjoy regional social gatherings, summer camp, and vacations that draw the dispersed southern Jewish community together. They celebrate their Jewishness and their shared heritage as southerners through food and fellowship. "We've tried to honor our forefathers, our ancestors," explains Joe Erber, whose grandfather was a charter member of Orthodox Congregation Ahavath Rayim in Greenwood, Mississippi. "We've never been perfect. We've done the best we can with what we've got."[1]

When Jews arrived in the South, two powerful culinary cultures met and created a distinctive, braided foodways tradition that includes dishes such as lox and grits, sweet potato kugel, Sephardic *burekas* [a savory spinach and cheese-filled pastry], collard greens with *gribbenes* ["cracklins" made from schmaltz, rendered chicken fat], sweet and sour shad, Sabbath fried chicken, Rosh Hashanah "hoppin john" (the black-eyed peas and rice dish traditionally served in January on New Year's Day), and barbeque brisket.

For over three centuries, Jewish Southerners have been tempted by regional foods that are among the most delectable, fattening, and pleasurable dishes in the world. When we consider that a high percentage of these foods have been officially "forbidden" to Jews since the time of Moses, we understand the predicament southern Jews face. In my work, I explore how Jews both embraced and avoided southern food through patterns of eating that date from the arrival of Jewish settlers in Savannah, Georgia, in the early 1700s. The southern Jewish experience at the dining table is one key to understanding Judaism in the South.

What people eat, the stories they tell about eating, and the foods they either embrace or reject define how southerners relate to their region. By eating or rejecting southern and Jewish foods, from barbecue to *kishka* [animal intestine or casing stuffed with meat, spices, and onions], Jews define their relationship to the American South. When they eat like other southerners, they become southern. When they prepare Jewish recipes passed down from Old World ancestors, they become Jewish. Eating between these two worlds requires a complex negotiation of regional, ethnic, and religious identity. Food events are the heart of the southern Jewish community and include home-cooked meals for visiting rabbis, Sabbath suppers at the Temple, community Passover seders at the synagogue, fried chicken at Jewish summer camp, "Ballyhoo" luncheons [the Atlanta, Georgia courtship weekend, popular from the 1930s-1950s], Sisterhood-sponsored fairs and food bazaars, Jewish golf tournaments, and temple barbecue fundraisers.

Southern Jewish foodways are like a braided challah. The strands of the challah reflect the distinctive food traditions, flavors, and textures of Anglo-American, African-American, and Jewish foodways in the South. They include French Creole cuisine and the cuisines of Germany, Alsace-Lorraine, Eastern Europe, Turkey, and the Isle of Rhodes. As food historian Damon Lee Fowler suggests: "Today it is almost impossible to separate the threads in the fabric of Southern cooking's many cuisines."[2] When the largest numbers of Jewish immigrants arrived in the South during the mid-1800s, they encountered a cuisine already closely associated with southern history. These foodways had an enormous impact on newly-arrived Jews who wished to embrace the Confederacy, southern nationalism, and the bounty of the southern table.

Did Jews become less Jewish by choosing to live in the South? Moreover, by choosing to eat the same foods as other southerners, did they contribute to creating the "Sahara" of Jewish culture, to borrow a phrase from H. L. Mencken's description of the South as a cultural and intellectual desert?[3] I would argue that neither grits nor barbeque led southern Jews astray, but rather, like Jews in other regions of the United States, southern Jews developed a distinctive religious identity that is an important part of the spectrum of regional American Jewish experience. Most Southern Jews do not view themselves as "Jewishly disadvantaged"; instead, they cherish the ethnic patterns and religious traditions of their region.[4]

When we observe how southern Jewish families eat, we encounter a regional experience that is unique in American Jewish history. The experience of southern Jewish immigrants—their small numbers, their geographic isolation, and their ties to white and black Protestant culture—is reflected in how food continues to define the southern Jewish experience today. Through their foodways, Jews became a part of southern life. My work focuses on Jewish families in Savannah, Georgia, Charleston, South Carolina, New Orleans, Louisiana, Atlanta, Georgia, Memphis, Tennessee, and the Mississippi and Arkansas Delta. What follows is a culinary sampling of food memories from these places that reflects the mixing of southern and Jewish worlds.

At the heart of every conversation about southern Jewish foodways is the "bread problem." The conversation focuses on the lack of good "Jewish" bagels, chewy rye breads, and cake-like challahs in the South. The problem is less serious today, now that crusty, European-style breads are baked in cities like Atlanta and Memphis. But in smaller cities and towns, southern Jews find only cornbread and biscuits, frosted layer cakes, and pies. This bread problem helps us understand the Jewish South. Why do full-service Jewish bakeries have difficulty surviving in cities with significant Jewish populations like Memphis and New Orleans?

My Jewish parents, my mother from Connecticut, my father from Arkansas, lived in Memphis for several years and lamented the closing of the last "real" Jewish bakery in the city.[5] "Their stuff wasn't even that good, but the bagels were okay, and the strudel was delicious," said my mother.[6] Carolyn Washer, my cousin and a Memphis native, added, "We're back to picking up bread and bagels out of town again."[7] "It doesn't make any sense," I reply. "You've got a significant Jewish community here—Temple Israel has over a thousand families. You have Conservative congregations and a healthy Orthodox community. Why can't Memphis Jews support a Jewish bakery?" My mother sighed, "They just don't know any better."[8]

But what southern Jews do know is how to blend their region's foodways with Jewish foodways. Just as generations of Jews in Eastern Europe, the Middle East, and central Europe adapted to the foodways of those worlds, southern Jews adapted to food traditions of the American South. As historian Hasia Diner explains, "Jews adopted local foodstuffs and adapted them to their laws. They created cuisines blending Jewish law and practice with the produce and styles of the lands of their dispersion."[9]

In Memphis today, there are kosher sections at the larger grocery stores and two independently operated kosher bakeries, Ricki's Cookie Corner and City Bread, which recently opened the only sit-in kosher café in the city. But unlike independently-owned kosher bakeries in most cities, these businesses do not advertise their kosher status and they do not include the word "kosher" in their store names. They are "quietly kosher," and this fact is insider knowledge within the Jewish community. Even with a healthy observant Jewish community in Memphis, these bakeries would find it difficult to survive without their Gentile customers. Owners and operators of kosher food businesses in Memphis understand that regional tastes are equally powerful for southern Jews. Kosher food businesses come and go in this southern city, revealing the Jewish community's mix of ethnic and regional food loyalties. A long-time member of Memphis's Anshei Sphard-Beth El Emeth Congregation commented to me, "Kosher places haven't lasted in Memphis. The Jewish people here just don't support them....I hope the new bakery does. I think we're ready for it."[10]

While the lack of traditional Jewish breads in Memphis and throughout the South clearly reflects assimilation, this lack does not signal an absence of ethnic identity.[11] Southern Jews blend their regional identity both as Jews and as Southerners through the foods they eat, the holidays they celebrate, and the products they buy.[12] To understand this phenomenon, we should consider Mimi Sheraton's study of the bialy, an onion-filled bagel once popular among Jews in Poland.[13] Sheraton observes that with the destruction of Polish Jewry in the Holocaust, Jewish bread traditions disappeared. No Jews meant no demand for bialys. Although the reasons are vastly different, in the American South the small Jewish population also could not sustain a demand for "Jewish-style" breads, bagels, and pastries. Nevertheless, unlike the Jews of Poland, southern Jewry has endured and even flourished. While bagel shops, Jewish bakeries, and delicatessens are rare in the region, southern Jews maintain a strong ethnic identity through other distinctive food traditions within their homes and their synagogues.

In his memoir of growing up in the Reform Jewish community of Charleston, South Carolina, author and founder of Algonquin Press, Louis Rubin, explains, "These people were part of the South, and their response to their experience was very much in terms of the Southern community....Cut off from what for their forebears had been a powerful historical and self-sufficient community tradition, in effect they replaced it with the intense heritage of their new home."[14] They bridged southern culture with Jewish culture at the dining table, and as a result they retained their Jewish identity as they embraced the South.

The foodways of Jewish southerners reflect a distinctive regional expression of American Jewish life that is defined by six primary factors: 1) Their religious observance and ethnic identity center on an entire region rather than on a specific community, city, or even state; 2) Jewish women accept African Americans as Jewish cooks and caterers after they learn Jewish traditions; 3) "Creative" interpretation of Jewish ritual and law is tolerated; 4) A high rate of synagogue affiliation and participation in Jewish organizations occurs throughout the region; 5) Non-religious cultural activities are invested with religious meaning; and 6) Loyalty to the South and its culture is demonstrated in ethnic identity and religious life.

Unlike the urban Northeast, where large numbers of Jewish immigrants settled in ghettos, Jews came to the South in small numbers and found themselves at the center of white and black Gentile communities in which they played an important, highly visible role as merchants and traders. In these worlds it was impossible for Jews to remain isolated from the history and culture of their region. Southern white and black cultures, explains George Tindall, "bubbled away side by side, with some of the ingredients spilling over from one into the other."[15] The diverse population of the colonial South merged into black and white "ethnic" groups "that had much in common, however reluctant they were to acknowledge kinship."[16] Similar cultural encounters also shaped the southern Jewish experience with their distinctive expression of American Jewish life.

Food both connects and distances Jews from their non-Jewish southern neighbors. From the antebellum South to the present, the foodways of southerners—white and black, Jew and non-Jew—defined a shared identity for the region. Some southern Jews argue that they have more in common with non-Jewish Southerners than with Jews who live outside the region, and food is central to their argument. As Leanne Silverblatt of Indianola, Mississippi, explains:

Growing up Jewish in the South is hard to explain to someone who is not from here and hasn't experienced it—because it's all mixed up and intertwined together. We are Jewish, but we're southern. And sometimes we feel more comfortable with southern Christians than we feel with Jews from another part of the country....Yet we have a very strong sense of Jewishness, and we are very adamant that we want to be Jewish, and we want our children to be Jewish.[17]

While southern Jews share the same religious heritage as urban Jews in the northeast, they are bound to non-Jewish Southerners by fried chicken, cornbread, and field peas.

Consider two contrasting examples from the food traditions of Jewish southerners. The first is centered in the rural South, in the Mississippi Delta, that rich agricultural land between Memphis and Vicksburg bounded by the Mississippi River. Delta food traditions reveal the complicated cultural interactions of this region and the challenges faced by Jews who live here. The second example is set in the urban South in Memphis, where Orthodox Jews have found a way to make peace with one of the South's strongest food traditions: barbecue.

Although far removed from Jewish butcher shops, bakeries, grocery stores, and synagogues, Arkansas and Mississippi Delta Jews frequently drive to Memphis, Greenville, Greenwood, Clarksdale, and Vicksburg to socialize, worship, and buy Jewish foods. Their foodways reveal how "country Jewish" life is distinctive from that of "city Jews" in Memphis, where it is possible to socialize almost exclusively with other Jews. Strong Jewish social ties in the Delta create a sense of Jewish community through monthly dinner clubs, Sisterhood and B'nai B'rith activities, Jewish golf tournaments, dances, and youth activities that reinforce Jewish identity.

"What was different about living in the Delta was not its rural character or the presence of a Gentile majority," wrote Rabbi Fred Davidow, a native of Greenville, Mississippi. "The difference lay in the willingness to settle in an area far from a center of Jewish population."[18] Jewish immigrants who moved to the Delta accepted the fact that they might never again see relatives left in New York and Eastern Europe.[19] Adjusting to a world seemingly void of Jewishness—of pickled herring, pumpernickel, and borscht—was a "fact of life."[20] Undaunted by this reality, Jewish women followed their peddler and merchant husbands into the Delta and re-created the tastes and traditions of Jewish life as best they could.

Russian-born Morris Grundfest came to the Mississippi Delta as a pack peddler in the early 1900s; he eventually opened a store with a cousin in the town of Rolling Fork. After the birth of six more children and a fire that destroyed their store, the Grundfests opened "M. Grundfest's" in the nearby town of Cary. They purchased two hundred and twenty acres of Delta farmland, establishing themselves as both shopkeepers and cotton planters. Betty Grundfest Lamensdorf, the great granddaughter of Mollie and Morris, with her husband Ben farms the original acreage, known as "the Grundfest place." "People are surprised you're Jewish and a farmer," said Ben Lamensdorf, who has raised cotton in the Delta for over forty years, "but we were farming a long time ago in Israel. We just went from sheep herders to raising cotton....Cotton has been good to the Jewish people who came to the Mississippi Delta."[21]

Ike Grundfest raised cotton in the Delta, ran his father Morris's store after his death in 1925, and married June Flanagan, an Episcopalian who, like Ike, was born in the Delta. At home, June Flanagan Grundfest supervised the work of African American employees, including Alice Watson, the family cook, and Edna Davis, the housekeeper and the children's nurse. June Grundfest's daughter, Ann Grundfest Gerache, described their daily meals as "southern country food." "Mother didn't like to cook," said Gerache. "She loved to garden. She did not like being inside cooking, because you worked a half a day for every meal, and then it was gone in thirty minutes."[22] Their African American cook Alice Watson prepared three meals a day, every day except Sunday.

Meals were bountiful at the Grundfest table. As was the tradition in the Delta, they included several meats, bowls of fresh vegetables, rice and gravy, hot biscuits and cornbread, preserves, and two or three desserts. The amount of food and the ritual associated with these meals grew oppressive to wives and daughters charged with overseeing this daily burden. When she married, Ann Gerache told her mother, "I'm not going to put all this food on my table. We're going to have one meat, two vegetables, and I don't know if I'm going to have dessert."[23]

Holidays were divided between June Grundfest's Episcopalian family in Blanton, Mississippi, where they celebrated Thanksgiving and Christmas, and Ike Grundfest's Jewish family in Greenville and Clarksdale, where they visited on Sunday afternoons and at Passover and High Holidays to attend religious services. The Grundfests belonged to temples in both Greenville and Vicksburg. At Christmas an elegant dinner overseen by June Grundfest's aunt, Elizabeth Darden, was prepared by three African American cooks, who served turkey with all the trimmings and a coconut cake and ambrosia for dessert. Ike Grundfest's sisters, Kate Grundfest Sebulsky and Hattie Grundfest Brownstein, worked in "ladies' ready-to-wear." During market trips to Memphis and St. Louis they bought kosher salamis, pastramis, and rye bread as treats to serve with homemade chopped liver when their family visited on Sundays.[24]

Food traditions in the Grundfest family reveal issues that have defined the Jewish experience in the Delta since the late nineteenth century. These issues, which continue to shape contemporary Delta Jewish life, include intermarriage, regional Jewish social networks, mobility, impact of the cotton economy, Jewish self-sufficiency, isolation from centers of Jewish population, and adjustment of religious practices.

Interviews with Anne Grundfest Gerache and her sister Betty Grundfest Lamensdorf reveal the important relationships of southern Jews and African Americans in home and synagogue kitchens. Cultural traditions and foodways passed easily back and forth between black cooks and their Jewish employers. Black women in the Delta baked sweet potato pies and biscuits for their Jewish employers and went home after holiday meals with leftover chopped liver and kugel.

Food events and food-related activities are central to southern Jewish communities. A unique southern Jewish food event takes place in Memphis, where for the past fourteen years the "world's only Kosher Barbecue Contest" has been sponsored by Orthodox congregation, Anshei Sphard-Beth El Emeth.[25] In the late 1980s, Melvin Katz and his friend Ira Weinstein approached officials at the "Memphis-in-May World Championship Barbecue Cooking Contest," now the largest barbecue competition in the world. Katz and Weinstein inquired about sponsoring a kosher event, but the idea was never approved. The congregants at Anshei Sphard-Beth El Emeth decided to go it on their own.

In a traditional barbecue contest, contestants bring their own customized grills, smokers, secret sauces, spice mixes, and meat purchased from suppliers. But in a kosher competition, they arrive empty-handed. Upon their arrival, the contestants find barbecue grills that the shul has purchased for each team; these grills are saved and used for future contests. On the Saturday evening before the Sunday competition, after the end of the Sabbath, the parade of kosher grills begins with yarmulka-clad male volunteers from the shul pushing grills from the social hall out onto the parking lot, where the contest takes place. For a fee of one hundred dollars, each team receives a slab of kosher beef ribs, a kosher brisket, and a certified kosher grill. Teams also receive ingredients for sauces, spice mixes, and marinades approved by the shul and purchased by a volunteer at a local kosher food purveyor.

Each team uses its own special recipe. Melvin Katz's recipe came from Rosie Niter, the African American wife of Robert Niter, a former employee at the Katz auto business.[26] Aware of her reputation as a fine cook, Katz asked Niter for help. "I need to know how to make a good barbecue sauce," said Katz. "That's no problem," said Niter. "I can show you."[27] When Niter showed up with Katz at the synagogue on the Thursday night prior to the first contest, Katz's friends accused him of "bringing in a ringer."

The contest has now grown from ten to thirty-two teams and, like the "Memphis-in-May Competition," has a corporate sponsor, Kroger's Supermarket, and celebrity judges, such as Memphian Barry Pelts, a Jewish co-owner of Corky's Barbecue, a local landmark famous for its pork ribs and shoulders. Awards are given not only for the best beef ribs, brisket, and chicken breast, but for the best booth, costumes, and team names. Memorable names include "The Holy Smokers," the "Alte Kookers" [*alter kocker* is Yiddish for "old man"], "Grillin n' Tefillin," the "Three Brisketeers," "Shofar Shogood," "Boychiks in the Que," the "Kosher Cardiac Cookers," and "So Fine Bovine."[28]

Rabbi Joel Finkelstein of Anshei Sphard-Beth El Emeth says that the kosher barbecue contest is the "ultimate in the integration of the great traditions of Jews and Southerners."[29] Raised in Brooklyn, Finkelstein admits his ignorance when it comes to preparing barbecue, but kashrut is another matter. The Rabbi distributes two pages of kosher rules to all contestants, including information on what to do if a team has no Jewish members. Although the event is open to all, Finkelstein requires non-Jewish teams to ask him or a Jewish friend to light their barbecue grill. "In order for most foods to be kosher," says Finkelstein, "they also need to be at least partially cooked by a Jew."[30]

Because the Rabbi wants guests to feel welcome, he keeps the "religious aspect of the barbecue contest low-key."[31] "Is there a special *bracha* [blessing] over the barbecue?" I asked the rabbi. "Almost every event has its *devar Torah* [commentary]," says Rabbi Finkelstein, but not so at the barbecue contest.[32] Any praying that day focuses solely on requests for sunshine and clear skies. The involvement of the Jewish community in the culture of barbecue—one of the strongest symbols of southern regional identity—reinforces their Southernness. It also brings together all segments of the Memphis Jewish community and strengthens their Jewishness.

As we explore the role of food among Jewish Southerners—from food prepared in Mississippi Delta Jewish homes like the Grundfests to kosher barbecue contests in Memphis—it is clear that food bridges southern culture and the Jewish experience. The experience of southern Jewish immigrants—their small numbers, their geographic isolation, and their ties to white and black Protestant culture—helps us understand why food continues to define the southern Jewish experience today. As middle and upper class white southerners and also as Jews, the foods southern Jews eat define them. By choosing either to accept or reject southern foods like fried chicken, treyf foods like pork barbecue, and traditional Jewish foods like kugel and kreplach, southern Jews define their ethnic boundaries.

Southern Jewish history underscores our nation's racial and religious diversity, and nowhere is this diversity better understood—and tasted—than at the dinner tables. Jewish southerners share a complex experience that is shaped by place and the interaction of diverse cultures within their region. Jewish southerners describe *shochets* [those who slaughter kosher meat] and storekeepers, African American cooks and caterers, and homes where food nurtured and defined their religious experience. Their foodways experience offers a richly detailed chapter in American Jewish history, where the tastes of matzoh ball gumbo, gasper goo gefilte fish, and "Big Momma's" kreplach all interact.

NOTES

[1] Joe Erber, Greenwood, MS, *Delta Jews*, dir. Mike DeWitt, 1999.
[2] Damon Lee Fowler, *New Southern Kitchen* (New York: Simon and Schuster, 2002) 25.
[3] H.L. Mencken, "The Sahara of the Bozart," in H.L. Mencken and James T. Farrell, *Prejudices: A Selection* (2nd series; Baltimore: John Hopkins University Press, 1996), xvii, 70. In this 1920 essay, Mencken claimed the South, once the "American seat of civilization," had become a cultural and intellectual desert. He believed that "poor white trash" had replaced the Anglo-Saxon elites of the antebellum South, and with this change, artistic and intellectual cultures in the South disappeared: "And yet, for all its size and all is wealth and all the 'progress' it babbles of, it is almost as sterile,

artistically, intellectually, culturally, as the Sahara Desert…It would be impossible in all history to match so complete a drying-up of a civilization." See also Fred Hobson, *Serpent in Eden: H.L. Mencken and the South* (Baton Rouge: Louisiana State University Press, 1995), 14-15.

[4] Gary P. Zola, "Why Study Southern Jewish History," *Southern Jewish History* 1 (1998): 7. In his essay exploring the need to document and explore the southern Jewish experience Zola wrote, "The history of what many consider to be a Jewishly disadvantaged region like the South may prove useful to those who are seeking ways to preserve the vibrancy of Jewish communal life in North America."

[5] Shalom Bakery, one of the few independently operated "Jewish" bakeries in Memphis, closed a few years ago. The business was bought by another bakery group. Seessel's, a grocery store chain that was the namesake of Jewish merchant Albert Seessel, recently was sold to another grocery chain, Snuck's, which closed the kosher bakery, but kept the kosher deli section in the stores. Kroger's Supermarket has a kosher deli which sells sandwiches and fresh kosher meat. A commercial kosher bakery, Manna, sells kosher bread and challahs to Kroger's in Memphis. City Bread and Ricki's Cookie Corner also sell kosher breads and pastries.

[6] Huddy H. Cohen, interview with Marcie C. Ferris, April 2001, Memphis, TN.

[7] Carolyn Washer, telephone interview with Marcie C. Ferris, 2 August 2002, Memphis, TN.

[8] Huddy H. Cohen, interview with Marcie C. Ferris, April 2001, Memphis, TN.

[9] Hasia R. Diner, *Hungering for America: Italian, Irish, and Jewish Foodways in the Age of Immigration* (Cambridge: Harvard University Press, 2001), 148.

[10] Interview by Marcie C. Ferris, Anshei Sphard-Beth El Emeth Congregation, October 2002, Memphis, TN.

[11] In her study of food and entrepreneurship among African-Americans, Italians, and Swedes in Chicago, Tracy Poe explains the evolution of theories regarding ethnic persistence. Earlier scholars Milton Gordon and Herbert Gans viewed assimilation and acculturation as a process that resulted in the inevitable loss of ethnic identity over time. Contemporary scholars like Lizabeth Cohen, Andrew Heinze, Jenna Weissman Joselit, Barbara Kirshenblatt-Gimblett, Colleen McDannell, Stephen Stern, John Allan Cicala, and Stephen Stern have questioned this notion in studies that examine the meeting of ethnic cultures and market forces. These works reveal the innovative, creative expressions of American ethnic identity expressed in foodways, patterns of consumption, material culture, and the ritual observance of holidays and life cycle events. Tracy Nicole Poe, "Food, Culture, and Entrepreneurship among African-Americans, Italians, and Swedes in Chicago" (Ph.d. diss., Harvard University, 1999), 25-26.

[12] Karen S. Mittleman, ed., *Creating American Jews: Historical Conversations about Identity* (Philadelphia: National Museum of American Jewish History, 1998), 8. Mittelman argues that cultural identity is "an ongoing creative struggle, reinvented by each generation. Cultural markers of identity that are rejected by one generation resurface with renewed power and a transformed meaning for a later generation

confronting a different America." She notes the importance of other factors such as gender, age, and geographic region in the shaping of American-ethnic identity.

[13] Mimi Sheraton, *The Bialy Eaters: The Story of a Bread and a Lost World* (New York: Broadway Books, 2000).

[14] Louis D. Rubin, Jr., *My Father's People: A Family of Southern Jews* (Baton Rouge: Louisiana State University Press, 2002), 2-3.

[15] George Tindall, *Natives and Newcomers: Ethnic Southerners and Southern Ethnics* (Athens: The University of Georgia Press) 23-24.

[16] *Ibid.*

[17] Leanne Lipnick Silverbaltt, Indianola, MS, *Delta Jews*, dir. Mike DeWitt.

[18] Rabbi Fred Victor Davidow, "Greenville, Mississippi," *Jews in Small Towns: Legends and Legacies* (ed. H. V. Epstein; Santa Rosa, CA: Vision Books International, 1997), 240.

[19] *Ibid.*

[20] *Ibid.*

[21] Quoted from the film *Delta Jews*, dir. Mike DeWitt, 1999.

[22] Ann G. Gerache, interview with Marcie C. Ferris, Vicksburg, MS, June 2001.

[23] *Ibid.*

[24] *Ibid.* Another Grundfest sister, Freida, married Jake Stein, and in 1945 they opened Stein Mart, a Greenville clothing store that grew from the one store to hundreds, which are located throughout the southeastern and southwestern United States.

[25] See David Waters, "People can't pig out at a kosher barbecue, but what's the beef?" in *The Commercial Appeal*, Memphis, TN, Oct. 16, 2002, B-1.

[26] Melvin Katz, interview with Marcie C. Ferris, December 2001, Memphis, TN.

[27] *Ibid.*

[28] Donna Reisman, interview with Marcie C. Ferris, December 2001, Memphis, TN.

[29] Rabbi Joel Finkelstein, interview with Marcie C. Ferris, October 2002, Memphis, TN.

[30] Rabbi Joel Finkelstein, "All About Kosher for the ASBEE BBQ Contest," October 2002, Anshei Sphard Beth El-Emeth Synagogue, Memphis, TN.

[31] *Ibid.*

[32] *Ibid.*

The Vegetarian Alternative: Biblical Adumbrations, Modern Reverberations

S. Daniel Breslauer

THE CHALLENGE OF BIBLICAL SACRIFICIAL AND DIETARY LAWS

Studies of biblical sacrificial law often conclude that the ancient Israelites had a primitive and materialistic faith. One of the pioneers in biblical study, W. Robertson Smith, went so far as to claim that the sacrificial rituals of the Bible point to the lack of spirituality in the "mass of Israelites."[1] One contributing factor to this evaluation lies in the dietary restrictions associated with sacrifices. Theodor Reik examines the contention that "you are whom you eat" and sees in sacrificial rituals and dietary taboos and concerns a suppressed cannibalism.[2] There is something dark and mysterious about the biblical laws of food. Many writers focus on this controversial and somewhat unsavory aspect of the Bible.

An equally controversial element in this discussion is the form taken by these ritual regulations. Myths are generally understood as stories, not as laws. Yet interpreters such as Reik suggest that the roots of the taboos in these regulations are mythic. The Bible suppressed the stories justifying the laws, but the laws themselves remain as remnants of a mythic way of thinking that the "higher" biblical purpose negates. Some thinkers, for example, claim that the Bible contributes to a growing scientific and rational approach to life. In that case passages that have elements of myth in them—such as those lurking behind the sacrificial rituals and their dietary restrictions—are retrograde and backsliding. G. Ernest Wright, respected as both a theologian and archeologist, so argues. Reviewing the comparative data, he insists on the absence of "myth" in the Hebrew Bible. While admitting that "modern theologians revive the term "myth" in explaining the Bible, he contends that such usage is derivative and "not primary or original." Israel's literature

79

"suddenly appears in history, breaking radically with the mythopoeic approach to reality." The Hebrew Bible dramatically alters the traditional mythology of ancient Near Eastern literature and introduces a theological innovation. By substituting history for myth, Wright suggests, Israelite thinkers advanced the cause of rationality. Since events followed predictable causes, not the whims of changeable gods, humanity could plan for the future. That rational predictability prepares the way for science: the process of creating general principles of causation based on practical experimentation. The biblical dietary laws are a contrast to the rational advance that Wright finds in the Hebrew canon more generally. [3]

This negative approach to ritual sacrifices, and in particular its dietary laws, reveals a deep-seated theological bias. How are scholars to avoid such a bias? One way has been to look at the biblical text as just another literary text to which an interpreter applies general categories of analysis. Applying these ordinary tools to the biblical text distances it from theological or even historical evaluations. These evaluative approaches tend to impose a religious or theological agenda. Literary criticism, many claim, makes the Bible less susceptible to theological readings. Norman Gottwald comments that literary criticism of the Bible has been forced to distance itself from other methods of analysis, especially the historical and the theological. He considers this "declaration of independence by biblical literary critics" a productive way to authorize their insights into the text. [4] How does the biblical critic become independent of these other approaches? One way is to look for the universal and, thereby, to discover some patterns in the text that are not unique to the religious tradition that holds it sacred. Instead of looking for the historical accuracy of a book or even for the theological ideas it conveys, an interpreter may try to understand it as a type of coded message. The key to understanding the method may lie in the genre used and the way that genre reflects certain generally human characteristics. This study seeks to find a useful method by which to decode apparently mythic elements in the sacrificial dietary system and trace these not only in the Bible but in later Jewish literature as well. An approach to myth that recognizes its power in both ancient and modern works provides a helpful perspective on the way literature codes and communicates a particular message.

STRUCTURALISM AND THE BIBLICAL SACRIFICIAL CODE

Mary Douglas' 1999 book analyzing the laws of Leviticus as literature suggests a direction to take.[5] Douglas has won fame for her anthropological study of systems of purity and impurity, including an illuminating study of the dietary laws in the book of Leviticus.[6] Her approach in this more recent book claims to be "literary" rather than purely "anthropological." A more or less traditional literary approach analyzes plot, character development, poetics, and aesthetic themes in the Bible. To this emphasis has been added the rejection of the text as a historically accurate document. Three characteristics separate this new literary approach from earlier ways of biblical interpretation. First, rather than look at meaning in relationship to historical context, this technique discovers meaning from within the confines of the text itself. Secondly, various elements within the text—deep structures, mythical references, and folkloric traditions—replace narrative and character development as the key to the message conveyed by the literary work. The truth of a text is said to lie within its hidden structure, in the implicit view of reality rather than the explicit claims expressed. Finally, there is an open-ended approach to meaning. No single idea predominates. This approach valorizes ambiguity and multi-vocality over against univocal and unequivocal meanings.

Within this general literary approach several alternative methods compete. Structuralism has given way to deconstruction; new historicism adds a distinctive perspective of its own. Douglas traces her use of this approach to the influence of Claude Lévi-Strauss.[7] After his studies on mythology, she claims, scholars must look to systems of meaning, must analyze symbols and references not as historical or philosophical but as parts of a greater structural pattern.[8] By literature Douglas seems to mean a text that uses words as symbols, that offers a glimpse at the deep structures of human experience through a coded linguistic usage. She turns to structuralism as a means of decoding "literature" as a type of language or, more specifically, as a special use of language. This approach has its limitations and needs the supplement of other ways of reading the biblical text. Nevertheless, its translation of the biblical text into a set of universal mythic elements leads to some useful insights and an ability to bridge the gap between the literature of the past and that of the present.

STUDYING THE BIBLICAL LAWS OF SACRIFICE AND FOOD
This present study takes Douglas' approach as one possible and
potentially valuable way of seeing how themes emerge in the biblical
writings and then reappear in later writings. More than that, it focuses
on texts associated with sacrifice and the consumption of food. Those
aspects of the Bible that seem most problematic will be examined here.
The experiment in this essay does not claim to illuminate everything
that should be said about the texts adduced. The ideas developed here
do show one avenue of thinking awakened by reading these texts. The
point is to bring into prominence an aspect of both the Hebrew Bible
and later Jewish writings that has been suppressed in much recent
scholarship. A second objective is to test the method of structuralism as
a means for uncovering new meanings not only in biblical texts but also
in other Jewish literature.

   How does Douglas uncover the implicit significance of biblical texts?
To achieve her aim, she ignores plot and narrative, looking instead to
structural aspects of the literature. She avoids looking for historical
explanations of the laws presented or seeking modern "scientific"
rationalizations for those rules and regulations. She contends that the
Bible has been misunderstood by most modern commentators because
they focus on the wrong type of questions. Douglas herself focuses instead
on "correlative" meanings and "analogy," reading the laws of the Bible
as elements in a secret code. When unraveled, this code shows Leviticus
to be a "modern religion" that evokes all the ambivalence and variety of
contemporary faiths.[9] For Douglas, reading Leviticus as literature means
reconstituting the language of symbols it entails and deciphering that
language. One continuing set of themes focuses on food, dietary laws,
and regulations for the offering of sacrifices and their consumption.

   Lévi-Strauss often looks to culinary matters as one example of mythic
patterns and their possible transformations. Dichotomies exist between
types of foods; for example, the raw and the cooked, cannibalism and
another kind of carnivorous diet, and carnivorous and vegetarian diets.
The latter distinction points in an interesting direction. Human beings,
as omnivorous creatures, stand midway between herbivores and
carnivores. As Lévi-Strauss puts it, "from the vegetarian point of view,"
humanity is "congruous with the macaws," while, "from the carnivorous
point of view," humanity is "congruous with the jaguar."[10] Each mythic
system balances in different ways the ambiguity of being human. Dietary

choices reflect the balance that a society has made for the mythic ordering of human tendencies.

The choice between a carnivorous and an herbivorous diet seems decisive for the symbol systems from which Leviticus developed. Walter Houston notes that this choice occurs as part of the social "code of meanings" adopted not only in Leviticus but "throughout the West Semitic world."[11] Houston declares that the dietary regulations found in the Hebrew Bible are similar to those habitual in the ancient Near East generally. The prohibition against pigs and dogs was, he thinks, related to the association of these animals throughout the "Canaanite-Aramaic world" as representative of the infernal world. Such animals, he thinks, "find themselves on the wrong side of the line that divides the good herbivorous domestic animals from the scavenging, blood-consuming carnivores."[12] Such a reading of the mythic code in the Bible makes it particularly straightforward and uncomplicated. To stress the primacy of the herbivores leaves open the question of why human beings are called upon to sacrifice (and to consume) animal products. Does human diet, being omnivorous, imply a lower and more "unclean" status for humanity than for the animals? A more careful look at the structure of the rules in the Pentateuch generally and in Leviticus in particular reveals a more ambivalent attitude toward both vegetarian and carnivorous diets.

Mary Douglas recognizes that ambivalence, but also yields to the temptation to reduce the tension and develop a unified mythic system to associate with Leviticus. She resolves the ambiguity by emphasizing the carnivorous rather than the vegetarian aspect of humanity. She suggests: "Whether humans should eat meat at all is a live moral question," but thinks that the sacrificial system in Leviticus answers it unambivalently. In her view, the biblical approach rejects vegetarianism. Since, according to her analysis, sacrifice becomes a means of gaining atonement through covenantal blood offering, it necessarily involves the consumption of meat.[13] In contrast to this exclusive use of a meat sacrifice, she points to Christianity, which uses vegetable sacrifice "without being vegetarian," and to Hindu cults in which vegetable sacrifice is the rule in practice although the ritual speaks of the sacrifice of a goat.

One important text concerning this question occurs in Lev 2. That chapter designates not only animal sacrifices, but also vegetarian ones; namely, a grain or "meal" offering. Perhaps because the traditions of ancient Israel combined agricultural and farming elements with shepherding and hunting, both meat and grain were considered valid sacrifices. Douglas recognizes that Lev 2 allows for a cereal offering, but she considers the shape and form of the ritual so parallel to the other offerings that there is "a common paradigm for vegetable and animal sacrifices."[14] Douglas is certainly correct to identify a valorization of the carnivorous over the vegetarian alternative in Leviticus. As a mythic element, however, the vegetarian alternative has several different meanings, each of which requires its own explication and understanding. Just as every variant of a myth must be considered before decoding an entire system, so attention must be given to every valence present in a particular symbol.

LITERATURE AND LANGUAGE

Why do Lévi-Strauss and Douglas approach religious texts as examples of myth? How does their understanding of myth enable interpreters to valorize what others castigate? How does it provide a key not only to the Bible but to later Jewish writings as well? Many scholars see in the development of language a cognitive advance. A language takes shape, they argue, through conceptualization and generalization. Several thinkers also identify what might be called a type of "cognitive pluralism" in which different types of languages, different means by which to communicate ideas, coexist. If, as this view suggests, several types of "notational systems" reflect different modes of symbolizing reality, they provide different prisms through which people form an understanding of their world. Language provides, according to Vera John-Steiner, the tools by which to "transform the fluctuating complexity of experience in the raw" into human significance.[15] Such a view of language suggests two different implications: first, different symbolic systems serve different purpose; second, behind all symbolic systems lurk some universal ways of perceiving reality. Uncovering the meaning of linguistic usage points beyond any particular case study to make a general statement about the nature of human beings and the nature of human communication.

One of the most influential approaches to language and its construction of meaning has been that of Ferdinand de Saussure.[16] Saussure distinguished between the constituent parts of a language: its grammar and structure (he calls this langue) as opposed to its individual elements, such as particular words (he calls this parole). He uncovered the logic of language as a system of signs, making use of dichotomous polarities such as the signifier and the signified or chronological time and simultaneous time. The approach to culture and literature that came to be called structuralism arose by applying Saussure's insights to a variety of symbolic systems, not only to those conventionally understood as language. History and texts turn out to be "symbols" no less than the alphabet, words, and grammatical forms. Understanding artistic works entails understanding them as part as a system of signified meanings. This suggests that not only language but other "social and cultural phenomena" are analogous to language because they too "do not have essences but are defined by a network of relations, both internal and external."[17] Different forms of literature use different types of symbolic notation. The systems employed by a literary genre require decoding as well as the literary works using that genre. To perform this task, the interpreter must look not only at the meaning conveyed by the words of a text but also to the symbolic system being used. This approach to "unpacking" a literary text is notoriously difficult and dangerous. Transferring a narrative or a set of rules to writing always leaves out more than it incorporates. Thus, a literary study must recapture that which has been excised in the writing of a text.

Claude Lévi-Strauss offers one of the most powerful transformations of Saussure's linguistics into a related field, that of mythology.[18] Lévi-Strauss posits that different types of language perform different types of functions. Not only do they differ in their notation and their vocabularies, but also in their functions. Ordinary language, for example, conveys the correspondence between things and that to which they refer. Such language may use generalizations and concepts, but only to communicate information about the outside world. Lévi-Strauss contends that this type of language seeks precision. It is characterized by flexibility and responsiveness as it tries to modify and adapt its usage to fit the reality perceived. Such a language absorbs external influences and changes itself to accommodate new situations. A spoken language is "alive" because it functions best when it can dispense with words and terms no longer useful and add newer words and constructions when they become needed. It serves its purpose only by providing an accurate accounting of the changing landscape of external reality.

Lévi-Strauss considers the language of music to be a useful analogy to mythic language because it uses a structure so obviously different from ordinary language.[19] By music he means not just the notation that records the notes that performers play (although he also calls attention to how future archaeologists, coming upon musical scores in a library, would of necessity have to learn to read them differently than other books), but also the musical performance itself. He thinks that the motifs and phrases that composers use convey emotion and attitudes through certain standard themes. They evoke feelings by using tropes that are associated with happiness or sorrow or some other emotion. In his view, music does not require precision but rather a generalized response. It often changes less radically than does ordinary language because associations and conventions do not need the precise accuracy of ordinary speech. He argues that music, at least in performance, tends to use broad patterns of sound and combinations of acoustic techniques to achieve rather static goals. In these ways, Lévi-Strauss thinks that "myth and music" share the characteristic of "both being languages" that, in their different ways, transcend articulate expression, while at the same time—like articulate speech, but unlike painting—seem to require "a temporal dimension in which to unfold." Thus music provides an analogy to myth, a different type of language whose grammar needs exposition.[20]

While myth shares much with music, it seems to Lévi-Strauss to be a third type of language. He understands myth as a narrative story that reveals, through its use of concrete images, the shape of reality. Myths tell stories, but these stories are not really accounts of events that have occurred in the past or in the present. Rather, these stories are complex systems of symbols that, in the way they put together certain basic elements, communicate attitudes toward the world in which human beings live. He sees any particular myth composed of smaller units (mythologems). When two or more versions of a story share similar mythologems, they show a concern with the same underlying realities. Lévi-Strauss wonders about the ways these structures develop, not because of their social or cultural environment but because of the limited options available to all human beings. He does not compare versions to put them into a historical context but as a way of spinning out the possible combinations human beings can devise. He understands himself as a linguist of myth, seeking not contextual perspective but rather the "mythic logic" behind the use of mythologems.[21]

For Lévi-Strauss, myth stands in contrast to both ordinary speech and to the language of music: it cannot be reduced to any empirical reference. It absorbs changes and external influences less easily than does the spoken language. However, it does alter itself in a way that musical language cannot. An entire mythic pattern may undergo a radical transformation; reversals and new combinations of mythic elements reflect a system that has confronted and adapted to some crucial challenge. He does not decode mythic language as either an attempt to give a precise rendering of reality or as a generalized set of emotional stimuli. Ordinary language is built out of a dialogue between words and reality; musical language as conveyed in its performance grows out of a dialogue between sounds and their emotional associations. Mythic language, he contends, is built out of simple dichotomies, binary dialectics that lie at the heart of human experience, such as male and female or cultural and natural. From that perspective, mythic systems are a means of communication, a type of language that conveys truths about human consciousness. In many ways, Lévi-Strauss argues, myth shares the general characteristics of language: it is made up of constituent units that take on meaning only through a "grammar," or set of rules for their usage. The language of myth, however, is not simply one language among many. Rather, it is a particular application of language, an application that shows significance as much by what it omits as by what it includes.

Lévi-Strauss argues that myth as language selects certain combinations of symbols and rejects others. To understand one mythic language, the scholar must know not only what it includes but also what it has excluded. Thus a structural analysis of any mythic language must take all variants into account.[22] The study of myth is the study of how the perception of human nature and its underlying binary possibilities have undergone transformation from one system to another. This emphasis reinforces the demand to take all variants into account. It also reinforces the view that myth conveys ideas more universal than those of ordinary language. Lévi-Strauss ignores some aspects of language that are clearly essential, primarily the literary impulse that experiments with words and grammar, that sets linguistic order on its head, and that delights in puns and word plays. The emotive aspect of literature, and even its social or moral agenda, receives little comment. In this analysis, content takes second place to form.

THE AMBIGUITY OF LEVITICUS 2 AND THE GENERAL BIBLICAL RECORD

The biblical exposition of the grain offering (Lev 2) presents a complex and varied perspective on the vegetarian alternative. The very term used for that sacrifice, minḥa, while often indicating an exclusively vegetable offering, is applied to meat offerings as well (see Gen 4:3-2 and Mal 1:11). Several questions arise from Lev 2 involving the use of honey, leaven, and salt, the meaning and significance of "first fruits," and different forms of cooking, whether in an oven, on a griddle, or in a pan. My examination here looks only at the nature of a vegetarian sacrifice: is it a supplement to the regular meat offering or an alternative, substituting for the meat offering? Three possibilities arise: the grain offering may be an independent supplement to animal offerings; it may represent a special type of offering, for example an expression of gratitude to the divine; or the grain offering could be seen as a useful addition that accompanies the regular meat sacrifice. The latter case would supply an additional element not normally found in the animal offering. The text of Lev 2, however, implies that the grain offering can substitute for the meat offering. Its preparation parallels that of the meat offering; its ritual effects the same divine responses. This view suggests that a grain offering may be an alternative to animal sacrifice, a type of cultic performance that replaces the burning of flesh.

Baruch Levine suggests that Lev 2 results from a growing adaptation of a ritual meant to supplement the meat offering to one that conforms to the same forms and purposes as that offering. Originally, he thinks, the offering of grain was treated very differently from the offering of animal sacrifices. While animal flesh was burnt on the altar and consumed either by the worshipers or by the priests, the vegetarian offering was meant to be "presented" or "shown." Rather than being consumed, it was left as a witness to the loyalty and faith of the individual or the community.[23] This use of the ritual suggests that it supplemented the burnt offerings with a different type of cultic performance. The sacrifice of animals was augmented by the displaying of a vegetarian offering.

Symbolically, such a ritualism points to the complexity of human nature. Human beings need to temper carnivorous behavior with recognition of the value of an herbivore heritage. Merely being vegetarian or being exclusively meat eating leaves something out of the human experience. As long as the meal offering was combined with, or seen as a supplement to, animal sacrifices, it appeared as a necessary reflection of human complexity.

Leviticus 2 as we now have it, however, seems to propose the grain offering as an alternative to the meat offering. Levine suggests that, as the vegetarian offering developed, it came to resemble, and even substitute for, the regular animal sacrifices. Like the burnt offerings, he notes, it was used in several different contexts, for a variety of purposes and occasions. It could replace the animal sacrifice if necessary. Levine comments that it "often served as a less costly alternative to animal sacrifices."[24] This suggests that the motivation for the substitution of the meal offering for the animal sacrifice was economic rather than ideological. This proposal makes sense and has considerable support from both traditional and modern commentators. Thus Jacob Milgrom argues that the minḥa is a duplication of the burnt offering meant for the poor, for "those who cannot afford a burnt offering of a quadruped or bird." According to this view, it represents a supplement to the ordinary sacrifices, instituted for a specific purpose.[25]

On this reading, the choice of a vegetarian alternative occurs because of necessity, in response to special circumstances, not as a value in and of itself. In the case of a substitution for economic reasons, animal sacrifice in and of itself is not rejected. Circumstances may dictate the offering of a vegetarian supplement now and then, but these circumstances do not invalidate the virtues of a meat offering. Using a vegetarian alternative may have dangers associated with it. By preferring grain, one may be rejecting the divine preference for meat. A sacrifice that is only agricultural, like that of Cain in Genesis 4, may anger the divinity. Using such a substitute must be done with caution and defensively. Symbolically, this approach focuses on the problematic nature of human beings, on their innate violence, and on the extraordinary situation that alone could allow for a relaxation of carnivorous behavior.

Nevertheless, Lev 2 itself never makes this purpose clear. The minḥa could be an entirely independent type of sacrifice, it could be a substitute for those who cannot afford an animal offering, or it could be an alternative to a blood sacrifice, a type of worship free of the need to kill any living creature. This latter represents an alternative view that valorizes the vegetarian alternative, insisting that slaughtering a life is problematic and that therefore a non-animal sacrifice is preferable to that of an animal. From this perspective, human nature should refrain from indulging in violent actions, even against animals. There is a virtue, accordingly, to transcending the need for animal sacrifice and remaining only with the display of a vegetarian alternative that does not require the slaughter of any living creature.

The symbolism of the vegetarian alternative found in the Hebrew Bible generally supports the interpretation that Milgrom and Levine provide—not because there is an explicit concern for changing ritual requirements because of economic necessity, but because the valorization of a purely herbivore existence is consistently considered suspect and problematic. Perhaps the most powerful expression of such a view occurs in the story of Cain and Abel in Gen 4. As the text describes it, these two sons of Adam divided between themselves the two basic types of human labor: agricultural cultivation and animal husbandry. At the "end of the season" both brought an offering [minḥa] to God—Cain, the farmer, brought the fruits of his labor as an offering, while Abel, the herder, brought the flesh and fat (milk?) of his flock. God reportedly favored Abel and his offering rather than Cain and his offering. In consequence, Cain eventually murders Abel in a jealous rage.

René Girard, using a structuralist approach to the Bible, claims that while Abel has an outlet for his aggression in animal sacrifice, Cain does not, and that this explains the murder Cain commits.[26] Girard sees the difference between Cain and Abel as that between the vegetarian and the carnivore. The story favors the carnivore and rejects the vegetarian alternative as self-destructive. God prefers Abel because Cain's sacrificing of vegetable offerings provides no outlet for natural human violence. A vegetarian proves himself to be a murderer because he cannot deflect his violent impulses from other human beings onto animals.[27] In this view, Cain is a proponent of the vegetarian alternative, an advocacy that inevitably leads to violence and danger.

The case of Noah seems to illustrate an understanding of human omnivorousness as occurring through dietary supplement rather than through choosing either a carnivorous or vegetarian alternative, but it also includes elements similar to those in the Cain story. Genesis 8:20-9:27 shows an interesting progression. Noah is chosen by God to survive the great flood visited upon the world. Part of Noah's task includes preserving the variety of animal life on the earth. Anticipating the necessity of slaughtering some of these animals for sacrifice, at least one version of the Noah story has the hero take enough animals of the "clean" type (those one is permitted to slaughter) to ensure the survival of the species. While thus prefigured in the text, the actual sacrifice of the animals seems to come as a shock. On leaving the ark, through which he had saved both human and animal life, Noah proceeds to slaughter some of that animal life as a sacrificial offering, yet God responds in an ambivalent way. Genesis 8:21 imagines God accepting Noah's offering, but notes inwardly that "man's impulse is wayward from youth onwards." In chapter 9 that inward musing takes on an explicit form. Humanity is permitted to eat every living creature as a supplement to a vegetarian diet. Certain restrictions apply to the manner of eating that life, but a sharp distinction is drawn between the permitted slaughter of animals and the prohibited killing of human beings. The passage concludes with a story about Noah's skill in horticultural endeavors. Noah plants a vineyard, becomes drunk, and disastrous consequences follow.

In the case of Noah, human slaughtering of animals comes as a response to human violence, precisely as Girard would suggest. The eating of non-animal nutrients is considered a natural and acceptable addition to the eating of meat. The vegetarian alternative, however, lurks in the background. Turning from this permission to slaughter animals, Noah experiments with agriculture. He plants the first vineyard and consequently reaps the first harvest of drunken misadventure. The biblical narrative is, perhaps intentionally, vague about these consequences, but Gen 9: 18-27 tells how, while Noah was in a drunken stupor, his son Ham "uncovered his nakedness." As a result, God curses Ham's son, Canaan. The text is notoriously difficult, but a comparison with the term "uncovered the nakedness of his father" in Leviticus, where the phrase invariably means to have sexual relationships with one's mother, clarifies the matter. The drunken orgy that Noah begins culminates in an incestuous relationship, resulting in the conception of a cursed bastard. Although the Bible as presently edited obscures this narrative, it still suggests that when men prefer wine to meat, they encounter disaster. The seductive danger of intoxicants rises to the surface in the story of Noah's drunkenness. While the vegetarian supplement to a carnivorous diet may be natural and expected, the text still raises the possibility of its danger.

From the ambiguity of Lev 2, the danger of avoiding animal slaughter in Gen 4, and the potential for misuse of the vegetarian supplement found in the story of Noah, a common consensus emerges. The first danger is that of ignoring human nature. When the vegetarian alternative becomes a self-sufficient offering, a ritual independent of all others, it seems to embody a purer and more perfect ritualism than the sacrifice of animals. Cain's sacrifice of his crops represents this approach. But the Bible marks that idealization of the vegetarian offering as an occasion for violence. Leviticus seeks to obviate that danger by melding the grain offering and the burnt offering into a single, harmonious ritual type. The second danger is that of homogenization. Leviticus 2 runs the risk of implying that only one type of offering is truly effective. It then seeks to overcome that implication by explicitly equating the effectiveness of the minḥa with that of the burnt offering. The story of Noah follows a similar pattern. It shows the dangers present in both a carnivorous and a vegetarian diet. This view of the vegetarian alternative focuses on the balance necessary for a full existence. Moving from one extreme to another is dangerous. While certain circumstances may legitimate using a vegetarian alternative, they do not obviate the danger inherent in leaving a carnivorous diet behind. An exclusively carnivore or herbivore orientation symbolizes a disruption of the natural order and signals the possibility for an outbreak of violence.

POST-BIBLICAL REFLECTIONS ON THE VEGETARIAN ALTERNATIVE

The double concern with the vegetarian alternative as either a sign of too high an idealism or too rigid a view of social behavior adumbrated in the Hebrew Bible finds expression in post-biblical Jewish thinking as well.[28] One theme often sounded in that material is vegetarianism as a symbol of some lost ideal, of a paradisiacal alternative that is no longer possible in the normal world of human life. This idea, echoing the lessons of the Noahide story and of the way Leviticus 2 disguises the originally independent nature of the vegetarian alternative, places vegetarianism as an unattainable value that stands over and against the compromises of daily life. The apocryphal book, the Testament of Levi, presents this view when claiming that the angels offer God a "reasonable and bloodless offering." Angels can afford to provide God with such a perfect gift. They do not face the temptations, the impulses, and the natural necessities that beset human experience. That angels constitute a bloodless cult implicitly criticizes human beings, who are forced to offer a sanguinary sacrifice. Vegetarianism, therefore, is a higher type of sacrifice, a more exalted and therefore appropriate offering to the divine.

Abraham Isaac Kook, the first Chief Rabbi of Israel and a noted Jewish mystic, expresses a similar ambivalence toward vegetarianism. Kook claims that Jewish law implicitly rather than explicitly condemns human carnivorous behavior. "There is," he states, "a hidden reprimand between the lines of the Torah in the sanction to eat meat."[29] The move from a vegetarian to carnivorous diet testifies to the problems inherent in human nature. In the messianic age, he suggests, such concessions will disappear. Returning to their original condition, people will no longer require the training and discipline of animal sacrifices. Kook imagines that in those days all animal offerings will be abolished. The vegetarian alternative will become realized as a sign that the messianic transformation has occurred.

By relegating vegetarianism to a future time, Kook indicates that it is inappropriate as a contemporary possibility. It has some value pedagogically—for example, it teaches people about their present condition in contrast to their original status—but it remains an impossible ideal in the contemporary period. Discussing the meaning of Jewish dietary laws and in particular those concerning animal slaughter, Rav Kook claims that they do indeed have a pedagogical purpose. Without the laws specifying allowable carnivorous behavior, he argues, human appetite would make no distinction between one type of meat and another. Not only would all animal life fall under the butcher's axe, but even human life as well. In periods of "moral destructiveness," he avers, people "would not have differentiated between man and animal, beast and fowl, and every creeping thing on the earth."[30]

This pedagogical view represents a post-biblical, pessimistic appraisal of human nature and accepts as inevitable compromise with higher ideals. Discussing the various views of vegetarianism "from a Jewish perspective," Alfred Cohen recognizes the validity in this symbolic statement. He rejects the validity of vegetarianism as a type of "higher" and "more humane" ethics. Such a view would relegate the Talmud and its legislation to a lower, more primitive moral ground. On the other hand, when vegetarianism is understood as a symbol of "the way the All-Mighty really wanted the world to be" and when not eating meat is a means of self-chastisement and recognition of one's own wayward nature, then "that person is acting well within the spirit of Jewish belief and philosophy."[31] The symbolism of the vegetarian alternative as a reminder of human limitations, already present in the biblical story of Noah, resounds throughout the post-biblical material as well.

This theoretical lack of differentiation was, in fact, attributed to the story of Cain and Abel by earlier rabbinic authorities such as Joseph Albo [circa 1380-1435], who argued that Cain became a murderer precisely because he saw no difference between human and non-human life. Once his reluctance to kill animals disappeared, he then became equally willing to kill human beings. For human beings to recognize their distinct and higher nature, they need to separate themselves from animals. The permission to slaughter animals achieves that purpose.[32] The restrictions differentiating animal and human life do not point to human waywardness. The laws of animal sacrifice make use of the fact of a carnivorous diet to teach people the distinction between the value of human life and the value of all other life.

This pedagogical purpose combines with the symbolism of vegetarianism as an impossible ideal. In both cases, human beings are in danger of overlooking their own nature. They are tempted either to understand themselves as angels and more exalted than they really are or to sink into a state in which both animal and human life is held in low esteem. In both cases, vegetarianism appears as a danger because it either ignores the realities of human existence or it denies any distinctiveness to that existence. Thus, as in the Hebrew Bible, vegetarianism poses a threat, raises assumptions about human beings, and challenges the social order. It stands as a symbol for several types of opposition to society and its values.

Such symbolism is occasional. It occurs when the eating of meat of any sort is a real human possibility. There are certainly cases in which a human being will be unable to afford any meat whatsoever. Rabbinic literature points to these cases as the ones for which the vegetarian alternative was originally intended. The Talmud notes that Lev 2 associates the minḥa sacrifice with the word nefesh [soul or person], claiming that when a poor man offers the grain offering, it is as if he were offering his own soul. The special types of preparation mentioned in Lev 2 are said to point to God's compassion for those who are poor. Like a king who takes particular care for an impoverished friend, so God take special care for those who are without wealth (b. Men. 104b). In connection with the different offerings listed in Leviticus, the same source notes God's concern for the intent rather than the substance of what is sacrificed: whether one offers much or little, what matters is that one directs attention to heaven. (110b). The vegetarian alternative here denotes both the inability of the poor to offer sacrifices as lavish as those of the rich and the irrelevance of that inability.

In this case the symbolic power of vegetarianism is its testimony to human difference and individuality. Human society depends on a variety of talents and resources. The supplement offered by those who can afford a meat offering is balanced by the supplement contributed by those whose faithfulness finds expression in a vegetarian sacrifice. Here vegetarianism symbolizes a pluralistic society in which those who live a more luxurious lifestyle must learn to recognize the validity of those forced to consume less indulgently. It thus addresses the danger of too uniform and undifferentiated a society. Vegetarianism is a supplement that allows those excluded from the practice of one kind of sacrifice to engage in an alternative. This use of the vegetarian alternative awakens an awareness of the need for variety within social life.

VEGETARIAN MEALS IN TWO STORIES BY DAVID GROSSMAN

The symbolism of the vegetarian alternative as a supplement that teaches about human nature and about the importance of variety and difference reappears in contemporary Hebrew writing. David Grossman evokes a universal humanism from the raw materials of such unpromising subjects as the conflict between Jew and Arab, an obsession with the Nazi Holocaust, or a strange exchange of letters between two Israelis working through the problems arising from their personal situations. His technique, as Nurith Gertz suggests, is to transpose static binary oppositions into several overlapping contraries, into "a pluralism of identities and viewpoints" in which aliens and natives, outcasts and insiders, socially central and socially peripheral individuals coexist.[33] This attention to dichotomies, this awareness of the variety of binary contradictions in human experience, makes Grossman's work amenable to analysis from a structuralist perspective. Grossman's own attention to myth as a central aspect of human existence adds to the sense that his symbolism is not accidental. His book, The Smile of the Lamb, seems to argue that precisely because Jews and Arabs share the same myths, they cannot understand one another. His study of the Holocaust evokes that myth in its destructive force but also as a means of transcending that destruction.[34] Storytelling itself becomes a mythic enterprise. The writing of a novel creates a type of magic that alters reality. This way of composing a novel, called by Leon Yudkin "magic realism," integrates myth and fact by applying the techniques of folklore and imagination to events of daily life.[35]

Grossman does more than evoke myth and the binary oppositions that structuralists find in every human culture. Through his focus on children, he also portrays a universal vision of humanity. Children reflect a transformation occurring within the State of Israel: becoming more multicultural, adapting to Western values in general and American values in particular, and holding an increasing individualism and self-expression.

This last point is crucial, since the role of the individual and the formation of individual character lie at the heart of the vegetarian alternative as it is classically understood. It may not be accidental that explicit references to that alternative occur in Grossman's more recent works, works that evoke not merely the myths that drive society but also the myths that generate personal identity.[36]

Grossman often uses children to articulate the message he seeks to convey (for example, Momik in See Under: Love and Nono in The Zigzag Kid). More recently, children have become a focus around which the story develops. In Be My Knife, the two protagonists, Yair and Miriam, are obsessed with their children. Miriam has a son, Yokhai, who suffers from a degenerative disease. Yair has suffered a terrifying childhood. His father always demanded that he act in a masculine way, that he defend himself, that he show how tough he could be, and Yair always felt he disappointed his father. However hard his father pushed, Yair could never go far enough, could never prove himself man enough. In training his son Ido, Yair hopes to avoid falling into that same pattern, but cannot escape the repetition of parental imprinting. The inability of these two central figures to aid each other or to overcome their own weaknesses underlines the unchanging nature of human beings and the traps that keep them locked in eternal patterns. The difficulty—perhaps the impossibility—of healing the wounds of childhood runs throughout the book.

Children can be the focus of hope, but they are also a danger. Grossman signifies this danger in a central event, in which Yair flees from Jerusalem to Tel Aviv just after an outbreak of the mumps; since he is an adult, he fears contracting the disease would be painful and result in impotence. A different but similar incident occurs with Miriam. She becomes enraged when two youths tie a cowbell around Yokhai's neck, and she attacks them in his defense. Yokhai, in response, merely laughs, dances, and jumps for joy. The child seems to understand and accept, while the adult feels only pain. Indeed, the enduring presence of pain seems to be the conclusion of the novel.

Be My Knife is divided into three parts. The first presents the letters of Yair to Miriam: Yair initiates an epistolary relationship as the result of an unguarded look he discerned on her face at a public gathering. The second part presents Miriam's reflections on the correspondence, showing her as more complex and insightful as well as more conflicted and self-doubting than Yair's correspondence would suggest. The final part, called "Rain," tells the chilling story of how Yair punishes Ido by forcing him to stay outside until he asks for forgiveness. Despite the ravages of a storm and the implied intervention by outsiders, Yair refuses to let Ido in. The novel ends as Miriam finds both Yair and Ido unconscious and blue from the cold, the two marvelously similar, the fingers of both rendered beautifully thin yet breakable. In this story, the fragility of children (and therefore of adults) finds symbolic expression through an explicit reference to the vegetarian alternative. Yair describes how he delighted in teaching Ido to speak—how every word Ido knew, he claims, came from him. But the stage during which Ido imitated his father perfectly quickly passed, superceded by a period of competition and struggles, one of which concerned the eating of meat. Yair laments:

> Why do I force him to eat meat that revolts him? Why does it set me off that he won't take his rung on the food chain and receive the accepted rule that this "fowl" isn't just a "dead bird." Instead I push it into his little mouth with my fingers just as my father used to push me day after day. Perhaps I should stop writing now? But tomorrow it will rain and erase everything.[37]

Here the child asserts authority and independence through refusing to eat meat. Like Cain in the biblical story, we have an absolute vegetarianism that equates a carnivorous diet with murder and killing. The struggle to civilize a child, to teach children to compromise with their spirit of independence, involves rejecting the absolutism of the vegetarian ideal. The mythic point presented here is that maturity entails accepting rather than denying the violent and murderous nature of humanity. The struggle over eating a dead bird parallels the struggle for a child's soul. The passage ends with a symbolic rain that obliterates the struggle, the reality, the very nature of being human. As the end of the story suggests, such obliteration comes at a terrible price. If humans adhere to an exclusively vegetarian diet, then they repress the powerful emotions that will eventually well up to destroy them.

In contrast to the somber and often frightening tone of Be My Knife, Grossman offers a more lighthearted portrait in The Zigzag Kid.[38] The Zigzag Kid is a "coming of age" narrative located in pre-Six Day War Israel. The hero, Amnon, nicknamed Nono, is about to become a Bar Mitzvah, entering his adulthood. His father, a detective in the Israeli police force, plans a surprise for him together with the woman who has stood as his mother since the death of his birth mother. The surprise is subverted by a man called Felix Glick (obviously a wonderful play on the respective Latin and Yiddish words for good fortune), who, unknown to Nono, is actually his grandfather as well as a notorious criminal. One escapade leads to another, until Nono finally confronts himself through a history of his past that has been kept from him. The story may be of a kidnapping disguised as a bar mitzvah present or a bar mitzvah present disguised as a kidnapping.

From almost the very beginning the hero must pursue the repetitive question, "Who am I?" Thinking the question irrelevant at first, he gradually learns that it represents the most important knowledge that he can achieve. His thinking zigzags from present to past to future, and he must learn that human beings want to deceive themselves and be deceived by others. Again and again he invents a plausible deception for himself, only to discover his error. By facing his past and owning up to his own ability to deceive and willingness to be deceived, Nono eventually recognizes the human truth that we create our own identity by choosing which stories to tell about ourselves. In order to gain the knowledge that allows him to choose, he must continually take risks. He slowly recognizes that it is indeed he himself who makes the decisions, that no external plan dominates the narrative of his story. Thus, it is his choice to follow the path of learning about his past if he is ever to understand his present. He grows into adulthood as he relinquishes the fantasies that have kept him from acknowledging how little he knows about himself and his past.

At the end of the novel, Nono provides an interpretation of his father's name—Yaakov—based on a pun untranslatable into English. The name, Nono thinks, is suitable for a detective because it means "walking in the footsteps" of someone who goes on ahead. That is what Nono has done. Throughout the story he has understood his experience as some sort of training given him by his father. He has followed his history back to its origins. Yet he has, as his father remarks, turned the skills he has learned from his father against his own teacher. Following in the footsteps of the past becomes a means of advancing into one's own future.

Several themes emerge throughout the story: individualism and imagination, the pluralistic nature of any genetic inheritance, the value of American individualism even in the collectivist setting of the nascent Israeli state, the relationship between music and self-consciousness. The vegetarian alternative takes shape as a major symbol that unites these themes. Nono, it appears, has a wild nature. Once he imagined himself the first Israeli matador. He and his friends decided to have a bull fight and attacked a neighbor's cow. Nono so injures the cow that it must be sold, and, to compensate, his father must give up the classic automobile on which he and his son had lavished great attention. Nono, regretting this disaster, decided to give up eating meat for seven years. Felix notices how Nono looks longingly at steaks but settles for a vegetarian meal. He hears the tale, applauds Nono's daring, and then proposes a strange "business proposition":

> And now listen to something else. This is a serious matter of what I would call "biziness"....Mr. Feuerberg [this is the formal address Felix uses for Nono during the first part of the book] has now decided that he will not eat meat for ten years so as to return at least one cow in the stead of the cow that was sacrificed in his Corrida....But Mr. Feuerberg especially prefers meat—I saw how you eyed the steaks in the restaurant, but he must control himself for about eight more years....So I will do a little "biziness" with Mr. Feuerberg. Felix will take on himself five of the years to come. What do you think? Shall we have an arrangement? Nu?[39]

Several themes coalesce in this proposal. First, Felix shows his sense of identification with Nono. He wants to take upon himself the restrictions that Nono has imposed as his own penalty. Secondly, vegetarianism is clearly a voluntary supplement to a carnivorous diet. It comes as a response to a particular incident, it seeks to correct a specific act of violence. This seems to parallel the rabbinic understanding of the minḥa as a substitute offered by those whose circumstances demand something other than a meat sacrifice. Finally, the resolution to refuse meat by someone attracted to a carnivorous diet has a special value, showing self-control and an awareness both of the temptations a person confronts and the power to meet them. Nono must ultimately reject Felix's offer. He is in search of identity, of learning who he is. What constrains him, what makes vegetarianism imperative for him, is not something that can be universalized or generalized to others. It is a matter of personal necessity and cannot be shared with others no matter how willing they may be to accept the burden.

Nono's valorization of the vegetarian alternative contrasts with Ido's perverse struggle with his father over eating "dead bird." Nono demonstrates flexibility and responsiveness. He does not idealize vegetarianism or despise a carnivorous diet. Instead, he accepts human complexity. While affirming the omnivorous nature of humanity, Nono's choice confirms the pedagogical value of transcending carnivorous instincts in the name of coping with some challenge in the environment. His vegetarian choice is valid and impressive not because it is free and voluntary, but rather because it is a necessary answer to a particular situation.

THE VEGETARIAN ALTERNATIVE: THE DIALECTIC OF BEING HUMAN

At this point the structuralist interpretation of the vegetarian alternative becomes most useful. Why symbolize human ambiguity through the dualism of a vegetarian and carnivorous diet? Why use that dichotomy as the key to understanding the nature of being human? Diet is a crucial metaphor because human beings cannot exist without nourishment. Food is essential to human survival. Meat, apparently, would seem more dispensable than non-meat nutrients. The vegetarian alternative would appear as the most purely voluntary of human actions. The rabbinic tradition, however, noted that the biblical laws of sacrifice contradict this intuitive observation. For them, the vegetarian alternative points not to choice but to necessity. The meat offering is preferred; the vegetarian alternative arises from specific needs and particular situations. The symbolism of human duality points, as well, to human constraints, to the inevitability of the human condition. Thus the structuralist does well to use such symbolism to point to the enduring, unchanging, and inherent ambiguities of being human.

The structuralist, however, may not go far enough in this analysis. It may well be that sacrifice mediates between the violence of the carnivore and the passivity of the herbivore. Nevertheless, the recognition that both are required, that balance rather than polarity is needed, introduces a third term into the binary opposition. That third term suggests that both violence and passivity serve a common purpose. Both gain significance by their relationship to life, by their part in ensuring human survival. The Hebrew Bible intertwines what, most probably, were two independent strands (one valorizing the farmer and the other the shepherd) because both are required for the continuation of humanity. Human society depends as much on the food provided by the farmer as on the channeling of aggression to a productive purpose. In this way, what could be called "divine violence" as well as "divine passivity" takes on new meaning. The sacrifice of life is not merely the satisfaction of a human desire for violence, but also a correction of violence, a sacrificing for the sake of justice and life. That new purpose, one that transcends both the carnivore's nature and the herbivore's messianic at-homeness, explains why both the offering of meat and of meal are done "in order to save life."[40]

NOTES

[1] W. Robertson Smith, *The Old Testament in the Jewish Church : A Course of lectures on Biblical Criticism* (London: Adam and Charles Black,1895), 242.

[2] Theodor Reik, *Myth And Guilt: The Crime and Punishment of Mankind* (New York: Grosset and Dunlap, 1970), 168-80.

[3] G. Ernest Wright, *The Old Testament Against Its Environment* (Naperville: Allenson, 1950), 19-21; compare his continuing argument, 21-45.

[4] Norman K. Gottwald, "Literary Criticism of the Hebrew Bible: Retrospect and Prospect," in *Mappings of the Biblical Terrain: The Bible as Text* (eds. V. L. Tollers and J. Maier; Lewisburg: Bucknell University Press, 1990), 29; see the entire essay, 27-44.

[5] Mary Douglas, *Leviticus as Literature* (Oxford: Oxford University Press, 1999).

[6] See her seminal work, Mary Douglas, *Purity and Danger: An Analysis of the Concepts of Pollution and Taboo* (London: Penguin, 1970; rev. ed.; New York: Routledge: 2002).

[7] See Claude Lévi-Strauss, *From Honey to Ashes: Introduction to a Science of Mythology: 2* (New York: Harper and Row, 1973); *The Raw and the Cooked: Introduction to a Science of Mythology* (trans. J. and D. Weightman; New York: Harper and Row, 1970); and *Structural Anthropology* (New York: Basic Books, 1963).

[8] Douglas, *Leviticus as Literature*, 22.

[9] *Ibid.*, 18, 2.

[10] Lévi-Strauss, *From Honey to Ashes*, 38.

[11] Walter Houston, *Purity and Monotheism: Clean and Unclean Animals in Biblical Law* (Sheffield: Sheffield Academic Press, 1993), 212.

[12] *Ibid.*, 193.

[13] Douglas, *Leviticus*, 67.

[14] *Ibid.*, 82.

[15] Vera John-Steiner, "Cognitive Pluralism: A Whorfian Analysis," in *The Influence of Language on Culture and Thought: Essays in Honor of Joshua A. Fishman's Sixty-Fifth Birthday* (eds. R. L. Cooper and B. Spolsky; Berlin: Mouton de Gruyter, 1991), 71; see the entire essay, 61-74.

[16] See Ferdinand de Saussure. *Courses in General Linguistics* (eds. C. Bally et al.; trans. W. Baskin (New York: The Philosophical Library, 1959).

[17] Jonathan D. Culler, *Structuralist Poetics: Structuralism, Linguistics and the Study of Literature* (London: Routledge and Kegan Paul, 1975), 4; see the discussion

throughout this book. Culler looks at the work of Lévi-Strauss and the Structuralist study of myth on 40-54 and in his *The Pursuit of Signs: Semiotics, Literature, Deconstruction* (Ithaca: Cornell University Press, 1981).

[18] See Lévi-Strauss, *The Raw and the Cooked* and *From Honey To Ashes.*

[19] See the discussion in Culler, *Structuralism.*, 212-13; Lévi-Strauss *From Honey To Ashes*, is organized on a musical model with a section "Toward Harmony" and several "variations." The same musical orientation is found in Lévi-Strauss, *The Raw and the Cooked.*

[20] Lévi-Strauss, *Raw and Cooked*, 15.

[21] See Culler, *The Pursuit of Signs*, 31, 103.

[22] Lévi-Strauss, *Structural Anthropology*, 209-17.

[23] Baruch Levine, *Leviticus: Va-Yikra: The Traditional Hebrew Text with the New JPS Translation* (Philadelphia: Jewish Publication Society of America, 1989), xiii.

[24] *Ibid.*, 9-10.

[25] Jacob Milgrom, *Leviticus 1-16: A New Translation with Commentary and Introduction* (New York: Doubleday, 1990), 196. See also the chapter in this volume, Gary A. Rendsberg, "The Vegetarian Ideal in the Bible," in *Food and Judaism* (ed. L. J. Greenspoon, et al.; Omaha: Creighton University Press, 2005).

[26] On Girard's approach generally, see Richard J. Golsan, *Rene Girard and Myth: An Introduction* (New York: Garland, 1993), especially "The Bible: Antidote to Violence," 85-105 and Robert G. Hamerton-Kelley, ed., *Violent Origins: Ritual Killing and Cultural Formation* (Stanford: Stanford University Press, 1987).

[27] Réné Girard, *Violence and the Sacred* (Baltimore: Johns Hopkins University Press, 1977), 4.

[28] See the various discussions in J. David Bleich, *Contemporary Halakhic Problems* (New York: Ktav, 1989), 237-50; Alfred S. Cohen, "Vegetarianism From a Jewish Perspective," in *Halacha and Contemporary Society* (ed. A. S. Cohen; New York: Rabbi Jacob Joseph School, 1983), 292-317, and Elijah Judah Schochet, *Animal Life in Jewish Tradition: Attitudes and Relationships* (New York: Ktav, 1984), especially 290-96.

[29] Abraham Isaac Kook, *The Lights of Penitence, The Moral Principles, Lights of Holiness, Essays, Letters, and Poems* (trans. and intro. B. Z. Bokser; New York: Paulist, 1978), 319. Bleich, *Contemporary Halakhic Problems.*, 243, discusses Kook's "four distinct arguments" against taking vegetarianism as a contemporary goal.

[30] Kook, *Lights of Penitence*, 318. See also the article in this volume, Jonathan Brumberg-Kraus, "Does God Care What We Eat?" in *Food and Judaism.*

[31] Cohen, "Vegetarianism," 304.

[32] See Bleich, *Contemporary Halakhic Problems*, 241, and Schochet, *Animal Life*, 290-92.

[33] See Nurith Gertz, "David Grossman's *The Smile of the Lamb*: In Search of Authentic Humanity," *Hebrew Studies* 34 (1993): 79-89.

[34] See Naomi Sokoloff, "David Grossman: Translating the 'Other' in 'Momik,'" in *Israel Writers Consider the Outsider* (ed. L. I. Yudkin; Rutherford, NJ: Fairleigh Dickinson

University Press, 1993), 37-56.

[35] See Leon I. Yudkin, *Beyond Sequence: Current Israeli Fiction and Its Context* (Northwood, Middlesex: Science Reviews, 1992), 63-73, 152-153 and *A Home Within: Varieties of Jewish Expression in Modern Fiction* (Northwood, Middlesex: Science Reviews, 1996), 170-75.

[36] Naomi B. Sokoloff, *Imagining the Child in Modern Jewish Fiction* (Baltimore: The Johns Hopkins University Press, 1992), 153-87.

[37] David Grossman, *Words Into Flesh* [*She Tihyi li ha-sakin*] [Hebrew] (Tel Aviv: Hakibbutz Hameuchad, 1998), 112-13. My translation: compare David Grossman, *Be My Knife* (trans. V. Almog and M. Gurantz; New York: Farrar, Straus and Giroux, 2001), 114.

[38] David Grossman, *The Zigzag Kid* (trans. B. Rosenberg; New York: Farrar, Straus, and Giroux, 1997); in Hebrew, David Grossman, *The Zigzag Child* (Tel Aviv: Kibbutz Hameuchad, 1994).

[39] Grossman, *Zigzag Child*, 157. Compare the translation in *The Zigzag Kid*, 159. The English translation fails to convey the Americanisms that Felix uses.

[40] Gideon Ofrat, *Jewish Derrida* (Syracuse: Syracuse University Press, 2001), 79.

In Memory's Kitchen: Reflections on a Recently Discovered Form of Holocaust Literature

Cara De Silva

Ten o'clock strikes suddenly
and the windows of Dresden's barracks darken. [1]
The women have a lot to talk about;
they remember their homes,
and dinners they made.[2]

A modest verse. Just five simple lines. But in context they are devastating. Part of a poem written by twelve-year-old Eva Schulzova while interned in the Czech concentration camp of Terezin, they depict a harsh and poignant element of the life led there and the need to talk about food by those who had so little of it. Exchanges such as those Schulzova writes about were very common.

But for one group of women in Terezin (called, in German, Theresienstadt), such recollections weren't limited to conversation. They not only talked about the "dinners they made," they wrote down recipes for them. As a result, they are the authors of a form of Holocaust literature that few were aware existed—the dream cookbook, the cookbook of remembering. Through the vitality of their food memories they defended themselves against oblivion; through their recollection of recipes the authors, consciously or unconsciously, struggled against the loss of self and found a way, against all odds, to leave a mark, a trace of their culture, their traditions, and themselves for those who came after.

They were not the only ones to undertake such an enterprise. But unlike the others, *In Memory's Kitchen*, as the manuscript came to be called, found a publisher.[3] Therefore, it is their particular story, and the story of the cookbook manuscript they created, that has touched people around the globe and allowed them to approach the Holocaust in a new way.

Food and food memories are able to transcend all boundaries and speak to us in an international language, a universal language that we can all understand and to which we can all respond. In the case of the Terezin manuscript, they tell a remarkable tale. On Yom Kippur, 1944, as one of its authors, Mina Pachter, lay dying of starvation in Terezin, she handed a parcel to a friend and asked that, if he survived, he get the package to her daughter Anny Stern in Palestine. There was only one problem. Because of the war, she couldn't give him an address.

Mina was in Terezin instead of with Anny because when Hitler came, she had refused her daughter's pleas to escape with her. "You can't move an old tree," Mina had said. And, "No one will hurt an old woman." Of course, she soon found out just how wrong she was.[4]

Her friend did survive, but because he was unable to deliver the manuscript, he simply kept it. Then, fifteen years after liberation, his cousin came into his shop and told him she was going to Israel. He recounted the story of his friend Mina and asked her to take the copybook with her, an attempt to keep his deathbed promise. But by the time she managed to get word of Anny and her husband, George Stern, it was to discover that they had just moved to the United States to be with their son, a scientist at NASA. Ten more years passed; then, one day, a stranger from Ohio—no one knows exactly who he was—arrived in Manhattan at a meeting of Czech Jews and asked if anyone there knew Anny Stern. "I think I do," answered one woman. With that, he handed her the parcel and she became the manuscript's final custodian. Later that day, a full twenty-five years after Mina Pachter died in Terezin, Anny's phone rang. "Hello. Is this Anny Stern?" said a stranger's voice. "Yes," said Anny. "Then," came the response, "I have a package for you from your mother."

For almost a decade after she received that package Anny was unable to look at it. "It was something holy," she told me. "It was like my mother's hand was reaching out to me from the past." The mother she was remembering with so much pain was born in Southern Bohemia in 1872. She was an art dealer, a fine cook, and had a memorable personality and character, qualities that apparently remained vital until her death.

That her individuality endured even when she was taken to Terezin is a great tribute to Mina Pachter, for this surrealistic concentration camp/ghetto, unique in the Third Reich, was, while not itself formally a death camp, still a bizarre and fearful place, a holding pen, a way station to the killing centers of the East, primarily Auschwitz, but also other camps. Of the 144,000 people who were sent there, many prominent professionals and artists (among them educators, engineers, lawyers, musicians, composers, painters, and writers), 33,000 died there, and 88,000 were sent to the death camps. Of the 15,000 children who went to Terezin, only a few hundred survived.[5]

A former garrison town, a walled city built by the Emperor Joseph II in the late eighteenth century and named for his mother, the Empress Maria Theresa, Terezin was, under the Reich, a pestilent and hideously overcrowded place (built for seven thousand and, by some accounts, periodically housing up to ninety thousand).[6] Rife with disease and misery, it was a place where people survived on slop and where at times as many as a hundred people a day died, their corpses often left lying around until they could be collected, usually by a hearse that was also used to transport food.

What made Terezin unique, however, was the fact that Hitler positioned this hellish place to the rest of the world as a city for the Jews, a model ghetto, or, as it came to be known despite the griminess and cruelty that lay behind its facade, the Paradise ghetto. Designed to fool those watching the actions of the Reich about Hitler's actual treatment of the Jews, it was the ultimate publicity ploy. On one memorable occasion, a beautification project was undertaken for an inspection visit by the International Red Cross. Before the visit, the ranks of those in Terezin were "thinned out" to reduce the appearance of overcrowding; that is, inmates were sent to the death camps to support the illusion that all was well. Children were dressed up to look adorable and were coached in their behavior. They were taught, for example, to run up to camp commandant Karl Rahm when the visitors came, saying, "Not sardines again, Uncle Rahm!"—implying that sardines were their usual fare, so common that they were tired of them.[7] The grounds of Terezin (the camp was built around a public square) were manicured, flowers were planted, and buildings painted. Food appeared in shop windows. A cafe was created, as was a synagogue. There were also several films made here supporting the model ghetto deception. After the filming on one of them was completed, all the actors, including the children, were sent to the gas chambers.

But the ruse also had another effect. Because it helped perpetuate the hoax, a blind eye was turned to many of the activities of the Terezin inmates. So here in a fever of endeavors—and despite their dire circumstances and the constant threat of the transports hanging over their heads—inmates put on plays, operas, composed music, drew, gave cabaret performances, assembled a library that held thousands of books, educated their young, and gave untold numbers of lectures. Mina Pachter, for instance, lectured on the Prague Baroque. And it was amid this astonishing cultural ferment that the Terezin cookbook—which for so many years lay barely touched in a drawer in Anny Stern's home—was born.

Eventually Anny did find the courage to examine the manuscript, a heartbreaking repository of food memories. Many years later, she even showed it to a friend named Dalia Carmel, a great collector of cookbooks. Carmel immediately realized that she was looking at a document of great importance, and asked Bianca Steiner Brown, an acquaintance, to translate a few of the recipes. Carmel knew Brown had been a professional cook and spoke Czech and German, the languages of the manuscript, but what she did not know was that Brown had bitter personal knowledge: she herself had been a prisoner in Terezin. Ultimately, and with painful appropriateness, Brown would also become the cookbook's official translator.

When I first held the manuscript, a frail, hand-sewn document filled with a variety of faltering scripts, I told myself I must feel like those who had first held Anne Frank's diary. But what I didn't yet grasp—and didn't begin to fully comprehend until I wrote an article about the manuscript for *Newsday/New York Newsday*—was that it was to tell a story that was every bit as horrific and poignant as the tragedy recounted in those pages. For, although the manuscript had taken the form of a cookbook, it was no ordinary cookbook. It was a memoir in recipes: recipes of fantasy, longing, wishing; recipes remembered from a time before the war when these women had husbands and children to feed and celebrations to prepare; recipes that, like all recipes, have a tale to tell, but that in this case, are particularly gripping because of the extraordinary and heinous circumstances under which they were remembered and recorded.

Called back into memory by the starving women who put the manuscript together, they recount not only the quality and robust, dessert-heavy nature of the cuisine native to them, but also reveal elements of the manuscript's creation. They tell us, for instance, that while the women who set them down may have been strongly Jewish in

some ways, they, or at least a number of them, were also highly
assimilated. As a result, we see many dishes that are not kosher. Some,
such as *Kriegs Mehlspeise* [War Dessert], directly reflect the fact that the
women experienced war before their internment. Rationing is also
reflected: several of the recipes, for example, call for coffee substitute;
others for margarine, which, originally, would certainly have been butter.

Actual shortages were probably much more severe. In his book called
Terezin, Karel Lagus writes:

> Even before the deportations began, the Jews were already being
> systematically starved under wartime rationing. Their ration
> books were stamped "J." On such ration books no white bread,
> meat, eggs, were issued. Jews were not allowed to receive any
> pulse, fruit, jam and marmalade, stewed fruit, cheese and other
> dairy products, sweets, fish and fish products, poultry and game,
> yeast, sauerkraut, onions and garlic, honey, alcoholic drinks
> including beer, etc.[8]

What, one might ask, was left?

In general, however, these remembered recipes tell us not of
deprivation, but of a world of people for whom matters of the table
were of great importance and who set their tables with dishes that, were
we reading their names in other circumstances, would surely make our
mouths water. Plum strudel, cream strudel, chocolate strudel, an
elaborate galantine of chicken, healthcake, potato doughnuts, glazed
fruits, farina dumplings, liver dumplings, cherry dumplings, apple
dumplings, poppy seed slices, goulash, breast of goose, onion kuchen:
all portray a culture of delight and indulgence. The names of the dishes
alone evoke a whole milieu, as they dramatically chronicle the contrast
between the world from which the authors had been torn and the one
in which they were living as they recorded these dream recipes.

Listen for a moment to Mina Pachter's recipe for Caramels from
Baden:

> Brown [caramelize] 30 decagrams sugar without water. Pour
> in 1/3 liter coffee extract [very strong coffee], 1/8 liter cream
> and bring it to a boil. Add 8 decagrams tea butter [best quality
> butter] and cook until the mixture is thick. Pour boiling into a
> buttered candy pan. With the back of a knife divide it before it
> completely cools. Then break it into cubes and wrap in
> parchment and also pink paper.[9]

The poignant contrast between this evocative recipe and Pachter's harsh circumstances makes the juxtaposition of the two almost unbearable. How can someone who is incarcerated and malnourished dream of tea butter and caramels, right down to the color of the paper in which the caramels should be wrapped? But in that paper and in its sugary contents lay her dream—and her memory—of life outside the prison walls. As the scene described in the Schulzova poem makes plain, though recipes were not always recorded, discussions of past meals and how to prepare them were common in the camps and in hiding. People even fought about the correct way to make a dish and over which version of a dish was better. Bianca Brown, for example, remembers a conflict between two women, one arguing the merits of chocolate cake from Prague, the other of chocolate cake from Vienna.

Until recently, food scholars rarely studied this aspect of chronic disaster. We may know that advances in food technology—such as the preserving techniques developed by Nicholas Appert for the armies of Napoleon—were developed in direct consequence of war. We may know about feeding the troops. We may know the consequences of protein deficiency. In general, we know little else, and perhaps because for most people the association of cooking with carnage is psychologically too difficult to address, that has also inhibited research. Whatever the reason, we simply have not had adequate information on the mental and physcial effects of food deprivation in time of warfare.

It certainly should not surprise us, then, despite the many personal accounts of the Holocaust that mention food and how people managed, that when the horrors are those not of traditional wartime, but of mass incarceration and genocide, we know even less.

In Memory's Kitchen is most valuable for the information it contributes to that important subject as well as for the moving testimony it provides about the indomitable nature of the human spirit and the capacity of food to sustain it. Among the things we learn from it are the important roles fantasy, memory, and imagination play in survival, roles attested to not just by the authors of this book but, as we have seen, by many others.

While visiting Terezin, I met a woman who said that every day in her division of Bergen-Belsen someone was assigned to make up a fantasy menu of remembered recipes to be discussed each evening. Another survivor said that inmates of Auschwitz talked and bickered constantly about the dishes of home. Most did what was sometimes dubbed "cooking with the mouth."[10] Others did what was often called "cooking in bed," just as the Schulzova poem describes, exchanging recipes with each other after the lights went out. And in a few cases, what sprang out of this constant remembering and talk of food was the creation of cookbooks.

When I first began to do research for the introduction to *In Memory's Kitchen*, I thought the Terezin manuscript was an anomaly. I had been told by Dalia Carmel that there were several cooking manuscripts in the library at Yad Vashem, the great museum of the Holocaust in Israel, but at first it never occurred to me that I was actually dealing with a genre of Holocaust literature. In the course of working on the book and also since the book's publication, it has become apparent that that is indeed the case. In fact, I have now come to suspect that wherever in the world people are literate and under siege and have writing materials available, such documents emerge. In any case, I now know of ten or twelve manuscripts from the Holocaust alone. Among them is one in Yad Vashem from Lenzing work camp (a sub-camp of Mauthausen). The author, Malka Zimmet, wrote on propaganda leaflets for the Third Reich. Recipes are scrawled around pictures of Hitler's face. Another was composed on a death march. Two more come from Ravensbruck, the women's camp. Yet another is written in Serbo-Croatian.

It is important to understand that the phenomenon also exists outside the Holocaust. American prisoners of war in Japanese prison camps in the Philippines had elaborate fantasies about food (one laid out an entire farm, though he had nothing to plant and no animals to raise;[11] others cut out pictures of food from magazines and used them as pin ups).[12] Moreover, POWs here also wrote a cookbook. Published in 1946, it was called *Recipes Out of Bilibid*.[13] Italian prisoners of war are also known to have recorded recipes.

Why, one might ask, do people choose to set food memories down in a time of such extraordinary privation and misery? Bianca Steiner Brown, the translator of the recipes in *In Memory's Kitchen*, explains it this way:

> In order to survive you had to have an imagination. Fantasies about food were like a fantasy that you have about how the outside is if you are inside. You imagine it not only the way it really is, but much stronger than it really is. I was, for instance, a nurse, and I worked at night and I looked out at night— Terezin was surrounded by walls, a garrison town. So I looked

out at all the beds where the children were, and out of that window I could look into freedom. And you were imagining things, like how it would be to run around in the meadow outside. You knew how it was, but you imagined it even better than it was, and that's how it was with food also. Talking about it helped you.[14]

Beate Klarsfeld, the Nazi hunter who brought Klaus Barbie to justice and who refers to this manuscript as a cookbook from hell, suggests in the jacket quotation she supplied for the book that:

to remain mentally alive in such conditions some people tried to think of happy moments they had known—the summer wind in their faces, the smile of a nice girl, the friends they had at school, a beautiful poem or a moving painting. What Mina Pachter and her friends remembered in the concentration camp of Terezin was their traditional foods.[15]

Dorothy Wagner, editor of *Recipes Out of Bilibid*, believed that the GIs who created the book while they were prisoners of war did so because "it strengthened their resolution to survive, if only because it made more vivid not what they sought to escape from, but what they were resolved to return to."[16]

No doubt that was also true of the women who created the Terezin cookbook. But I think for them, and possibly for others who wrote cookbooks, such recipes are not only symbols of hope for the future, reminders of a gentler time in the past, and a means of going home. They are also something else—a form of psychological resistance.

Food is a powerful metaphor for life as well as a powerful identity marker. Noted French historian Pascal Ory writes in *Realms of the Senses: The Contruction of the French Past*:

Cuisine is one of the most distinctive expressions of an ethnic group, or, in modern times, a nation. Frequently, the last sign of an individual's attachment to his roots before total assimilation into the host community is the consumption of distinctive kinds of food. [17]

Might not the same be true not only before total assimilation but also before total annihilation?

Wherever and whoever we are in the world, what we eat and with whom we eat it and how we eat it, what the foods of our celebrations encompass, are all things that define us and are among the most forceful components that make up who we are personally. Barrie Kavasch, writing of her Native American grandmother, says, "Long after my grandmother traveled the 'spirit' path I can still see and feel her patient hands. Through the lens of memory I can look into the old oven and see Ma's biscuits rising, ghost biscuits from spirit batter and cloud dough tantalize my senses and transform the food of my soul."[18] Moreover, though remembering takes many forms, few things are as evocative of our loved ones as the tastes we associate with them, the dishes we prepare to keep their memories alive.

The mother of a friend of mine died some time ago; at the funeral, one of the mourners handed out a recipe for the delicious meatballs for which her mother had been celebrated among family and friends. It was a way of making sure she was remembered even better. A man I met told me that his mother had always made soup, that his father especially loved it, and that when she died it was the soup they had in the freezer that provided the most sustenance, not only physically, but spiritually. "In a way, it offered us encouragement," he said. "It was as though being able to eat her soup extended her life for us."

But not everyone eats the foods that are left behind. In fact, my favorite story of all was told to me by a woman who said that her grandmother had always made her *pirogen*, a popular Eastern European dumpling. The woman loved them and would freeze some so she always had them on hand for herself and her family. Then one day her grandmother made her a batch and three days later she died. The woman couldn't eat them. They were the last vestige of a deep connection to her grandmother, the food that embodied her best, the food she remembered her by. So she maintained the connection by keeping them in the freezer, even taking them with her to her next house when she moved. At the time she told me the story she had had them for fifteen years.

For me, that connection came in a little green pot, an old-fashioned enamel pot with funny black handles that stuck out like ears. But it was magic. Out of it came my grandmother's dense, delicious matzo balls and her heavenly potted chicken, a mahogany-brown bird nestled in a bed of what I later came to know as caramelized onions, but which were then just plain old stewed onions to me. When my grandmother died, the pot was lost, gone in the welter of detail that temporarily distracted those who were left behind. But the chicken lingered on, in a different pot and with a slightly different taste, made now by my mother in memory of hers.

Think about your own memories as well as memories in the making—about your grandmother's irresistible chicken fricassee and how much you loved it, about the *rugelach* (a beloved Jewish pastry) she would always make for special occasions and store in boxes on top of the armoire, about your father's special lasagne recipe and the way you would beg him to make it, or your mother whipping off the *bletlach* [wrappings for blintzes] while you struggled to learn to make crepes, about sitting around with your sisters topping and tailing string beans, about your son's favorite chocolate cake, a constant on his birthday, about the fragrance of the challah that was always on the table for Shabbat, about your recipe for the best-ever chili, or about how you lay your table for the holidays.

To recall such things in time of oppression—and to create, as these women did, a manuscript cookbook of the kind women in Europe traditionally gave their children—is a means, whether conscious or unconscious, of using memory to reinforce identity when surrounded by those who want to obliterate you, your culture, your traditions, and your people. It is to use as weapons, not grenades or bazookas or machine guns or bombs, but the memory of dumplings and *zvetschken* [plum] streudel and *erdapfel dalken* [potato doughnuts] and caramels from Baden.

Not surprisingly, then, the recipes themselves show battle scars. Sadly, those who were remembering them remembered imperfectly. Many of these are broken recipes, whose defects most often cannot be accounted for by normal explanations. For, while it is true that European recipes have traditionally been written in a much terser manner than recipes as they appear in American cookbooks today, that is not sufficient to explain their problems. And though it is also true that women who shared a culinary culture might use a kind of shorthand with each other, that too does not explain the state of some of these recipes, which have missing ingredients and missing or reversed instructions, and sometimes just trail off into space.

What may be sufficient to explain them is the condition the four or five women who wrote the manuscript were in: what they seem to show is the decline in mental faculties caused by starvation. Almost certainly, all the authors were elderly, like Mina Pachter, and for the elderly Terezin was a particularly terrible place. The Jewish Council of Elders, the group forced by the Nazis to make such decisions as who went on the transports to the death camps, also had to make some other soul-destroying decisions.

Among them was a decree about food rations. Faced with a shortage of even the thin, nasty gruel and stale bread on which they generally survived, the Council of Elders decided that workers had to be given a larger share of the food and so did the young, for whom, if they could only keep them alive, there might be a future. The elderly, on the other hand, already closer to death, would have to make do with less. Predictably, the results were horrifying. "Starving elderly men and woman begged for watery soup made from synthetic lentil or pea powder, and dug for food in the garbage heaps rotting in the courtyard of the barracks," writes Zdenek Lederer in *Ghetto Theresienstadt*:[19]

> In the morning, at noon, and before nightfall they patiently queued up for their food clutching saucepans, mugs or tins. They were glad to get a few gulps of hot coffee substitute and greedily ate their scanty meals. Then they continued their aimless pilgrimage, dragging along their emaciated bodies, their hands trembling and their clothes soiled.[20]

As a result of eating the raw peelings, many of the elderly developed severe enteritis and diarrhea, a chronic camp condition but especially common, and especially serious, among the aged. "The decision [to reduce their rations]," writes Berkley, "transformed many of the elderly into scavengers and beggars. They would ...pounce on any morsel of food such as a pile of potato skins, food considered fit only for pigs."[21]

And almost certainly, it would not just have been their bodies that were affected. In his book, *Grass Soup*, an account of his life in a Chinese labor camp, the Chinese writer Zhang Xianliang talks about the impact of food distribution on a prisoner:

> Whether or not a man kept on living, or whether he was able to live one more day or two, appeared to depend on whether he [happened to be] given two extra, or two fewer, grains of rice. [Obviously,] one's survival did not depend on the vitamins or protein in one or two grains of rice—but it did depend on the spiritual sustenance, the encouragement, those grains gave a man.[22]

We cannot know whether this state accurately describes the life of Mina and her co-authors, but the errors found in the recipes do indeed suggest that they have been marred by fear, illness, starvation, and the mental debility caused by all three.

Of course, these mistakes were left intact for publication. They are part of the historical record. But of equal, or greater, importance, they bear witness to the heinous events that produced them. Therefore, it is critical that readers of *In Memory's Kitchen* focus on what is wrong with the recipes as well as on what is right, for in a sense it is those errors, those incarceration-induced mistakes of memory, that are the most telling—and, of course, the most bitter—part of the story. It is in them, as well as in the aromas, textures, and history the recipes evoke, that the voices of Mina Pachter and the women of Terezin can be heard again. Listen and you will hear them rising above the abyss.

NOTES

[1] Dresden here refers to a barracks for prisoners. Buildings in Terezin were named after German cities.

[2] Eva Schulzova, "An Evening in Terezin," in *I Never Saw Another Butterfly: Children's Drawings and Poems from Terezin Concentration Camp, 1942-1944* (New York: Shocken, 1993), 42-43.

[3] Cara De Silva, ed., *In Memory's Kitchen: A Legacy from the Women of Terezin* (Northvale: Aronson, 1996).

[4] The chronicle of Anny's family, and of the Terezin cookbook appear here as they were related to me in private interviews with Anny Stern in 1994 and 1995, and concur with the way she had told the story for the last dozen years of her life. However, there are some uncertainties in the account that cannot be reconciled because too many of those involved are no longer now alive.

[5] Michael Berenbaum *The World Must Know: The History of the Holocaust as Told in the United States Holocaust Memorial Museum* (Boston: Little, Brown 1993), 87.

[6] *Ibid.*

[7] George Berkley, *The Story of Theresienstadt* (Boston: Branden, 1993), 171.

[8] Prague: Council of Jewish Communities in the Czech Lands, 1965, 16 .

[9] One decagram equals ten grams.

[10] Susan Cernyak-Spatz, a survivor of Terezín and Auschwitz, described people in both places as speaking of food so constantly that this term, "cooking with the mouth," became a camp expression.

[11] Jan Thompson. "Prisoners of the Rising Sun: Food Memories of American POWs in the Far East during World War II." (Paper presented at the Oxford Symposium on Food & Cookery, Oxford, England, September 8-10, 2000).

[12] Sue Shephard, "A Slice of The Moon." (Paper presented at the Oxford Symposium on Food & Cookery, Oxford, England, September 8-10, 2000).

[13] Dorothy Wagner, ed., *Recipes Out of Bilibid* (New York: George W. Stewart, 1946).

[14] De Silva, *In Memory's Kitchen*, xxviii.

[15] *Ibid.*, book jacket.

[16] Wagner, *Recipes Out of Bilibid*, 9.

[17] Pascal Ory, "Gastronomy," in *Traditions* (vol. 2, *Realms of Memory, The Construction of the French Past*; ed. P. Nora and L. D. Kritzman; trans. A. Goldhammer; New York: Columbia University Press, 1997), 443-67.

[18] Barrie Kavasch. "My Grandmother's Hands," in *Through the Kitchen Window: Women Writers Explore the Intimate Meanings of Food and Cooking* (ed. A. V. Avakian; Boston: Beacon Press, 1997), 106-107.

[19] Zdenek Lederer, *Ghetto Theresienstadt* (New York: Howard Fertig, 1983), 48-49.

[20] *Ibid.*

[21] Berkley, *The Story of Theresienstadt*, 55.

[22] Zhang Xianliang, *Grass Soup* (trans. M. Avery; Boston: David R. Godine, 1995), 161.

Does God Care What We Eat?
Jewish Theologies of Food and Reverence for Life

Jonathan D. Brumberg-Kraus

In this paper, I intend to explore the presumptions behind our justifications for killing or not killing animals for food. I contend that we presume the existence of something: life, vitality, something not completely reducible to the chemical composition of its parts, a quality of existence that previous generations called "the soul." Eating (or not eating) food that was alive is a way of perpetuating these presumed qualities and their rank in a hierarchy of being. I show here how I think Judaism does this, and I put forth some ideas and models to stimulate thinking about these issues. What, for example, are the ethics of dealing with "souls" or whatever comparable term one might use for these phenomena?

So, does God care what we eat? Yes! Kashrut—obviously. But why does God command us, as it says in the Torah, to "distinguish between the unclean and the clean, between the living things that may be eaten and the living things that may not be eaten?" (Lev 11:47). One of the main reasons God commanded the dietary laws was to distinguish the Jews, God's chosen people, from all the other nations of the world. Thus, one thirteenth-century medieval Spanish rabbi, Bahya ben Asher, the author of an ethical manual on eating, characterized the Torah as a "Regimen of the Pleasures" [*dat sha'ashuim*], a rule of spiritual health intended for the Jews alone as a remedy for Adam's sin:

> *We are distinguished by our regimen of the pleasures from the nations who err, rebel and sin.* For we found our Rock in the desert in the land of souls, and there He set for us a table against the nations, and thus David, peace on him, said, "Set before me a table against my enemies" (Ps 23:5).[1]

A second reason was that God wanted us to be mindful and intentional about how we eat, in order to distinguish ourselves from animals. For Rabbenu Bahya, as for many of his medieval intellectual contemporaries—Muslim and Christian doctors and scientists as well as Jews—people who eat indiscriminately and without thought are no better than animals:

> It is well known of the majority of the children of Adam, that their hearts are asleep and slumber, they eat with the blood, they spill blood themselves. *Like an ox eats straw* they eat their bread, and their souls are wasted and devastated, full of the wine of lust and empty of the wine of intellect. Their drunken excess turns against them, hard in pursuit of tangible pleasures, far from the way of truth. How many are those who serve their senses, to fulfill their desire, who gather to drain their cups to please their gullet! And how few are the elite who eat to sustain their body for their Creator's sake! There are some, witless and ignorant, the shifty man, who enjoy without blessing, neglect blessings. There are some fools who spit the good of the world into their vessels; the light of their calm will flash away like lightning, they forget the point when they eat at their tables, if they drink from their bowl. But unique is the one who fears and delights in the Lord even over a dinner of vegetables.[2]

In this view, people who are ruled by their animal desires to eat and drink are incapable of showing proper respect for God. Rules about food, particularly prohibitions against eating blood and requirements for blessing food, transform our ordinary animal instinct to nourish ourselves. They become opportunities to serve and respect God; thus, a third reason for the dietary rules is to promote proper reverence and gratitude toward God. It is within this context that I shall examine the prohibition against consuming blood. The prohibition against eating meat with the blood in it is the paradigmatic example of a fourth reason for the rules of kashrut: to teach reverence for life. But what exactly is the nature and quality of the life that these *mitzvot* are intended to teach us to revere? How can killing animals for food possibly be construed as a way of fostering reverence for life?

The answer to this question can be found in the Torah's equation of blood and life in its prohibition against eating meat with the blood in it. This command appears first in Gen 9:4: "You must not however eat flesh with its life-blood in it" and is reiterated in Lev 17:14: "For the life of all flesh—its blood is its life. Therefore I say to the Israelite people: You shall not partake of the blood of any flesh, for the life of all flesh is its blood. Anyone who partakes of it shall be cut off." I should note here that the Hebrew word translated "life" in these Biblical passages is *nefesh*, which in later medieval texts comes to mean "soul," as in the terminology for the tripartite medieval Platonic conception of the human soul: vegetative soul [*nefesh tzomahat*], animal soul [*nefesh behemit*], and rational soul [*nefesh sekhlit*].

Rabbenu Bahya, in his *Commentary to the Torah*, quotes a long passage from his better-known teacher, Nahmanides (Ramban), to call attention to the Torah's frequent and emphatic equation of blood and *nefesh*. Bahya gives Nahmanides' four explanations of the reason for the prohibition against eating blood. *Nefesh* has different connotations in Biblical and post-Biblical Hebrew. In Biblical Hebrew it means something like "life" or "vitality." Its interpretation as "soul" (implying a dualistic view of body and soul) belongs to later rabbinic and medieval Jewish thought. R. Bahya and Nahmanides knew the difference. Accordingly, I will leave *nefesh* untranslated, though I will use "life" in contexts that seem to refer to its biblical sense [its *peshat* meaning] and "soul" when a text refers to its later philosophical meaning. In this quotation, note especially Nahmanides' rejection of the position of the foremost medieval Jewish philosopher, Maimonides:

Because the *nefesh* [life] of the flesh is in the blood, and I have set it on the altar for you (Lev.17:11). Nahmanides wrote that there are many reasons for the prohibitions against blood. The first is because it is the Lord's portion, like the fat, because just as one burned the fat as incense, as it is written, "All the fat belongs to the Lord" (Lev. 3:16), so they poured the blood on the altar, and accordingly, the Torah prohibited both the fat and the blood, because it was the Exalted One's portion....And another reason was because it is the *nefesh* [life], and the Holy One Blessed Be He never permitted the [consumption of] *nefesh* [life]. And so we found with Adam that all living creatures were prohibited to him and only the grasses and fruits were permitted to him for food, until Noah came and the Holy One Blessed Be He permitted him all the living creatures, since they would not have been saved were it not for him. But what he permitted to him of them was specifically the body and not the *nefesh* [soul], and if so, the *nefesh* still stands under the first prohibition. And another reason is because the blood is the animal soul [*nefesh behemit*]; it is not fit for its nature to be mixed with our nature. We receivers of the Torah require that we be pure of body and fit to receive intelligible things, and we have been commanded to cultivate [lit., grow] our nature to be mild and merciful, not cruel. Were we to eat the blood it would impregnate our soul with cruelty and a coarseness of nature, and make it nearly like an animal soul, because a thing which is eaten turns into the flesh of the body of the eater, and impregnates him with a nature just like him. But blood is not like the rest of foods that change with digestion. Accordingly it says, "The *nefesh* [life] of the flesh is in the blood, and I have set it as an expiation on the altar for you" (Lev.17:11). All these reasons come from the Rabbis. And Maimonides, may his memory be a blessing, wrote on the reasons for the commandments that the prohibition of blood was a way to distance people from engaging in practices with demons, for when Israel went out of Egypt, who were expert in this wisdom, and they grew accustomed to it from the Egyptians, who were drawn to it. Some of their sages when they wanted to gather them, would make a pit and pour blood there, and the demons would collect around the edges of the pit, and when they wanted to prophesy the future they would eat the blood, and this is what Scripture warned against when it said don't eat over the blood....This is the opinion of the Teacher, may his memory be a blessing, in the *Guide to the Perplexed*...but Nahmanides wrote about this that if this was the main reason, why does Scripture say "*nefesh*" every time it mentions the blood prohibition? Therefore, even if Maimonides' explanation makes logical sense, the language of the scriptural verse does not mean this, and so he [Nahmanides] explained it according to what I just wrote.

These two [quotes from] the verse [Lev 17:14] teach that the *nefesh* is in the blood and the blood is in the *nefesh*, that the two are mixed together—like wine mixed with water, where the water is in the wine and the wine is in the water, each in its partner. Accordingly he [Nahmanides] explained and said that [where it is written], "The blood of all flesh do not eat, because the life of all flesh is its blood" [Lev.17:14], comes to explain that the blood is the *nefesh* [soul] itself, that

they became one flesh, they shall not be separated, and that no
blood is found without *nefesh* [soul] and no *nefesh* [soul] without
blood, like matter and form in everything that has a body, that
one is not found without the other.[3]

Bahya goes on to differentiate between blood that pours out of a
wound and blood that flows through a body. I think he is trying to
account for the fact that a certain amount of blood can pour out of a
wound before a person or animal dies from blood loss, and, technically
speaking, the quantity of blood up to that point is not exactly equivalent
to the life; it is not exactly "life-blood." In any case, one is prohibited
from eating both types of blood, presumably out of reverence for the
life-blood it could be.

Thus, it is clear that both the Bible itself and its medieval
interpreters presumed a quasi-scientific theory equating life, blood, and
soul behind the prohibition against eating meat with the blood in it. In
other words, we show respect for life by not eating the "life" part of
permitted animals. However, if that were the case, why doesn't the
Torah forbid meat eating altogether? Nahmanides brings as one of the
reasons for the blood prohibition the rabbinic tradition that it was
God's original intention that humans be vegetarian.[4] Only with Noah
did God allow as a concession the right to eat animals, provided that
the life, specifically the blood, was removed from them. This view comes
from a talmudic tradition that interprets Gen 9:3-4 in relation to Gen
1:29-30 in exactly this way:

> Rabbi Judah said that Rav said, "The first human being was
> not permitted to eat meat, as it is written, "For you it shall be
> to eat, and for every animal on the land" (Gen 1:29-30), and
> not, "Every animal on the land for you [to eat]," and when the
> children of Noah came, [He] permitted them [to eat meat], as
> it is said, "Like the green grasses, I am now giving you everything
> [to eat]" (Gen 9:3). It is possible that this doesn't exclude not
> eating a limb from a living animal, so [in the following verse]
> the Torah teaches, "But the flesh with its *nefesh*, its blood, you
> shall not eat" (Gen 9:4).[5]

Therefore, if meat eating according to kosher law does not appear
to be God's original intent, does God ultimately want to wean us away
from meat eating, or is meat eating the way to fulfill God's Torah?
Essentially, does God want us to be vegetarians or meat eaters? Within
this question lies the issue of God's justice; positions for both meat

eating and vegetarianism have certainly been taken in the tradition. For purposes of comparison, let us examine the relative positions of Rabbi Joseph Gikatilla, another thirteenth century Spanish kabbalist and contemporary of R. Bahya, and the pro-vegetarian position of Rav Abraham Isaac Kook, the first chief rabbi of Israel from this past century.

R. Gikatilla does a kind of end run around the tradition, positing that God changed his intention with Noah. He does this by offering a story that took place during the time of creation and that he feels justifies the morality of God's permission to kill animals for food. R. Gikatilla's position assumes a theory of reincarnation:

And now I have a great key to open this matter. What did the Lord (may He be blessed) see to command in the Torah the slaughter of animals for human beings to eat? For is it not written, "The Lord is good to all, and His mercy extends to all His works" [Ps 145:9]? And if He acts mercifully, why did He command that beasts be slaughtered for human beings to eat— where is the mercy in that? But the secret is in the beginning of the verse, which said, "The Lord is good to all," good in fact, and accordingly "His mercy extends to all His works."

During the work of creation, an agreement was reached with the cow, to be slaughtered, and she said, "Good." And what was her reason? Since the cow had no higher soul to conceive of the work of *HaShem* and His powers, the Lord (may He be blessed), when He was creating the world, told all the beasts to stand before Him, and He said, "If you consent to be slaughtered, and to have human beings eat you, then you will ascend from the status of a beast that knows nothing to the status of a human being who knows and recognizes the Lord (may He be blessed)." And the beasts replied, "Good. His mercies are on us." Whenever a human being eats a portion of the portions of a beast, it turns into a portion of the human being. Here the beast is transformed into a person, and her slaughter is an act of mercy, for she leaves the torah of beasts and enters into the torah of human beings. Death is life for it, in that it ascends to the degree of angels—and this is the secret of "Man and beast the Lord will save"[Ps 36:8].

If you really reflect on the secret of slaughtering animals, then everything comes from the side of His mercy and love for all His creatures. And thus reflect on the reason why our rabbis said in tractate *Pesaḥim* of the Talmud, "It is forbidden for an 'am ha-'aretz [illiterate person who cannot study] to eat meat." For it was not commanded in the Torah to slaughter a beast unless one knows the "torah of beasts, wild animals, and fowl." And whoever engages in Torah is permitted to eat meat. Thus an 'am ha-'aretz does not eat meat because he is like a beast without a soul, and he is not commanded to slaughter a beast only so that another "beast" can eat it, but rather, if so, it [the beast] becomes like carrion and prey [in other words, it is forced to a lower, "unfit" status, to which it presumably would not consent].[6]

For this position, eating meat is a necessary behavior that maintains the hierarchy of status differentiating us from irrational animals bereft of a rational soul and incapable of raising their spiritual status on their own; in this activity we are also brought nearer to the image of God. This interpretation lends new meaning to the "torah of beast and fowl...to distinguish between the living things that may be eaten and the living things that may not be eaten" (Lev 11:46-47). The "torah of beast and fowl" becomes an active Torah, for beast and fowl are to be eaten by those who engage in their torah; eater and eaten are thus distinguished from one other by their relative position in a spiritual hierarchy.

In his vegetarian position, Rav Kook stressed that God wishes to involve us in the process of unifying the differentiated reality, rather than to perpetuate or justify this differentiation. Being weaned from the "torah of beast and fowl" to a vegetarian torah is part of this process of *tikkun* [repair].[7] Richard Schwartz, a professor of mathematics and Orthodox Jewish activist for vegetarianism, summarizes Rav Kook's pro-vegetarian position in this way:

Rav Kook believed that the permission to eat meat was only a temporary concession; he felt that a God who is merciful to his creatures would not institute an everlasting law permitting the killing of animals for food[8]....According to Rav Kook, because people had sunk to an extremely low spiritual level [in the time of Noah], it was necessary that they be taught to value human life above that of animals, and that they first emphasize the improvement of relationships between people. He felt that if people were denied permission to eat meat, some might eat the flesh of human beings instead, due to their inability to control a lust for flesh. He regarded the permission to slaughter animals for food as a "transitional tax" or temporary dispensation until a "brighter era" dawns, when people will return to vegetarian diets[9]....Rav Kook writes that the permission to eat meat "after all the desire of your soul" was a concealed reproach and an implied reprimand. He argues that a day will come when people will detest the eating of the flesh of animals because of a moral loathing, and then people will not eat meat because their soul will not have the urge to eat it.[10]

The permission to eat meat is circumscribed by the many laws and restrictions of kashrut. Rav Kook suggests that the reprimand implied by these regulations is an elaborate apparatus designed to keep alive a sense of reverence for life, with the aim of eventually leading people away from meat eating.[11]

Probably to acknowledge the fact that the time had not yet arrived when humanity would return to the vegetarianism that God originally intended for it, Rav Kook used to eat a token amount of chicken every Sabbath. Moreover, Rav Kook felt that the "moral struggle" against one's inclination to eat meat until the time when God would make victory possible was a good thing:

The only way you would be able to overcome your inclination would be through a moral struggle, but the time for this conquest is not yet. It is necessary for you to wage it in areas closer to yourself. The long road of development, after man's fall, also needs physical assertion, which will at times require a meat diet, which is a tax for passage to a more enlightened epoch, from which animals are not exempt....The advantage of the moral sense when it is linked to its divine source [is that it] knows the proper timing for each objective, and it will sometimes suppress its flow in order to gather up its strength for future epochs, something that the impatient kind of morality that is detached from its source would be unable to tolerate.[12]

Rav Kook's gradualist vegetarianism is perhaps his way of reconciling the tension between God's desire to have us both differentiate and unify the manifold aspects of creation. Thus, on the one hand, restraint in eating animals comes from the moral imperative to recognize that they are like us:

The regulations of slaughter, in special prescriptions, to reduce the pain of the animal registers a reminder that we are not dealing with things outside the law, that they are not automatons devoid of life, but with living things....The feelings of the animal, the sensitivity to its family attachment implied in the rule not to slaughter an ox or a sheep "with its young on the same day" (Lev 22:28), and, on the other hand, the caution against the callous violation of the moral sense in an act of cruelty shown particularly in the breakup of the family implied in the directive concerning a bird's nest, to let the mother bird go before taking the young (Deut 22:26-27)—all these join in mighty demonstration against the general inequality that stirs every heart.[13]

On the other hand, Rav Kook says that human beings "excel" over their fellow creatures with a "firm spiritual superiority."[14] Thus, it seems that the crucial difference between Rav Kook's vegetarian position and the meat eating one of R. Bahya and Gikatilla has to do with the moral implications of human beings' spiritual superiority over animals, on which all three seem to agree. For Rav Kook, the consequence of our spiritual superiority is that we will not eat animals despite our higher rank in the chain of being. For those who make a case for eating meat, the spiritual superiority of humankind over animals (epitomized by *talmidei hakhamim* [those who engage in Torah]) is precisely why at least some of us are entitled to eat the "flesh of beast and fowl."

In conclusion, Jewish theological discussions over whether or not to eat meat assume that both animals and humans have souls. The difference of viewpoint about what God wants us to eat depends on whether one believes that the superiority of human souls entitles people to eat animals or that humans ought to be above eating them. Neither of these positions shares the belief of many contemporary ethical vegetarians and animal rights activists, that human beings and animals are of equal moral status. Nevertheless, both Jewish positions, the meat eating and the vegetarian, find it abhorrent to eat the vital life force, the *nefesh*, that animates animals when they are alive, believing that it is the same vital force that animates us human beings. The traditional Jewish sources, following the Bible's identification of the *nefesh* with the blood, determine that this life force must not be eaten. However, once the term *nefesh*, under the influence of Greek philosophical views of soul/body dualism, takes on the post-biblical connotation of an immaterial soul qualitatively different from the body that houses it, there is a difference of opinion whether or not that sort of soul/*nefesh* is, as it were, "edible." The meat eating position of the thirteenth century Spanish kabbalists understands the eating of meat with the right spiritual intentions to be a kind of reincarnation, in that it raises the souls of the lower animals to a higher rational, spiritual level as they are integrated into the souls of the Torah scholars who eat them.[15] Naturally, any animals with sense would have agreed to this process, as the story of the animals' assent told by Gikatilla conveniently assures us. In this "gastronomic theory of metempsychosis," animal sacrifices in the Bible serve as a powerful metaphor for this process.[16] Just as the fires of the sacrificial altar raise the animal flesh into a refined bodiless odor that is pleasing to God [*re'ah niho'ah*], so the right-minded intentions of the Torah scholar transform the animal souls he eats into higher souls—circumventing even the need to involve female creatures in the rebirth process.[17]

Obviously, an important part of this theory is the privileging of rationality over the animal and vegetative capacities of the soul. In this view, our rationality, so long as it is in accord with God's reasoning (specifically, the Torah), gives us the right to kill and eat creatures with only animal and vegetative souls. However, if it is in fact the case that animals do not have rational souls, how could they then have had the capacity to consent to be slaughtered for food; how could they know what it would mean to have their souls raised? The vegetarian position avoids this paradox by drawing a different conclusion about rational souls: rational, spiritually enlightened souls will not eat other souls because they will not "taste good" to them. For Rav Kook, the perfected soul by its very nature "will detest the eating of the flesh of animals because of a moral loathing, and people [with such a soul] will not eat meat because their soul will not have the urge to eat it."[18]

Both carnivorous and vegetarian diets can find support in the traditional Jewish sources about the nature of the *nefesh*. Remember the traditions Nahmanides assembles, in which he uses both "high" and "low" views of the soul to explain the prohibition against eating blood without really trying to reconcile them with one another. Some souls seem to have a taste for flesh, some do not. In the philosophical realm of souls, it may well be that the old Hebrew saying applies: *al ta'am ve-re'ah ayn le-hitvake'ah* [there's no accounting for taste].

Both the vegetarian and meat-eating positions in the classic Jewish sources base their moral conclusions about what to eat on a belief in some sort of immaterial, eternal, God-like "soul." In other words, these moral imperatives to eat or not to eat meat presuppose a medieval hierarchical and dualistic conception of the soul that presumably we modern people do not share. Moreover, it is significant that both these classic Jewish positions are based on a mystical understanding of the process of eating, where eating is an act of *tikkun,* of cosmic repair, a way of raising the status of souls, not only of the diner, but also in some cases of one's dinner.

Whether or not we share these assumptions, Jewish mystical attitudes about food raise important questions about our own modern, scientifically informed assumptions and experiences of what it means to be alive. Does it make sense for human beings to sacrifice the lives of other beings—animals—for food, clothing, medical experimentation, or for other activities intended to enhance our lives, without the assumption of a hierarchy of being or "souls" like that implicit in these classic Jewish theories about food? It is arguable that the kabbalistic interpretation of meat eating and animal sacrifices shows "reverence for life" by striving to raise all forms of life to the highest possible level, even if that means consuming it.

On the other hand, most vegetarians sense, on an intuitive level, that killing something to eat it is inherently disrespectful. Thus in certain "exo-cannibalistic" cultures that ate their defeated enemies, "there was no more certain way to insult someone than to say, 'I will use your head as a cooking pot,' or to refer to a man or a part of him as 'cooked,' or to give some dish the man's name."[19] This is essentially what meat eaters do to the animal flesh they eat; this also serves as an expression of precisely the low moral level Rav Kook says we human beings will grow out of when the messianic era comes. So, is the idea of higher and lower forms of life—upon which classic Jewish ethics of reverence for life is based—morally sound or even empirically demonstrable? Must any sort of ethical claim to revere life necessarily believe in a soul—a *nefesh*—the vital life force that animates human beings and animals alike? It seems that the very thing that we share with animals, the *nefesh*/life-force/blood, is precisely that part of the animal the Bible says we must not eat.

This raises the question as to why is it wrong to eat the animal's *nefesh*. Is it because the animal with its *nefesh*/life in it is too much like us; if we eat their living limbs with the *nefesh*/blood still in it, we would be like cannibals and murderers (Gen 9:3-4)? Or because the *nefesh* is precisely that part of humans and animals that is not ours to give and take; is it the case that the *nefesh* is God-given, intrinsically sacred, and therefore must not be dishonored in this way? The evolving meaning of *nefesh* over time makes sorting out responses to this question ever more complicated.

Regardless of how we answer these questions, one thing is clear: Jewish ritual and mystical traditions intentionally transform eating into moral philosophy. In turn, that moral philosophy transforms our eating into divine service, as if we were offering sacrifices to God in the Temple. As it says in *m. Avot* 3:3: "At every table over which three have eaten and have spoken words of Torah over it, it as if they have eaten from the table of God."

NOTES

[1] Bahya ben Asher ben Hlava, *Shulhan Shel Arba* in *Kitve Rabenu Bahya* [*Kad ha-kemah—Shulhan shel arba—Pirke avot*] (ed. Charles B. Chavel; Jerusalem: Mossad Harav Kook, 1969), 459. The citations of R. Bahya are based on this Hebrew edition of *Shulhan Shel Arba*; the translations of this and other post-Biblical Hebrew texts are mine, unless otherwise indicated.

[2] Bahya ben Asher, *Shulhan Shel Arba*, 460.

[3] Bahya ben Asher ben Hlava, *Be'ur al ha-Torah*. (ed. Charles B. Chavel; Jerusalem: Mossad Harav Kook, 1968) v. 2:506-7.

[4] See also in this volume, Gary Rendsberg, "The Vegetarian Ideal in the Bible," in *Food and Judaism* (vol. 15 in Studies in Jewish Civilization; ed. L. J. Greenspoon, et al.; Omaha: Creighton University Press, 2005).

[5] B. Sanhedrin 59b.

[6] Joseph Gikatilla, *Shaare Orah* (ed. Joseph Ben Shlomo; Jerusalem: Mossad Bialik, 1981) 2:11-12. See also R. Bahya, *Shulhan shel 'Arba*, 496:

> Our sages taught, It is forbidden for an *'am ha-'aretz* to eat meat, as it is written, "This is the *Torah* of the beast and fowl.'[Lev. 11:46] All who engage in Torah are permitted to eat the meat of beasts and fowl, and all who do not engage in Torah are forbidden to eat beast and fowl [*b. Pes.* 49b.]. The explanation of this among the enlightened is [that] when we set aside a soul for a soul, this is nothing other than the animal [lit., mobile] soul that we annihilate for the intellectual soul. But because one is an *'am ha-'aretz* and has no intellectual soul, you have it that he is forbidden to eat meat, since [in him] we have nothing to set aside and annihilate the animal soul, since he is someone who has no intellectual soul, and understand this.

I discuss this tradition at length in "Meat-Eating and Jewish Identity: Ritualization of the Priestly 'Torah of Beast and Fowl' [Lev. 11:46] in Rabbinic Judaism and in Medieval Kabbalah," *Association for Jewish Studies Review*, 24:2 (1999) 227-62.

[7] See especially Abraham Isaac Kook, "Fragments of Light: A View as to the Reasons for the Commandments" in *Abraham Isaac Kook—The Lights of Penitence, Lights of Holiness, The Moral Principles, Essays, Letters, and Poems* (trans. and intro. B. Z. Bokser (The Classics of Western Spirituality; New York: Paulist, 1978) 317-20.

[8] *Ibid.*, 318.

[9] *Ibid.*

[10] *Ibid.*

[11] Richard H. Schwartz, *Judaism and Vegetarianism* (New York: Lantern Books/Booklight, Inc., 2001) 3,4,10,11.

[12] Kook, "Fragments of Light," 318.

[13] *Ibid.*, 319.

[14] *Ibid.*, 317.

[15] Brumberg-Kraus, "Meat-Eating and Jewish Identity," 257.

[16] *Ibid.*

[17] *Ibid.*, 259.

[18] Kook, "Fragments of Light," 318.

[19] Margaret Visser, *The Rituals of Rinner: The Origins, Evolution, Eccentricities, and Meaning of Table Manners* (New York: Penguin, 1991) 15.

Nebraska Jewish Charitable Cookbooks, 1901-2002

Oliver B. Pollak

I handed her some community cookbooks from her home state, Iowa. Books typical of the kind that are compiled to raise money for churches, schools, and other organizations. To her amazement, the young woman found that one of the cookbooks was from a neighboring county and she was able to recognize the recipes and the names of some of the contributors. She too had found her place and her people in a cookbook.[1]

Cookbooks reveal culinary culture, family and religious values, technology, and domestic economy. The "compiled cookbook," "fund-raising cookbook,"[2] or "charitable cookbook" is an American genre dating from after the Civil War. Margaret Cook identified about two thousand charitable cookbooks published before 1915, twenty-three of which were Jewish.[3] Untold thousands more have been published since. Lacking copyright and ISBN identification, they elude library cataloguing and comprise "a vastly underutilized resource."[4] Nebraska Jewry produced about twenty-five Jewish charity cookbooks, only four of which are listed on the electronic library data base WorldCat. This essay explores Jewish foodways in Nebraska through the collective efforts of women raising money for building funds, scholarships, and other causes. It comprises a record of social interaction and prosopography.[5]

Cookbooks are normally organized around the order of the meal, beginning with appetizers and ending with desserts; they are also organized according to spiritual and seasonal cycles. Kashrut is not the defining standard of Jewish cookbook. Kashrut marks social boundaries within the Jewish community and the larger community. Social mobility challenged the observance of kashrut inside and outside the home. Cookbooks articulated different visions of J ewish life. Maintaining separateness from the larger community reinforced religious precepts. About seventy percent of the Nebraska Jewish cookbooks observed kashrut.

German-language Jewish cookbooks predated the English volumes by several decades. The first English-language Jewish cookbook, *The Jewish Manual, or, Practical Information in Jewish & Modern Cookery with a Collection of Valuable Recipes & Hints Relating to the Toilette,* appeared in London in 1846. Esther Levy published the first American-Jewish cookbook, *Jewish Cookery Book: On Principles of Economy,* in 1871, in Philadelphia. Levy quoted Proverbs to describe the model woman who "riseth while it is yet night and giveth provision to her household" [Prov 31:15]. She suggested about ninety necessary kitchen utensils including coal scuttle, jagging iron, lamp cleaner, and wedge for breaking ice.[6] *Jennie June's American Cookery Book* offered seven pages of twenty-six Jewish "receipts," including white stewed fish and Purim fritters.[7]

The first Jewish charity cookbook, *The Fair Cookbook,* appeared in Denver in 1888.[8] *The Settlement Cook Book, The Way to a Man's Heart,* by Lizzie Black Kander, appeared in 1901 under the aegis of the Milwaukee National Council of Jewish Women in Milwaukee; it was a marvelous NCJW fundraiser. The 182-page 1903 edition contained matzos and shellfish recipes. The 623-page, 1947, 28th enlarged and revised edition contains a chapter for Passover and also has pork recipes.

The Passover Seder is central to Jewish identity. Synagogue and commercial pamphlets, Passover sections in the supermarket, community workshops, a miniature Seder table at the Jewish Community Center, eradicating *hametz,* eating unleavened bread, and avoiding *unpesadiche* food fostered a creative profusion of recipes for a limited number of dishes. Kugel is ubiquitous. Janet Theophano asserts: "Every Jewish family has its own recipe for haroseth, the apple and cinnamon dish meant to represent the Jews' bondage in Egypt, or gefilte fish, which some claim should be sweet and others insist must be savory."[9] Ruth Reichl writes, "Every girl should know how to make gefilte fish."[10] Although the homemaker may prepare gefilte fish from scratch, she may also purchase it jarred, canned, or frozen, or decide to eat out.

Learning to make matzo balls involves visual, verbal, aromatic, tactile, and textual cues, encompassing tradition, conventional wisdom, and innovation. Ingredients for matzo balls since 1846 have included chopped suet, pepper, salt, ginger, nutmeg, eggs, oil, onions, suet fat, chopped parsley, goose fat, and chicken grease. Cooks can follow the

Manischewitz, Streits, Rokeach, or Shmuras directions to make their own matzo balls, or, as with gefilte fish, they can find matzos balls frozen, canned, or in a jar. Guests at the Seder table may have been longing for matzo balls for several days. The cook may worry about how they will turn out. Words like light, fluffy, golf balls, and soft balls, combined with requests for second helpings, pepper the dinner conversation. Vikki Weiss and Jennifer A. Block reveal additional significance to food in their book, *What to Do When You're Dating a Jew: Everything You Need to Know from Matzoh Balls to Marriage.*[11]

Temple Israel, a Reform congregation founded in Omaha in 1871, published a 78-page book in 1901, titled, *Cook Book Compiled for the Benefit of Building Fund.* Contributors included Mrs. Nathan Rothschild, Mrs. Charles Rosewater, Mrs. L. Kirschbraun, Mrs. B. Newman, Mrs. J. L. Brandeis, and Mrs. Arthur Brandeis, comprising the wealthy Jewish elite. The chapter, "Easter Desserts," actually covers Passover desserts. A dessert section in German used Gothic typeface. Some German recipes were translated into English.[12] Heavy on cakes and pastries, the book included not a single matzo ball recipe, but there were several recipes for oysters, lobster, and shrimp. Among the advertisements was a testimonial from Rabbi Isaac P. Mendes of Mickva Israel, Savannah, Georgia, stating that Wesson's cooking and salad oils were appropriate for "Israelites who are strict in the observance of their Dietary Laws."

In 1916, Temple Israel Sisterhood published *The Greater Omaha Cook Book*, which sold for $1.00.[13] Mrs. Edward Treller and Mrs. Charles S. Elgutter, heads of the Book and Recipe committees for the Temple, presented the book "to the housekeeper with the confidence that it contains many new and carefully selected recipes of appetizing dishes, which have been tried and tested." The individual recipes are anonymous. The section "Matzos or Passover Dishes" replaced those for "Easter Desserts," but there were still seventeen oyster recipes, as well as directions for clams, lobster, bacon, and ham.

In the mid 1960s Temple Israel produced a tin recipe box containing 109 three-by-five recipe cards. Mrs. Donald (Mickey) Sturm wrote in the Preface, "We are proud to offer you this treasury of special favorite recipes....We hope it will be a continuing part of our Sisterhood program...Good Health and Happy Cooking." Each recipe card provided the name and telephone number of the recipe contributor. "Herring & Sour Cream Appetizer" by Joan Rips was again followed by several crab and shrimp dip recipes. Traditional Jewish recipes included

Kamish Bread, Rose Weiner; Esther's Piroshkes, Gigi Osten; Hamantaschen, Lyra Monasee; Passover Bagel and Beet Borscht by Ruth Garber; Lockshin (noodle) Pudding by Ruth Wise; and Kreplach and Never Fail Matzo Balls by Frances Cohn.

Theophano suggests Jewish cookbooks negotiate the complex relationship of multiple Jewish identities, "American, Jew and Zionist in a multicultural society."[14] This is evidenced when, one hundred and one years after publishing its first cookbook, Temple Israel published *Unleavened, A Collection of Passover Fare*.[15] Marked by these two books, the century starts by exemplifying the foodways of Reform Judaism assimilation and ends with a reinvigorated traditional dedication to Passover. *Unleavened* provides five matzo ball recipes, accompanied by the loving text of its creators. Judy Zweibeck writes: "I ask the person who uses a book to sign his or her name and the year. The books hold very special memories—particularly the ones with the name of those who share our Seders in spirit." While not a kosher cookbook, it goes out of its way to avoid non-kosher foods. A modern note is hit in a gefilte fish recipe that calls for frozen tube gefilte fish.

Beth El, Omaha's Conservative congregation established in 1929, never produced a full-scale cookbook. It participated in three smaller recipe projects, starting with a 22-page pamphlet produced in the mid-1950s, *A Hopechest of Jewish Recipes, 18 Traditional Dishes*. In May 1974, the Mid-west Branch of National Women's League, part of the Conservative Movement, met in Waterloo, Iowa, and produced a mimeographed multi-congregation cookbook, *Memories Meichals* [special personal recipes]—*Midwest Style*. Delegates came from Denver, Des Moines, Kansas City, Marshalltown, Mason City, Minneapolis, St. Joseph, St. Louis, Sioux City, Waterloo, and Winnipeg. Lincoln delegates Mrs. Irv Goldenberg and Mrs. Elmer Shamberg provided blintzes and strudel. From Omaha, Mrs. Benjamin Wiesman and Ilene Klein provided Passover Appplenut Cake and Chopstick Tuna. Brief histories of women's work in the congregations accompanied the recipes.

In 1994, Beth El produced *The Simcha "Just Deserts" Cookbook, A Collection of Recipes from the Sisterhood of Beth El Synagogue*. This ninety-one page booklet contains many recipes by Lucy White, who is not Jewish but has been directing food service at Beth El since the 1960s. About "Grandma's Cinnamon Rolls" she says, "I made these rolls, they are delicious—very, very good," and of "Walnut Spice Cake" she enthuses, "A very good cake—everybody just loves this cake." Karen Pollak

contributed baklava and "Aunt Sara's Recipe" for "Graham Wafer Bars."
Mary Arbitman Fellman contributed her mother's hamantaschen recipe.

Lincoln's Tifereth Israel, founded in 1913, is a Conservative
congregation whose Sisterhood published *Bagels to Blintzes* in 1984[16]
The cookbook committee of twelve women stated in the "Expression of
Appreciation": "Many of these recipes reflect our traditional Jewish way
of cooking handed down from mother to daughter, generation to
generation." A two-page glossary, "Bagel to Yom Kipper" gives this
definition of kosher:

> The recipes in this cookbook conform to the laws of Kashruth
> (kosher). These laws mean the use of pork, certain cuts of beef,
> lamb and veal, shellfish, and other fish which do not have scales
> are prohibited. The mixture of dairy products with meat or
> meat products is also not allowed. Some foods may be used
> with either. There foods are called "pareve" and are neither meat
> (fleishig) or dairy (milchig). Fruits, vegetables, fish, and eggs
> are examples of pareve foods.

Bagels to Blintzes includes recipes from Helene Krivosha, wife of Norman
Krivosha, former Nebraska Supreme Court Chief Justice, and Jan, Sarah,
Sonia, and Tillie Breslow, related to the Republican State Auditor, John
Breslow. The cookbook also reflects mobility within the state. Lincolnites
Hanna DeBruin and Phyllis Silberstein moved to Omaha. Brenda
Friedman, who teaches at the University of Nebraska at Lincoln,
contributed a recipe for "Passover Nut Balls." There are Chinese, French,
Greek, Hawaiian, Israeli, Italian, Korean and New England offerings.

Frances Groner, wife of Benjamin Groner, the spiritual leader of
Orthodox Beth Israel from 1953 to 1965, published a twenty-six page
Passover Parade of Recipes, probably in 1955. In 1967, the Beth Israel
Sisterhood published *Happiness is Good Food.*[17] Mrs. Jay (Esther) Stoler,
president of the Sisterhood, stated that *Happiness is Good Food* is the
sisterhood's "labor of love." Their goal "is to make available traditional
kosher recipes handed down by 'our mothers' as well as offerings of our
modern day cooks." Fifty people were involved in production. Two pages
were devoted to the Dietary Laws of Kashrut, The Fitness of Food, The
Method of Slaughter, The Koshering (salting) Process, and Meat and
Milk.

Mrs. Max (Ida) Sacks provided 103 of the 520 recipes and a few
editorial comments, such as Gefilte Fish (Like Mama Used to Make)
and Strudel (like "Bubbie" used to make). Ida, an assistant in a television

cooking program, gave cooking demonstrations at Beth Israel. She tested many of the recipes on her family. She did not cook unless she had sour cream, real butter, schmaltz [chicken fat], and sugar. Her refrigerator was full with at least ten good things to eat.[18] Ida's husband Max owned an army surplus store.

Mrs. Isaac (Jeannette) Nadoff, the rabbi's wife, exhibited the family's Yemenite background in String Beans (Yemenite-Style). Mrs. Isadore Elewitz provided twenty-six recipes. Mrs. Ignac (Miriam) Grossman provided one recipe, "Moist Apple Cake." Theo Richmond recorded Miriam's larger story in *Konan*.[19] Only two recipes were accompanied by commentaries. Mrs Harold (Lucille) Zelinsky, a social work professor at the University of Nebraska, provided the following with Gramma Polly's Casserole:

> Once upon a time when I was a little girl, my grandmother used to serve a delicious ONE-DISH meal on cold winter nights that lingered in my memory with aroma and "tamme." I could never figure out when and how she had time to make it, because my grandmother was never home. She was a real "yente." She went to meetings and belonged to at least three card-playing groups, to say nothing about belonging to every Jewish Women's Organization in town. When it appeared evident that I was arriving at the stage of life when many afternoons would be spent in going to meetings, etc., I confronted Gramma Polly for her recipe of this long-remembered dish.

Synagogue kitchens catered bar and bat mitzvahs, weddings, and other congregational events. Cooking for hundreds of people requires a coordinator, volunteers, and tried recipes. Beth Israel included a chapter, "Beth Israel Kitchen," with salad, kugel, and other dishes for large groups. A chapter titled "Celebrities" included recipes from opera stars Richard Tucker, Roberta Peters, Robert Merrill, as well as Sammy Davis, Jr., Abigail Van Buren, Theodore Bikel, and Arthur Goldberg, President Lyndon Johnson's United Nations ambassador. The first edition sold out. The Sisterhood reissued *Happiness is Good Food* in 1971, deleting the thirty-nine page "Shopper's Guide" consisting of advertisements and the index.[20]

Happiness is Still Good Food appeared in 1993.[21] President Georgia Ann Steinberg repeated the litany, "Many of these recipes reflect our traditional Jewish way of cooking—having been handed down from mother to daughter, generation to generation." The 1993 edition, produced using a word processor and sold in a three ring binder, expanded the 1967 edition.

These were significant additions. The new generation took their own names in the 1970s. Mrs. Annette Fettman, an artist and the wife of Hungarian-born Cantor Leo Fettman, provided "Cheesecake without Guilt" and "My Hungarian Loves it Lasagna." Recipes were presented by Mrs. Iz Elewitz and Frieda Elewitz. Julie Katzman, wife of synagogue president Rick Katzman, provided "Curry Dip." Sophie Katz Schulman provided Red Lentil Soup. Susan Paley liked to build recipes around family and contributed "The Ben and Audrey Dessert" and "The Nikki Salad (for 12)," named after her daughter. An unsigned gefilte fish recipe had the additional description "(Food Processor Method)." Notable deletions from 1967 volume were two recipes for *Pitcha* (jellied calves' feet) by Mrs. Haskell Morris and Mrs. Max Sacks; tastes had changed, vegetarianism was more popular, and the city no longer had a kosher butcher.

Omaha's secular Jewish life was organized around the Omaha Hebrew Club, Hadassah, B'nai B'rith, National Council of Jewish Women, ORT, Jewish Community Center, and Jewish Federation. Hadassah and Council raised funds by producing an annual yearbook listing all members, with addresses and telephone numbers, first name of spouse, and advertisements.

Hadassah was created in 1912. In October 1927, Mrs. M. F. Levenson, who headed a committee of sixteen married women, pleaded for "more and more kosher recipes." In 1928, the Omaha chapter published *Hadassah Kosher Cook Book*, which sold for $1.00. The book opens with a statement about Hadassah's program and goals. This is the first of over fifty Hadassah cookbooks and the only volume until 2002 to include "Kosher" in the title. Full page ads were purchased by National Laundry Co. and People's Coal Co.[22]

In 1954, Council Bluffs Hadassah published a forty-eight page booklet, *What's Cooking in Hadassah?*, edited by Mrs. Ben Telpner, introduced by president Mrs. Oscar Greenberg, and illustrated by Mrs. Joe Katelman. The Jewish community in Council Bluffs had a synagogue, B'nai B'rith, and Jewish Community Center. The aging Hadassah chapter was decommissioned in May 2002.

B'nai B'rith, established in 1843, arrived in Omaha in 1884 and provided lodge fellowship and insurance. Omaha loomed large through the leadership of Henry Monsky and Philip Klutznick and the creation here of the youth organization AZA.[23] In 1952, B'nai B'rith Women produced the *B'nai B'rith Year Book*, which appeared almost annually though changing its name to *B'nai B'rith Souvenir Year Book, 1953, and Recipe Book*; starting in 1956, the *B'nai B'rith Annual Souvenir Recipe and Year Book* appeared. Nine issues were published from 1952 to 1963, describing the organization's activities, listing officers, committees, published ads, and recipes.

B'nai B'rith represented a wide spectrum of Omaha Jewish life. The 1959 issue contained recipes by Mrs. Sidney (Jane) Brooks, wife of Temple Israel's rabbi, Mrs. Myer (Dorothy) Kripke, a children's story writer and the wife of Beth El's rabbi, and Mrs. Max Sacks, Beth Israel's indefatigable cook. The publication in 1963 of *Eppes Essen* [Something to Eat], by forty members of B'nai B'rith Woman and their daughters in B'nai B'rith Girls, replaced the annual recipe and advertisement books.[24] A kosher cookbook, it is the only one to contain recipes in Yiddish. The last two pages had broiled fish, stuffed broiled potatoes, plum and apple pie, beat borsht with meat, fish baked in tomato sauce, and traditional *kreplakh*.[25] A second edition of *Eppes Essen*, appeared in 1972.[26] Although "A Word of Thanks" is extended to "our Mothers, Mothers-in-law, Grandmothers, and friends who helped by contributing many traditional recipes," the recipes are anonymous. This is the last cookbook containing advertisements.

The New Women's American ORT (Organization for Rehabilitation through Training), founded in 1880 in St. Petersburg, produced hardbound cookbooks in 1959, 1972, and 1980. The Omaha chapter, formed in 1972, produced in 1982, 1983, 1985, 1990 and 1992, "cooking pamphlets" ranging from eleven to sixty-one pages and titled *Taste'n Tell, Taste & Tell* and *Taste and Tell*.

The National Council of Jewish Women, founded in 1893, arrived in Omaha in 1896, and reemerged again in 1920. Many NCJW members belonged to Temple Israel. In 1960, NCJW produced a 168-page wirebound *Council Cooks* as part of the fortieth anniversary celebration. The Council Cooks Committee included Mrs. Ernest Hochster, Max Granat, Robert Levine, Maurice Feldman, Harold Garber, and Edward Milder. Their motto, "Faith and Humanity," was attested by two photographs depicting assistance to the blind and the aged. The last three pages identified about 450 contributors and donors. In 1973, NCJW produced *Council Cooks* in a three-ring looseleaf binder with chapter illustrations by Civvy Roffman.[27] Thirty women served on committees (including a "Low Calorie Recipe" committee), and fifteen typists produced the book. Recipes included ribs, clams, crabs, and shrimp. Bernard Schimmel, innkeeper and chef of the famous Blackstone Hotel, Harold Farber, Lloyd Friedman, Sol S. Parsow, Justin Horwich, Eddie Tepperman, Harold Slosburg, and David Fredricks contributed twenty recipes to the chapter entitled "From Men Only."

The Kitchen Connection appeared in 1983.[28] Edited by Sandy Kutler, it had two hundred contributors, thirty-four committee members, eleven proofreaders, and one typist. The authors declared that their book "represents the best of what we have received from our mothers and grandmothers. It is our hope that you will enjoy using these recipes as much as we have enjoyed collecting them." It avoided *trefe* ingredients. Ten thousand copies were printed. Initially priced at $11.95, volumes were given away as part of the welcome package at the August 2002 Maccabi Games.

The Jewish Federation of Omaha, formed in 1903, built a downtown Jewish Community Center in 1926. It moved to the western suburbs in 1973 and remains the center for non-synagogue Jewish life in Omaha. In April 1981 and March 1983, the Jewish Cultural Arts Council sponsored Passover preparation workshops. Participants in 1981 were Frieda Elewitz, A. M. Goldkrand, Sandy Kutler, Joyce Cohen, Marci Gallner, Mary Fellman, Steve Riekes, and Judy Rosenblatt. Contributors in 1983 were Carol Katzman, Susie Drazen, Margie Gutnik, Doreen Lerner, Annette Fettman, and Sharon Greene. In 1984, the Jewish Cultural Arts Council's College of Jewish Family Learning and twenty-two contributors produced the thirty-six page *Passover Cookbook and Contemporary Guide to Pesach.* Doreen Lerner, chairman of the College of Jewish Family Learning, wrote: "The Jewish Cultural Arts Council would like to present to you this collection of recipes from our community as well as a few suggestions on making your Pesach more enjoyable."

In 2001, the Jewish Federation of Omaha produced *L'Dor V'Dor, The Untested Cookbook.* One hundred fifty-one pages in length, it sold for $10.00. Sheryn Joffe, Suzanne Pocras, and Andrea Siegel, the 2001 Women's Event co-chairs, offered the cookbook with the "hope that *The Untested Cookbook* will be a treasured souvenir, and that it brings you fond memories of the past and present as you celebrate with food 'from generation to generation.'" It includes "Mama Stamberg's Cranberry Sauce," read annually around Thanksgiving on National Public Radio. Little about this cookbook is specifically Jewish other

than an Orthodox contributor mentioning "parve." Some recipes invoke
the names of mothers, aunts, and grandmothers. Lucy White's recipe
for baklava is included. The last page contains a disclaimer: "The recipes
in *The Untested Cookbook* may or may not meet the standards of kashrut.
Substitutions may be made to adapt recipes."

The following cookbooks, although not charity cookbooks, reveal
Jewish contributions to community cookbooks. In 1933, the *Omaha
Bee-News* published the *Prudence Penny's Homemakers Guide and Cook
Book*. A Depression-era work, it contained recipes by Mrs. Nate Mantel,
Mrs. David M. Newman, Mrs. S. G. Saltzman, and Mrs. H.
Mierendorff. The *Centennial Cook Book of Omaha, 1854-1954*,
published in 1954 by the Womans' Division of the Omaha Chamber
of Commerce, contained Mrs. David Adler's recipe for "Pineapple
Raspberry Cake" submitted by Mrs. Izadore Elewitz. However, *100
Years of Republican Cooking in Nebraska, 1867-1967*, introduced by
Mamie Doud Eisenhower, contained no Jewish names.

In 1947, Lillian Chapman Gottstein produced *Aunt Lil's Famous
Tested Recipes*.[29] Lillian, born in Centerville, Iowa, came from a family
of seven girls and three boys and felt quite comfortable cooking for large
groups. She served as a housemother from 1942 to 1947 at a sorority at
the University of Illinois and the ZBT, the Jewish fraternity at the
University of Nebraska. Gottstein explained, "My friends have been
asking me for years to compile a cookbook, and it was not fair for me to
keep my recipes from being used, so that is why I am sharing my food
treasures with you."

In 1974, the Ethnic Committee of the Omaha/Douglas County
Bicentennial Commission published *The Melting Pot, An Ethnic
Cookbook*. None of the twenty-four person committee and associates
appears to be Jewish. Jewish recipe contributors included Cheryl Kraft,
Mrs. Max Sacks, Esther Meiches, Miriam Soshnik, Joan Margolin, Judy
Tully, Sandy Kohll, Miriam Simon, Liberty Faier, Tina Palmisano, Mrs.
Seymour Goldston, Mrs. Morris Becker, Mrs. Isaac Nadoff, Marilyn
Abraham, Lorraine Silverman, Ginny Becker, Josephine Fraenkel, and
Mrs. E. R. Simon. Nebraskans were exposed to "Aunt Ida's Onion Rolls,"
and recipes for bagel, water bagel, honey cake, cheese blintzes, apple
kuchen, easy strudel, *hamantaschen*, *mandelbrodt*, carrot *tzimmes*,
chopped chicken liver, *knishes*, spinach borscht, beet borscht, holiday
chicken soup, *knaidlach*, onion soup, *lokschen* kugel, latkes, and potato
kugel. Indian, Czech, French, German, Greek, Italian, Japanese, Korean,

Lithuanian, Mexican, Polish, Scandinavian, Scottish, Serbian, Ukrainian, and West African cooking were also represented.

Religion-based cookbooks frequently contain a recipe for life, a composite of ideals, inspiration, and solidarity. Rabbi Martin J. Zion provided "A Rabbi's Recipe" to *Council Cooks*:

Take an overflowing measure of cheerfulness and add the milk of human kindness. Leaven with constantly rising good spirits and fold in plenty of patience. Season with common sense and a lot of laughter. Do not let the mixture stand, but stir continuously in the cup of your life. When ready, bake in the warmth of your heart, over a high flame of faith. Do not cover with the icing of selfishness or indifference. Instead, spread thickly with love, and serve large and generous portions daily to your friends and family.

B'nai B'rith Women revealed their ten ingredients and Guaranteed Recipe for the Success in *Eppes Essen*.

Advertisements identify the prevailing technology, modes of transportation, power sources (coal, gas, electricity), merchandizing, and longevity of businesses. Materialism, labor saving devices, consumer services, and household activities are amply represented. Advertisements provided social and economic information about Omaha businesses.

Temple Israel's 1901 cookbook predates the automobile. Advertisers included wagon dealers, livery supplies, harness shops, horse shoeing, and bicycle shops. The Union Pacific, Burlington, Chicago, Milwaukee and St. Paul, Missouri Pacific, North-Western railroads published train schedules. Utility companies promoted the efficiency of gas and electricity. Household matters included Nebraska Clothing Company, tailors, alterations, furrier, hats, storage, upholstery, lumber, hardware, rubber goods, sewing machines, liquor distributors, and breweries. Comestibles included baking powder, yeast, flour, and Wesson oil.

Temple's 1916 cookbook contained fifty-two advertisements for clothing, food, health, home maintenance, money management, tailors, clothiers, dry cleaners, furriers, coal, ice, window shade cleaning, flowers, candy, liquor, beer, flour, corn starch, matzos, baking powder, meat, grocers, prescriptions, dentists, plumbing, pianos, insurance, banks, real estate, investments, theaters, and photo studios. Brand names included Karo syrup, Jello, Knox Gelatin, and Shredded Wheat. Merchants offered electric appliances, refrigerators, and electric cars.

Hadassah's 1928 cookbook included Roberts Sanitary Dairy, Butter-Nut coffee and tea, Baker Ice Machine Co., Omar Baking Company, Kraft Cheese and Nucoa Nut Margarine, Gilinsky Fruit, Somberg Delicatessen Stores (3 locations), Sunset Tea Room, Candyland and Crystal Candy Company, Advo Coffee, Loose-Wiles Biscuit Co., Alamito Dairy, Old Settler Rye Bread, Ernest Buffett, The Buy-Rite Grocer of Dundee, Harding's Ice Cream, Fairmont Icecream, Hinky Dinky, National Laundry Co., People's Coal Co., home landscape, flowers, Omaha Lace Laundry, Omaha Laundry, Fischer Millinery, drapery shop, Pillow Co., I. Berkovitz fur storage, home furnishings at Union Outfitting Company, Royal Rug Cleaning Co., Dutch Cleaner, silk, upholstering, loans, extermination and insecticides, coal and feed, plumbing and heating, Pittsburg Plate Glass Co., lumber, Sam Tarnoff Painting, Paperhanging and Decorating, Sol Lewis, State Furniture Co, Creamery Butter, Nebraska Power Co., J. M. Opper Motor Co. carrying the Reo line, and Spangenberg & Beauchesne auto painting.

The 1954 Council Bluffs Hadassah cookbook had 289 advertisers, including Nebraska Furniture Mart, Shaver's Food Mart, Master Furniture and Appliance, and Iowa Clothiers. Beth El's 1955 book contained three advertisements: Sol Lewis, "Over 30 years Westinghouse Headquarters" with downtown, Crossroads, and Bellevue locations; Nebraska Furniture Mart with locations in Omaha, Lincoln and Council Bluffs; and Pepsi-Cola.

The 1960 *Council Cooks* contains 89 advertisements. Familiar advertisers included Nebraska Furniture Mart, Omaha Public Power District, Milder Oil Co., Buffett and Son, Albert's Salad Dressing, and H. Z. Vending & Sales Co. Edward Zorinsky (of H. Z. Vending) became mayor of Omaha and a United States senator. Advertisers no longer in business include Peter Pan Bread, Armstrong Cleaners, N. S. Yaffe Printing ("The best recipe for GOOD Printing"), Levenson's "We Kill Pests," Jolly Giant Stores, Manny's Record Shop, Graystone Dairy, Ross' Steak House, and Shaver's.

The 1963 B'nai B'rith cookbook contained fifteen restaurant advertisements; only Johnny's Café, the Village Inn Pancake House, and the Bohemian Café are still in operation. It contained seven ads for wholesale and retail liquor. The 1967 Beth Israel cookbook "Shopper's Guide" contained 173 advertisements. The ads raised $1,600, and the book sold for $4.50. B'nai B'rith's 1972 book, *Eppes Essen*, had seven full-page ads: Cris Rexall Drugs, Grace-Mayer Insurance, Nebraska

Furniture Mart, David A. Baxter & Son, electrical contractors (which became Baxter Kenworthy Electric, Inc.), and Sterling Distributing Co.

The 1972 B'nai B'rith book was the last to include advertisements. Between 1901 and 1972 family businesses might pass to the next generation, change names, incorporate, merge, consolidate, go bankrupt, or simply go out of business. Retirement and death were the leading causes of business closings. Surviving multi-generation businesses include Capitol Liquors, Pulverente Monument, All Makes, Nogg Bros, Pitlor, Bakers (purchased by Fleming Foods), Milder Oil, Criss Rexall Drug Store, Wolf Bros, Borsheim (now part of Berkshire Hathaway), Carl S. Baum, I-Go Van & Storage, OPPD, Dean's Camera, Max I. Walker Cleaners, Hinky Dinky, Roberts Dairy, and Jacobson Fish Co. Significant transitions in ownership include the sale of Mastercraft in early 2002.

Businesses that ceased to exist include Shaver's Food Marts, Central Market and Grand Central Market, Aaron Ferer & Sons scrap metal, Conant Hotel, Fontenelle Hotel, Youngtown, Ray Gain Florist, N.S. Yaffe Printing Company, Crandell Furs, Nebraska Kosher Meat Market, Friedman's Bakery, Storz Brewing, Baskin-Robins 31 Flavor Ice Cream, Rubin-Ford Mercury in Plattsmouth, Brandeis Flower Shop (which later sold out to Younkers), Rosen-Novak Chevrolet, and Rose Bowl Lanes. The absence of advertisements in the half dozen cookbooks appearing since 1972 may reflect lack of volunteers to approach businesses, the prevalence of busy two-income families, the groups being sufficiently well funded (does that ever happen?), and the idea that the book itself was of such importance that the commercialism should not detract from the propagation of the faith through food.

CONCLUSION

Like a Haggadah spotted with wine, a cookbook with marginalia, interleaved notes, newspaper clippings, and recipe cards evokes the memory of years of use.[30] Cookbooks are frequently designated to pass on to a child, grandchild, or niece. The story of Jewish food in Nebraska is not limited to Jewish charity cookbooks. The weekly *Omaha Jewish Press* has a food column.

Jewish cooking does not loom large in midwestern foodways. *The Best from Midwest Kitchens* published in 1946 mentions the immigrant melting pot, but there is no Jewish recipe. The chicken soup recipe calls for one can of chicken and rice soup and one #2 can of cream-style corn.[31] Varonikas is the sole recipe attributed to Jews in Kay Graber's 1974 *Nebraska Pioneer Cookbook*.[32] Lynne Ireland, in describing Great Plains cooking, does not identify Jewish cooking. She states: "Ultimately, the fate of traditional plains foods will rest with the plains people who call those traditions their own. Even where the tongue of the Old Country is silent, the old songs forgotten, the food remains."[33]

Home cooking reflects ethnic, national, social and religious identity. Janet Theophano, assaying Chinese culinary traditions in America, suggested that it "wants to evoke a way of life that no longer endures, a way of life that exists, perhaps, only in the author's imagination, an imagination born of dislocation and memory." She characterized it as a "literature of exile, of nostalgia and loss."[34] Bonded to faith and ritual, Jewish cooking can anticipate change and longevity.

Advertisements in Jewish charity cookbooks open windows on merchandising. The illustrations provide visual images of family, food, and faith. They reveal the vitality of midwestern Jewry as Temple Israel moves from assimilation to firm independent Jewish identity, and Beth Israel maintains the tradition of the kosher kitchen. The Jewish charitable cookbook attempts to memorialize nostalgia with the prayer that foodways raise money for worthy causes. No cause is worthier than preservation of the faith.

ACKNOWLEDGMENTS

I thank my wife, Karen Pollak, for her encouragement and culinary knowledge. Research was assisted by Don Cunningham and Lynne Ireland at the Nebraska State Historical Society. I thank Jane Brooks, Mary Fellman, Mrs. Lois Friedman, Beth Ginsberg, Estelle Goldston, Joan Lehr, Mrs. Rabbi Isaac (Jeannette) Nadoff, Caryn Rifkin, Stacey Rockman, Civvy Roffman, Mrs Jay (Esther) Stoler, and others cited in the notes who graciously lent their cookbooks, the Nebraska Jewish Historical Society, Temple Israel, Mort Kulesh (Phoenix, Arizona), Jeanne Abrams (Rocky Mountain Historical Society, Denver, Colorado), and Leo Greenbaum, archivist at YIVO, for translating Yiddish recipes.

NOTES

[1] Barbara Haber, *From Hardtack to Home Fries* (New York: The Free Press, 2002), 221.

[2] Lynne Ireland, "The Compiled Cookbook as Foodways Autobiography," *Western Folklore* 40 (1981): 107.

[3] Margaret Cook, *America's Charitable Cooks: A Bibliography of Fund-Raising Cookbooks Published in the United States (1861-1915)*, (Kent, Ohio: 1971).

[4] Haber, *From Hardtack to Home Fries*, 3, 5.

[5] Janet Theophano, *Eat My Words, Reading Women's Lives Through the Cookbooks They Wrote* (New York: Palgrave, 2002), 8, 11, 13.

[6] Esther Levy, *Jewish Cookery Book* (Bedford, MA: Applewood Books, 1988, reprint), 3-4.

[7] *Jennie June's American Cookery Book* (New York: The American News Company, 1878), 319-25. Jennie June is the syndicated pen name for Jane Cunningham Croley, the daughter of an English Unitarian preacher.

[8] *The Fair Cook Book* (Denver: Congregation Emanuel, 1888, 49 pages). See Barbara Kirshenblatt-Gimblett, "The Moral Sublime: The Temple Emanuel Fair and Its Cookbook, Denver, 1888," in *Recipes for Reading*, Community Cookbooks, Stories, Histories (ed. A. L. Bower; Amherst: University of Massachusetts Press, 1997), 136-53.

[9] Theophano, *Eat My Words*, 50.

[10] Ruth Reichl, *Tender at the Bone, Growing up at the Table* (New York: Random House, 1998), 207.

[11] Vicki Weiss and Jennifer A. Block, *What to do When You're Dating a Jew: Everything You Need to Know from Matzoh Balls to Marriage* (New York: Three Rivers, 2000).

[12] Barbara Kirshenblatt-Gimblett indicates that designating Passover as Easter was not uncommon in Reform cookbooks. "The Kosher Gourmet," *Journal of Gastronomy* 2(Winter 1986-87): 87, n. 41.

[13] *The Greater Omaha Cook Book* (Omaha: Burkley Printing Co., 265 pages).

[14] Theophano, *Eat My Words*, 52.

[15] *Unleavened* (Omaha: Kinko's, 2002, 92 pages).

[16] *Bagels to Blintzes* (Lenexa, Kansas: Cookbook Publishers, Inc., 1984, 150 pages).

[17] *Happiness is Good Food* (Omaha: 1967, 308 pages).

[18] Telephone interview with daughter in law, Monica Sacks, August 23, 2002. She referred to her as Bubby Ida.

[19] Theo Richmond, *Konan, A Quest* (New York: Pantheon Books, 1995), 269-94.

[20] *Happiness is Good Food* (2nd printing 1971; Omaha, 1967, 267 pages).

[21] *Happiness is Still Good Food* (Audubon: Jumbo Jack's Cookbooks, 1993, 301 pages).

[22] *Hadassah Kosher Cook Book* (Omaha: Omaha Lino-Slug Co. Commercial Printers: 1928, 87 pages). Saul Graetz, born in 1910, and married to Esther since 1934, thinks the "Cheese Torte" recipe by Mrs. S. Graetz is his grandmother's. "Hadassah Wants More Cook Book Recipes," *Omaha Jewish Press*, October 13, 1927, 1-4; *Omaha*

Chapter Hadassah, Annual Report, 1929-1930, 32, Nebraska Jewish Historical Society, Archives; Oliver Pollak, "Hadassah's First Cook Book, Cornhusks'n All," *Forward,* June 6, 2003, 8.

[23] Oliver B. Pollak, "The Omaha Hebrew Club, 1982-1953: The Immigrant Search for Security," *Memories of the Jewish Midwest* 7(1991): 1-15, and "100 Years of B'nai B'rith," *Memories of the Jewish Midwest* 4 (1989).

[24] *Eppes Essen* (Omaha: Unionist Publishing Co., 1963, 106 pages). See Oliver B. Pollak. "B'nai B'rith in Omaha: 1884-1989," *Memories of the Jewish Midwest* 4 (1989) and "The Education of Henry Monsky, Omaha's American Jewish Hero" in *Crisis & Reaction: The Hero in Jewish History* (Omaha: Creighton University Press, 1995), 151-80.

[25] On the status of Yiddish, see Oliver B. Pollak and Leo Greenbaum, "Jewish Youth and Yiddish Culture in Omaha, Nebraska, 1922-1926" *Western States Jewish History* 33 (2001): 99-119.

[26] *Eppes Essen* (2nd rev. ed.; Omaha: Unionist Publishing, 1972, 126 pages, $3.00).

[27] *Council Cooks* (Omaha: N.S. Yaffe Printing Co., Omaha Section, National Council of Jewish Women, 224 pages, $5.00).

[28] *Kitchen Connection* (Memphis: Wimmer Brothers Books and National Council of Jewish Women, Omaha Section, 1983, 302 pages).

[29] *Aunt Lil's Famous Tested Recipes* (rev. and enlarged ed.; Omaha: Campbell Printing and Publishing, September 1947, 164 pages). Courtesy Mrs. Lois (Novit) Friedman, born in Sioux City, a lifelong National Council of Jewish Women member, married Lloyd Friedman in 1947 and received it as a wedding gift.

[30] H. J. Jackson, *Marginalia, Readers Writing in Books* (New Haven: Yale University Press, 2001).

[31] Ada B. Lothe, Breta L. Griem, Ethel M. Keating, *The Best from Midwest Kitchens* (New York: Gramercy, 1946) 26.

[32] Kay Graber, *Nebraska Pioneer Cookbook* (Lincoln: University of Nebraska Press, 1974) 90.

[33] Lynne Ireland, "Great Plains," in *Smithsonian Folklife Cookbook* (ed. K. Kirlin and T. Kirlin; Washington: Smithsonian Institution Press, 1991), 218.

[34] Theophano, *Eat My Words,* 263.

Public and Private in the Kitchen: Eating Jewish in the Soviet State

Alice Stone Nakhimovsky

All sorts of threads can bind someone to his homeland—a great culture, a mighty people, a glorious past. But the strongest thread goes from the homeland to the soul. That is, to the stomach.[1]

For the seventy years of its history, Soviet conditions shaped the public and private lives of Russian Jews. Living in a totalitarian state with enforced atheism and periodically intense anti-Semitism, Jews learned to keep their Jewishness hidden. Ultimately, separation from their religious identification was almost total, and while other forms of identification persisted (Jews gravitated to certain professions and shared some characteristic approaches to education, language, and humor), the Jewish content of these behaviors is hard to pin down.

In the arena of food, however, Russian Jews by and large agreed on which foods were Jewish and which Russian. Jewish foods were private foods, prepared in the home, and constituted one of the few content-laden aspects of Jewish life that was transmitted (even as it changed) over generations. How Russian Jews thought about Jewish foods, when they ate them, and with whom, reflect the changing nature of Russian-Jewish self-consciousness. It is a story that involves not only abandonment and retention, but a surprising intensity of purpose.

FROM 1900 THROUGH THE 1920s: DISLOCATION AND POSSIBILITY

For Jews of the Russian Empire, the early twentieth century was a period of dislocations and possibilities. Enlightenment trends, Jewish and non-Jewish, had reached the world of the shtetl. While many Jews continued

149

a life of religious observance in Russia or left for America to do so, others became Yiddish-speaking socialists, Russian-speaking socialists, Hebrew-speaking Zionists, or Russian-speaking professionals. The association of language with particular ideological outlooks shows that all of these choices came with recognizable patterns of behavior. And since, as Hasia Diner has observed, "food in the Judaic tradition stood at the very center of the sacred zone," the choices that people made were reflected in what they ate.[2]

For an insider's view of this changing situation we can turn to contemporary writers, for whom Jewish food was a rich source of associations and meaning. In the opening chapter of *Tevye the Dairyman*, written in 1894, Sholem Aleichem shows a Jewish world that is still intact. In this chapter, Tevye, not yet a dairyman, gives a lift to a pair of wealthy ladies and is rewarded with money and food: soup, a pot roast, a goose, a jar of chicken fat. Tevye is poor; his benefactors are rich. But they are all Jews, and the food that the wealthy ladies eat is exactly the food that Tevye would eat if only he had the means. Later in the Tevye stories, that world comes apart. In "Shprintze" (1907), Tevye's fourth daughter is courted by a well-to-do young man, Aharonchik. Aharonchik (his mother calls him Arnold) is assimilated. He has never even eaten a blintz. The split between rich Jew and poor Jew is now a split in food, including knowledge about food.

Another observer of an intact food world is the Russian writer David Aizman. In his story "Landsmen," a Russian-Jewish family living in rural France invites a Russian woman over for Shabbat.[3] Aizman makes it clear that the woman would not ordinarily have socialized with Jews, but in France the Russianness of her hosts outweighs their Jewishness. As they progress through the meal (consisting of two challahs, gefilte fish, chicken soup with noodles, chicken and stewed fruit) the Russian's anti-Semitism abates and finally disappears altogether. "Where is the kugel?" she asks at last, using the Jewish word.[4] Aizman's point is that Russians and Jews can be landsmen and that mutual understanding can occur not only without Jews giving up their food, but even by means of Jewish food.

Aizman's view of Shabbat dinner as a cure for Russian anti-Semitism was as unusual in literature as it was in life. Far more frequently encountered was the opposite situation, in which assimilating Jews express an aversion to the food of their childhood. In a story published in 1902, in the Russian-language Zionist journal *Budushchnost'*, a young woman who has married a rich, presumably assimilated, Jewish husband in St. Petersburg, returns on a visit to her rich but unassimilated home somewhere in the Pale. Her alienation from Jewish life is characterized by her reaction to Jewish food. Unlike Aizman's openhearted Russian, this Jewish heroine looks on askance as a kugel is brought in. "Eat your chopped liver, you used to love it" [*Kushai zhe rublenuiu pechenku, ved' ty liubila*] cries out her mother, but the heroine's deracination has progressed too far.[5]

If we turn from this obscure story to some very well-known Soviet writers of Jewish origin, we find two characteristic paths. Some writers recorded a sensual aversion to Jewish food, a physical reflection of their own desire to flee. To this category belong the famous lines of Osip Mandelstam in *The Noise of Time*: "The smallest hint of Judaism permeates a whole life with its strong odor."[6] Taken to Riga on a rare visit to his observant grandparents, Mandelstam remembers his grandmother's only Russian word, "Eat," and the "spicy old people's cake" that she served him and that he did not like.[7] Mandelstam's contemporary, Eduard Bagritskii, who unlike Mandelstam actually grew up in a shtetl, was no more reconciled to it. To his friend, the non-Jewish writer Paustovskii, he complained about the "acrid sourness" that permeated all the food, even the tea.[8] "And my childhood passed/ They dried it up with unleavened bread" runs a line in his poem, "Origins."[9] Neither Mandelstam nor Bagritskii fled altogether—both have strong verses expressing identification with Jews—but for both writers, food images are negative.

For other Russian-Jewish writers, Jewish food in a Russian context is comic. The source of the comedy can be the clash between Russian literary language and the lower class lifestyles of unassimilated Jews (Isaac Babel's "Odessa" stories are famous for this) or between the new age of scientific socialism and retrograde Jewish traditions, including culinary ones. Jewish food is inherently funny in Il'ia Ehrenburg's *The Adventures of Lazik Roitshavenets*, a satire that the author, after a deep and courageous involvement in documenting the Holocaust, refused to reprint in the aftermath of that event. But when it was written in 1927, Jewish habits, including Jewish foodways, were associated with an old world about to be cheerfully superceded. Ehrenburg's Lazik is a representative of that world. Imagining the good life, he says of food:

I ate, for example, chopped liver with eggs. That's for starters. I ate *gribenes* [he uses the Russian word *shkvarki-AN*], I ate

kneidlakh, I ate *p'tcha* [he uses the Russian word *studen*]. That's
five. But why keep a stupid count? I ate a hundred dishes. The
chicken! But how can I be such an idiot, I forgot the gefilte fish!
It came with red horseradish, and then there was "kugel" with
raisins, "tsimis" with prunes and turnip with ginger. But why
rush ahead? We can talk a little more about those goose necks.[10]

Behind Ehrenburg's comedy lies an ideological point. Revolution
is liberating, and in the case of Jews Ehrenburg imagines it as offering a
revolutionary shift in their diet in the abrogation of Jewish dietary laws.
Ehrenburg knows these laws, he assumes his readers have an idea that
they exist, and he has fun with the notion of overturning them. At one
point, Lazik and a fellow ex-Jew, who has renamed himself after a Slavic
prince, go to a restaurant where Lazik imagines them having "rabbit,
that is to say meatballs in sour cream."[11] In another food-connected
episode, Lazik, pretending to be a rabbi, persuades the owner of a Jewish
restaurant to serve pork fried in butter.[12] In Ehrenburg's presentation,
the freedom of the revolution is the freedom to eat like a Russian.

The picture created by writers is of course not always reflective of
life as it was lived. In the case of Soviet writers like Babel and Ehrenburg,
the gap between literature and everyday life can be considerable. While
Ehrenburg and Babel imply that Jewish life and Jewish food are
inappropriate in a modern, public, Russian environment, historical
sources suggest that ordinary Jews were using the period from 1900 to
1918 to develop a public life, including restaurants, in major cities.
Looking at Jewish life in St. Petersburg, where before the revolution
most Jewish residents lived or traveled illegally, the scholar Mikhail
Beizer notes the presence nonetheless of twenty-six Jewish restaurants
and food shops dating from approximately 1910 to 1918; he gives the
addresses of illegal kosher restaurants during the 1920s and even into
the 1930s. One was non-kosher, but "Jewish-style." Another sold kosher
vodka for Passover.[13]

A picture similar to Beizer's emerges from the memoirs of an
American journalist, Marguerite Harrison, who talked her way into the
Soviet Union during the civil war that immediately followed the
revolution. Not Jewish herself, but interested in what people ate,
Harrison gives accounts of recognizably Jewish meals served by Jews
working for the revolutionary government. The Jewish head of medical
services at Krupki "regaled me with roast goose and baked apples in his
billet."[14] A few pages later, the Jewish chairman of the *Orshcha Ispolkom*

[roughly, the mayor] treats her to a dinner: "*Tschi*, a Russian vegetable soup, roast goose with potatoes and onions, Jewish style, pancakes with sour cream, tea and cakes and apples for desert."[15]

Unlike Ehrenburg's super-striving assimilationists with their hare in sour cream, this real-life chairman has abandoned dietary laws without being overly demonstrative about it. Both the chairman and the doctor have gone public with their Jewish foods—in fact, they seem to be using Bolshevik funds to cook Jewish foods for themselves and for a non-Jewish guest. In other words, if in literature Jewish food was a private, possibly comic, and certainly obsolescent preference, in reality it was moving in the opposite direction—outside the home. We see here the nascent stage of what Jenna Weisman Joselit, Hasia Diner, and Donna Gabbaccia have described for Jewish immigrants to the United States:[16] Jewish food habits are being secularized, and they are moving from the private to the public sphere. But this movement will be abruptly stopped. It is telling that the final reference to Jewish food in Harrison's memoir is a description of a meal in an illegal, privately-owned restaurant in Moscow: gefilte fish and roast goose with apples. She concludes: "Occasionally these places were raided, their owners arrested and their supplies confiscated, but others were always springing up to take their places."[17] Eventually, this life-affirming battle with the authorities would stop because the stakes were just too high. For many decades to follow, Soviet Jewish food would become an attribute of strictly private life.

THE 1950s AND 60s: A FUGITIVE WORLD

By the 1950s and 1960s, the period when Soviet Communism seemed eternal, Jewish food was part of a hidden world. It represented a certain Jewish commitment, though in no way a religious one. Some Jews continued to see Jewish food as a mark of a low-status non-Russian world and avoided it, or avoided talking about it. Others went to great lengths to prepare it.

For reasons both external and internal, the postwar decades were hardly conducive to public displays of Jewish identity. The combination of social and official anti-Semitism made Jews across the population try to appear as Russian as possible. Jews strove to erase all overt signs of Jewishness except the most indelible: the last name, the nationality notation in the passport, and—the only really immutable factor of this trio—the face. Jewish religious practice was largely abandoned and Jewish religious knowledge ceased to be transmitted—a phenomenon with obvious implications for Jewish eating patterns. While anti-religious laws abetted this failure of education (it was, for example, illegal to provide religious instruction to anyone under the age of eighteen),[18] it is worth noting that even before the war, Jews had taken to atheism with more alacrity than other religious-ethnic groups. Census data from 1937 show that only seventeen percent of Jews over the age of sixteen expressed a belief in God, as opposed to 53 percent of other adults, and this was before the Holocaust, which disproportionately affected religious Jews who lived in and around the old Pale of Jewish Settlement. Russian Jews who came of age after the war compounded atheism with ignorance. The Russian Israeli novelist Dina Rubina captures the phenomenon in the succinct analysis of a cynical Jerusalem tour guide:

> Best of all was a juicy group of ex-Soviet technologically educated atheists. These knew nothing at all. They mixed up Jesus Christ with the God of the Hebrews, the Virgin Mary with Mary Magdalene, asked blasphemous questions, crossed themselves at the Wailing Wall and were happy with whatever the tour guide told them.[19]

Jewish writers working during and immediately after the war reflect the public tendency of Russian Jews to stress their essential Russianness. A case in point is Vasilii Grossman, whose *Life and Fate*, an early and long-unpublishable novel about the battle of Stalingrad and the Holocaust, gives its major Jewish characters Jewish fates but Russian interests. Grossman's huge book is singular for its era in discussing Jews at all, but it brings up Jewish food only once. The food in question is gefilte fish, which functions in the story as a trigger point that could unleash an episode of anti-Semitism, but does not. In Grossman's oppressive world, Jewish ethnicity is best ignored. A Russian officer's benign indifference is as good as it gets.

Some ten years after Grossman's *Life and Fate*, a young writer named Felix Roziner wrote a sensational underground novel, *A Certain Finkelmeyer*. Among the many forbidden aspects of *Finkelmeyer* was the presence of a Jewish hero, a poet who despite his extravagantly Jewish name is culturally Russian. Roziner uses food to show the poet's alienation from his Jewish background. Finkelmeyer's first romance is with a Russian woman. She gives him food that is unkosher, yet psychologically nourishing: "bread, butter, cheese and an aromatic sausage."[20] Later, quite by accident, the poet marries a Jewish girl. She feeds him a Jewish meal that even retains the separation of meat and dairy. The narrator, a well-disposed Russian, observes both the food and the poet's response to it:

A salad, fish and *p'tcha* [a Jewish food given in Russian, *kholodets*] sweet wine, chicken soup and *pirozhki* (with meat or cabbage and onion); goose! Why was he given such a great Jewish nose, if he couldn't appreciate the aroma of such a goose? thought Nikolskii.[21]

While post-war novels express one part of the Jewish picture, they do not reflect its entirety. Outside of fiction, Jews in the postwar decades continued to eat Jewish food (among the private connoisseurs was none other than Vasilii Grossman).[22] Certain trends begun in the pre-war period intensified now, among them the retreat of Jewish foods into the privacy of the extended family and the dissociation of these foods from religious restrictions and the ritual calendar. Entirely new, and possibly a product of the war, was the commitment displayed by cooks to the continuation of culinary tradition. In a setting in which ingredients were not easy to obtain and in which families lived in single rooms in communal apartments, ordinary Jews went to singular lengths to cook the foods of their childhoods.

The secretiveness that attached to Jewish foodways was part of a broader phenomenon affecting Jews in public life. "Jew" was a word best avoided in polite, mixed company. The essayists Piotr Vail and Aleksandr Genis put this rather well:

Jews were perhaps the biggest secret of the Soviet Union. Perhaps only sex was hidden more assiduously. It's no accident that Jews and sex are connected here. Society found a noticeable link between these two subjects. Both of them could exist only in the sphere of shameful silence, only in the form of euphemisms.[23]

The silence and the euphemisms extend, not surprisingly, to cookbooks. In 1955, the Soviet Ministry of Trade came out with a major cookbook, the 960-page *Kulinariia*, which would serve as the mother of all Soviet cookbooks to follow.[24] It has recipes for chicken soup (considered by Russians to be Jewish) and for gefilte fish, but the book that celebrates all other Soviet ethnic foods is notably silent about the Jewish ones. This is not, however, the entire story. Looking at the editorial board (chief editor M. O. Lifshits, associate editor A.A. Kaganov, and assistant editor N.A. Aizenshtein), we can break the silence at least partially: the Jews were present, but they knew their place. Another silence waiting for interpretation appears in a cookbook of 1973, which also has no recipes labeled as Jewish. It does, however, have some recipes for stuffed cabbage, which can be both Russian (made with meat and sour cream) and Jewish (meat but without dairy). The first stuffed cabbage recipe is classically Slavic. The second separates the meat from the sour cream and uses instead a typically Jewish sweet and sour sauce. Not wanting to write "Jewish," the editors—perhaps cynically, perhaps as a secret greeting to those who recognize the source—call the recipe "Stuffed Cabbage, Oriental Style" [*golubtsy po vostochnomy*].[25]

Foods that were not mentionable in public were consumed in private. One woman to whom I spoke in preparation for this essay responded to a question about what Jewish foods she prepared by declaring that the family "ate Russian food like everybody else." But when specific foods were brought up, she remembered them well and was happy to supply recipes for chopped liver and *tsimmes*. Her reticence has the same roots as the embarrassment of the man who remembers that as a child he hated to bring Russian playmates home with him because his mother might be serving chicken soup, and he was quite aware that Russians would recognize the soup as Jewish. This same man remembers that his mother, who was in other respects very distant from her Jewish background, did not cook other Jewish foods and avoided visiting the one set of relatives, his father's sisters, who did.

The eating of Jewish foods was sometimes combined with other clandestine Jewish behaviors, like the use of Yiddish or the singing of Jewish songs. One observer, the artist Grisha Bruskin, remembers the combination of food, guests, and singing as a fragile moment that was not destined for continuity: "the remnant of a Jewish Pompeii."[26] Another woman stressed the subversive content of the songs: "There were three Jewish families in one [communal] apartment. Uncle Boria had a connection with this apartment; they would get together and sing anti-Communist songs in Yiddish. My mother didn't like it."[27] Like this informant's mother, not all participants were comfortable with the situation. Some feared that their privacy would be breached. Others, like Grisha Bruskin, felt as a child that the whole event was too openly Jewish: "When I was young I didn't like those evenings. Embarrassed by the shtetl demeanor of the guests, I felt that I had nothing in common with them and tried to get out of the house."[28]

Of these private behaviors, one that was conspicuously absent was Jewish ritual. Not surprisingly, the foods themselves were dissociated from their religious context. Kashrut was not an imperative either religiously or as a matter of ethnic style; people commonly substituted butter for chicken or goose fat in meat dishes because it was easily obtainable and there was no reason not to. In a recent paper by anthropologists Maria Yelenevskaya and Larisa Fialkova, two informants recall delicious sandwiches of matzo and pork fat. One of these men was served the sandwich by a Russian who had been presented with the matzo by a Jewish friend and didn't know its context; the other made the sandwich himself as a convenient food for a camping trip.[29] The separation of foods from dietary laws went along with their separation from their traditional places in the holiday calendar. Challah, one of the few Jewish foods obtainable in stores, was not a food for the Sabbath, nor was gefilte fish. Honey-based sweets like *teiglakh* lost their connection with Rosh Hashanah.

While in some families Jewish food could be eaten at any time, in other families their appearance was restricted to special times of the year, as recounted in the following interview:

Q: "When did you eat these foods?"

A: "Holidays. Uncle Iosif brought gefilte fish, Aunt Rakhil' brought *teiglakh*."

Q: "What holidays?"

A: "The October holiday. The first of May. The eight of March. Birthdays."[30]

The migration of Jewish foods from the religious to the Soviet political calendar may not have been common. But their appearance at birthdays was widespread. This recurring private celebration is in Russian practice not a children's amusement, but an obligatory celebration for the extended family. And if that family was a Jewish one, the event became by extension an obligatory Jewish event.

Asked about birthdays, a man who on any index would not come across as Jewish-affiliating, emphasized the difference between Russian and Jewish takes on the same event:

Russian birthdays were disorderly. Big things were placed on the table, big pies, just as they came out of the oven. Jewish foods were always prepared, cut up. Among Russians guests were random. Some would be from work; they'd be present one year and absent the next. Among Jews it was always the same people, always the family. Russians made a big deal about the birthday girl or boy or person—they sang "*mnogoe let*" ["Live

Long," a birthday song]. With Jews, the birthday person was
pretty much forgotten. It was a family event.[31]
Another informant emphasized the enormity of the preparation: "It
was an incredible effort. The apartment had to be cleaned. There was
an incredible amount of cooking, and times were hard. For gefilte fish,
you had to get pike and carp."[32]

Evident in both these comments is the importance and effort put
into the Jewish birthday, an expenditure of energy made all the more
important when we keep in mind the absence of religious imperative,
the disaffection of the younger generation, and the need for privacy. To
these barriers we have already mentioned, more could be added. Many
people lived in communal apartments, sharing their kitchens with
arbitrary neighbors who may or may not have been tolerant of Jews.
Many people did not have telephones. That they nonetheless made
these dinners happen, cooking and often transporting across town
complicated dishes like *teiglakh* and gefilte fish, is testimony that
something very important was at stake.

The peculiar combination of intensity with disassociation is
strongest in the matter of Passover matzos. While the baking of matzos
was quite restricted, Jews across the Soviet Union went to great efforts
to get them from a synagogue or bake them at home. One characteristic
arrangement was to choose a family "delegate" to get the matzo, someone
old and hence not likely to suffer repercussions at work. One informant,
from Odessa, remembered that his family would get three packages
from Moscow through his grandmother, who was a doctor for the railroad
and was able to transport them herself or have them transported by
people she trusted. Another already elderly family member would get a
single package from the Odessa synagogue, for a total of four packages:
a huge haul.[33] The procurement of matzo was not without its dangerous
side. In 1959, 1960, and 1961, the baking of matzo was prohibited in
Kiev, Odessa, Kharkov, Rostov, Kishinev, and Riga. In July 1963, four
people were tried for "profiting" (in Soviet parlance, "speculating") frp,
the illegal baking of matzos, even though they declared at their trial
that they had handed out the matzo free of charge. Three of these people
were sentence to prison terms from six months to one year; the fourth,
who was 82, was let go for reasons of age and health.[34]

While many Jews tried hard to get matzos, few had Seders in any
traditional sense.[35] When asked what his family did with the four
packages of matzo obtained with great effort from two cities, the Odessan

informant said that they ground it up into matzo meal and cooked with it; he especially remembers matzo meal latkes. The cooking was under the supervision of his grandmother, who, over the same two-week stretch, also baked Russian *kulich* [leavened Easter cake] and helped the children color Easter eggs. Grisha Bruskin remembers his grandmother getting matzos "baked under the supervision of Moscow Rabbi Fishman" and then hiding them to give out to children "as treats"; their meaning was not discussed.[36]

What can we make of this? For several thousand years, food was the necessary and central component of the Passover story; explaining why it was present was the starting moment of the retelling of the Exodus. The Passover Seder, abbreviated, altered, and sometimes abandoned by secularizing American Jews, was in Soviet Russia abruptly cancelled and lost over the course of one single highly-pressured generation. The story was not told, but the food remained. And however it was used (reinvested, apparently with the single uncomplicated meaning "We are Jewish"), its importance remained.

THE PRESENT: RECLAMATION

After decades of Sovietization, some of it forced, some of it pursued and desired, Russian Jews resembled neither their Jewish ancestors nor their Russian neighbors. Separated from full-blood Russians by an expectation of anti-Semitism, a discomforting sense of not belonging, and an unremitting outgroup pride, Jews were left with very little knowledge of Jewish traditions. The resurgence of national consciousness, beginning with the 1967 Arab-Israeli war and continuing through emigration and the dissolution of the Soviet state, began to change this equation in directions that were almost completely positive. But Jewish self-awareness remained separate from most forms of Jewish knowledge.

Writing about this phenomenon ten years ago, I used the phrase "empty label" to describe the persistence of Jewish identity in the absence of Jewish content.[37] Recent sociological studies of Jewish attitudes inside Russia confirm that little has changed. "We are confronting an astonishing phenomenon," write the sociologists Zvi Gitelman, Valerii Cherviakov, and Vladimir Shapiro. "People classify themselves as Jews but do not feel that they are at all Jewish."[38] In her conclusions to a different study of Russian Jews, Rozalina Ryvkina concludes similarly: "People consider themselves Jews, although their behavior doesn't seem to back this up."[39]

While Ryvkina's respondents did not show a strong involvement in Jewish culture (7 percent felt strongly involved, 31 percent somewhat, 58 percent not at all),[40] the Gitelman-Chevriakov-Shapiro study gives a different and more complicated picture. The Russian Jews they questioned from 1992-1993 were not interested in religion. Only one percent of them believed that a Jew had to know the basics of Judaism, and not a single one, when asked to list important components of Jewish identity, mentioned keeping kosher.[41] At the same time, their regard for Judaism was much higher than for Christianity, which is embedded in Russian culture and which, beginning in the 1970s, had attracted a number of prominent Jewish converts.[42]

The picture emerging from the Gitelman-Chevriakov-Shapiro study is that of Jews who feel an emotional attraction to Jewish identity and who seek a variety of non-religious ways to express it.[43] Aware of their lack of knowledge, thirty percent consider it "obligatory" and sixty percent "very desirable" to learn more about Jewish traditions.[44] About half of the respondents acted on this desire by declaring themselves as participating in Jewish cultural life to some degree.[45]

What sociologists have distilled from surveys is recognizable in contemporary fiction. In Gary Shteyngart's recent novel, *A Russian Debutante's Handbook*, we have a wickedly satiric take on post-Soviet Jewish identity that uses food as a commentary on the hero's predicament. Shteyngart's hero Vladimir is a classic fictional Jew. Unathletic and verbal, cynical yet desiring to belong, Vladimir rises to the top of a number of unlikely social contexts, but feels at home in none of them. The combination of rootlessness and striving is nowhere more visible than in his meals.

Vladimir doesn't eat Jewish food, ever. The sentimental food of his childhood is a Soviet potato salad with a French name: *Salat Olivier*. Now, as a young man on the make, his meals are extravagantly and meaningfully non-kosher. In one example among many, he goes from a Russian Orthodox Church service (having tried to pass himself off as "half Russian-half Greek")[46] to a fancy restaurant, where he is the guest of a Russian mafioso. The meal is a yuppie variant of Ehrenburg's hare in sour cream. It begins with squid, followed by "braised hare in pimento reduction" and "lobster claws in kiwi puree"; at the meal's end, Vladimir has to take the lobster claw to coax his drunken host out from under the table.[47]

Jewish food names have a role in Shteyngart's novel, but they are attached incongruously to people. An episodic character in chapter one is called Ms. Charoseth, and Vladimir's soon to be discarded chubby girlfriend is called Challah. Of course, when Shteyngart dissociates the food from its meaning, he is full of conscious irony. But a website devoted to Russian-Jewish food displays the same disjunction, this time wholly without irony, when it accompanies a recipe for charoseth with the proud explanation: "Traditional dessert. Delicious of taste and exotic of great people, surely, will obtain success."[48]

Shteyngart's focus on these two foods as emblematic of post-Soviet confusion is not accidental. Charoseth is also singled out in a recent illustrated dictionary intended as an introduction to Jewish life for Russian-Jewish children. Here, a drawing of charoseth is accompanied by an account of its meaning. It is interesting that charoseth is one of only two foods included in the dictionary. The other one, also illustrated, is challah.[49]

Unlike Vladimir, for whom Jewish food is out of reach and not desired, many Jews have sought it as a retrievable representation of their lost culture. Evidence of this comes in the proliferation of Russian-Jewish cookbooks since 1991. It may be significant that all of the books I have seen or seen reference to have been published for Jews who have chosen to remain in Russia, and not for émigrés. The émigré community has two traditions (Jewish and Soviet Russian) to be nostalgic about; judging from the foods in émigré groceries, it is the latter, the harder to reproduce in America, that has predominated. The wonderful book *Russian Cuisine in Exile*, by the émigré essayists Petr Vail' and Aleksandr Genis, acknowledges the presence of Jews as Russian eaters, but the food world it evokes is overwhelmingly Russian.[50]

Russian-language Jewish cookbooks published in Russia after the fall of the Soviet Union are engaged quite consciously and often touchingly in cultural restoration. Of the six books I have studied, not one evokes "my mother's" or "my grandmother's" kitchen, a staple of such books in the West.[51] Nor do they refer to specialties of individuals or communities. The reasons for this are obvious: mother's kitchen is assumed to be inauthentic, and community groups were closed by decree in 1918.

The most frequently republished of these books is Z. M. Evenshtein's *Evreiskaia kukhnia* [Jewish Cuisine]. While it celebrates Jewish food ("Who in Europe or America does not know of a delicacy like stuffed fish Jewish style? Or the no less delicious Jewish boiled fish with sauce from horseradish and apple?"), Evenshtein's book is notable for its distance from the Jewish calendar. Foods are present by time of day, as appropriate for breakfast, dinner (hors d'oeuvres, soups, main course, and dessert), and supper. There is no mention of holidays, though a set of pictures inserted into the book are full of religious symbolism. The first picture shows a Seder plate and a bottle of Carmel concord wine. The second has another bottle of concord, a Torah (in Russian), a dish of honey, a shofar, a tallis, and a whole gefilte fish. Light from candles shines onto the Torah, the honey, and the fish. The religious settings are never explained. In the final picture, a cornucopia of fruit spills to the edge of a Talmud, whose Hebrew writing is backwards; the mistake is reproduced from edition to edition.

Evenshtein's emphasis on nutrition frequently conflicts with his goal of enabling "every reader to cook a dish in the same manner in which it was cooked (boiled, steamed or fried) many hundreds of years ago." The source of the conflict is the goose or chicken fat that is traditional for many meat dishes. A curiosity of this book is that when advising the cook to avoid chicken fat, it suggests not vegetable oil, which is used in Russian cooking and which would maintain the Jewish separation between meat and dairy, but butter or sour cream. A recipe for chopped liver lists chicken fat among the ingredients, but concludes: "The nutritional value of chopped liver will improve if the onion is not fried (especially not in chicken fat), and if instead of bullion, you make do with water or even milk."[52]

A similar unapologetic blend of Russian and Jewish practices can be seen in a recipe for stuffed cabbage. This is a classic Jewish sweet-and-sour dish: tomato sauce, lemon, and sugar. As with the chopped liver, Evenshtein's desire to make it more nutritious leads him to recommend the inclusion of dairy:

> Since the stuffing for the cabbage uses boiled rather than raw meat, it is equally appropriate for a health-conscious diet, particularly if you substitute melted butter for the solid beef fat. In preparing the sauce, bullion can be replaced with sour cream.[53]

It's not that Evenshtein is completely unaware of Jewish dietary laws; he just sees them as irrelevant to Jewish cooking. A case in point is a recipe for matzo balls [in Russian, *shariki iz matsemela*], which concludes this way:

This, like other dishes made with ground matzo, is the peculiar indulgence [*svoeobraznoe poslablenie*] of a religious believer. Dumplings made in a similar fashion, but from flour, cannot be used during the fast, while dumplings from matzo meal can.[54]

Evenshtein concludes by once again advising nutritionally conscious readers to withhold the chicken fat and "serve [the matzo balls] in a dish with sour cream or pieces of butter."[55]

Other Russian-Jewish cookbooks do not follow Evenshtein's approach. Aware of the gap between Soviet Jewish and Jewish practices, including religious tradition, they attempt to bridge it by providing information about holidays and explanations of concepts like "meat," "dairy," and "parev." Some of the cookbooks include Israeli recipes like *sufganiyot* [Hannukah doughnuts], thus expanding the concept of "Jewish food" beyond the ancestrally Russian; another authenticizes the tradition with excerpts from Sholem Aleichem, who was, after all, a Russian Jew. While occasional mistakes creep in, the recipes in general maintain the separation of dairy and meat.[56] As a group, they are distinguished by their seriousness and humility; their tendency to look outside Russia for explanations of religious concepts; and, as noted earlier, a certain impersonality. Aside from Sholem Aleichem, the recipes are not contextualized in any real life setting.

The confusion in the cookbooks reflects a changing cultural landscape and a variety of approaches among real life cooks, each of whom can be said to uphold a particular Jewish tradition. A poignant example of this comes in a set of responses to a recipe for chopped liver that appeared on a website devoted to Russian-Jewish cooking. The recipe, from a pre-revolutionary Russian-Jewish cookbook, is presented in English:

Wash liver and peel off the skin, chop it into small pieces and fry in oil until cooked. Grind liver pieces with a soaked in water white bread slice. Fry finely chopped onion until light brown and add it with salt, pepper and melted fat to beef mince. Stir thoroughly. Serve in a deep plate and decorate with slices of hard-boiled eggs and chopped green. Ingredients include 250 g beef liver, 1 ea white bread slice, 2 tbs chicken fat, 2 ea eggs, 1 ea onion, 30 g spring onions, salt, pepper.

Three responses follow from visitors to the website, all in Russian:

1. Chopped Liver.

Jewish cooking has always been distinguished by the fact that it is maximally healthy and extremely delicious! Chopped liver proves this.

2. An Addition to the Recipe

If you leave out the white bread and fry the onion together with the liver, put the mixture through the meat grinder, add a little heavy cream and butter and only then put the pate through a sieve, this will be the most correct recipe.

3. In Response

I'll add only that in Jewish cooking there is such a thing as kashrut—it is forbidden to mix meat and dairy. So in place of the butter use margarine, and as for the cream, don't even think about it.[57]

For the first respondent, food is a material representation of Jewish pride. The second and third disagree about what is authentic: Soviet practice or Jewish tradition before and outside of the Soviet Union. For all three, Jewish food is invested with value. No longer comic, no longer relegated to a pre-revolutionary past, and no longer confined to the family, for anyone so inclined it can be a matter of public debate.

NOTES

[1] Petr Vail' and Aleksandr Genis, *Russkaia kukhnia v izgnanii* [Russian Cuisine in Exile] (Moscow: *Nezavisimaia gazeta*, 2002), 26.

[2] Hasia Diner, *Hungering for America: Italian, Irish, and Jewish Foodways in the Age of Migration* (Cambridge: Harvard University Press, 2002), 150.

[3] David Aizman, *Krovavyi razliv I drugie proizvedeniia, kniga pervaia* (Jerusalem: Seriia Pamiat', 1991).

[4] *Ibid.*, 261.

[5] M. L. Brianskii, "Dinochka priekhala," *Budushchnost' nauchno-literaturnyi sbornik* 1-2 (January1900-April 1902): 148.

[6] Osip Mandelstam, *Sobranie sochinenii v trekh tomakh v. II* (ed. G. P. Struve and B. A. Filippov; New York: Interlanguage Literary Associates, 1971), 56.

[7] *Ibid.*, 32.

[8] Konstantin Paustovskii, *Povest' o zhizni v dvukh tomakh v.II* (Moscow: Sovetskaia Rossiia, 1966), 586-87.

[9] Eduard Bagritskii, *Stikhotvoreniia i poemy* (Moscow: Sovetskii pisatel', 1964), 106.

[10] *Ibid.*, 199.

[11] Il'ia Erenburg, *Staryi skorniak I drugie roizvedeniia,* v. 1, (Jerusalem : Pamiat', 1983), 156. The name of Lazik's friend is Riurik Abramovich.

[12] *Ibid.,* 232.

[13] Mikhail Beizer, *The Jews of St. Petersburg: Excursions through a Noble Past* (Philadelphia: The Jewish Publication Society, 1989), 307-309. I have no specific information on Jewish restaurants in Moscow, but a similarly intentioned attempt to a Jewish University there, with instruction, in Russian and Yiddish, on Jewish history, law, literature and other subjects is described in A. Levitova, "Evtreiskii narodnyi universitet v Moskve 1918-1921 (Moscow-Jerusalem: Vestnik Evreiskogo universisteta v Moskve 3 (7) (1994): 107-120.

[14] Harrison, Marguerite, *Marooned in Moscow* (New York: George H. Doran, 1921), 29.

[15] *Ibid.,* 37

[16] In addition to Diner, see Jenna Weissman Joselit, *The Wonders of America: Reinventing Jewish Culture 1880-1950* (New York: Hill and Wang, 1996) and Donna R. Gabaccia, *We Are What We Eat: Ethnic Food and the Making of Americans* (Cambridge: Harvard University Press, 1998). Also see the article in this volume, Jenna Weissman Joselit, "Food Fight: The Americanization of Kashrut in Twentieth Century America," in Leonard J. Greenspoon, et. al., eds., *Food and Judaism* (Studies in Jewish Civilization 15; Omaha: Creighton University Press, 2004).

[17] Harrison, *Marooned in Moscow,* 137.

[18] Z. Gitelman, V. Chervyakov, V. Shapiro, "Iudaizm v natsional'nom samocoznanii rossiiskikh evreev," Vestnik evreiskogo universiteta v Moskve 3(7): 1994, 122. In the case of Judaism, the easy linkage with Zionism made it dangerous to give instruction to adults as well

[19] Dina Rubina, *Vot idet messiia!* (St. Petersburg: Retro: 2001), 35.

[20] Feliks Roziner, *Nekto Finkel'maier* (London: Terra, 1990), 57.

[21] *Ibid.,* 275.

[22] Semen Lipkin, Zhizn' i sud'ba Vasiliia Grossmana, (Moscow: Kinga, 1990), 30.

[23] Petr Vail' and Aleksandr Genis, *60-e: Mir sovetskogo cheloveka* (Ann Arbor: Ardis, 1988), 269.

[24] M. O. Lifshits, ed, *Kulinariia* (Moscow: Gostorgizdat, 1955.

[25] I. I. Guba, ed, *Priglashaem k stolu* (Dneporpetrovsk: Promin, 1973), 82.

[26] Grisha Bruskin, *Proshedshee vremia nesovershennogo vida* (Moscow: Novoe Literaturnoe Obozrenie, 1991), 63.

[27] Conversation with Tatiana Garger, June 20, 2002.

[28] *Ibid.*

[29] Larisa Fialkova (University of Haifa, Israel) and Maria Yelenevskaya (Technion-Israel Institute of Technology, Haifa) unpublished paper, "Culture-Specific Meaning in Personal Narratives," 2004

[30] Conversation with Bruskin-Rokhinson family, March 19, 2002.

[31] Conversation with Paperno family, June 20, 2002.

[32] Conversation with Tatniana Garger, June 20, 2002

[33] Conversation with Serebrayanikov family, June 22, 2002.

[34] Leon Shapiro, "Evrei posle Stalina" in *Kniga o russkom evreistve 1917-1967* (New York: Soyuz russkikh evreev, 1968), 356-7.

[35] It is hard to find reliable data on how many Jews had Seders in which the Passover story was narrated. Robert J. Brym, in Robert J. Brym and Rozalina Ryvkina, The Jews of Moscow, Kiev, and Minsk: Identity, Antisemitism, Emigration (ed. H. Spier; New York: New York University Press, 1994), 25, found that forty percent of Jews in those cities celebrated Passover, which seems high and does not make sense in the light of data from surveys done by Zvi Gitelman, Valerii Chervyakov, and Vladimir Shapiro in 1992 and 1997. Jews in those surveys were not asked whether they celebrated Passover, but when asked "what is the most important thing required of a person in order to be considered a genuine Jew?" only 3.2 percent in 1992 and 1.4 percent in 1997 cited "Know Jewish traditions." All other possible religiously connected responses were even less popular, for example, in 1997: "Know the basics of Judaism": 0.7 percent; "Circumcise one's son: 0.1 percent (Zvi Gitelman, "Thinking about Being Jewish in Russia and Ukraine," in *Jewish Life After the USSR* (ed. Z. Gitelman et al.; Bloomington: Indiana University Press, 2003) 51. It seems to me, based upon my less systematic conversations, that Russian Jews felt they were celebrating Passover by virtue of obtaining matzo, so that if asked the question, "Do you celebrate Passover?" anyone who made the effort to get matzo into the house would say yes.

[36] Grisha Bruskin, *Proshedsee vremia nesovershennogo* vida, 54; further elucidation in conversation with the author. My husband, Sasha Nakhimovsky, is from Leningrad, and remembers getting matzo from relatives in Vilnius. In his family also, the meaning of the matzo was not explained to the children.

[37] See the discussion on the "contentless" nature of Soviet Jewish identity in the chapter "Enlightenment, Disappearance, Reemergence" in Alice Nakhimovsky, *Russian-Jewish Literature and Identity* (Baltimore: The Johns Hopkins University Press, 1992), 1-44.

[38] Gitelman, Chervyakov, Shapiro, 129

[39] Rozalina Ryvkina, *Evrei v postsovetskoi Rossii—kto oni?* (URSS: 1996), 52.

[40] *Ibid.*

[41] Gitelman, Chervyakov, Shapiro, 134-35.

[42] *Ibid.*, 135. Christianity, in second place among major religions, was named by almost three times fewer people.

[43] *Ibid.*, 141.

[44] *Ibid.*, 133

[45] *Ibid.*, 127.

[45] Gary Shteyngart, 264.

[46] *Ibid.*, 265-69.

[47] Cited June 18, 2003. Online: http://www.russianfoods.com/recipes/group0001F00002/default.asp.

[48] Vol'pe M L ,*Evreiskie traditsii* (Moscow: Izdatel'stvo dom Podkova, 2001.

[49] Petr Vail' and Aleksandr Genis, *Russkaia kukhnia v izgnanii*. See also the article in this volume, Eve Jochnowitz, "Smoked Salmon Sushi and Sturgeon Stomachs: The Russian Jewish Foodscapes of New York," in *Food and Judaism* (vol. 15; Studies in Jewish Civilization; ed. L. J. Greenspoon et al.; Omaha: Creighton University Press, 2005).

[50] I. A. Avakh, *Evreiskaia kukhnia* (St. Petersburg: Karavella, 1995); L. Fronina, A. Kharitonova and L. Botiva, *Evreiskaia klassicheskaia kukhnia* (Moscow: Elista, 1999); *Aromaty evreiskoi kukhni* (Moscow: Gersharim, 1996); Z.M. Evenshtein, *Evreiskaia kukhnia* (Rostov na donu: Feniks, 1998); Gennadii Rozenbaum, *Luchshie retsepty evreiskoi kukhni* (Moscow: BAO Press, 2001); M. Gershovich, *120 bliud evreiskoi kukhni* (Tallinn: Kooperativ "Iana," 1990).

[51] Evenshtein, 54.

[52] *Ibid.*, 129.

[53] *Ibid.*, 204-5.

[54] *Ibid.*, 205.

[55] Consider, for example, A. Avakh's *Evreiskaia kukhnia*. Ingredients for recipes separate meat and dairy. But an introduction to the section on soups, written from the point of view of an experienced cook, recommends dipping a piece of hard cheese in a meat soup, for taste (40); in another section, dumplings made with butter (66) are advised as an accompaniment to a meat soup. These carry-overs from Soviet practice contradict the advice given in the introduction.

[56] Cited June 18, 2003. Online: http://www.russianfoods.com/recipes/item000E8/default.asp.

Kashrut: The Possibility and Limits of Women's Domestic Power

Ruth Ann Abusch-Magder

Kashrut is a basic Jewish observance that is traditionally incumbent on all Jews, regardless of sex, age, or marital status. These laws add a rich set of ritual patterns and theological meanings to the everyday acts of eating. In the second half of the nineteenth century, in the wake of a period of great social, economic, and political change of the German-speaking Jews of Europe, every aspect of traditional Jewish life and observance was up for discussion and debate, including kashrut. The particular involvement of women in foodways, in Jewish culture in specific and in western culture more broadly, gave German-speaking women in the second half of the nineteenth century a particular role to play in the realm of Jewish observance. As household managers, cooks, wives, and mothers, Jewish women took stands regarding kashrut, stands that were both enabled and limited by their position in the home.

This paper seeks to expand our understanding of the relationship of community, women, and home to the enactment of the Jewish observance of kashrut. The responsibilities placed upon women involving food and domestic life meant that women gained a certain amount of power over decisions relating to food. In contrast to limitations put on women in other aspects of rituals life, the assumptions of the legal structure of kashrut ceded women a degree of religious authority in kitchen and food matters, which subsequently translated into influence over and expression of personal visions of Judaism. I believe that these rabbinic assumptions shaped the reality of Jewish foodways. However, I also believe that there were fundamental differences between the legal ideal and the day-to-day enactment of Jewish ritual seen in halachic ideas of kashrut observance. Finally, I would like to suggest an alternative model that better reflects lived experience. By applying that model to kashrut observances for German-speaking Jews in Europe during the second half of the nineteenth century and in early years of the twentieth century, I will highlight how the communal context in which kashrut is observed or forsaken influences the relative importance of the home in ritual life and the power of women to influence Jewish expression. These were times when the historic authority of the rabbinate over Jewish life was challenged in many ways; yet, as I will show, even within more traditional communities, the power of the rabbi was not as absolute as portrayed by halachic codes. Further, modernity did not in every instance stand in opposition to Jewish tradition.

In order to understand how and why kashrut came to be a means through which women gave voice to their own ideas about Jewish life, it is helpful first to understand something of the particular ways in which women in the nineteenth century were tied to food production. While all members of the household partook in the consumption of what women produced, the overwhelming responsibility for foodways belonged to these women. And while many of the women's tasks in the home were time-consuming and important, those connected with food stood apart. Whereas children grew up and stopped needing constant attention, a woman was called upon to attend to duties connected with food for as long as she ran a household. The production and consumption of food were inescapably at the core of daily domestic life. Unlike laundry, food could not be attended to only once a week. Moreover, the work of feeding a family was laborious, occupying much of women's time and energy.

Kashrut added practical responsibilities and layers of religious meaning to these already weighty responsibilities. The complex dietary laws are meant to govern every bite eaten by Jews, regulating which animals may be considered fit for consumption, the manner in which they are killed, and how they may be consumed. Many examples are well known: only animals with split hooves that chew their cud and fowl that do not eat carrion are permitted. Four- or two-legged creatures must be killed according to Jewish slaughtering laws [*shechitah*] to be kosher. Permissible fish must have scales and fins. Pork is prohibited; milk and meat may not be eaten at the same time, prepared together, or served in the same cookware. With few exceptions, only Sabbath-observant Jews may handle wines. Observed to their fullest, these dietary laws force Jews to consider the origin, preparation, and content of everything they put into their mouth. The everyday act of nourishing the physical body is thus transformed into a statement of spiritual expression and communal identification.

Women were excused by law from the obligation to go to the synagogue to pray three times a day, but were obliged by custom to feed their families kosher fare three times a day. In fact, Jewish law itself accords women a great deal of responsibility for the upholding of kashrut. As historian Hasia Diner has described, the rabbis imagined the role of women in the process of kashrut observance as part of a complicated "communal infrastructure." Diner explains the basic structure of this system, which I call the "halachic kosher food pyramid":

> Ideally it functioned well. In "traditional" Jewish societies, a kind of pyramid existed with rabbis and rabbinic courts at the top, adjudicating problems of kashrut and determining how to feed the community's poor. At the bottom, the wide base of the pyramid, were the individual women in their homes (with husbands hovering on the sidelines) buying, cooking and serving as the front line sentinels of observance. In the middle stood the merchants and the community functionaries, beholden to both the women as consumers and the rabbis as final arbiters.[1]

The tasks assigned to women by this model assure their centrality in the observance of kashrut. As the primary purchaser of goods, they must remain vigilant regarding the purity of ingredients. As workers in the kitchen, they must guard against the accidental mixing of meat and dairy ingredients or the utensils used for each. As menu planners, they must be sure to serve together only those dishes that are permitted to be consumed at the same time. And while halacha generally did not consider women reliable or knowledgeable to bear witness on legal matters, when it came to questions of kashrut arising in the kitchen, the male rabbis considered the testimony of a woman as valid. In the view of Jewish eating espoused by Jewish law, women were both essential and valued members of the system.

Nonetheless, the position of women is significantly controlled. Although the essential nature of the tasks women are to perform in the service of kashrut observance make women essential to it, the halachic kosher food pyramid placed that work within a hierarchical system that privileged male rabbinic authority over that of women. As the ultimate judges of what was considered kosher, this legal system not only credits rabbis with more expertise but also with the ability, arguably even with the obligation, to enter into what might otherwise be considered a private female realm. In the halachic model, the female power emanating from the kitchen is distinctly secondary to the male authority ruling over the entire structure.

It is important, however, to keep in mind that the halachic kosher food pyramid is primarily a legal construction. Prior to the modern era, Jewish communities existed as separate entities within the non-Jewish societies within which they lived. Within the Jewish context, halacha served as the official legal code that structured Jewish life. In these halachic communities, Jews turned to rabbinic courts for the adjudication of legal quarrels. Such communities were increasingly rare in German-speaking lands in the second half of the nineteenth century. Even in places where Jews continued to follow the customs handed down over generations, the reality of kashrut observance did not always follow the precise roadmap set out by the rabbinate. Halacha is a system that allows for little personal choice regarding observance. The halachic kosher food model assumed that women would defer to the rabbis as a matter of course whenever appropriate. In reality, the responsibility and authority ceded to women by the male rabbinate created opportunities for women to exercise choice and control. In contrast to the halachic model, actual deference of women to rabbis was not always as automatic as the law assumed.

Choices about Jewish living had also been limited in the past by restrictions put on Jews by the non-Jewish societies in which they found themselves. Jews were limited in their social, political, and economic activity even where non-Jewish rulers affirmed the role of the rabbis to enforce law and order in the Jewish community. But in Central Europe during the second half of the nineteenth century, the historic constraints placed on Jews were in many instances being challenged and eliminated. The ideas of the Enlightenment led to new approaches to citizenship and to role of religion in communal life. Jews could now be involved in social, economic, and cultural worlds that had previously been closed to them. Increasingly, Jews could also reject Jewish observances and still remain connected to the Jewish world.

In an era of greater freedom to exercise individual preferences vis-à-vis Jewish observances, the halachic model no longer accurately reflected the reality of Jewish eating among German-speaking Jews, whether or not they lived in a more traditional community. Writing about the shift away from the traditional Jewish society, Diner wonders: "[Given what] we know from countless studies of Jewish communities that [show that] modernity involved the breakdown of communal authority...how much did the breakdown of kashrut rob that power elite of its base of authority?"[2] Diner is correct in asserting that moves away from kashrut observance challenged the rabbinic power assumed in the halachic kosher food pyramid and the halachic system generally; she also correctly observes that the possibility to opt out of this central ritual obligation further challenged the applicability of the halachic model to lived daily life.

To better help us understand the way in which the lived experiences of kashrut challenged not only the halachic hierarchy but also the place and role of women and the home in kashrut observance, I offer a new model, "the Jewish food chain." "Jewish" is used rather than "kosher" to allow for the possibility that not all food eaten by Jews was kosher. The Jewish food chain differs from both the halachic pyramid and the scientific concept of a biological food chain, in that the Jewish food chain is a lateral model. The term chain in this model suggests how component parts are linked, the ease with which the links can be broken, and the·impact on the endeavor as a whole if one of the links is broken. The three primary links in the Jewish food chain are, in order, those who supplied kosher food into the Jewish home, those whose work in the kitchen transformed supplies into dishes, and, finally, the Jews who gathered around tables inside Jewish homes to consume those dishes. For those who still valued kashrut, rabbinical authority continued to play a role in its observance. Rabbis, however, did not have an automatic role in the supply of Jewish food. They sat outside the Jewish food chain, but could be linked to any of the links through consultation that had become more or less voluntary, depending on the beliefs of those involved in each link.

To understand how the Jewish food chain functioned, we must begin with the supply of kosher goods. To keep kosher, one must have a supply of kosher foods. In nineteenth century Germany and America, the majority of foodstuffs were made at home. Even bread, among those items most readily available for purchase, could be made at home if there were no kosher bakeries. Making food at home may have been time-consuming, but limited reliance on a supply of kosher goods. Meat was another matter altogether. For this, the kosher housewife relied on a kosher butcher. A vegetarian diet would bypass the need for kosher meat and make the observance of kashrut possible even when meat was not available. Jews did not always have the financial means to afford meat. Nonetheless, poultry and meat were valued parts of the Jewish diet, making the strictly vegetarian option most undesirable and, indeed, unlikely. Given the social and cultural import assigned to meat within the diet of German-speaking Jews, a supply of kosher goods was a necessary first link in the chain of kashrut observance.

Supply of kosher items might be essential to kashrut observance, but it was by no means sufficient. If supply of kosher foods and services was the first link in the chain of kashrut observance, the kosher kitchen was the next necessary link. In both the halachic pyramid model and the Jewish food chain model, women's role as keeper of the kitchen makes her indispensable for the observance of kashrut. Both models assume that women were responsible for purchasing foodstuff and transforming them into the dishes consumed by the family, making woman's cooperation essential to maintaining a kosher home. Even in a traditional setting, it was the commitment of the individual woman to kashrut that assured the upholding of the strictest halachic standards on a practical level. The rabbi might in theory have the right to stand in judgment over kashrut matters, but in practice it was the woman who made the decision about whether or not to bring a given question to the rabbi. Within certain limits, the woman was, practically speaking, the highest authority.

Paradoxically, the control and responsibility ceded to women by the halachic kosher food pyramid only amplified their control over this central observance in an era in which Jews could opt out of the halachic system altogether. In a time of choice, women were not simply the arbiters of how to keep kosher, but whether to keep kosher. Even if kosher food was available, it was now up the individual woman to decide whether or not to buy kosher meat. Within her own kitchen, she could follow the letter of the rabbinic law, disregard it completely, or create a middle path of her own. The halachic food pyramid may have assumed women would serve as the front line sentinels of observance, but by the late nineteenth century the observance of kashrut relied on the voluntary compliance of individual women.

KASHRUT: THE LIVED REALITY

Among the nineteenth century memoirs that include a discussion of kashrut, that of Adolf (Aaron) Hoenig stands out. By his own accounting, Hoenig's childhood, lived not in the prosperity of Berlin, Hamburg, or Vienna, but on the eastern reaches of the Austro-Hungarian Empire, was filled with family, tradition, and mischief. Looking back over his life, Hoenig wrote about a life on the margins. He was a younger child in a family rich in children but poor in possessions. He relied in part on the kindness and generosity of relatives for his care and the support of his education. Born in 1837, he was part of a generation that knew the structures and institutions of traditional Jewish life, but who also had the opportunity to experience the promises and potential emancipation of modernity.

Despite (or perhaps because of) his position at the edges of an empire, a family, and a rabbinic way of life, Hoenig's memoir captured many of the complexities and nuances of Jewish life in the nineteenth century. He was an uncanny observer, one who set the stories of his life within the social and political contexts in which they occurred. In particular, he was uniquely situated to relate the complexity of daily home life. As mentioned above, Hoenig experienced firsthand the rhythms of more than one household. His detailed reports of these homes make clear that within the framework of day-to-day living, matters revolving around food, particularly kashrut, held both practical and symbolic significance.[3] Two of the specific incidents he described help to illuminate the complexity of kashrut observance at the time.

The first took place before his bar mitzvah, while he was living away from his parents in a small village with his Aunt Rachel and his uncle, whom he called "Reb Itzig." Rachel and Itzig were not wealthy, but were God-fearing and traditional. Rabbinic rules and customs guided their lives. Daily prayers, learning, and keeping kosher were givens. Young Aaron, as they called Hoenig, was sent to study in a *cheder* [Hebrew school]. Itzig was a salesman who traveled every week. Rachel, on her own, took care of the boy and tended to the work of the house.

The kitchen demanded particular attention. For Rachel, as well as other women who kept a kosher home, the issue of fat was especially demanding. Butter, derived from milk, could not be used with meat or poultry. Neutral fats derived from plant substances were expensive and relatively hard to come by. Observant Jews could not, of course, rely on pork lard, which was plentiful and a favorite of non-Jewish cooks. Instead, Jewish cooks relied on kosher animals for a supply of cooking fat. Chickens provided only limited amounts of fat. Geese were far superior not only because their relative size over the chicken, but also because this naturally fatty bird only became more so as it increased in size and weight. Caring for and fattening geese in order to harvest their fat, while rewarding, took time and attention.

Throughout the winter of 1849, Aunt Rachel fattened geese "in order to prepare the necessary amount of koscher [sic] fat for her kitchen."[4] One particular goose took well to the process and was a "true masterpiece," weighing in at 15 pounds, which according to Hoenig was "fully three pounds above the ordinary."[5] As Hoenig told it, other women envied her this prize and Rachel was proud of her accomplishment.

Her hard work, however, was nearly offset by the events that followed. The time for slaughter came. Even animals that can be eaten by observant Jews may not ultimately be permissible, if they are slaughtered incorrectly or found not to have been in perfect health. The goose was killed without incident. The feathers were removed. Rachel carried out a careful inspection of the now naked bird. The procedure revealed a blue spot on the leg of the bird, potentially a sign of ill health. Though knowledgeable about many of the finer points of keeping kosher, Rachel "did not feel enough of an authority to decide" the status of the bird.[6] She sent the goose with twelve-year-old Aaron to the senior local rabbi for a ruling on its status.

From Hoenig's description, it seems Reb David was a kind man. Understanding the importance of declaring the bird unkosher, the rabbi was not hasty in his final judgment, but ultimately pronounced the goose *trefah* [not kosher]. The rabbi's wife, the rebbetzin, who had also "anxiously waited for the result of the test," understood the tragic implications of this ruling and could only shake her head in distress.[7]

Hoenig was also distressed. His interest lay less in the fat than in the meat of the bird, a prize in and of itself. The thought of not eating this particularly succulent creature was too much to consider; he "could not submit so easily to the sentence."[8] On the way home he passed the house of Reb Dowidleb, the secondary rabbinic judge. Hoenig was knowledgeable about the law and knew that once a rabbinic opinion had been received, a second opinion was not to be sought. Still, he was willing to overlook the finer points of law if there was hope "for a slice of the longed-for roast." Without mentioning the first ruling, he asked the second rabbi for an opinion. Again law books were consulted, but this time the ruling was "Kosher!"[9] The boy jumped up and ran home, reporting only the second ruling. Friday came. Rachel portioned and begun preparing the meat and Reb Iztig returned to town. Hoenig greeted his uncle in the street telling him about the marvelous goose.

That evening they welcomed the Shabbat with joy. The goose was consumed without comment or incident.

The next morning, the rebbetzin, Reb David's wife, sat next to Aunt Rachel in synagogue. After services, the rebbetzin "felt compelled to express her regret concerning the wonderful goose which her husband, unfortunately, had had to pronounce *trefah*.[10] Rachel, shocked, denied the claim. An argument ensued. Rachel was left to question the truth of her nephew's report and was unsure of the status of the bird. Returning home, she did not mention the incident or her doubts. Not wanting to ruin the Shabbat, the meal including the goose was served and eaten. She continued to keep her own counsel, allowing her husband to peacefully take his afternoon nap. Nonetheless, the burden of the secret was too great, and when Itzig awoke her concerns burst forth. The boy was summoned. Hoenig tried to allay concerns by pointing out that Reb Dowidleb had pronounced the bird kosher. Aware of the laws regarding second opinions, Reb Itzig knew that this by no means improved matters. They all set off to Reb David's to address the matter.[11]

Reb David was expecting the call. Upon returning from prayers, his wife had informed him of the situation, "not without adding some items of her own, such as that the goose had already been boiled, broiled, roasted, and partly consumed by Aunt Rachel, so that the whole house was 'trefah.'"[12] Despite his own concerns, Reb David tried his best to calm Itzig, who "convinced of having partaken from a 'trefah' food— believed to feel already pains in his stomach."[13] Reb Dowidleb and Reb Vigdor, the *cheder* teacher, were summoned. Reb Vigdor joined with Dowidleb in a kosher verdict, explaining that he thought the spot the result not of ill health but of the excessive weight carried around by the bird. "This argument convinced even Reb David. Reb Itzig, however, refused for his person to partake anymore of the bird."[14]

Hoenig's second tale took place in 1854, when he, having completed his apprenticeship in a small town, set off to Budapest to set up in trade. There he sought out his older brother Henry, whom he had last seen years earlier. Henry was pleased to meet this young brother and brought him home to meet his wife Julka and their children. The apartment was in a courtyard, which gave Aaron the "feeling of having entered a market square."[15] Unexpectedly faced with two extra mouths to feed, Julka complained that all she had prepared were "American sandwiches."[16] Placating Julka, Henry announced that "his wife should not go through any trouble, he would take care of the supper." He then left the flat in search of lodgings for Aaron.[17]

While Henry was out, an old man entered the apartment and was introduced by Julka: "This is my father—till a hundred years." Her blessing was undercut by the sharp words that followed:

> He does not live with us, but with my sister. He takes also his meals there because we are not enough kosher for him. My goodness, I cannot waste my time with observing all these old rules of the *Schulchan Aruch* [from 1564, the standard code of Jewish law and practice]: make the meat kosher, salt it, water it... that alone takes time enough. And the cooking! The children have to return to school on time, and besides, we live in the year 1854. Nobody takes that kosher business so seriously any more![18]

Her cutting remarks and tone were answered in kind: "'Will you kindly shut up,' the father till a hundred years raised his voice. 'Even in 500 years from now honest and orderly Jews will eat kosher food. And even in a thousand years there will be Jewish daughters who will not laugh at their fathers.'"[19]

The content and the style of discussion must have been familiar to father and daughter, for "this dispute continued for quite a while," ending only when Henry returned carrying a large package of store-bought food for dinner. Excitedly he told the family that "*lechoved den Orach*" [in honor of the guest], he had purchased, on credit, a fresh seven-and-a-half pound roast goose at the kosher butcher shop of Chaim Boskovitz. It is unclear from the account what caused Henry to make this specifically kosher purchase. Perhaps it was his mother's admonitions to make a good Jew out of Aaron. Perhaps he believed that it mattered greatly to Aaron himself. Maybe, despite his wife's opinions, kashrut mattered to Henry himself, or maybe it was simply an unusually generous gesture to include his father-in-law in the celebration. Whatever the reasoning, it mattered little to Julka's father. Claiming that neither Chaim Boskovitz nor the rabbi that supervised his shop was trustworthy, he left without tasting a morsel.

The players and the settings in these two stories were quite different. There was no question about Aunt Rachel's and Reb Itzig's commitment to halacha. They valued their connection to traditions of Judaism; the rhythms that shaped Jewish life; for generations were the essential organizing principles of their own lives. They lived in a small town, where the lives of the inhabitants were strongly intertwined with each other and where even the walls of your own home did not shield you from the scrutiny of others. In contrast to Itzig, Henry did not pedal his wares from town to town as many Jews historically did; rather, he had one of the new white-collar jobs that became a sign of Jewish entrance into the modern world.[20] Julka's speech about kashrut left no question as to her willingness to abandon even key elements of traditional Jewish life. The family's small flat was located in the midst of a block of similar apartments, in a large modern city bustling with action and diversity. No matter how close the neighbors might be, here it was possible to eat what one wanted without fear of social recriminations.

Focusing on the differences in these stories conceals a key element shared by these two tales: the role of the women. On the one hand, they are clearly different. Where Rachel readily took on the obligation and work that come with kashrut observance, Julka was articulate and adamant in her rejection of both the obligation and work involved with kashrut. On the other hand, though they fundamentally disagreed with each other, in both cases it was their opinion that for the most part shaped the observance of this mitzvah—not only for themselves, but for their entire household. Although the rabbis envisioned a pivotal but circumscribed role for Jewish women in kashrut observance, what they did not expect was that women would not always adhere to halacha. Nor did they imagine that under certain circumstances the role of women role would lead to a variety of results, some of which directly challenged the importance of halacha. Though very different in their personal visions of Judaism, both women used their place in the kitchen to shape the observance of others. Whether in breach or in observance, far from being minions of rabbinic will, these women were gatekeepers of a central religious ritual.

In many respects, Julka and her approach to Jewish living represent the antithesis of the rabbinic vision of Jewish life. As discussed in the introduction to this paper, the rabbis who codified Jewish law did not imagine a time when Jews would have the power to completely reject Jewish custom and practice, nor did they afford much agency to women in making decisions or expressing opinions about Judaism. Julka did precisely this, and hers was not a random choice. She made it clear that not observing kashrut gave expression to her own personal concerns about Jewish life; for her, tradition stood in opposition to modernity. By abandoning kashrut, she embraced modernity.

Her explanation of this to Hoenig and the ensuring argument between herself and her father indicate that something other than the dichotomy between modernity and kashrut is being played out. On the one hand, it is easy to understand Julka's practical considerations. For example, soaking and salting meat are labor-intensive and time-consuming. For her children, their modern schools undoubtedly did not take dietary needs into account when setting the school timetable. Yet, had kashrut continued to be a valued observance for Julka, she may well have found a means of adapting to the modern school day. In a similar memoir, Eduard Silbermann recounts how his mother was faced with a similar concern about being able to accommodate the children's school schedule and the midday meal. The exact nature of the conflict is unclear from the memoir; perhaps the customary meat meal was considered too formal and time-consuming, or the process of salting and kashering fresh meat in the days before refrigeration meant a later start to a meat meal. According to her son, Mrs. Silberman chose to prioritize kashrut, solving the conflict by serving a dairy meal.[21] Had the amount of work been the only consideration for Julka, she could probably have found one kosher butcher among the several on her block who would have been willing to soak and salt the meat for her. As Hoenig wrote, Julka and Henry lived on a street where there were several kosher meat markets and "even a delicatessen offering roast geese and other specialties."[22] Ironically, the availability of kosher takeout food and multiple kosher establishments were themselves modern conveniences. Additionally, kashrut was not so outmoded in1854 that it was irrelevant to Julka's sister or the other women who supported the multiple kosher meat markets in the neighborhood.

If kashrut was not incompatible with modernity, neither was kashrut as timeless as "Father—till a hundred years" suggested. While some of the practical advantages of modern city life seem to have made kashrut observance easier, the forces of modernization were obviously also making it possible for women to move away from these rituals. And while Father was correct in assuming that kashrut would continue into the future, Julka was by no means unique in availing herself of the unprecedented opportunity to abandon kashrut without fear of communal repercussions. Joseph Adler wrote of his mother's moral character in the most glowing terms, yet she was "not a pious person," and kashrut and Jewish holidays were not observed in her home. However, her parents, Adler's grandparents, still observed kashrut. In contrast to Julka's father, Adler's grandfather seemed to accept that normative Judaism and even observance of kashrut were changing. On one particularly memorable occasion, the grandfather took Joseph to a beer garden to eat. The older man bought the boy a piece of bread, butter, and mustard, but Adler explained, "As he only ate Kosher food he did not join me in the delicacy."[23]

Jewish life in the later part of the nineteenth century was more open to internal introspection than it had been in earlier times, and women did use this openness to opt out of one of their central obligations as understood by halacha. Such actions not only flew in the face of the rabbinic model of Jewish eating, but were also a fundamental repudiation of the centrality of halacha to Jewish life. Another view into the shift away from kashrut observance can be seen from several of the personal recipe collections that survive from this period. Recipes for dishes mixing meat and milk or containing pork could be found in some of the private collections of Jewish women.[24]

Jewish women were not necessarily shy about failing to endorse kashrut. Lina Morgenstern was well known for her philanthropy and as a public figure on issues concerning domestic life in Germany. Though she was the author of a Jewish prayer book for young people, she was apparently also quite comfortable about not keeping kosher.[25] In the early twentieth century she was the author of a weighty cookbook that made no pretense to be either Jewish or kosher.[26]

Despite her prominence, the cosmopolitan and powerful Morgenstern was not representative of all Jewish women. In some cases, especially in the middle years of the nineteenth century, there were still those for whom kashrut was not a matter of choice. The degree to which kashrut was a value enforced by the community at large is demonstrated in an episode when, attacked by a bully, the nearly thirteen-year-old Aaron Hoenig was forced to eat pork sausage. When the incident came to light, instead of supporting the boy in his trauma, the community turned against him. Concerned that the pollution caused by his consuming pork would infect the entire community, the boy was banished from the town and forced to return to his parents' home. It is hardly surprising that Hoenig's Aunt Rachel had no choice in the matter of practicing kashrut.

The story of Aaron's banishment was extreme and exceptional, yet it also points to the centrality of kashrut in the fabric of everyday life in traditional settings. Others who wrote of childhood or family in small towns in the middle of the nineteenth century often went into great detail about the variety of other ritual observances, but did not afford kashrut the same attention. It is highly unlikely that this omission points to lack of commitment to kashrut. On the contrary, for these memoirists kashrut was so central to the fabric of daily life that it did not provoke special attention. For example, Esther (Hildesheimer) Calvary, born in 1855, was a daughter of Rabbi Esriel Hildesheimer, one of the founders of modern Orthodoxy. She wrote extensively about the ritual observances of her childhood. In contrast to Rosh Hashanah, Hanukah, or Shabbat, kashrut merited no section of its own. Instead, as a testament to the all-pervasive importance of the dietary laws, kashrut appeared throughout her memoir, but always incidentally as part of a larger theme.[27]

We should also not assume that keeping kosher was merely a reflection of a lack of social or dietary alternatives or that it was merely part of a traditional, pre-modern lifestyle. Kashrut was not only a rural phenomenon, limited to Jews entirely ensconced in a culture shaped by halacha. And keeping kosher was not a choice made only by women who were ignorant of another way. Urban Jews, aware of the possibilities of modern life, exposed to a variety of lifestyles, and aware of cultures that did not revolve around halacha continued to uphold the dietary laws. Born in London in 1892, Flora (Strauss) Rosenthal spent her childhood shuttling back and forth between England and Frankfurt. Her mother was worldly, with "musical interests and civilized surroundings." She also kept "a kosher household."[28] In contrast, kashrut was not an issue in the childhood home of Flora (Rother) Goldschmidt. Her family was not observant in the least, celebrating Sunday rather than Saturday as their day of rest. However, growing up in Breslau in the late 1850s and 60s, one of Goldschmidt's best friends was Fanny Freund, whose family "strictly observed Jewish Orthodox rituals."[29] The Freunds may have been Orthodox, but they were also aware of other Jewish families like Flora's; their choice to observe kashrut was made with the knowledge of other possibilities.

In making an active choice to keep kosher, these women made as strong a statement about Jewish identity as Julka did in rejecting kashrut. They could give voice to their personal commitment to Jewish law. They actively chose to buy kosher meats and goods, they chose to prepare dishes in accordance with the dietary strictures, and they chose to serve kosher menus. By controlling the kitchen, they daily reiterated their commitment to Judaism. Though these women, like the women who chose not to keep kosher, showed a measure of agency not inherent in the structure of the kosher food pyramid, their choices served to reinforce the rabbinic ideals of Jewish living.

But making that choice did not always signify a strong commitment to halacha. Living in Cologne in the early years of this century, Ella (Leubsdorf) Levison maintained a kosher kitchen. Though the family maintained some elements of traditional Jewish living, attending synagogue on holidays and lighting candles on the Shabbat for example, Jewish law was by no means the dominant organizing principle for their family life. Her daughter-in-law, Engel Levison, explained Ella's personal commitment to the mitzvah as stemming from respect for her mother. Though Ella's mother, Billa (Bürger) Leubsdorf, lived in Duesseldorf with her other daughter, Fanny, Ella wanted to be sure that her mother would feel welcome to visit at any moment.[30] In contrast to Julka and her father, here kashrut was a means of connecting one generation with another.

Even among those committed to kashrut observance, the rabbis were not always actually invested with the degree of power envisioned by the halachic system. Clearly Aunt Rachel participated actively in the legal structure that upheld rabbinic authority; nonetheless, even she found ways to negotiate the system. It was her own recognition of the importance of halacha and the admission of the limits of her own authority that initially brought her to send the goose for rabbinic inspection. This was not done lightly, given all that was at stake should the goose be pronounced not kosher.[31] But when the rebbetzin informed her that the goose was *treyf*, she chose to overlook the questionable status of the bird. Choosing not to go back to the rabbi immediately, as she should have, she took the matter into her own hands. She did not question Hoenig even to learn that there had been a second ruling. She had concerns other than kashrut. Having no other food prepared to feed her family, she decided that Shabbat peace and provisions were more important than kashrut. She fed her family and did not raise the concerns until after the food had been consumed and the afternoon nap completed. By her actions, she overruled the rabbi and upset the hierarchy of power.

Rachel was not alone among women who upheld and challenged the halachic structure. However, because women rarely recorded the process by which they decided food was fit for family consumption, it

is hard to find records of this process of negotiation within the larger
halachic framework. One story from Eduard Silbermann's memoir is
particularly revealing. Silbermann's childhood was different in many
ways from that of Aaron Hoenig. Born in 1851, in Komsdorf, Upper
Franconia, Silbermann grew up in Bischheim, then in Upper Franconia,
and later in Bamberg. His was a thoroughly German childhood. In
contrast to Hoenig, Silbermann received schooling in a German school
as well as a Jewish one. The Silbermanns had good relations and contact
with their non-Jewish neighbors. Still, as was the case with Hoenig,
Jewish tradition permeated Silbermann's childhood home.

As we saw earlier with the discussion of lunch time meal
accommodations, kashrut was of particular importance to Silbermann's
mother. It was so significant that the family had a saying meant to
assure that even gifts of food, prepared outside of the watchful eye of
Silbermann's mother met her strict standards: "*Wenn eine heisst 'Bele'
(judischer Frauenname) darf ich essen aus ihrem 'Kele' und 'contraris' bei
Christen darf man nicht essen*" [When she is named Bele (a Jewish woman's
name) I may eat from her ladle, and on the contrary, when she is a
Christian woman, one may not eat (from her ladle)].[32] Thus, gifts of
food were to be sorted by their kitchen of origin, and only Jewish
kitchens could be trusted as suppliers of food.

In the 1850s and 1860s, the family regularly received gifts of
doughnuts from their Christian neighbors on *Kirchweih Tag* [Church
consecration day], not an uncommon practice. At first, the Silbermanns
strictly held by their maxim and would not eat them. This is hardly
surprising, since the doughnuts had likely been fried in pork lard. As
the years passed, Eduard's mother reassessed the situation. Upon further
consideration, the homes of the non-Jewish neighbors were deemed
reinlich and the Silbermanns could eat from their kitchens. Unfortunately,
Silbermann does not explain how his mother came to this conclusion or
precisely what she meant. One possible reading relies on one of the
Yiddish meanings of *reinlich* as "pure." Among the many connotations
of the word pure are those that imply holiness or sanctity, states
associated with kashrut, for kosher foodstuffs are considered to uphold
standards of holiness. Perhaps Mrs. Silbermann found the circumstances
of her neighbors' kitchens to be pure enough to be considered kosher
on some level and as a result eating food produced there would not have
challenged her standards of observance.

I believe that Mrs. Silbermann's concerns lay more with cleanliness than with kashrut. To be *reinlich* in the German sense of the word meant to be tidy or clean, qualities that the German housewife valued greatly. In such a case, Mrs. Silbermann must have decided that, upon inspection, her neighbor's kitchen was *reinlich* enough, meaning clean enough, to be considered on a par with other, clean Jewish homes. This suggests that, at least in this matter, cleanliness trumped kashrut.[33]

Whatever the reason for the reversal of the decision, what is clear from this incident is that Mrs. Silbermann created standards by which to judge the fitness of the food supplied to her family's home. Whether those standards somehow took kashrut into consideration or, as I believe, overlooked it entirely, the role of the rabbi as arbiter of what was fit for consumption by Jews was entirely bypassed, supplanted once again by the judgment of the woman of the house.

Nineteenth century German Jewish cookbooks offer another view into the relationship between Jewish women and the rabbinate. Jewish cookbooks were a new literary genre. Though they appeared first in the early part of the century, they gained real popularity only in the second half of the 1800s. No less than eight German-language, Jewish, commercial cookbooks appeared between 1850 and 1910. Words like "Israelitische" or "Judische" in the titles proclaimed the Jewish origins of these popular volumes. Often they were reprinted several times; the most successful enjoyed publication through the end of the Weimar period. Notably, all of these specifically Jewish commercial cookbooks adhered to traditional standards of kashrut.

This uniformity regarding kashrut clearly did not reflect the practice of the mitzvah among the audience for whom these books were intended. Yet there were reasons for this homogeneity regarding kashrut. German-language, Jewish cookbooks varied little from book to book. As a rule they were large volumes, both in scope and heft. With the apparent belief that more is better, they contained anywhere from 300 to over 3,500 recipes. Aside from recipes, they usually included an introduction, a table of contents, and menu suggestions. The dishes themselves bore strong similarities from book to book. Kashrut seems to have been one of several prerequisites for inclusion in a fairly uniform genre.

There were of course advantages to upholding kashrut, regardless of religious outlook. Until World War I, German Jewish cookbooks were always commercial ventures intended to and usually succeeding in appealing to a broad audience. A kosher cookbook could be used equally

by those who observed dietary laws and those who did not. Indeed,
even women who did not keep kosher found use for a book like Marie
Elsasser's *Ausführliches Kochbuch für die einfache und feine jüdische Küche*
[Detailed cookbook for the simple and pure Jewish kitchen].[34]

Whatever the reasons, these books embraced kashrut; in so doing,
they publicly positioned women as halachic authorities. Without
exception, the authors of these cookbooks were women. In each volume,
women took the expertise they had amassed through their own experience
in their own kitchens and moved out of their homes to share this
information in the broader arena. By stating that their cookbooks were
guides to "cooking by the ritual laws," as kashrut was often described,
these authors claimed to know not only the mechanics of how to put a
dish together or organize a meal, but also what constituted kashrut.
In this way, they provided information about kashrut that, although
based on the male rabbinic tradition, was unfiltered by male supervision.
Flora (Pfeffer) Wolff's right to write with expertise about domestic areas
of Jewish law was reinforced by the title *Frau Prediger* [preacher's wife]
on the title page of the book. She provided her readers with a great deal
of information regarding how to observe the general principles of dietary
law. She even went so far as to endorse particular products; for example,
she vouched for a brand of mustard made by the Pintus-Brandenburg
company. Unlike other mustards, this one, she asserted, was produced
without the addition of gelatin or rennin and could therefore be used
"without objection" by even "strictly believing" Jewish women.[35] Here,
it was the rabbi's wife and not the rabbi who authenticated particular
supplies.

Most women did not have marriage to a rabbi to lend credence to
their claims about kashrut, but they did not need one. With the
exception of the widow of Joseph Gumprich, these women wrote under
their given names and without the endorsements of rabbinic leaders or
other male communal figures.[36] In contrast to the ideal set out by the
halachic kosher food pyramid, these women used cookbooks to give
public voice to their authority as the ultimate arbiters of kashrut.

Lack of male rabbinic involvement gave women some room to assert
ideas about kashrut and Judaism that may not have been fully in step
with orthodox rabbinic ideals. Though committed to Orthodoxy, the
widow of Joseph Gumprich was aware that even those women who
observed kashrut were not always beholden to the norms established by
men. A small note to the readers of her *Vollstandiges Kochbuch für die*

jüdische Küche [Complete Cookbook for the Jewish Kitchen], first printed in 1888, explained that, after investigation, neither the coloring agent cochineal nor gelatin could be used according to strict orthodox regulations. That she felt the need to boldly make such a claim suggests that even women who kept kosher were making use of these new uncategorized ingredients in contradiction to the interpretations put forward by the male authorities.[37] Cookbooks, as a new genre, reflected the growing importance of foodways in shaping identity. This importance also provided a small group of Jewish women with the opportunity to take the power ceded to them by rabbinic law far beyond the boundaries envisioned by halacha.

The power instilled in the women as gatekeepers in the chain of Jewish eating can also be seen in the few cases where conflicts arose between the woman in charge of the kitchen and those seated at her table. Anna Auerbach's grandmother, for example, was a devout woman who had observed kashrut all her life. In the last quarter of the nineteenth century, as an old woman, she came to live with Anna's family. Anna's mother did not keep a kosher home; at first, the grandmother did not eat the same food as the rest of the family, but partook of special meals prepared in a kosher kitchen outside the home. However, given the practical complications involved, the older woman ultimately surrendered her observance of kashrut and succumbed to the practice as defined by Anna's mother.[38]

In contrast, young Hugo Carl Plaut felt hemmed in by the kosher diet imposed upon him in his mother's house in Leipzig. While recovering from an illness, he hankered for the distinctly unkosher taste of roast hare and dispensed a servant girl to a local inn to procure the forbidden meat. He consumed his treat and placed the plate under his bed. Subterfuge was the only way to circumvent the kosher norms of his mother's kitchen. Later, when the nanny entered the room, "she smelt the illegal meal and his misdeed was revealed!"[39] Those at the family table had little choice but to partake in the food, kosher or not, coming from the family kitchen.

As we have seen, even within the home, the influence of women as gatekeepers was not absolute. Just as the position of rabbis in a traditional Jewish society did not always guarantee their control over all aspects of kashrut, so women's involvement in foodways did not always guarantee their control over those whom they fed. In rejecting Rachel's power as well as the rabbi's to gate-keep for him and determine what was kosher,

Itzig's refusal to further partake of the suspect goose asserted his authority as well. Conversely, while Julka made clear that she would not keep a kosher home, her husband asserted his preference and rarely ate at home. We will never know if the restaurants he frequented were kosher establishments, but we do know that when he brought home a meal for Julka and Aaron, he brought kosher food into Julka's unkosher kitchen, thereby challenging her proprietary role as gatekeeper of kashrut for the household.

Ultimately, because women's power derived from their work in and influence over the home and kitchen, it was a power that was circumscribed by the boundaries and structure of the home. If women had a measure of control over what those at her table ate, that control weakened significantly when they left her home. When Joseph Adler's mother lived in her mother's home, she undoubtedly ate the kosher food her mother served. On leaving her mother's home and setting up her own, she was obviously no longer obliged to observe the dietary laws.[40] Eduard Silbermann's mother, as we saw earlier, cared a great deal about keeping kosher (even if she was willing to interpret the laws without rabbinic consultation) and took great care to assure that her children kept kosher. Her brother, in contrast, had no wife to keep house or kosher for him and took his meals at the apparently unkosher restaurant *Brauerei Lang*. Once, on an outing with his uncle, Silbermann joined his uncle in eating at the *Brauerei*. Upon learning of this infraction, his mother was terribly upset.[41] But what was she to do? Even when leaving Eduard in the care of a close relative, once the boy left her house she had no real ability to control what he ate. Although she worked to instill the importance of kashrut in her children, when Eduard eventually left her home and set out on his own, she ceased to be his gatekeeper. Outside of her home and realm of influence and able to decide for himself, Silbermann moved away from many observances, among them keeping kosher.[42] In the vastness of the entire world, power that was tied to the finite geography of a given home was indeed limited.

CONCLUSION

Kashrut derived from a legal system that assumed the centrality and authority of rabbinic law. The kosher food pyramid envisioned a hierarchical society that preserved the position of the rabbi and halacha. However, the way in which kashrut was enacted by late nineteenth and early twentieth century German-speaking Jews differed from this rabbinic model. Jews participated in a Jewish food chain, whether kashrut was observed in practice or in breach. Though rabbinic ideas about food strongly influenced Jewish foodways, the Jewish food chain was significantly more lateral than the rabbinic ideal. Jewish eating depended on connections between the supplier of food to Jewish homes, the purchasers and preparers of those foods, and Jewish consumers. Though the rabbis could, and often did, play a part in this system, they were by no means guaranteed a role.

Women, on the other hand, were essential to the Jewish food chain. Their central position, derived in part by gender norms, also, ironically, obtained in no small measure from the authority and responsibility placed upon them by the rabbinic structure of kashrut observance. Jewish and general social custom placed home-based, food-related tasks almost exclusively in the hands of women and those who served under them. Because kashrut observance relied on the work done in purchasing, preparing, and serving food that was primarily consumed at home, Jewish women were in a unique position to influence this particular ritual practice. Within the kosher food pyramid, the role of women was subject to the hierarchical rabbinic structure. In reality, the position of women was much more powerful. Though power derived from food and home were limited by the boundaries of home, within the reality of the Jewish food chain, the position of individual Jewish women was raised to that of gatekeeper of Jewish identity as expressed through food. No matter what a given Jewish woman thought about keeping kosher, whether she saw it as non-negotiable, a positive choice, something to be rejected, or of no consequence whatsoever, her opinion shaped the preparation of food and the enactment of law for of all those who gathered around her table. Though the power women derived from both the religious structure and the social roles that tied them to the kitchen was significantly limited in scope, Jewish women found ways to engage it and give voice to their own approach to Jewish observance.

ACKNOWLEDGMENTS

I would like to thank David Abusch-Magder, Maria B. Baader, Julie Burch, and Jane Rothstein for the help and insights they contributed in the development of this essay.

NOTES

[1] Hasia Diner, "Looking at the Home to Find a Home" (paper presented at the Jewish Theological Seminary, New York, 17 October, 1999), 8-9.

[2] *Ibid.*, 9.

[3] Adolf Hoenig, *Memoirs: Part One, 1915* (trans. A. Fried; Cincinnati: American Jewish Archives).

[4] *Ibid.*, 66.

[5] *Ibid.*, 67.

[6] *Ibid.*

[7] *Ibid.*

[8] *Ibid.*

[9] *Ibid.*, 68.

[10] *Ibid.*

[11] *Ibid.*, 71.

[12] *Ibid.*, 70.

[13] *Ibid.*, 71.

[14] *Ibid.*, 72.

[15] Adolf Hoenig, *Memoirs: Part Two, 1915* (trans. A. Fried; Cincinnati: American Jewish Archives), 14.

[16] *Ibid.*, 15.

[17] *Ibid.*, 16.

[18] *Ibid.*, 18.

[19] Ibid.

[20] David Sorkin, *The Transformation of German Jewry 1780-1840* (New York: Oxford University Press, 1999).

[21] Eduard Silbermann, *Erinnerungen 1851-1917* (M.E. 601/1; New York: Leo Baeck Institute, 1916?) 12-13.

[22] Hoenig, *Memoirs Part Two*, 15.

[23] Joseph Theo Adler, *The Family of Joseph and Marie Adler, Jews in Germany, German Jews in America* (M.E. 971; New York: Leo Baeck Institute), 16.

[24] Steiner, *Erprobte & Disktierte Kocherecepter Meiner Lieben Mütter Eva Berl 1912* (Hedi Levenback Collection; New York: Leo Baeck Institute) and *Kochbuch Für Der Frau Schnebel Und Nachträge* (A.R. 10843; Dora Schocken Collection; New York: Leo Baeck Institute). Katie Jonas, *Untitled Cookbook* (AR 6268; New York: Leo Baeck Institute, 1908).

[25] Lina Morgenstern and Immanuel Heinrich Ritter, *Glaub, Andacht Und Pflicht* (Berlin: Julius Springer, 1863). I would like to thank Maria B. Baader for bringing this little-known work to my attention.

[26] Lina Morgenstern, *Illustriertes Universal Kochbuch Für Gesunde Und Kranke: Enthält Nahrungsmittellehre, Theorie Der Kochkunft, Sowie Nahe an 3000 Erprobte Un Bewährte Rezepte Für Die Bürgerliche, Die Feinste Und Die Krankenküche* (12th ed.; Berlin: W. Herlet, 1907).

[27] Esther Calvary, *Kindheitserinnerungen* (M.E. 79; New York: Leo Baeck Institute). While Calvary explains the particulars of many home based rituals but only obliquely mentions keeping kosher when she mentions that women would bring chickens to her father so he could judge their kashrut. For another example of a similar treatment of kashrut look at the memoir of Arthur Kahn who was born in 1850. He writes in great detail of small town life filled with rituals but includes only incidental mentions of kashrut observance. Arthur Kahn, *Lebenserinnerungen Eines Juden* (M.E. 741; New York: Leo Baeck Institute). Julius Frank's memoir of Steinach similarly shows how kashrut could be part of the fabric of Jewish village life as late as the 1890s. Julius Frank, *Reminiscences of Days Gone By* (M.E. 142; New York: Leo Baeck Institute).

[28] Nora Rosenthal, *Opus One 1973-6* (ME 534; New York: Leo Baeck Institute), 4.

[29] Flora Goldschmidt, *Jugenderinnerungen Von Flora Goldschmidt Geb. Rother* (M.E. 191; New York: Leo Baeck Institute), 13-14.

[30] Billa (Bürger) Leubsdorf died in 1924. It is unclear whether or not Ella (Leubsdorf) Levison maintained a kosher kitchen after that point. It seems unlikely, however, that she did so after the family emigrated to the United States in the 1930s. Engel Levison, interview with author, South Orange, New Jersey, February , 2000.

[31] Rachel was not alone in respecting the importance of halacha or acknowledging the limits of her authority. Nor was the importance of the goose particular to her case. Esther (Hildesheimer) Calvary recounted that after Chanukah when it came time to slaughter the geese, it was quite common for women to come for a rabbinic ruling about the status of the birds. This, she reports, was always stressful because a ruling of unkosher meant a tremendous financial loss. Calvary, *Kindheitserinnerungen*, 21.

[32] Silbermann, *Erinnerungen 1851-1917*, 152. Translation by the author.

[33] For a complete discussion of Eduard Silbermann and the doughnuts, see Ruth Abusch-Magder, "Eating 'Out': Food and the Boundaries of Jewish Community and Home in Germany and the United States," *Nashim* 5 (2002): 61-63.

[34] Marie Elsasser, *Ausführliches Kochbuch Für Die Einfache Und Feine Jüdische Küche Unter Berrucksichtigun (with consideration of) Aller Rituellen Vorschriften in 3759 Rezepten* (4th ed.; Frankfurt: J. Kauffmann, 1901). The first volume I have come across is dated 1901. That edition, however, is already marked as a fourth edition. The book was reprinted at least until 1930. Two copies of this book given to me belonged to families who did not keep kosher homes.

[35] Flora Wolff, *Koch Und Wirthschaftsbuch Für Jüdische Hausfrauen* (Berlin: Siegfried Cronbach, 1889), xxiv.

[36] Witwe Joseph Gumprich, *Vollstandiges Kochbuch Für Die Jüdische Küche: Selbsgeprüfte Und Bewährte Rezepte Zu Bereitung Aller Speisen, Backwerke, Getränke Und Alles Eingemachten Für Die Gewöhnliche Und Die Feinere Küche, Sowie Anleitung Über Tischdecken Und Servieren (Mit Abbildungen)* (6th ed.; ed. P. Münz; Frankfurt: J. Kauffmann, 1914). The first edition of this book appeared in 1888 and as late as 1914 included the original introduction and, I suspect, most, if not all of, the same recipes.

[37] *Ibid.*, 6

[38] Anna Auerbach, *Chronik Unserer Familie, 1905* (M.E. 707; New York: Leo Baeck Institute), 2.

[39] Rahel Liebeschuetz, *Hugo Carl Plaut: Part I 1858-1890* (ME 847/1; New York: Leo Baeck Institute), 15.

[40] Adler, *The Family of Joseph and Marie Adler,* 16.

[41] Silbermann, *Erinnerungen 1851-1917,* 66.

[42] *Ibid.,* 134.

Holy Kugel:
The Sanctification of Ashkenazic
Ethnic Foods in Hasidism

Allan Nadler

There are many incredible Hasidic tales of the sort that one will not find in the renderings of Yehudah Leib Peretz, Micha Yosef Berdichevsky, Martin Buber, Elie Wiesel or in any of the other well-known, romantic reconstructions of Hasidism. Nor have the academic historians and theologians of Hasidism taken account of the most internally popular genre of primary Hasidic sources. This is quite understandable. Those studying, or romancing, Hasidism from a respectful distance would almost certainly find these tales to be disconcertingly grotesque. Many— like some colleagues with whom I've discussed these materials—would insist that the sources dealt with in this paper cannot possibly be authentic and are probably in fact anti-Hasidic satires. They are not. They abound in Hasidic writings since the mid-nineteenth century. The examples immediately below, just the tip of the iceberg of a vast popular Hasidic literature dealing with the most mundane of things, are all narrowly concerned with a single, apparently trivial subject: the praise of kugel, the humble potato or noodle pudding commonly eaten by eastern European Jews on the Sabbath:

> The zaddikim proclaim that there are profound matters embedded in the kugel. For this reason they insisted that every Jew must east the Sabbath kugel. Rabbi Menachem Mendel of Rimanov recalled that once, when he went out for a walk with the holy rabbi of Ropshitz, all that they talked about for three hours were the secrets that lie hidden inside the Sabbath kugel.[1]

The Seer of Lublin taught that just as one's respective mitzvot and transgressions are weighed in the balance in the process of our final judgment in the heavenly courts, so too they weigh all of the kugel that one ate in honor of the Sabbath.[2]

Reb Shmelke of Selish used to immerse himself in the mikvah [ritual bath] after the Mussaf service, before the eating of the kugel.[3]

Reb Itiskel of Pshevorsk taught that there is a special chamber in the heavens in which the particular reward for eating kugel on the Sabbath is distributed; even one who ate kugel only out of base material motives, because he craved it, would receive his reward.[4]

Rabbi Aaron Roth of Meah Shearim, revered throughout the Hasidic world as Reb Arele, in a work devoted entirely to the "Sanctity of the Table," establishes the eating of kugel as a theological imperative deriving from Judaic monotheism. For Reb Arele's Hasidim, as they are known throughout contemporary Israel, kugel has become a veritable sacrament to the oneness of the God of Israel:

Kugel is the one special food that all Jews eat, one food in the service of the one God [*ma'akhal ehad, ve-ovdin bo le-Eyl ehad*], so that anyone who does not eat kugel on the Sabbath in this country [Israel], should be investigated [for heresy].[5]

Finally, in one of the most disturbing of these tales, the power of kugel is proclaimed to be so great that it served, for the Belzer rebbe, to be an effective antidote even for the extreme horrors of the Holocaust:

The Rachmastrivker rebbe, who now lives in Jerusalem, recounted an awesome tale about the Holy rebbe Arn of Belz. When Rabbi Isser Zalman Meltzer, of blessed memory, visited the Belzer rebbe after the Second World War, among the things he asked him was how he passed the years of horror. The Holy Belzer rebbe—who lost his wife and all of his children and grandchildren and all who were dear to him and remained alone, naked and stripped of everything that had been his and had endured years of wandering and terribly difficult homelessness— (the rebbe) answered R. Isser Zalman joyfully and serenely with the following words: "Thank God, I had kugel to eat every Shabbes."[6]

THE HASIDIC TISH: THE REBBE'S TABLE

What is going on here? In order to understand this bizarre sanctification of potato or noodle pudding, among many other traditional Eastern European Jewish foods, one must begin with the Hasidic rebbe's sacred meal, or tish, which has long been the unique central ritual of Hasidic communal life. The Sabbath table of the zaddik—the rebbe's tish—is the most enduring and significant public ritual in Hasidic life. The tish originated, in embryonic form, with the followers of Rabbi Israel ben Eliezer, or the Baal Shem Tov [Master of the Good Name, also familiarly called The Besht], the founder of Hasidism, who held court regularly at the third Sabbath meal.[7] It remains to this day the most important communal gathering for most Hasidic groups, one that allows for a unique spiritual encounter between the rebbe and his followers.

The specific rituals of the tish showcase the central myths that animate Hasidic society: the charisma and spiritual powers of the rebbe are on public display at the Sabbath table, as is his followers' adoration of him. The monarchical status of the rebbe is symbolized by his throne-like chair at the head of the tish and by his royal, gold-laced *tish-bekeshe* [table-robe] worn only on this special occasion. Even more dramatically, the rebbe's priestly powers are manifested during his administration of the sacramental rites of sanctifying, eating and then distributing to the assembled the *shirayim* [remains] of his Sabbath meal. The status of the zaddik [righteous man] at his Sabbath table, as the equivalent of the ancient Israelite priest offering sacrifices in the Temple, is a regular motif in Hasidic accounts of the tish. An illustrative example is the following description of the tish of the leader of the Belorussian Hasidic sect of Karlin:

> Once, R. Monele Karliner entered the tish of R. Shmuel of Karlin and the Ratner Maggid was cutting the meat for him. His face was burning like a torch, and he took a piece of meat and put it in his mouth and said: I eat this with the same intent as the High Priest in the Holy Temple would eat the sin offering; then he took another piece and said, this one, as a burnt offering etc.[8]

The intense interaction between the rebbe and his Hasidim that takes place at the tish serves as a demonstration of yet another classical Hasidic notion: the descent of the zaddik to the masses and the deeply personal relationship he enjoys with each and every one of his disciples. Tales of the ability of the rebbe to see into the hearts and divine the thoughts of individual Hasidim assembled around the tish abound. While the specific rituals vary widely among different Hasidic sects, the custom at most tishen is for each Hasid to "receive a *le-Hayyim*"; that is, to raise a glass of wine with the rebbe in order to receive his personal benediction.[9]

This focus on the ritualized consumption of food reflects the early Hasidic practice of *avodah be-gashmiyouth* [serving God through earthly pleasures]. In the context of the tish, the rebbe engages in this corporeal worship on behalf of his entire community by elevating the sparks of holiness embedded in his food back to their divine source and then sharing his sanctified meal with the assembled. Beyond the doctrinal significance of the specific rituals of the tish, some of the most celebrated aspects of Hasidic folklore—particularly Hasidic music and dance—[10] are on public display here as in no other arena of Hasidic life, as is the Hasidic emphasis on *dibbuk haverim* [spiritual intimacy within the Hasidic fraternity].[11]

Finally, and most importantly for the history of Hasidic literature and thought, the tish (again, specifically at the third Sabbath meal) has been since the earliest years of Hasidism the principal venue for the public discourses of the rebbe, and thus the main source for the dissemination of Hasidic doctrine. The bulk of the classical texts of Hasidic theology emerged from the Hebrew renderings of the oral Yiddish discourses of the zaddikim at the third meal. The timing of this meal, at the Sabbath's twilight, lent itself to the task of remembering the rebbe's sermons and faithfully committing them to writing. The fact that Hasidim tend to extend this ritual well into the evening, past the normative time for the Sabbath's end, often allowed for designated individuals, who had already recited the evening prayers proclaiming the end of the Sabbath in advance of the rest of the community, to take notes discretely (or, as is the practice today in many Hasidic courts, to record) the rebbe's discourses.

Given the obvious importance of the tish in hasidic life and the doctrinal centrality of the mystical beliefs and myths reflected in its rituals, it is particularly odd that it has not yet been systematically explored either by critical scholars or even in traditional hasidic writings.[12] Although there are many hasidic books and pamphlets that explain and justify unique hasidic customs and despite the fact that the tish is regularly referred to in the Hasidic literature, most particularly in the tales of the zaddikim, the tish itself is almost always merely the mise-en-scène for some other hasidic doctrine or miraculous occurrence and is rarely treated as a significant subject in itself. One thing I have found particularly surprising is the absence from Hasidic sources of any systematic treatments of the central, most striking and repercussive ritual of the Hasidic tish; namely, the distribution of the *shirayim*, whereby Hasidim share the remains of the rebbe's Sabbath meal. Most hasidic sources that discuss *shirayim*, as well as other aspects of the tish, are found scattered in the liturgical pamphlets for the Sabbath table songs, or *zemirot*, published by the various Hasidic sects[13] or in general compendia of customs specific to each of those sects.

There were some attempts by later Hasidic authorities to find a normative basis in halachic—rather than mystical or Hasidic—literature for the practice of *shirayim*. So, for example, the Munkaczer rebbe, Hayyim Elazar Shapira, suggested a classical Rabbinic source as its basis:

> Regarding the custom of Hasidim to take *shirayim* from the food of their rebbes: I have found its source in the story in the Jerusalem Talmud of how Rabbi Yochanan used to gather crumbs left over [from the meal on the eve of the New Moon] and eat them.[14]

Clearly, that is not the immediate source for the Hasidic practice of *shirayim*. Similar attempts to justify this uniquely Hasidic custom by reference to normative rabbinic sources are occasionally found in contemporary Hasidic literature. It is not simply that the source for the custom of *shirayim* is in some doubt; the chronological origins in hasidic history of what has become the most evident, and in many ways the most grotesque, practice of Hasidism remain obscure.

THE ORIGINS OF THE COMMUNAL SABBATH MEAL IN HASIDIC SOCIETY

Some form of a communal tish at the third Sabbath meal was apparently already instituted by the Baal Shem Tov himself. An early Hasidic source describes the alleged origins of the Besht's public celebration of the third Sabbath meal in a deliciously populist way:

> Once, the Besht and his minyan spent the Sabbath in a certain village. When the time for the third meal arrived, the village's proprietor gathered numerous people from the nearby farms and sat and ate and drank together with them, in song and celebration. And the Besht perceived that this found great favor in the heavens. So he called that farmer after the meal and

asked him the reason that he invested so greatly in the third meal. And the farmer answered the Besht: for I have heard the verse quoted: let my soul depart while I am among my people Israel; and I have heard furthermore that on the Sabbath each Jew possesses an additional soul [*neshama yeterah*] which departs from him at the termination of the Sabbath. So I said: let my additional soul also depart while I am in the company of the people of Israel. That is why I gather these Jews together.[15]

Whatever its source, the third Sabbath meal conducted by the Besht and his disciples was apparently a genuine communal gathering, a celebratory feast that emphasized the significance of the gathering "in the company of the people of Israel," as indicated in this story as well as many other Hasidic legends. Both the early Hasidic sources and the classical Mitnagdic [rationalistic] polemics indicate that, for the Hasidim, the communal third meal was primarily an occasion to indulge together with the rebbe in much food, hard drink, and merriment, and then to hear the rebbe's discourse. The description of the early Hasidim's celebration of the third meal by the enlightened Galician satirist of Hasidism, Joseph Perl, in his notorious work *Vesen Der Sekt Hasidim* (ca. 1816), is fairly typical of the early external accounts of the Tish by many other critics and opponents of Hasidism:

> Though the entire Sabbath is considered a time of special divine favor which is best spent in the rebbe's court, it is the period of the third meal which is thought to be the most desirable time for the bonding of the Hasid with his rebbe. On each and every Sabbath, following the afternoon prayers, the local Hasidim, along with visitors from other places, gather in the home of the rebbe; and when there is no rebbe present in the city, they gather in the home of a prominent Hasid, for the third meal. There they eat and drink a lot of wine, sing and dance. And it is during this time that the zaddik delivers before the assembled his interpretations of the Torah and Talmud.[16]

Though these early gatherings included many of the basic elements of the tish that have endured to this day, some obvious changes have occurred. The most conspicuous of these changes has been the development of the custom of *shirayim* [the remains of the rebbe's meal]. The introduction of *shirayim* symbolizes the gradual transformation of the tish from a genuinely communal meal into a symbolic sacrament, in which the masses of Hasidim no longer really feasted but rather ended up nibbling on tiny, symbolic morsels of food provided for them by the rebbe. Not entirely unlike the Eucharist, *shirayim* constitute the sacrament that allows the Hasid to attain intimacy with the Divine. Many Hasidic sources discuss the concentration of divine powers in the most minuscule portions of the most common foods that had been sanctified by the rebbe. The following tale is illustrative of this phenomenon:

> I heard this from the Holy rebbe, Benzion of Bobov. When his holy grandfather, the author of *Divrei Hayyim* [Rabbi Hayyim Halberstam of Zanz], was visiting the Ropshitzer rebbe together with rabbi Shmuel of Kaminka, the two of them split and shared a single grain of kasha that had come to them from the *shirayim* of the Ropshitzer rebbe. [17]

No eighteenth-century sources that describe the Hasidic gatherings at the third meal refer to the custom of *shirayim*. Moreover, when this practice is first alluded to, so far as I have been able to discover, it takes place not at the third meal, but at the first Sabbath meal on Friday evening. The tale I have in mind refers to the interaction between the Yehudi of Pershsyzcha (d. 1814) and the Maggid of Koznitz (1733-1814) , as narrated by the latter's grandson, Hayyim Meir of Mogielnica:

> The Yehudi visited the Maggid of Kozhnitz several times, and it was his custom not to partake of the food at his table, since he used to recite the *Kabbalath Shabbat* prayers after the meal of the holy Maggid. But it was the Maggid's practice to seat the Yehudi next to him and to hand to him the *shirayim* to distribute to the assembled. So once, when the Yehudi came to Kozhnitz, they complained to the holy Maggid about the fact that he did not partake of the anything from his table, and that this was a sign of disrespect....Later that night, the Yehudi paced back and forth and wondered aloud: What does the Maggid think, that I have come to "get Hasidism" from him ? No, no, it is only because he is a weak man, that I come to help him with his worship. [18]

As the story of the contention between the Maggid of Koznitz and the Yehudi indicates, the practice of *shirayim* was not immediately universally accepted. A similar tale by R. Hayyim Meir of Mogielnica, this one involving the Yehudi and the Seer of Lublin (1745-1815), illustrates the fact that the Yehudi was not terribly impressed with the importance of *shirayim* or more generally with the role of eating in the spiritual life.[19]

It is therefore not until the early nineteenth century that we find evidence of two significant additions to the original Hasidic celebration of the third meal, neither yet universally practiced by Hasidic rebbes. The first was a public meal, or tish, with the rebbe on Friday night, in addition to Saturday evening; the second was the practice of distributing *shirayim* to the assembled Hasidim, which developed into a sacred ritual instead of a genuine communal meal. I believe that these two developments are closely related. The earliest references to the Friday night tish and the *shirayim* are vague. However, in the later sources there is evidence of an increasing, almost magical concern with the specifics of the rebbe's meal, the exact nature of the food he distributed, and the techniques by which he ate and handed out his *shirayim* on Friday night. Along with this, there is both a quantitative diminishment of the meal itself and an increasing emphasis on the Torah discourse delivered by the rebbe at the table.

These changes directly correspond to the increasing conservatism of Hasidism over the course of the nineteenth century regarding the boldest mystical teachings of the movement's founders. The ideal that each and every Jew serve God through eating and drinking—which is, after all, the theoretical basis for the tish—was quite prominent among the disciples of the Besht and the Maggid of Mezeritch. In his treatment of this aspect of the doctrine of *avodah be-gashmiyouth* [serving God materially], for example, Levi Isaac of Berditchev (d. 1810) presents the practice democratically, as accessible to every Jew, requiring only that he maintain the correct spiritual attitude towards food and drink. Moreover, Levi Isaac and his contemporaries instructed that each Jew is providentially led to eat specific food whose divine sparks correspond to the spiritual needs of his own soul.[20]

A similarly populist view of sacred eating can be found in the writings of Menachem Nahum of Tchernobyl (1730-1787), who writes:

When a man fully believes with a true and complete faith that this is holy food in which the Lord our God Himself is to be found, truly robed therein, and when he focuses his heart and mind on the internal holiness of the food, then he is able to raise the holy spark that was until then in a state of brokenness and exile back up to God, may He be blessed, and he will derive deep pleasure from it. For this is the very essence of our divine service. Therefore, every servant of the Lord must delve into the interior of each physical matter so that all of his actions will be for the sake of heaven, especially when it comes to eating and drinking, in order to rescue and elevate the holy sparks from their broken state.[21]

During the nineteenth century, however, as Hasidism became more elitist, there was a clear tendency to limit the mystical activity of sanctifying of food and drink to the zaddikim. Rabbi Israel of Rizhin (1797-1850), for example, spoke often of the great difficulty of serving God through eating. R. Israel went so far as to suggest that this form of worship is more sublime, esoteric, and difficult than either prayer or Torah study and must therefore be limited to a small number of the spiritually gifted:

The worship of God through eating and drinking and all similar matters where some physical pleasure is involved, in which one must pierce through the pleasure in all these things in order to find therein the divine vitality and the power of God who animates it and dwells therein, and then one must extricate the divine essence and return all of it to its holy sources; this kind of worship is far more difficult than the divine worship of prayer and Torah study. Not every Jew is capable of this, and it is to be limited to the chosen few.[22]

The trend towards restricting the practice of sacred eating to the religious elite naturally led to the practice of the rebbes' sanctification of the food on behalf of the masses of their followers, to whom the necessary mystical techniques were allegedly inaccessible. Moreover, it is now the rebbe who is said to have the ability to direct specific morsels of food to specific Hasidim gathered around his table, based on his divination of their individual spiritual needs.

Whereas in the earliest accounts of hasidic feasting—particularly those found in mitnagdic sources—the Hasidim are portrayed as engaging in gluttonous behavior, in later hasidic sources, along with the restriction of "holy eating" to the zaddik, there is a glorification of the smallness of the portions of food involved in the *shirayim* that each Hasid received. R. Hayyim of Zanz (1793-1876) is reported to have taught that the zaddik transforms all of the food from which he partakes into a highly concentrated form of purity, in which the tiniest amounts have the same sustaining power as large quantities of food that had not been so transformed. That is why "even the tiny morsel that a person eats accomplishes for him an enormous amount of good."[23] Phinehas of Cracow adds to this the idea that the tiny crumbs of *shirayim* that the Hasidim eat at the tish can retroactively transform and raise the sparks of the substantial meal the Hasidim had "mundanely consumed" at home earlier that evening.[24] *Shirayim* were also used for other medicinal and magical purposes. It is told of R. Hayym Zanzer that he wrapped *shirayim* in cloth and used them as a salve for an inoperable brain tumor.[25]

As the portions of Sabbath foods that reached the common Hasidim assembled at the tish continued to diminish, the parallel phenomenon of gluttonous, sometimes obese zaddikim emerges in Hasidism. Rabbi Abraham Joshua Heschel of Apta, who was known, and often mocked, for his gluttonous behavior, is reported to have justified it as follows:

> Some serve God through Torah study and prayer. But others serve God through eating, drinking and other material pleasures. There are those who criticize the latter conduct. But why did God create such a zaddik [who serves God through eating]? Because most people fail in this and become distracted and corrupted by the earthly pleasure. But when the true zaddik worships God in this way, he raises up all of the people of Israel....Such a zaddik, insofar as he is connected with the "hidden world"...can serve the Lord through much eating and drinking.[26]

THE SANCIFICATION OF THE REBBE'S "MENU"

The focus on the rebbe's eating, the idea that the divine sparks of the entire community are concentrated in his food, and the vicarious nature of the tish eventually led to a very narrow focus on, and obsessive interest in, the specific items on the rebbe's plate. In the many compendia of customs [*sifrei minhagim*] issued by individual Hasidic sects, while there is scant, if any, theological explanation of the general concept of *shirayim*, there is a virtually totemistic focus on the specific items on the rebbe's plate. Every dish on the menu, how it was prepared, and the specific way in which the rebbe ate it became the subject of elaborate kabbalistic speculation. For example, intense speculation concerns the fish eaten at the tish.

While there is a rich history of Rabbinic and kabbalistic expositions on the importance of eating fish on the Sabbath, this interest was taken to unprecedented extremes in later hasidic thought.[27] Stories abound regarding various Hasidic rebbes' obsession with fish; some insisted on seeing the live fish before the Sabbath and choosing the "holiest fish" for the tish. Others, such as R. Aaron of Belz, would be presented with a silver plate filled with fish on Erev Shabbat, from which they would choose the holiest one.[28] Some tales relate how the rebbes would remove the eye of the fish and eat it first,[29] while Rabbi Yosef Meir Weiss, the Spinker rebbe, is described as removing the eye and placing it in his pocket.[30] Kalonymous Kalman Epstein, the author of the popular Hasidic biblical commentary, *Maor Va-Shemesh*, and apparently a man of fine taste, proclaims that the holiest fish of all is lox, since salmon has very large scales: a sign of its kashrut.[31]

Many Hasidic tales refer to the esoteric, mystical power inherent in the rebbe's every move during the course of his meal. Take, for example, the description of the Bialer rebbe's consumption of his fish-chowder:

> Before the end of the *zmira* [song], they brought before him two bowls, one with his fish and the other with soup. And it was tangibly evident that there was here a most exalted service. And who can enter into the secrets of the Holy? For he would break up the little challa into seven pieces and put it in the soup and then he engaged in a great and holy service with the spoon in the bowl while he was completely absorbed in angelic contemplation. So that even those who couldn't enter into his secret realm, behold they saw before them a glorious worship. In the same way he would mix the crumbs from the challa into the holy fish broth.[32]

OTHER DISHES

Garnishes and side dishes were not exempt from being imbued with intense kabbalistic symbolism.[33] So, for example, R. Yechiel of Komarno (1806-1874) taught that, because the gematria [the numerical value of the Hebrew letters] of onions [*bezalim*] is equivalent to *eheye elohim adonai* [I will be the Lord, your God], it is important to mix onions into the fish so as to spice them with the divine presence.[34] Fanciful speculation regarding the significance of the food at the tish is by no means limited to fish; each and every item on the menu became subjected to intense, elaborate kabbalistic interpretations by the Hasidim. The changing interpretation of the rituals of the tish reflect its narrowing from a genuine feast to a symbolic mystical sacrament.

Particularly important in this shift was the increasing focus on every item of the rebbe's menu as specific emanations of the different kabbalistic *sefirot* [cosmic divine orbs]. This notion is clearly expressed by R. Shalom of Koidonov:

> I will now reveal to you the secret of the Sabbath foods, for in my humble opinion they hint at the ten holy *sefirot*. My source for this is holy wonder of our generation, Israel of Rizhin, who taught that eating kugel symbolizes the *sefirah* of Yesod. So that I say that each of the foods is symbolic of one of the ten *sefirot*. The fish we eat symbolize the first three *sefirot*, as is well known; onions in oil and other things that sweeten the onions symbolize *hesed* & *gevurah*; for onions which have a sharp taste refer to *gevurah* while the oil and other things that sweeten them refer to *hesed*. The [chicken] leg we eat symbolize *nezach* & *hod*, as is known. The tchulent [*maaseh kederah*] hints at *malkhuth*...while the food in the pot along with the sauce contains the secret of the scripture, "blessed be the glory of God's Holy name forever and ever."[35]

THE HOLY KUGEL

Of all the Sabbath foods, the greatest significance was attached to the kugel. Employing very eclectic exegesis and imaginative kabbalistic hermeneutics, the Hasidic theoreticians "figured out" that kugel corresponded to the *sefirah* of *yesod*. Some important, and startling, conclusions were derived from this association. Since, in most systems of kabbalistic symbolism, the *sefirah* of *yesod* corresponds to the phallus of Adam Kadom, or primordial man, kugel was believed to harbor generative, or creative, powers. More to the point with regard to the powers on display at the rebbe's tish was the longstanding Hasidic association of *yesod*—manifested in the Sabbath kugel—with the zaddik, based on the biblical verse, "And the righteous man [zaddik] is the foundation [*yesod*] of the universe" (Prov 10:25).

For this reason, many Hasidic sources assert that the rebbe achieves the height of his powers of leadership during the distribution of the *shirayim* of the kugel at the tish. The following story about the last rebbe of the Slonimer dynasty, Rabbi Solomon David Joshua, who was murdered by the Nazis in 1941, is fairly typical:

> He would distribute the kugel to all of the assembled from his own hand, specifically indicating and directing which person should receive each and every piece of kugel. It was evident to the assembled that he was involved in a very high form of

worship, in that he had a deep spiritual connection with each
and every person to whom he sent the kugel, and he would
often at that moment tell them what they had to fix in their
lives. Many waited all week long for this very moment,
particularly if they were confused or lost. Now, with one word,
he made it right and they knew what they must do....Is it even
possible to describe the holiness with which they then ate the
kugel ?[36]

This attribution of sanctity to the specific Sabbath dishes was more
than merely symbolic; it was often taken quite literally and applied
practically, thus affecting the actual etiquette of the tish (to the extent
that it existed at all). Take, for example one of the truly grotesque Hasidic
tish stories, regarding Rabbi Aaron of Koidonov:

I once asked [Rabbi Aaron] why he eats all of the Sabbath foods
with his hands instead of a fork; yet the kugel he always eats
with a fork. He answered that it is said in the name of R. Israel
of Rizhin that all of the Sabbath foods correspond to the supernal
orbs [*sefirot*], as it is written in the holy book *Tikkunei Zohar*.
Now kugel, since it is the principal additional dish in honor of
the Sabbath, contains the mystery of *mussaf* [addition or
procreation]; now since *mussaf* corresponds to the *sefirah* of
Yesod...therefore it is forbidden to touch the kugel with one's
hands since, as is well known, one is not allowed to handle
one's own *Yesod* [penis].[37]

The question of how to handle kugel appropriately is addressed in
numerous other hasidic texts. A somewhat sanitized variation on this
story is found in the following exchange between two of the leading
Hasidic rebbes of the late nineteenth century:

It is told that the Holy rebbe of Apta [R. Abraham Joshua
Heschel of Opatow], may his merits protect us, once asked the
holy Ruzhiner [R. Israel of Ruzhin] if it is true that he ate the
kugel with his bare hands. The Ruzhiner retorted by asking
him, Well, how do you eat the kugel? The Apter rebbe
responded: It is my custom to eat all the [Sabbath] dishes with
my hands, except for the kugel, which I eat with a fork. He
then went on to explain the reason for this: You see, the kugel
is the most important Shabbes dish, and it is symbolic of the
spiritual influence of the Sabbath, something that comes directly
from the hand of the Holy One, Blessed Be He. So it says in

the holy Zohar; namely, that from the Sabbath all the other days of the week are blessed. If so, how can anyone dare to take [kugel] directly from the hands of God, and so I eat the kugel with a fork. To this the Rizhiner responded: If indeed we have this opportunity only once in the course of the week when the Holy One extends to us his spiritual influence directly with His hand, why should we not take it directly with our hands rather than use a medium?[38]

The difference between the Apter and Ruzhiner rebbes on the appropriate etiquette pertaining to handling the kugel clearly reflects more general spiritual tendencies. The Apter's modesty and reticence contrast with the famously bold and independent Ruzhiner's personal confidence and iconoclastic approach to the realm of the Divine.[39]

As for the fact that many hasidic rebbes handle the food at the tish with their hands, it would appear that this is the natural outcome of the belief that it is in the intimate physical handling of the food, as well as in its consumption, that the zaddik sanctifies it and elevates the holy sparks within. A tale regarding the founder of Hungarian Hasidism, R. Moshe Teitelbaum (1759-1841), illustrates this point:

Once, Rabbi Zevi Hirsch of Zidichov was sitting at the meal of the holy Rabbi Moshe Teitelbaum, and the latter picked up a fork in order to take a piece of meat. The Holy Rabbi of Zidichov then told him: Rabbi! Is there not more holiness in your ten fingers than in that piece of metal? R. Moshe immediately let go of the fork and took the meat with his bare hands.[40]

Clearly then particular holiness was attributed to the kugel that the rebbes distributed to their Hasidim at the tish. Whereas the sanctity of fish is not new to Hasidism and has many earlier kabbalistic sources, the specific attribution of holiness to kugel, and to other ethnic dishes specific to Eastern European Jews, is as original as it is remarkable.

The revolutionary nature of Hasidic leadership represented by the rebbe is perhaps most graphically illustrated in the distribution of the kugel to particular Hasidim at the tish. Often in Hasidic descriptions of the rebbes's officiating at the tish, and particularly with regard to the kugel, the rebbes were, as we have seen, compared to the priests officiating in the Jerusalem Temple. This veneration of kugel in particular is clearly captured by the following tradition ascribed to the post-Holocaust Hasidic rebbe of Antwerp: "The distribution of the kugel was, for Reb Itsikl, just like the most difficult and exalted forms of priestly worship in the Holy Temple."[41]

Of course, kugel was not the only Sabbath delicacy that was sanctified in Hasidic culture. Hasidic sources attribute mystical attributes to a stunning array of dishes. Aside from eating fish on the Sabbath, a custom long sanctified in pre-hasidic kabbalistic lore, special holiness is ascribed to each of the Sabbath delicacies including *lokshen*, soup, farfel, liver, *tsimmes*, and *tchulent*. Examples of the attribution of spiritual significance to these foods abounds.[42] Still, kugel receives by far the most attention and is credited with the most power and spiritual benefits.

A recent Yiddish anthology of Hasidic Sabbath customs, compiled by a widely respected Satmar Rabbi, devotes an entire section to the glorification of the various Sabbath dishes, with by far the greatest attention—more than fourteen pages—accorded the holy kugel.[43] Aside from itemizing the various benefits of eating kugel, which range from health and financial security to messianic redemption, this anthology includes an array of tales intended to illustrate the degree to which the zaddikim venerated kugel.

It is well known that rebbes from different Hasidic courts argued about many "exalted" things, and kugel was no exception. While the majority seemed to hold that potato kugel was the real deal, some zaddikim insisted that the only true kugel was *lokshen*, or noodle, kugel. Reb Itsik of Psheworsk, a kugel pluralist who nonetheless preferred the noodle form, resolved the dispute with the following fair-minded formulation: "*Lokshen* kugel is the principal kugel, while potato kugel is just another Shabbes food." One major Hasidic authority was most forcefully unilateral in his preference, going so far as to imbue the *lokhsen* kugel with Biblical authority: "Rabbi Meir of Premyshlan declared: *lokshen* kugel was ordained at Mount Sinai."[44]

How are we to understand the unique importance that these many Hasidic rebbes attached to the kugel? Why would they engage in these tortuous mystical hermeneutics in order to arrive at the conclusion, for example, that kugel corresponds to the Divine phallus, or *yesod*? There are two approaches to this question. One would be to take the Hasidic claims about the kabbalistic significance of this simple food at face value and search for oblique references to kugel in the earlier kabbalistic literature. Perhaps some messianic significance to kugel might be unearthed in a medieval manuscript of Moses de Leon or Abraham

Abulafia. We will leave this unpromising avenue of research to other scholars.

A simpler and more obvious, if somewhat disappointing, answer readily suggests itself. Kugel was, quite simply, the most popular and common of the Sabbath dishes. Hasidism's task, since its very inception, was precisely to imbue the most common experiences of the simple masses of Polish Jewry with spiritual significance. In many respects, the sanctification of the kugel can serve as a metaphor for the manner in which the Hasidic movement read holiness into the most common of mundane things. And there is little question but that kugel was the most common and popular of the Sabbath victuals. Moreover, unlike many other dishes originating in the cuisine of their gentile neighbors that eventually became staples of the Eastern European Jews' diet, there is evidence that kugel was always viewed as a uniquely Jewish food with no equivalent to be found on Christian tables. In fact, a book published under Polish Jesuit auspices in both Warsaw (1724) and Vilna (1728) – just prior to the emergence of the Hasidic movement – banned Christians from "eating kugel and other such Jewish dishes."[45]

In his decidedly non-mystical ethnographic study of Jewish foods in Eastern Europe, *Yiddishe Maykholim,* the Yiddish scholar Yehuda Elzet devotes several pages to describing the rich varieties of Sabbath kugel. Elzet begins this discussion as follows: "Now we come to the crown of all the Sabbath foods, to the kugel."[46]

Elzet describes the variety of kugel and cites numerous Yiddish authors who sing the praises of kugel. He also refers to a number of folk customs and Yiddish expressions regarding kugel that suggest just how central, and respected, a place it occupied not only in the Jewish diet, but also in Eastern European Jewish folklore generally:

> When the kugel rises in a Jewish woman's [stove] it is said that a hot angel has baked a kugel for her. A Jewish woman therefore spares no wood for the oven, so as to assure that she will have a hot angel in honor of the holy Shabbes. And the neighbor, Trayne, will say of her that she is a *koshere yidene,* [a kosher Jewish woman] and that a hot angel has cooked for her a kugel in honor of Shabbes.[47]

Elzet further cites an abundance of folkloric expressions regarding kugel. For example "*A Shabbes on Kigel iz vee a faigel on a fligel*" [The Sabbath without kugel is like a bird with no wings]. Or "*Az a yidene ken kayn kugel nisht makhn kunt ihr a get*" [A Jewish wife who cannot make kugel deserves to be divorced]. Of a Jew who tries in vain to hide his identity and pass as a gentile, it is said: *"Der kugel ligt im af'n ponim"* [You can see the kugel on his countenance].[48]

Elzet's extensive folkloric descriptions of the centrality of kugel both to the Sabbath diet and even to the very identity of the average Eastern European Jew go a long way in explaining how kugel came to acquire pride of place in Hasidic ritual life and mystical doctrine. In fact, some Hasidic traditions overtly explain the importance of kugel as deriving from its universal popularity among Jews. In that spirit, the Shinever rebbe applied Rashi's commentary to Deut 33:19 to kugel:

> Rashi interpreted this verse to mean: The nations of the world will be attracted to the mountain [of God] by the industriousness of Zevulun. The merchants of the idolatrous nations will travel to Jerusalem to see why this nation inspires such fear and what are its deeds. Then they will see how all of Israel worships a single God and eats the same food. Not like the idolatrous nations who have different gods and eat different foods. Then they will say, there is no more righteous nation that this one, and they will immediately convert [to Judaism]. The reference here is clearly to the kugel that all Jews eat on the Sabbath.[49]

This Hasidic tale, clearly establishes kugel as the universal and distinctive Jewish food, thus confirming Elzet's definition of kugel as "the unique and quintessential Jewish food."

That the most common and simple of all the Sabbath foods— kugel—became the most elevated and imbued with mystical significance in Hasidic lore is entirely consistent with Hasidism's original nature as a populist movement that sanctified the mundane experiences of the simple, untutored Jewish masses. In discussing the Sabbath foods, R. Yitzhak of Komarno establishes the principle that every custom of the tish, even the way the fish is salted, contains deep secrets. This principle applies to every food and by extension to all of the physical activities, no matter how apparently trivial, of the zaddik: all of them are saturated with the very deepest of mystical secrets. [50]

It is difficult, when reading these Hasidic texts about the sanctification of food at the tish, not to think of a wide array of parallels to this literal conception of certain foods as the embodiment of the divine. Such parallels run a wide spectrum, from the totemist practices of the primitives studied by anthropologists like Claude Levi-Strauss[51]

and Raymond Firth[52] to Mary Douglas's anthropological re-casting of
the traditional Christian understanding of the Eucharist.[53]

While I am not engaging in this paper in a comparative
anthropological study of the religious phenomenology of the tish, such
parallels, of the kind that emerge by way of rather casual or random
association, are often quite striking in their details. To take but one
example, the question raised in several Hasidic tales about the appropriate
way in which to handle food at the tish brings to mind the mid-twentieth
century controversy in the Roman Catholic Church regarding the
handling of the wafer of the Eucharist. The belief that, through the
priest's sacrament, the wafer becomes the body of Christ influenced the
eventual liturgical mandate that the priest not touch the host with his
hands and that communicants receive it on the tongue, restrictions
that since the 1960s have been relaxed in most Roman Catholic churches.

CONCLUSION

The Hasidic tish originated as a public feast—a tangible communal
manifestation of the early Hasidic ideal of serving God joyfully and
through material indulgences. The earliest accounts of these Hasidic
gatherings suggest a sumptuous third Sabbath meal in which all the
Hasidim sated themselves together with their rebbe and received his
teachings. Over time, as Hasidism became more conservative and limited
the application of its more radical mystical doctrines to the exclusive
prerogative of zaddik, the communal eating at the Hasidic table
diminished, becoming more symbolic than real and focusing increasingly
on the rebbe's plate as a symbolic sacrament.

During the early decades of the nineteenth century, the Friday night
tish emerged, and this meal lent itself naturally to symbolic and
derivative, rather than active, "holy eating" on the part of the Hasidic
masses. For, on Friday night, the Hasidim would have their actual meal
at home and later that evening become vicarious participants in the
rebbe's mystical meal, partaking only of the smallest morsels of his
food, which served to sanctify all they had mundanely eaten before.
This movement from the horizontal to the vertical, from the tish as
communal feast to the restricted focus on the rebbe's food led in turn—
inevitably, I believe—to an intense fascination with the specific
symbolism and mystical significance of every portion of his meal. The
Hasidic leaders themselves viewed their role less as hosting a communal

meal for their followers than as priests officiating at a mystical sacrifice on their behalf.

Another factor at play here is the tendency, beginning in nineteenth century Hasidism, towards narrower, literal applications of classical, grand Hasidic concepts, such as the immanence of God in all things and the mystical imperative to raise the sparks of the Divine hidden in the material universe. From a manifestation of the general panentheistic idea in early Hasidism that all Jews can serve God through feasting and celebration of the material world, the tish eventually became a perfect illustration of the deepening conservatism of Hasidic thought and the growing elitism of the institution of the zaddik. It also reflects the narrowing and marginalization of genuine mystical experience in Hasidic society since the early nineteenth century. At the same time, the intense interest in and sanctification of the most common Ashkenazic ethnic foods remain perfectly consistent—albeit in the most trivialized fashion—with the Hasidic doctrine of panentheism. The circle of the Besht emphasized the presence of God in all things and encouraged mystical consciousness based on a heightened awareness of divine immanence. By the middle of the nineteenth century, this originally sublime mystical conception came to be so narrowly focused and so literally—some might argue primitively—applied that Hasidim feared handling a piece of kugel lest they be violating the divine phallus.

NOTES

[1] David-Dov Meiseles, ed., *Oytser Ha-Shabbes* (Yiddish; Brooklyn: Yofi Publishing, 2000), 273.

[2] Haym Grunfeld, ed., *Sefer Pardes Ha-Melekh* (Manchester: privately published, 1999), 445. This anthology of the customs emanating from the Hasidic sect of Ruzhin-Sadigura includes an entire section devoted exclusively to the religious significance of kugel, titled, "*Kuntres Ma'achal Ha-Meyuhad Le-Shabbat Ha-Nikra Kugel,*" 439-53. It is one of many Hasidic anthologies with such extensive "theological" discussions of specific food eaten in the context of the "rebbe's tish," or holy table.

[3] *Sefer Pardes Ha-Melekh*, 443.

[4] *Sefer Le-Atar Petura: Zemirot Beit Shineve* (Brooklyn: privately published, 1988), 27.

[5] Aaron Roth, *Shulhan Ha-Tahor*, (9th ed.; Jerusalem, 1989), sect. 177, par. 3. Hebrew: "*bodkin aharav.*"

[6] *Sefer Pardes Ha-Melekh,* 445.

[7] The Third Sabbath Meal was accorded unprecedented importance in Hasidic theology, a status that began during the Besht's lifetime. Legends regarding the unique holiness of the Third Meal are scattered throughout *Sefer Shivhei Ha-Besht.* For some of the more striking of these legends see in particular, *Shivhei Ha-Besht* (Kopys, 1814), nos. 101, 124, 153, 173, 234, and 238. Subsequent Hasidic lore is replete with odes to the special holiness of the Sabbath twilight, which in Hasidic thought is generally considered *eyt ratson* [a time of unique divine favor].

[8] Moses Midner, *Kitvei (Kodesh) Ramam* (Jerusalem: undated), 158.

[9] For a full treatment of the various customs relating to the *Le-Hayyim* ritual in Hasidism, see Hanina Yom-Tov Lipa Braun, *Sefer Berakha Le-Hayyim* (Jerusalem, privately published, 1954). An interesting discussion of the details of this custom can be found in Moshe Aryeh Freund, *Zmirot Le-Shabbat Kodesh: Ateret Yehoshua* (Brooklyn: privately published, 2001*),* 108. This compendium of Sabbath songs and customs contains one of the most vivid general descriptions of the rebbe's tish; see 93-123.

[10] Although there is a wealth of material about Hasidic musicology, very little has been written about Hasidism's internal mystical interpretations of the significance of the singing that takes place at the rebbe's table. An unusually rich source for such material, from the court of Jerusalem's R. Arele Roth is *Perush Gaaguay Nefesh: Al Ha-Nigunim She-Yasad Maran Rabenu Be-Vet Midrasheynu,* (Jerusalem: privately published, 1993). For a traditional explication of many aspects of Hasidic song and dance, see Yeshaya Meshulem Rottenberg, *Sefer Zamru Lishmo* (Jerusalem: Or Chadash, 1996).

[11] For a discussion of the concept of *dibbuk haverim* in early Hasidism, see Joseph Weiss, *Studies in East European Jewish Mysticism* (Oxford: Littman, 1985), 154-69. See also the remarkable description of the practice of this ideal within the Hasidic fraternity by the Hasidic rebbe of Piasecne, Kalonymous Kalman Shapira in *Hachsahrat Ha-Avrechim* (Jerusalem: 1962), 58b-63a. A contemporary hasidic treatment of the importance of *dibbuk haverim* can be found in the work of the late Slonimer rebbe, Shalom Noah Beresovsky, *Netivot Shalom,* (Jerusalem: 1982), 305-14.

[12] The only scholarly treatment of the sanctity of food in Hasidism is Louis Jacobs, "Eating as an Act of Worship in Hasidic Thought," in *Studies in Jewish Religious and Intellectual History Presented to Alexander Altman on the Occasion of his Seventieth Birthday* (ed. S. Stein and R. Loewe; University of Alabama Press, 1979), 157-66. Jacobs refers to the tish and the custom of *shirayim* only in the very last paragraph of this essay, which deals mainly with the early treatment of this concept in the writings of Rabbi Levi Isaac of Berditchev.

[13] In preparing this article, I have consulted the following Hasidic collections of *zemirot,* all privately published by the respective Hasidic sects, as indicated: Hayyim Halberstam, ed., *Seder Zemirot Le-Shabbat Kodesh: Bet Tsanz* (Bnai Berak, 1996); Hayyim Yosef Biderman, ed., *Zemirot Shabbat Mi-Darkhei Moshe* (Lelov; Bnai Berak, 1988); Meir Wiener, ed., *Sefer Shirat Ha-Shabbat* (Biala; Bnai Berak, 1988); *Sefer Le-Atar Petura: Zemirot Le-Shabbat Kodesh* (Shineve/Tseshinov; Brooklyn, 1988); Moshe

Aryeh Freund, *Zemirot Le-Shabbat Kodesh: Ateret Yehoshua* (Brooklyn, 2001); Gedalia Apfel, ed., *Zemirot Simkha Ve-Ora Le-Shabbat U-lekhol Moadei Ha-Shana* (Satmar; Kiryat Yoel, 1980); *Zemirot Avodat Ha-Levi: Tosh* (Boisbriand, Quebec, 1999).

[14] Hayyim Elazar Shapiro of Munkacz, *Sefer Darkhei Hayyim Veshalom* (Munkacz, 1940), 123. Compare *Sefer Divrei Torah* (Munkacz, 1933), pt. 3, sect. 42.

[15] *Keter Shem Tov* (Lemberg, 1823), pt. 2, no. 21.

[16] Joseph Perl, *Uber Das Wesen Der Sekte Chassidim* (ed. from the mss. by Avraham Rubenstein; Jerusalem: Israel Academy of the Sciences and Humanities, 1977), 111.

[17] Abraham Chaim Frankel, ed., *Shabbat Beyt Rophsitz* (vol. 1; Jerusalem: privately published, 1994), 181.

[18] Hayim of Mogolience, *Sefer Sihot Hayyim* (Lublin, 1926), 8b.

[19] *Sefer Sihot Hayyim*, 24a.

[20] See Louis Jacob's discussion of R. Levi Isaac's ideas on this issue in "Eating as an Act of Worship."

[21] Menahem Nahum Twersky of Tchernobil, *Me'or Eynaim* (Polnoe, 1816), 43a.

[22] Israel of Ruzhin, *Irin Kadishin* (Warsaw, 1885) commentary to *Haazinu,* 74. See *Irin Kadishin Tinyana: Likkutim* (Bartfeld, 1907), 46. On Rabbi Israel of Ruzhin, see the excellent biography by David Assaf, *The Regal Way: The Life and Times of R. Israel of Ruzhin* (Stanford: Stanford University Press, 2002). Assaf discusses R. Israel's uniquely materialistic approach to Hasidism at great length, especially in chapters 10 and 13.

[23] *Sefer Le-Atar Petura: Beyt Shineve Ve-Tseshinov,* (Brooklyn, privately published, 1988), 45-46.

[24] See *Sefer Beit Pinhas* (Jerusalem, privately published, 1978), sermon on *Parshat Noah.*

[25] *Sefer Halikhot Hayyim* (Brooklyn, Munkatch Yeshiva: 1983), 151. See also the article in this volume, Joel Hecker, "The Blessing in the Belly: Mystical Satiation in Medieval Kabbalah," in *Food and Judaism* (vol. 15 Studies in Jewish Civilization; ; ed. L. Greenspoon, et. al.; Omaha: Creighton University Press, 2005).

[26] *Irin Kaddishin*, 49.

[27] The fullest treatment of the importance in the Jewish tradition, of eating fish on the Sabbath is Moshe Halamish, "*Achilat Dagim Be-Shabbat: Ta'amim Upishreyhem,*" in *Alay Shefer: Studies in the Literature of Jewish Thought* (Bar Ilan University Press: Ramat Gan, 1990), 67-87.

[28] *Minhagei Kevod Kedushat Rabotaynu Mi-Belz* (Jerusalem, Belz Publishing, 1974), 22.

[29] This was the custom of Rabbi Eliezer Zeev, founder of the Kretshinev Hasidic dynasty. See *Raza De-Uvda* (Jerusalem, privately published, 1972), 31.

[30] *Sefer Minhagei Spinke* (Bnai Berak: Spinker Yeshiva, 1981), 25.

[31] Kaloymous Kalman Shapira, *Maor Va-Shemesh al ha-Torah* (Krakow, 1842), 76b.

[32] Meir Viner, ed., *Sefer Shirat Ha-Shabbat* (Bnai Berak: privately published, 1988), 8. Rich material regarding the various customs of other Hasidic rebbes regarding

eating fish on the Sabbath can be found in vol. 2 of Y. Z. Moskowitz, *Sefer Oytser Ha-Shabbes* (Brooklyn: Beir Yehidah Publishing, 2000), 66-77.

[33] See Hecker, "The Blessing in the Belly."

[34] Yitzhaq Isaac Yehuda Yechiel Safrin, *Netiv Mitzvotekha* (Lemberg, 1858), 61.

[35] *Sefer Mishmereth Shalom* (Warsaw, undated), 40b. The highly personalized distribution of *Shirayim*, where by each and every morsel that left the rebbe's plate was specifically directed to the soul of one of his Hasidim, is described in great detail as a fundamental principle that guided the practice of this ritual by the Hasidic rebbe Elizezer Zeev of Kretchinev in *Raza De-Uvda* (Jerusalem, 1972), 32-33.

[36] Yair Shvartzman, ed., *Sefer Yehi Or: Elu Maaseyhem Shel Tsadikim* (Jerusalem, 1998), 394-95.

[37] Shalom Aryhe Shtam of Horodok, *Zekher Zaddik* (Vilna, 1908), 9b.

[38] *Sefer Pardes ha-Melekh*, 455. See vol. 2, *Oytser Ha-Shabbes*, 277.

[39] On the complex nature of the relationship between these two men, see Assaf, *The Regal Way.*

[40] Zvi Hirsch Friedman, *Sefer Darkhei ha-Yashar Veha-tov* (Munkacz, 1909-10), 23.

[41] *Shabbes Beys Ropshitz*, I. P., 276.

[42] See, for example, vol. 2 of *Sefer Oytser Ha-Shabbes*, 299-311, for discussions of the mystical significance of various traditional Sabbath foods such as egg salad with onions, tsimmes, chicken fat and tchulent.

[43] See the extensive discussions of the mystical symbolism of the traditional Sabbath foods kugel in the recently published Yiddish compendium of Hasidic lore by Rabbi David Dov Meisels, *Sefer Oytser Ha-Shabbes* (vol. 2; Brooklyn, 2000), 39-90 and 259-80. On kugel specifically, see 83-84 and 271-79.

[44] *Sefer Pardes Ha-Melekh*, 443.

[45] See Gershon David Hundert, *Jews in Poland-Lithuania in the Eighteenth Century* (Berkeley/Los Angeles: University of California Press, 2004), 63.

[46] Yehuda Elzet, *Yiddishe Maykholim* (Warsaw: Lewin Epstein Press, 1920), 35.

[47] Ibid., 37-38.

[48] *Ibid.,* 117.

[49] *Sefer Le-Atar Peturah*, 81.

[50] *Netiv Mitzvotekha* (Jerusalem, 1995), 61.

[51] See Claude-Levi Strauss, *Totemism* (Boston: Beacon Press, 1963).

[52] See the extensive discussion of the symbolism of native foods in Raymond Firth, *Symbols, Public and Private* (Ithaca/New York: Cornell University Press, 1975).

[53] The fullest treatment of Mary Douglas's reinterpretation of the Eucharist is found in Michael Jindra, *Reading Mary Douglas: The Radical Cultural Theory of a Catholic Anthropologist* (London: Routledge, 1999).

"As the Jews Like to Eat Garlick": Garlic in Christian-Jewish Polemical Discourse in Early Modern Germany

Maria Diemling

The association of garlic with Jews is clearly illustrated in the conflict between two eminent German poets. When, in 1828, Heinrich Heine and August Graf von Platen argued over which of them was the leading poet of the day, they did not hesitate to attack the other well below the belt in witty and masterfully written verse. Both were in their way outsiders in Germany; each was aware of the other's weak point and exploited it relentlessly. Von Platen wrote, putting words into the mouth of a close friend of Heine, that he would certainly be Heine's good friend, but "would not want to be his lover, since his kisses exude the smell of garlic." Heine, for his part, replied through the words of the naive but sincere convert Hirsch Hyazinth: "Some like to eat onions, others show more feelings for warm friendship, and I, as an honest man, have to admit openly that I like to eat onions and I prefer a hunched crone to the most handsome lover of beauty."[1] The contemporary audience, following closely this clash of two brilliant minds, easily understood what this coded language meant. Heine was alluding to Von Platen's homosexuality (the ambiguous "warm" still denotes homosexual attraction in today's colloquial German),[2] while von Platen used the image of garlic to denounce the convert Heine as a Jew.

In the following, I shall explore from where the association of garlic with Jews derives, and why and how Jews and garlic were linked together in Christian consciousness. In addition, I will show the use of garlic in Jewish-Christian polemical discourse in the early modern period.

I.

Food is culture-specific.[3] It functions as a distinguishing mark of all societies, whose members learn from childhood to eat a certain kind of

215

food. Persons from other cultures, unaccustomed to that food, may find the consuming of it incomprehensible or even disgusting. Mocking people's strange taste in food is quite common, but even in so doing, the identity of a distinct group is recognised. The Germans are nicknamed "Krauts" by Americans, the Italians "Makkaronifresser" by the Austrians, the French "Frogs" by the English, and the Inuit "Eskimo" (which derives from an Indian word for "those eating meat") by all the others.

Following Michel Foucault, I shall argue that food, like the body whose functioning depends on food, is directly related to the political field and to power relations.[4] Here I am interested in the question of how the notion of food and food-related body images is used from the outset in the not exactly even balance of power between Christians and Jews.[5]

It is well known that in Judaism as well as in Christianity the sharing of meals is central and holds deep religious significance. The weekly Shabbat meal is an essential part of religious ritual, as are the Seder meal on Pessach and shared meals on other holidays.[6] The breaking of bread, symbolising the Eucharist, is the central part of Christian religious service. However, for both religions, food practices also serve as a means of distinction. Jewish dietary laws not only state which types of food are permitted for consumption and how they are to be prepared, but they also separate Jews from Gentiles, since they make the sharing of meals much more difficult. Several biblical passages stress that the Israelites should not share the food of other peoples. Ezekiel (sixth century BCE) introduced the notion of forbidden food in the Babylonian Exile and referred to the impurity of food of other peoples (Ezek 4:13-14). The book of Daniel (around 165 BCE) forbids the consumption of wine prepared by non-Jews and objects to Jews sharing a meal with them (Dan 1:8-16). The book of Tobit (composed in Egypt in the third century BCE) hints that Israelite dietary laws were designed to set them apart from the Gentiles (Tob 1:10-11). Rules such as these set clear boundaries and strengthen the identity of a minority; indeed, they may have the "special significance for the survival of our people" attributed to them.[7] For the early Christians, many of them still culturally identified as Jews, Jewish dietary laws proved a challenge. Paul refutes Jewish dietary laws on theological grounds and thus estranges the two communities from each other.[8] When the Church gained political power in the fourth century, sharing meals with Jews became a standard prohibition.[9]

Warnings against drinking with members of the other religion, accepting gifts of fruits from Christians after a fast, or accepting unleavened bread from Jews after Pessach were uttered throughout the Middle Ages. Numerous sources, however, demonstrate that such friendly customs of neighbours living in great proximity to each other would continue, much to the dismay of religious authorities on both sides, who were aware that eating together is an affirmation of kinship. They feared fraternization that could eventually lead to losing a soul, intermarriage, losing a member and possibly a loss of control and power within the community.

II.

In the light of the fact that sharing food between Christians and Jews was strongly discouraged by both religions, it comes as less of a surprise that a seemingly innocent bulb could become at some point a topic of polemical discourse. Let us first, however, examine the anecdotal evidence of the association of garlic with Jews. *Allium Sativum*, garlic, has been cultivated in the Middle and Far East for at least 5,000 years and was popular with Chinese, Indians, and Egyptians. Egyptian tomb art shows the consumption of garlic; the Codex Elsers, an Egyptian medical papyrus (ca. 1500 BCE), lists more than twenty garlic remedies against a variety of disorders.[10]

The earliest Jewish reference is the biblical verse in Num 11:5, where the Israelites, wandering in the desert and becoming impatient with the rather monotonous menu, complained about the food supplied by God from heaven [*manna*] and expressed their longing for the spices of Egypt, wanting their onions, garlic, and leeks back on the menu. What they missed was apparently the diet of the Egyptian working class.[11]

Jews seem to have reverted to former eating habits in Mishnaic times. Here, two examples will suffice: When acknowledging the difference between Jews and Samaritans, the Mishnah says that although Samaritans do not go up to Jerusalem for worship, they keep Shabbat and eat garlic as the Israelites do.[12] Garlic skin serves as a measurement for a very thin unity, which can be important when deciding if something is still kosher or not, an indication that garlic was readily available.[13]

The Talmud acknowledges garlic as well. It quotes ten regulations that are by tradition attributed to Ezra. Apart from the rule that the Torah should be read aloud in the afternoon on Shabbat and that courts should go into session on Monday and Thursday, it also states that "garlic should be eaten on Fridays." This is explained by the requirement that sexual relations should take place on Friday night, thus acknowledging the aphrodisiac quality of garlic. Why one should eat garlic is explained further: "Our rabbis have taught on Tannaite authority: Five statements have been made in regard to garlic: it satisfies, it warms, it brightens the face, it increases virility, it kills parasites in the intestines." And then they add rather lyrically: "Some say, 'It brings love and takes away jealousy.'"[14] The Talmud also recommends enjoying a fish dish with garlic on Friday night to "increase the delight of Shabbat."[15] Since fish is associated with fertility[16] and garlic with virility, there was hardly any doubt as to what kind of delight the rabbis were referring. In a more profane context, the Talmud also mentions several times the use of garlic, garlic leaves, and the skin of garlic as a remedy.[17]

Moreover, garlic could also inspire poetry. The first sonnet ever written in Hebrew praises its virtues. The Jewish-Italian poet Immanuel of Rome (1260–c.1328 CE), the most important Hebrew poet of Medieval Italy, refers in his poem to the biblical verse mentioned above.[18]

Garlic was consumed by Jews living in Ashkenaz as well; Jews from other countries even referred to them as "garlic eaters"[19] or mocked their liking of it, as did the fifteenth-century Karaite scholar who complained that Ashkenazic students "eat their dishes with garlic which ascends to their brains."[20] According to the great Jewish scholar Rashi, garlic may be chopped during Jewish holidays.[21] A well-known medieval example that shows Jewish appreciation of garlic is the acronym "Shum" ["garlic" in Hebrew] for the three important Ashkenazic communities Speyer, Worms, and Mainz. Their resolutions, the so-called "Takkanot Shum," were accepted by the rest of the Jewish communities in Germany. It is generally assumed that the well-known picture of a sixteenth century Jewish couple represents members of one of these prestigious and influential medieval communities. Both of them are depicted in typical garments with the yellow ring marking them as Jews, while the man holds a bag of money and a garlic bulb. As the purse stands for the typical Jewish occupation of money lending, so the garlic not only refers to the "Shum communities," but also symbolises the food associated with Jews. The woman holds a goose, an animal that Christians also believed was cooked frequently in Jewish kitchens.[22]

Garlic seemed to have been a regular part of life, as food addition and as a symbol. The *Sefer Chassidim* [Book of the Pious], a very influential thirteenth century ethical treatise, recommends roasted garlic, eaten warm, as a remedy against impotence.[23] The name of the *Parnas* [the community leader] of Wiener Neustadt, an important Austrian Jewish center in the fourteenth century, was Josef Knobloch, bearing the German word for garlic as a surname.[24] "Knophlaich" was still known as a family name in Vienna a century later.[25] In the prosperous community of Frankfurt, Jews lived in the early modern period in houses with names such as "flower," "dragon," or "oak," but there was also a house that bore the name "garlic" and most probably also had, as was customary, a sign symbolising garlic.[26] Jews bought garlic together with onions, cabbage, turnips, and fruits from Christians at public markets, and they could do so—unlike the purchase of fish, for example—whenever they wished.[27] Thus, for Jews garlic was a very common addition to food, eaten frequently, and with no negative connotations for them.

But garlic did not feature only in the Jewish kitchen. In the Middle Ages, garlic was also well loved by Christian Europeans. Many staples of food common today had not yet been introduced to Europe, such as potatoes, rice, and tomatoes. The main dish for the vast majority was a simple grain mush. Vegetables, herbs, and spices, if one could afford them, had to satisfy the craving for strong flavour and smell. Onions, garlic, leeks, and chives were cheap, readily available, and widely used in the kitchen. Garlic figures both in cookbooks of Austrian monasteries and in the kitchen of English peasants' cottages. Everyone could afford it and everyone used it, so much so that it inspired the saying, "the mortar always smells of garlic."[28]

III.

The development of the printing press, which made books readily available to a broader reading public, together with an increasingly scientific perspective, encouraged, among many other fields, medical writing and observations about proper food.[29] The Renaissance rediscovered the writings of Galen of Pergamon, the famous Greek physician (130–200/201).[30] Based on his teachings about the system of "humoural" physiology, many books were published with "scientific advice" about what should be eaten and by whom. One was supposed to aim for the right balance between hot and cold and dry and moist body temperature; to be healthy one should choose food accordingly to the quality of one's body, combined with the qualities inherent in each food. Garlic was perceived as a very hot food, having a powerful influence on the body. It was recommended by many dieticians for good blood circulation or as an aphrodisiac for men. It could also serve as an emergency corrective for impure water.

During the late sixteenth and seventeenth centuries, food theories continued to be discussed, but shifted in emphasis. Writers adhered less to Galenic principles of bodily harmony and related more to local customs that deemed certain foods appropriate for certain classes and professions. Some authors believed that garlic would be especially suitable for sailors, since it purified their water and tobacco, helping to prevent scurvy and diminish hunger. It also helped against seasickness.[31] On the other hand, garlic and onions, whose smell was thought to smother the intellect and understanding, were not to be eaten by students and scholars.

Food was increasingly invested with social meaning; by the seventeenth century, these differences were described obsessively.[32] It is not surprising that food seen as appropriate for sailors but harmful to scholars did not get a very high social ranking. While physicians used garlic as a remedy well into the nineteenth century,[33] it lost some of its attraction in the kitchen. Although garlic was still eaten by middle and upper classes, it came to acquire a connotation of low social status.

Furthermore, it has been suggested by historian Ken Albala that many of the authors writing about proper diet and food at this time had a strong sense of nationality based on stereotypical eating habits and increasingly warned against the strange tastes and customs of neighbouring countries. One can notice a heightened awareness of cultural differences and of food prejudices between the 1570s and 1650s. Most English authors of this time would describe the Spanish, with whom they were at war, as hot-tempered and boastful garlic-eaters, which was definitely not meant as a compliment.[34]

IV.

It was at exactly that time, when garlic lost some of its appeal as a food staple, that it and the distinctive odour it leaves on those who eat it became a pungent topic in Christian-Jewish polemical discourse. Smell, of course, is not simply a biological and psychological phenomenon. Smell—like food—is cultural, hence a social and historical phenomenon. Odours are invested with cultural values and employed by societies as a means of and model for defining and interacting with the world. The intimate and emotionally charged nature of the olfactory experience ensures that such value-coded smells are internalised by the members of a society in a deeply subjective way. The idea of what is considered a pleasant fragrance or an unbearable stench draws clear boundaries between cultures and individuals.[35] As it happened, the smell of garlic was to become an odour separating Jews and Christians.

In the course of the polemical argument that has continued since Christianity split from its mother religion, Jews and Christians have frequently accused each other of bearing unpleasant smells. A Midrash contends that the smell of Jacob (who symbolises Judaism) was distinguishable from the smell of Esau (who stands for Rome and later on for Christianity) and even that the bones of a non-Jew smell differently than those of a Jew. The odour of "the righteous" is so pleasant that it is even compared to Paradise. In another Midrashic source, the non-Jewish nations are referred to as a "bad smell."[36] In the Middle Ages, Jews consistently mentioned baptism in contemptuous terms, such as being "befouled by putrid waters,"[37] or by using the Hebrew word *tzachanah* [stench], a code every Jew would understand.[38]

Christians made similar claims about Jews. In an edifying medieval story, after listening to her father debate with a priest, a Jewish girl left her home, converted to Christianity, and entered a monastery. When her father arrived at the convent in order to bring her back to her mourning family, "the maiden…began to perceive a very evil odour, so that she said openly, 'I do not know whence it comes, but an odour as of Jews is troubling me.'"[39] We see that even this newly-converted Christian is aware of the unpleasant smell of the Jews, a smell she apparently no longer carries.

Smell and stench are frequently related to a change of religion.[40] Jews claim that the water of baptism smells badly, and Christians hold that Jews are able to get rid of their bad, namely "Jewish" smell only through baptism. The satirical letters of "The Obscure Men," first published in 1515 by a group of German Humanist scholars to defend the Hebraist Reuchlin,[41] make this entirely clear when they target the convert Johannes Pfefferkorn, stating that somebody who encountered him "does not believe that Pfefferkorn is still a good Christian, since he saw him a year ago and he stank like every other Jew, although it is said that Jews don't stink when they are baptised."[42] This is obviously a satire, but medieval blood libel accusations, as a result of which numerous Jews were tortured and killed because they were believed to need the blood of Christian children in order to get rid of their inherent stench, demonstrate how serious the notion of smell could become.[43]

V.

"As man esst nischt Knobel, stinkt man nicht," goes a Yiddish saying.[44] German Jews did eat garlic, and German Christians in the early modern period did not like it. They did not like the smell of garlic-eating people and blamed the Jews for having it. The main claim in Christian works dealing with Jewish customs and religion, however, was that eating garlic was a deliberately anti-Christian action.

The well-known Hebraist and theologian Johannes Buxtorf, one of the most eminent scholars in seventeenth century Basle, a translator and editor of rabbinical works and censor for books printed in Hebrew, gives in his book, *Synagoga Judaica,* a detailed account of Jewish life and religion.[45] He knows of the ten regulations of Ezra in the Talmud, but does not explain why Jewish men should eat garlic on Thursday (he says Thursday and not Friday as in the Talmud).[46] When describing the food on the Rosh Hashanah table, however, he mentions all the traditional sweet dishes of his holiday and explains their meaning. For Buxtorf, garlic, eaten as well, is a reference to the enemies of the Jews who should be cut off the earth and perish. He gives a linguistic explanation[47] for the use of garlic and adds that after eating garlic, one would say *"jichretu seneenu* [all who hate us should be cut off]."[48] The Christian scholar invests the celebration of the Jewish New Year, celebrated in the privacy of a family behind closed doors, with an expressive anti-Christian meaning. Garlic serves as the means of uttering a coded statement of hatred against "the enemies," who are the Christians among whom them they live.

Another author making a connection between a holiday, the consumption of garlic, and anti-Christian sentiments is Samuel Friedrich Brenz, who converted from Judaism to Christianity in 1610. He claims that "the Jews also devour much garlic, especially on Christmas night. If one asks for the reason the answer is so that the *tola,* the hanged one [a derogative expression for Jesus], is despised or to stink even more than usual."[49] Now it is a Christian holiday on which Jews are accused of eating garlic as an expression of their anti-Christian attitude.[50] Brenz' polemical book, *Judischer abgestreiffter Schlangenbalg* [Jewish Shed Snake Skin], published in 1614, a catalogue of vitriolic anti-Jewish statements, did not pass unnoticed. A rabbi, R. Salman Zwi of Aufhausen, prepared a detailed reply in which he attempted to refute each accusation brought forward by the convert.[51]

For Brenz' claim that Jews would eat garlic as a strong anti-Christian statement, Aufhausen gives a sober explanation:

> Concerning the garlic. We have inherited this from our ancestors who also liked it as is shown in Numbers 11....But the Germans don't like garlic that much. So we found the solution to eat garlic when we have a holiday or when they have a holiday, when we don't meet Christians and have contact with them. It may happen that people eat garlic on Christmas night, because the Christians celebrate for several days and don't trade with us. But not because we want to despise Jesus *Notzri*. Who could believe such nonsense![52]

R. Salman, who does not at all deny that Jews are fond of garlic, describes the life of a minority that has had to adapt itself to the standards of the environment and tried to balance its own habits with the expectations of the surrounding society. He even provides a rational, medical justification that is based on rabbinical authority as well as on Christian scholarship:

> Garlic is healthy. According to our Talmud, garlic is a wholesome food. For five reasons garlic is healthy, especially for us Jews who wander and don't eat warm dishes and drink water from puddles....Buxtorf, Professor in Basle, writes in his book why we eat garlic [referring to Buxtorf's mentioning of the ten regulations of Ezra]. In Italy, France and Spain, noblemen eat garlic as well as common people....Why would we want to feast and drink and be merry on Christmas night? *Sheker*, a lie, the opposite is true, we should be mourning, because of Joshua *Notzri*, born in that night, much pain and sorrow has come over us. If it happens that Chanukah falls on the same night, we feast and play, but not because of Jesus as the convert claims. Can the convert begrudge us the poor, stinking garlic when he, as a former Jew, now eats blood sausages and pork whenever he gets them?[53]

As much as he tries to keep his temper, one certainly feels the anger and pain of R. Salman Aufhausen in these sentences. The need to defend Jewish habits in public against attacks from a former Jew is something educated Jewish authorities were well aware of. Accusations that Jews secretly despised Christianity could endanger a whole Jewish community; when the needs of the moment demanded, one had to react quickly and decisively before certain claims motivated threatening actions.

The polemic between the Jewish convert and the rabbi was published by the Christian theologian Johann Wülfer in 1681. Despite having a clear Christian agenda, he tries to validate both positions and adds his own commentary to their writings. He does not appear to be convinced by Brenz' specific claims, which seem to him to be just "obvious calumnies," since:

> I fail to see what kind of contempt attaches to our most holy Jesus from this single practice, that they eat garlic, since it is not just on that night; rather, they have a habit (and one long habitual to their race) of eating garlic the whole year through, and just as much [as on Christmas Eve]. It makes a far more substantial charge [that] they befoul their minds by this practice during the whole year than on one night only, a charge which Brenz himself does not dare to advance against them.[54]

Wülfer echoes the scientific opinion of his day that eating garlic smothers the intellect and mind and should thus rather be avoided, but he dismisses the claim that the consumption of garlic is to be interpreted as an anti-Christian act. In his view, Brenz loses credibility with such slanders with educated Christians.[55]

Another convert, however, a certain Paul Kirchner, wrote in 1717 in a book about Jewish ceremonies[56] that Jews eat garlic on the fast day of Tisha b'Av.[57] Again, the author construes the eating of garlic as an anti-Christian action:

> Why they keep the 9th of August [sic], [commemorating] the destruction of Jerusalem and eat garlic and carry garlic, salt and bread tied in a kerchief to their neck....They eat garlic, because the smell of the garlic takes away the power of those who don't eat any when it comes to them. So the smell is supposed to go from them to the Christians to weaken them and make the Jews powerful and strong. And as the garlic emits a strong odour, a pleasant odour is to come down from heaven which should last until the temple is built again and the fragrances of the temple shall be smelled until the end of the world.[58]

What can we make of this statement? Kirchner ignores the fact that Tisha b'Av, mourning the destruction of the temple in Jerusalem, is a strict fast day during which no food is consumed. The *seuda mafseket*, the last meal before the fast begins, traditionally reflects the sombre mood of the day; food for mourners, such as hard-boiled eggs, cold foods, and fruits, is eaten. Food is eaten that "causes one to feel cold" and that does not sexually arouse, since sexual relations are forbidden for this day.[59] However, the apotropaic use of garlic for the traditional visit to the cemetery on Tisha b'Av is documented. People would take garlic and salt with them when visiting the graves to ask the deceased to intervene for them, and they would scatter the garlic on the cemetery to keep evil spirits away.[60]

Kirchner does hint of Jewish "superstitious" practices, but his main claim is that Jews pray for a change in the balance of power. They pray for their Christian oppressors, in whose domain they had to live for lack of their own country, to lose their political power and religious superiority. The strong smell of garlic should help them to overthrow Christian authority or, at least, serve as a reminder that this misery will not last forever and as a hope for better days to come.

An echo of this claim is found nearly a century later in a fascinating correspondence between a rabbi and a Christian scholar. R. Eleazar Fleckeles (1754-1826) of Teplitz, Bohemia, and the Christian censor and translator Karl Fischer (1755-1844) used to exchange letters in Hebrew. In a letter sent from Prague in 1812, Fischer asks the rabbi if it were true that Jews refrained from learning Torah, but ate much garlic on Christmas Eve. In his polite reply, R. Fleckeles denies that claim, but adds that he remembers from his childhood in Moravia that old women would peel a number of garlic cloves, according to the number of their small sons and daughters, and put them on the gravestones during Tisha b'Av. He distances himself from this custom by stressing not only that it was done by old women a long time ago, but also by adding a rather contemptuous remark on mindless habits and customs.[61]

Karl Fischer states in his letter that he, as a censor apparently expert in "Jewish matters," was asked if there was any truth to the claim that Jews would not study the Torah on Christmas Eve.[62] Christians seem to have been aware of such rumours, but they could not prove them. It can hardly be expected that R. Fleckeles would share with Mr. Fischer, who worked for the government, information on an anti-Christian custom, even if they appear to have been on very friendly terms with each other.

Jews did react apologetically to these claims, but there were more garlicky matters to come. So far we have seen that, for more than a century, the consumption of garlic by Jews was interpreted as an act with a clear anti-Christian meaning. Christians had maintained for centuries that an anti-Christian attitude is inherent in Judaism. They accused the Talmud of containing blasphemous remarks about Jesus and the Holy Virgin and pointed at controversial passages in Jewish prayers.[63] That even such a trivial and ordinary act as eating a certain kind of food could be interpreted as a hostile attack against the religion of the dominant majority marks a new stage in the polemic. It is interesting that Jewish converts, claiming that they have "true knowledge from within" of Judaism, most strongly stress this anti-Christian meaning. If we followed their lead and accepted their claim of consumption of certain foods as a political act, we might discern an easy and, according to the emotional reactions it aroused, quite powerful way for a threatened and underprivileged minority to express its opposition to the religious and political authority, thereby strengthening its own group identity through sharing a coded ritual. It would be possible to see in this the tactics of a weak group attempting to survive in the face of overbearing power; indeed, it might represent a kind of "resistance not as the assumption of power and dominance but as resistance *to* the assumption of dominance," as Daniel Boyarin has put it.[64]

At about the same time that Paul Kirchner claims that Jews would use garlic to topple Christian authority, Johann Jacob Schudt (1664—1722), oriental scholar and the gossipy headmaster of a school in Frankfurt, composed his fascinating *Jüdische Merckwürdigkeiten* [Jewish Peculiarities]. The four volumes are a collection of the odd and curious, mainly Jewish habits and customs of the local Jewish community of Frankfurt, but they also cover Jewish history and customs all over the world.[65] Several pages are dedicated to our topic. Schudt states explicitly that "garlic is the reason for the bad smell of Jews." It is not true that Jews need Christian blood to get rid of their inherent smell as was claimed in the Middle Ages, since Italian Jews do not smell badly; only the common German and Polish Jews, who are not used to a clean lifestyle and household, do. Their fondness for garlic does not help, since they eat lots of it. He maintains that at the fair in Jaroslaw, Jews ate garlic and onions worth 20,000 guldens, an amount so huge amount it would naturally make them thoroughly stink. Schudt seems to love juicy stories, and he hastily adds one of a sick Jew whose sweat had such a strong smell of garlic that his doctor nearly fainted. Schudt's basic claim is that poorer Jews consume garlic for a variety of reasons, but mainly as a cheap remedy to keep healthy. Jews who were more prosperous and were able to keep up with Christians and share houses with them, as many of them were forced to do after the Jewish quarter in Frankfurt was destroyed in a big fire, acquired skills in keeping a household clean and tidy; they also changed their dietary habits to a certain extent.[66]

Schudt is not much interested in the religious meaning of garlic consumption, but he introduces the notion of social classes to the debate. Christians are superior in their hygienic habits to most Jews, he asserts, and as long as Jews do not imitate the Christian way of life, they will be less honourable because less clean. Even wealthy Jews still have a long way to go, as long as they do not renounce garlic: "The palaces of the Jews may be most elegant and furnished with exquisite furniture and delicate decorations, but when one enters one finds Jews smelling of garlic there."[67]

This marks an important change in attitude towards Jews; it was the code poet August Graf von Platen, who was himself from a noble family, used when he attacked Heinrich Heine to put him in his place and to remind him that he, despite all his mastery of the German language, was actually a poor, smelly Jew. Heine, with all his ambiguities about his identity, still felt confident enough to return fire. His contemporary, German-Jewish convert and writer August Lewald, who wrote a novel at about the same time with strong autobiographic allusions (*Memoiren eines Banquiers*, 1836), is much less enthusiastic about his Jewish cultural heritage. He admires the Christian lifestyle, praises the tidiness of his wife as a "Christian" virtue, and is appalled when, being invited to a wealthy Jewish home, he does not find it up to his expectations. He is impressed that many of the guests are prominent Christians, but wonders "what faces those elegant ladies and gentlemen will make when they start to taste the food cooked in oriental manners, strongly spiced with garlic," alongside the "overly peppered roasts, the saffron-coloured soups and the sweetened vegetables. For in the home where I dined, the style of the food was decidedly Old-Testament."[68]

For nineteenth-century German Jews, assimilation to Christian society did not necessarily mean adopting its religious beliefs, but rather accommodating to its cultural and social demands. To keep a house clean and tidy and to eat bland and colourless food was a main step towards acculturation. The smell of garlic no longer symbolised a religious anti-Christian attitude, but rather offensive vulgarity. It was clearly "Old Testament," to use Lewald's expression, and thus not up to the expectations and demands of a sophisticated bourgeois lifestyle.

It is hardly surprising that one of the most popular German anti-Semitic songs of the nineteenth century links Jews once more with garlic. It "praises" in mock Yiddish the virtues of garlic, which gives the "real, kosher Jewish smell," improves the appetite and cleans the stomach, fortifies sexual desire, and strengthens power and courage.[69] The underlying message comprises the most notorious of anti-Semitic claims of that time; namely, that Jews are stinky, gluttonous, lecherous, and behave in a cowardly manner.

German Jews would learn the lesson, change their eating habits, and refrain from eating garlic. Early twentieth century German-Jewish cookbooks rarely use garlic in their recipes.[70] When Orthodox rabbi Dr. Alexander Carlebach travelled from Cologne to Poland to support East European Jews during World War I, he hired a local Jew as a cook and had him wear a clean, white apron.[71] In one of his letters to his family back home, he described how amused he was by seeing him in his new white outfit and his high boots. But he also complained about the food with which the poor cook tried to please his employer:

> Yesterday evening our whole house stank so terrible, so horrible of onions since he cooked gefilte fish for dinner and all rooms were filled with Polish [Jews]. We could not stand the smell and I forbade him once and for all the use of onions. He is very unhappy about it. Of course he won't keep to it anyway. To give us special *naches* this morning, he served a roll larded over and over with onions. He does not take our horror of onions seriously and finds it so foolish that he believes that we are joking.[72]

It is somewhat ironic that German Jews, for about three centuries under attack for eating garlic and onions, expressed a similar disgust with the strong smell when facing "Ostjuden" [Eastern European Jews], whom they often believed to be less refined and cultured.[73]

CONCLUSION

What people eat is often a reflection of what they want to be. When Jewish converts mocked the eating habits of their former coreligionists in public, they tried to distinguish themselves from a past that embarrassed them. Similarly, when Jews adopted the eating habits of the surrounding non-Jewish society, their feeling of successful integration was strengthened, just as when they mastered the language and acquired the dress code of the target culture to which they wanted to belong. To represent the food eaten by another group as a dangerous act of religious and political antagonism is quite a different matter. When writers did so, they must have been fully aware of the consequences such statements could have for the Jewish community. Such an interpretation invested even the most mundane matter of Jewish daily life, food and holidays, with a hidden—and thus potentially dangerous—meaning, hinting at dark secrets carefully hidden from the scrutinising Christian eye.[74]

Christian scholars, stressing their perception of Jewish food habits as appalling, seemed to express a strong desire for clear social borders, for keeping people in "their proper, namely inferior place." Until the seventeenth century, a Jew could get rid of the smell attributed to him or her by the cleansing water of baptism. Afterwards one would expect from a true convert the adoption of social norms, such as getting rid of his or her "Jewish accent," adopting certain standards of cleanliness, and, as we have seen, changing his or her diet. However, this was a difficult mission, as Heinrich Heine was continually reminded. One of the greatest poets of the German tongue, he could never really get rid of his Jewishness and the faintly lingering smell of garlic.

NOTES

[1] Heinrich von Heine, "Die Bäder von Lukka," in *Heinrich Heine. Historisch-kritische Gesamtausgabe der Werke* (ed. M. Winfuhr; Hamburg: Hoffmann und Campe, 1986), 7/1: 125–52. For an interesting discussion of this dispute, see the chapter "The Conflict between Heine and Platen" in Hans Mayer, *Outsiders. A Study in Life and Letters* (trans. Denis M. Sweet; Cambridge: The MIT Press, 1982), 175–89. I am grateful to my friend and colleague Prof. Itta Shedletzky for this reference.

[2] For some contemporary references, see Jacob Grimm and Wilhelm Grimm, *Deutsches Wörterbuch* (Leipzig: S. Hirzel, 1912), 13: 2031.

[3] The literature about food and culture has become rather vast: for a helpful introduction see Carole Counihan and Penny Van Esterik, eds., *Food and Culture. A Reader* (New York: Routledge, 1997).

[4] Michel Foucault, *Discipline and Punish: The Birth of the Prison* (trans. A. Sheridan; London: Penguin, 1991), 25-26.

[5] One of the few studies to address the question of relations between Jews and Christians via food relations is Winfried Frey, "Jews and Christians at the Lord's Table?" in *Food in the Middle Ages: A Book of Essays* (ed. M. W. Adamson; New York: Garland, 1995), 113–44.

[6] Jacob Neusner, *A Short History of Judaism: Three Meals, Three Epochs* (Minneapolis: Fortress, 1992).

[7] Isidor Grunfeld, *The Jewish Dietary Laws* (London: Soncino, 1972), 4.

[8] Christoph Heil, *Die Ablehnung der Speisegebote durch Paulus. Zur Frage nach der Stellung des Apostels zum Gesetz* (Bonner Biblische Beiträge 96; Weinheim: Beltz Athenäum, 1994).

[9] See Amnon Linder, *The Jews in the Legal Sources of the Early Middle Ages* (Detroit: Wayne State University Press, 1997).

[10] Kenneth F. Kiple and Kriemhild Coneé Ornelas, *The Cambridge World History of Food* (vol. 1; Cambridge: Cambridge University Press, 2000), 256.

[11] W. Gunther Plaut, "Numbers," in *The Torah: A Modern Commentary* (New York: Union of American Hebrew Congregations, 1981), 1091.

[12] *m. Ned.* 3:10.

[13] See, for example, *m. Kelim* 9:1; *m. Ohal.* 6:5; *m. Neg.* 9:2; *m. Parah* 5:8; *m. Miqw.* 6:9.

[14] *b. B. Qam.* 7:82a. I cite the American translation of Jacob Neusner, "Tractate Baba Qamma,"in *The Talmud of Babylonia* (Brown Judaic Studies 248; vol. XX. B: ch. 4–7; Atlanta: Scholars, 1992), 195–96.

[15] *b. Shabb.* 118b.

[16] Herman Pollack, *Jewish Folkways in Germanic Lands (1648-1806): Studies in Aspects of Daily Life* (Cambridge: The M.I.T. Press, 1971), 158.

[17] See, for example, *b. Git.* 69a for garlic as a remedy against toothache. For further examples see Julius Preuss, *Biblical and Talmudic Medicine* (2nd ed.; trans. and ed. F. Rosner; New York: Hebrew Publishing, 1983), 125, 238, 291, 566–67.

[18] Claudia Roden, *The Book of Jewish Food. An Odyssey from Samarkand and Vilna to the Present Day* (London: Viking, 1997), 436–37.

[19] For a detailed account of garlic in Jewish sources see Immanuel Löw, *Die Flora der Juden* (vol. 2; Vienna: R. Löwit, 1924–34), 138–48.

[20] John Cooper, *Eat and Be Satisfied. A Social History of Jewish Food* (Northvale: Jason Aronson, 1993), 85.

[21] *Machsor Vitry* (ed. S. Hurwitz; Berlin: J. Bulka, 1923), 91, 290.

[22] Ken Albala, *Eating Right in the Renaissance* (Berkeley: University of California Press, 2002), 204.

[23] Jehuda Wistinetzki, *Das Buch der Frommen* (2nd ed.; Frankfurt/Main: M.A. Wahrmann, 1924), 293.

[24] *Leket Joscher des Joseph b. Mose* (vol. 2; ed. J. Freimann; Berlin: M'kize Nirdamim, 1903–1904), 40. I would like to thank Dr. Martha Keil for this information.

[25] Samuel Krauss, *Die Wiener Geserah vom Jahre 1421* (Wien: Braumüller, 1920), 158-59.

[26] Johann Jacob Schudt, *Jüdische Merckwürdigkeiten Vorstellende was sich Curieuses und denckwürdiges in den neuern Zeiten bey einigen Jahr-hunderten mit denen in alle IV. Theile der Welt/ sonderlich durch Teutschland/ zerstreuten Juden zugetragen* (vol. 3; Frankfurt: Hocker, 1714–17), 151 for the year 1611/12.

[27] Schudt, *Merckwürdigkeiten*, 3: 125–126 and 168 for Jews living in Frankfurt in the years 1560, 1588 and 1617.

[28] Bridget Ann Henisch, *Fast and Feast. Food in Medieval Society* (University Park: Pennsylvania State University Press, 1976), 107.

[29] For the following paragraphs, I am indebted to Albala, *Eating Right*.

[30] For an introduction to Galen's medical system, see Rudolph E. Siegel, *Galen's System of Physiology and Medicine. An Analysis of His Doctrines and Observations on Bloodflow, Respiration, Humours and Internal Diseases* (Basle: Karger, 1968).

[31] Albala, *Eating Right*, 203. The English diarist and founder of the professional Navy, Samuel Pepys (1633–1703), discovered that the French Navy would provide their sailors with garlic and brandy rations to prevent scurvy and keep them warm. The British Admiralty adopted this custom. G.R. Fenwick and A.B. Hanley, "The genus *Allium*. Part 1," in *Critical Reviews in Food Science and Nutrition* 22 (1985): 199–271.

[32] Albala, "Food and Class" in *Eating Right*, 184-216.

[33] For the use of garlic in medicine, see J. Worth Estes, "Food or Drug? The Example of Garlic," in *The Cambridge World History of Food* (vol. 2; Cambridge: Cambridge University Press, 2000), 1547-551.

[34] Albala, *Eating Right*, 224–25.

[35] For a useful introduction to smell as cultural phenomenon, see Constance Classen, et al., *Aroma. The Cultural History of Smell* (London: Routledge, 1994).

[36] Sacha Stern, *Jewish Identity in Early Rabbinic Writings* (Leiden: E.J. Brill, 1994), 68.

[37] Abraham M. Habermann, *Sefer Gezerot Ashkenaz v'Tzarfat* (Jerusalem: Tarshish, 1945), 11, 12, 25, 27, 31, 32, 36.

[38] Elisheva Carlebach, *Divided Souls. Converts From Judaism in Germany, 1500–1700* (New Haven: Yale University Press, 2001), 18.

[39] Quoted in Ivan Marcus, "Images of the Jews in the Exampla of Caesarius of Heisterbach," in *From Witness to Witchcraft: Jews and Judaism in Medieval Christian Thought* (Wolfenbütteler Mittelalter-Studien 11; ed. Jeremy Cohen; Wiesbaden: Harrassowitz, 1996), 255.

[40] For further examples, see Joshua Trachtenberg, *The Devil and the Jews. The Medieval Conception of the Jews and its Relation to Modern Antisemitism* (New Haven: Yale University Press, 1943), 48-50.

[41] For a brief overview of this affair, see Charles G. Nauert, Jr, *Humanism and the Culture of Renaissance Europe* (Cambridge: Cambridge University Press, 1995), 141-2.

[42] Wilhelm Binder and Peter Amelung, *Briefe der Dunkelmänner* (Munich: Winkler, 1964), 178.

[43] For a helpful summary of medieval blood libel and ritual murder accusations, see Norman Roth, ed., *Medieval Jewish Civilization. An Encyclopedia* (New York: Routledge, 2003), 119-21 and 566-70.

[44] "If you don't eat garlic, you won't smell badly." *Deutsches Sprichwörter-Lexikon.* (vol. 2; Leipzig: Brockhaus 1869), 1433.

[45] Johannes Buxtorf, *Synagoga Judaica: Das ist/ Judenschul: Darinnen der gantz Jüdische Glaub und Glaubens=Übung/ mit allen Ceremonien/ Satzungen/ Sitten und Gebräuchen/ wie sie bey jhnen offentlich vnd heimlich im Brauche* (Basle: Sebastian Henricpetri, 1603). On Buxtorf and his scholarship, see Stephen G. Burnett, *From Christian Hebraism to Jewish Studies. Johannes Buxtorf (1564–1629) and Hebrew Learning in the Seventeenth Century* (Leiden: E. J. Brill, 1996). A useful newly translated and annotated version of Buxtorf's book is available on the internet. Alan D. Corré, "Synagoga Judaica by Johannes Buxtorf" [cited 10 May 2004]. Online: <http://www.uwm.edu/~corre/buxdorf/>.

[46] Buxtorf, *Synagoga*, 290-91.

[47] "Garlic symbolises their enemies, who should be cut off the earth and exterminated, Because garlic, or rather chives, is Crate [in Aramaic] which comes from the word meaning to cut off." The custom of eating leek for "Crate" is mentioned twice in a collection of customs edited by pupils of the eminent Jewish scholar Jacob ben Moses Moelin (Maharil). See Jacob b. Moses Mulin, *The Book of Maharil. Customs by Rabbi Yaacov Mulin* (ed. S. J. Spitzer; Jerusalem: Mif'al Thorat Hahmei Ashkenaz, 1989), 277. See note 8:gimmel for a manuscript variant, "lomar lema'an yicartu son'einu," which reflects Buxtorf's words. Maharil used to eat leek also on the morning of Rosh Hashanah. There are at least three extant manuscripts that refer in this context to enemies that should be cut off. See note 12:alef on page 279. Many thanks to Dr. Yaacov Deutsch for this reference.

[48] Buxtorf, *Synagoga*, 502.

[49] Samuel Friedrich Brenz, *Judischer abgestreiffter Schlangenbalg. Das ist: Gründtliche entdeckung unnd verwerffung aller Lästerung und Lügen/ derer sich das gifftige Judische Schlangenzifer und Otterngezicht/ wider den Frömbsten/ unschuldigen Juden Christum Jesum/ und sein gantzes theuer erkaufftes Heiligthum/ theils in den verfluchten Synagogen/ theils in Häusern und heimlichen zusammenkunfften pflegt zugebrauchen* (Nuremberg: Scherff, 1614), 7.

[50] For Jewish customs on Christmas eve, see Marc Shapiro, "Torah Study on Christmas Eve," in *The Journal of Jewish Thought and Philosophy* 8 (1999): 319-53.

[51] R. Salman Zwi of Aufhausen, *Jüdischer Theriack*, Chapter 1, § 20, 29. I quote from the edition edited by Johann Wülfer as *Theriaca judaica ad examen revocata sive scripta Amoibaea* (Nürnberg: Andreas Knorzius, 1681). For some information on R. Salman's effort to have his book published, see Stephen G. Burnett, "Hebrew Censorship in Hanau: A Mirror of Jewish-Christian Coexistence in Seventeenth-Century Germany," in *The Expulsion of the Jews: 1492 and After* (Garland Studies in the Renaissance 2; ed. R. Waddington and A. Williamson; New York: Garland, 1994), 208-209.

[52] R. Salman Zwi of Aufhausen, *Theriack*, 29.

[53] *Ibid.*, 29.

[54] Wülfer, *Theriack*, 90.

[55] For an interesting discussion of this case, see Shapiro, "Torah Study," 340-43.

[56] Paul Christian Kirchner, *Jüdisches Ceremoniel, D. i. Allerhand Jüdische Gebräuche, Welche Die Juden in und ausser dem Tempel, bey allen und jeden Fest=Tagen, im Gebeth, in Opffern, in Beschneidungen, in Copulation, in Auslösung der Erstlinge, im Sterben und Begräbnissen, in Erbschafften, in Essen und Trincken und dergleichen mehr pflegen in acht zu nehmen* (Erfurt: Weinmann, 1717).

[57] For a medieval reference on the type of food eaten before the fast begins, see *Sefer Minhagim of the School of Rabbi Meir Ben Baruch of Rothenburg* (ed. I. Elfenbein; New York: Beit Hamidrash Harabbanim beAmerika, 1938), 33.

[58] Kirchner, *Ceremoniel*, 122–23.

[59] Pollack, *Folkways*, 193.

[60] *Ibid.*, 193-95.

[61] Shapiro, "Torah Study," 350-53.

[62] For possible explanations of this intriguing custom, see Shapiro's article, "Torah Study."

[63] See Amos Funkenstein, "Basic Types of Christian anti-Jewish polemics in the later Middle Ages," in *Viator. Medieval and Renaissance Studies* 2 (1971): 373–82; Samuel Krauss and Wilhelm Horbury, *The Jewish-Christian Controversy from the Earliest Times to 1789* (Tübingen: J.C.B. Mohr (Siebeck), 1996).

[64] Daniel Boyarin, "Masada or Yavneh? Gender and the Arts of Jewish Resistance," in *Jews and Other Differences: The New Jewish Cultural Studies* (ed. J. Boyarin and D. Boyarin; Minneapolis: University of Minnesota Press, 1997), 315.

[65] See note 24 for the full bibliographical reference.

[66] Schudt, *Merckwürdigkeiten*, 2: 350-56.

[67] Schudt, *Merckwürdigkeiten*, 4: 278. References to Jews "whose mouthes smelled of garlic" are made in more sources that can be mentioned here. For further examples see, among others, Nicoline Hortitz, "Die Art kan nicht nachlassen...(Rechtanus 1606)— rassistisches Denken in frühneuzeitlichen Texten?" in *Aschkenas* 8, 1 (1998): 71-103.

[68] Deborah Hertz, "The Lives, Loves, and Novels of August and Fanny Lewald, the Converted Cousins from Königsberg," in *Leo Baeck Institute Yearbook* 46 (2001): 105.

[69] Quoted in Eduard Fuchs, *Die Juden in der Karikatur. Ein Beitrag zur Kulturgeschichte* (Munich: Langen, 1921), 282–83.

[70] Löw, *Flora*, 4: 314–15. It is striking that American-Israeli philosopher Susan Neiman experienced many garlic-related incidents when living in the then West-Berlin in the late 1980s. She mentions in an autobiographical account uneasiness towards garlic-eating by Jews living in Germany and by Gentiles who would still refer to it as something Jewish, despite there hardly being any Jews living in Germany. See the

chapter "Garlic" in Susan Neiman, *Slow Fire. Jewish Notes from Berlin* (New York: Schocken, 1992), 185-209.

[71] On concepts of modern hygiene propagated by German Jews, see Jenna Weissman Joselit's contribution in this volume.

[72] Alexander Carlebach, "A German Rabbi Goes East," *LBYB* 6 (1961): 80–1.

[73] When Heinrich Heine travelled to Poland in 1822—several years before von Platen attacked him as a garlic-smelling Jew—he noted the "dirty furs, unkempt beards, garlic smell and jargon" of the Polish Jews, but stressed that he preferred them to others who live a wealthy, but stunted and unfree life. Heinrich von Heine, "Über Polen," in *Gesamtausgabe* (ed. M. Winfuhr; Hamburg: Hoffmann und Campe, 1973), 6: 62.

[74] See Elisheva Carlebach, "Attribution of Secrecy and Perceptions of Jewry," in *Jewish Social Studies* 2 (1996): 115–36.

Separating the Dishes:
The History of a Jewish Eating Practice

David Kraemer

TALMUDIC ROOTS

For modern Jews, kashrut is most immediately associated with two practices: eating kosher meat and maintaining separate dishes for dairy and meat. In fact, Jewish population studies that seek to measure levels of observance often include questions about these practices ("Do you have separate meat and dairy dishes?" "Do you buy only kosher meat?") as stand-ins for the more general question, "Do you keep kosher?" We take for granted that keeping kosher demands separate dishes (accompanied by pots, pans, and utensils), and many guides to kashrut go so far as to recommend separate ovens and separate sinks—at least for those who can afford this luxury. Indeed, one kitchen designer has reported to me that many religious Jewish families demand this as a necessity, assuming that anything less is virtually prohibited.

Yet, when one examines the literature of the rabbis who instituted the meat-dairy prohibition, one finds no evidence of such a practice. Nowhere in all of talmudic literature is there a hint that the rabbis demanded a systematic separation of dairy and meat utensils. Nor do we find such a requirement in the vast medieval literature that interprets and codifies talmudic precedents. In fact, not until modernity does a rabbinic authority describe such a comprehensive separation. This is not to say that no separation was demanded. Authorities clearly required that certain utensils, having been used in certain ways, must be kept apart. But the comprehensive, systematic separation we take for granted is a relatively late development.

The Mishnah institutes a variety of requirements pertaining to the separation of meat and dairy: they could not be cooked together, consumed side by side on the same table, or carried in such a way that they might come into contact with one another (*m. Ḥul.* 8:1-2). But, crucially, the Mishnah makes no mention of cooking or serving utensils

in this connection. "Dairy" or "meat" describes qualities of foods, not
of utensils, and it is the foods that must be kept apart. In the Mishnah's
view, this will be accomplished by assuring physical separation of the
foods. This is all it requires, nothing more.

The earliest rabbinic document to suggest that a utensil might take
on the quality of the food for which it has been used is the Tosefta. In its
language, quoted several times in the Talmud, "A pot in which he cooked
meat, he should not [then] cook milk in it, [if he cooked] milk, he
should not cook meat in it…and if he did cook, [it is prohibited] when
it gives taste" (*t. Ter.* 8:16, with parallels at *b. Ḥul.* 96a and 111b, *b.
Zeb.* 96b). This teaching stands essentially alone in recording such a
regulation, so it is difficult to know precisely what it means. Considering
its language alone, it is possible to read this as a declaration that once a
pot has been used for either meat or dairy, it takes on the quality of that
food and must be reserved for use with that category of food and not
the other.

But, in light of its isolation in the corpus—if this were its meaning,
we would expect many other similar regulations—other readings are
more likely. The concern of the legislator here seems to be for the
transmission of the taste of one category of food to the other. Having
used a pot (generally made of clay in that period)[1] for one category, a
person should not immediately use it for the other category, thus mixing
tastes that should not be mixed. In that case, what must be done before
the pot is used for the other category of food? Perhaps a certain period
of time should elapse (the Talmud assumes that the passing of a day
will eliminate the taste). Perhaps only a thorough washing is required.
Regardless of how one chose to eliminate the taste of the food, clearly
there is little here on which to hang the hat of separate dishes.

In one talmudic discussion, this Tosefta is quoted in the company
of other teachings that may help illuminate its meaning. At *b. Ḥul.*
111b, we find the following teachings in relatively close sequence:

A. R. Nahman said [that] Samuel said: A knife that he used to
slaughter, it is forbidden to cut hot food with it.

B. R. Judah [in mss: Nahman] said [that] Samuel said: A bowl
in which he salted meat [to remove its blood], it is forbidden to
eat hot food in it.

C. Is it not taught: A pot in which he cooked meat, he should
not [then] cook in it milk, and if he cooked [milk in it, it is
prohibited] when it gives taste.

D. It has been said: Fish which were put in a bowl [that was used for meat], Rav said—it is forbidden to eat it in milk pudding, and Samuel said—it is permitted to eat it in milk pudding.

The first two teachings are concerned with blood—the consumption of which is prohibited by the Torah—that might have been absorbed into a utensil, either during slaughtering or the salting done afterward to remove residual blood. If the utensils are then used with hot food, the blood they absorbed might be emitted and consumed. Absorption, therefore, is a factor in the law, and it may be of concern with relation to other prohibited foodstuffs as well. This concern will help us make sense of the latter two teachings, both of which are similarly worried that the taste of a prohibited absorbed substance might be emitted. The last teaching is particularly interesting in the present context because it extends the concern to dishes. However, in light of the limited application of the concern, we must assume that it is speaking of hot fish used in a bowl that had, shortly before, been used for hot meat. This is a specific case, exhibiting a limited concern. But it is still not a prescription for maintaining separate dishes. Might we understand how the concerns expressed here come to be expanded into more general prohibitions? Surely. But such an extension will take many centuries. There is nothing natural or foreordained about it. When we witness this later extension of the law, therefore, we will have to struggle to understand what ultimately served to generate it.

THE MIDDLE AGES

Rabbinic authorities in the period following the completion of the Talmud—the Geonim—have relatively little to say about matters of separation. The center of their focus, when it comes to Jewish eating practices, is the status of gentile wine. The great library of documentary materials that testifies to everyday Jewish practices in North Africa and Palestine (along with Lebanon and Syria) in the tenth and eleventh centuries—the Cairo Geniza—similarly reveals little about this practice. S. Goitein, in his general observation, declares "the dichotomy of the kitchen into a meat and a milk section... is unknown in Jerba and never mentioned in the Geniza."[2] It is never mentioned simply because such a practice was unknown at the time. The silence of the sources, as so often is the case, is reflective of an absence in reality.

But when we come to the high Middle Ages and beyond, both in Ashkenaz and Sepharad, the matters we are now exploring merit more substantial comment. Once again, however, we will find nothing like the systematic separation of dishes. For example, a scholar of the school of Rashi (1040-1105), instructs briefly, "It is forbidden to eat milk with spoons with which they ate hot meat foods" (*Sef. Ha'oreh* 110). This is a readily understandable extension of the brief talmudic teachings seen above, though it shares with them a lack of clarity concerning its precise meaning: Is this authority's intent to prohibit such use in close succession? Does he mean to suggest that spoons, once used for hot meat, should forever be kept separate? In view of the specificity of the instruction, the latter seems unlikely. But the ambiguity of his teaching must be admitted.

The same is true of the rulings of Rabbi Simha ben Samuel of Vitry (d. 1105), a student of Rashi. In his *Mahzor Vitry*, R. Simha writes:

(54) The law concerning "milking" dishes which he washed in a pan of meat, or the opposite: if both of them were used on the same day, it is all prohibited. But if one was not used on the same day and the other was, it is all permitted... and the same is the law with respect to dishes of meat, used on the same day, that were washed in boiling water, in the boiling vessel, with "milking" dishes that were not used the same day.

(44) If a spoon is "milking" and he inserted it in a pot filled with a meat stew, or the opposite, when the spoon has not been used the same day, the spoon is prohibited and the stew is permitted.

(65) The law regarding a knife with which he cut meat and he wants to cut cheese with it, or the opposite, the knife must be inserted into the ground ten times [in order to eliminate the taste of what it cut first].

R. Simha's formulations might be taken to suggest that utensils or cooking vessels take on the quality of the category of food with which they are used, at least until active steps are taken to remove that quality. If this were correct, then we could translate "milking" as "dairy" or, to use the Yiddish term, *milchig*; "of meat" would be rendered "meat" or *fleishig*. But this is not, obviously, what the pertinent Hebrew terms mean. I have intentionally translated the Hebrew *holevet* as "milking" in order to preserve the strangeness of this term, thus preventing us from too quickly assuming its meaning. The Hebrew term is an active verb—a participle—and it would be literally translated as "milking" or "giving milk." It suggests, in other words, that the vessel or utensil has recently been in contact with dairy and has absorbed at least its taste, and perhaps even its substance. Still, R. Simha also uses the term for a utensil that has not been used on the same day, so the terminology— and hence the category—seems to stick. But without going into the technical details of the present rulings, it is still evident that the status of a utensil is closely connected to its recent use. Thus, if one category of utensil was not used on the same day, then, when samples from the two categories are washed together, even in boiling water, all are permitted. So, while there is a hint of categorization here, it remains only a hint. The rabbinic author is, in the end, concerned with individual knives, spoons, and dishes (bowls). We do not yet have evidence here of a requirement of systematic separation.

Maimonides, in his monumental codification of the law, adds almost nothing to earlier precedents. In a stunningly ambiguous ruling, he merely repeats word for word the language of the earliest pertinent talmudic teaching. He writes: "A pot in which he cooked meat, he should not [then] cook in it milk, and if he cooked [milk in it, it is prohibited] when it gives taste" (*Mishneh Torah*, Prohibited Foods, 9:11)]. He says nothing about a time limit, nor does he use language suggesting that the pot becomes a "meat pot." Neither does he use such a label elsewhere in his codification. Crucially, Yosef Caro, in his later commentary, assumes that the prohibition, as understood by Maimonides, applies only on the same day. Whether or not this is an accurate reading, it is clear that Maimonides neither imagines nor requires a permanent categorization of cooking pots, let alone other utensils or vessels.

The question of the status of the pot "in which he cooked meat" is a point of major contention among authorities of this period, however, and attention to their opinions is essential. For obvious reasons, the question of the ongoing status of the pot and of the food cooked in it will be crucial in determining the contours of the observant Jewish kitchen and what actions may be performed in it. If a pot may be used for foods of the opposite category in relatively short order, then there will be no need to designate pots as "meat" or "dairy." But if a pot retains its status, then, for all practical purposes, it will be a meat or dairy pot. We shall carefully examine discussions of this question below, as we begin to witness the formation of bona fide categories, at least for cooking pots. This will be one of the first steps in the creation of the kosher kitchen as we know it.

The great Spanish talmudist, Rabbi Shlomo Ibn Aderet (the Rashba, 1235-1310), addresses at length several practical questions of separation. In an opinion quoted by his younger contemporary, R. Jacob b. Asher, Aderet expands and clarifies the talmudic ruling concerning cooking pots: "If one cooked vegetables in a pot of meat [a pot that had been used for meat], one is permitted to cook cheese in it afterward because the power of the absorbed meat had been diminished and weakened to the point that it is not appropriate to apply to it the prohibition of meat and milk" (*Tur, Yoreh Deah*, 93)].

According to Aderet, if a pot was first used for meat and then for a neutral substance such as vegetables, it would be permitted to be used for dairy without taking any further steps. Aderet may well be assuming here that if such an intervening step were not taken, the pot would retain the quality of what had been cooked in it. But, in practical terms, the present scenario creates the opportunity for enormous flexibility. Of course, according Aderet's ruling, one must be aware for what purpose one has most recently used a pot. At the same time, one need not have separate pots for meat and dairy. In fact, given conditions at the time, even a single pot could have sufficed. Of course, common people were unlikely to have had the means or the space to accumulate more than a few pots. Furthermore, though meat consumption in Europe would increase considerably after the Black Death, at this stage common people would not have regularly eaten meat. In Aderet's day, therefore, it would not have been difficult to keep track of those occasions when meat had been cooked in a pot or of the sequence of other foods for which it might have been used. It would have created little hardship to insist upon cooked vegetables (the most common of foods) after the occasional meat and before dairy. Thus, the sufficiency of a single pot is no exaggeration. Multiple pots, differently assigned, were certainly unnecessary, probably not easily obtained, and therefore not part of the imagination.

In another, more lengthy comment, Aderet does demand several steps of separation. In one of his responsa (76), Aderet forbids the eating of cheese on a cloth on which one has eaten meat (or vice versa) because there might be small pieces or drippings from the meat or because a knife used for cutting the meat might have been wiped on the cloth. He further forbids the use of a knife "with which one regularly cuts meat" for cutting cheese because "most of the knives, the fat of the meat is congealed on it." His concern, clearly and rather explicitly, is the actual contact of the particular food items. He assumes a reality in which food is placed directly on the cloth, there are no personal plates, and the danger of contact and combination is immediate. He therefore requires that the cloth be washed before it is be used for food items in the other category. In the same world, knives are not well washed, so they are typically covered with the remains of meat and therefore may not be used for dairy. But having demanded these real steps of separation—and even requiring what we might call a meat knife—like his predecessors Aderet cannot be said to know of a systematic division between meat and dairy utensils.

Rabbi Jacob ben Asher (1275-1340), in his ground-breaking halakhic composition, the *Arba'ah Turim*, returns to the question of the status of the pot. For the first time, he formulates the ruling with reference to the factor of time:

A pot in which he cooked meat, he should not [then] cook in it milk, and if he cooked [milk] in it within a twenty-four hour period, it is prohibited. But if he waited twenty-four hours before he cooked in it, it gives an undesirable taste and is [therefore] permitted (*Yoreh Deah* 93).

At this point in his comments, it appears that the status of the pot becomes irrelevant after twenty-four hours. But R. Jacob goes on to quote several recent authorities who debate the ongoing status of the pot. According to one of these, if one category of food was cooked after the other even within twenty-four hours, he may continue to use the pot for the second category of food. According to another, if the pot was made of pottery, he may never use it again. According to a third, Ba'al Ha-Ittur (1122-1193), he may use it for either category. According to Rabbi Peretz (d. 1295), if he used it for the other category after twenty-four hours, the pot should not be used again (though food cooked in it would be permitted) unless, in the case of a metal pot, it was first kashered. If the pot was pottery, it would have to be broken and not used again.

What emerges from this combination of near-contemporary opinions is the recognition that there are ongoing and significant differences of opinion in the law. According to some, there would be no need to assign cooking pots to permanent separate categories. According to others, there clearly would be. For these latter figures, a pot in twelfth through fourteenth century France or Spain would be meat or dairy, if not in name then surely in practice. But even for these figures, such a separation applies primarily to pots, not to kitchens as a whole. And, given their regular exposure to heat, it is easy to understand why pots might be subject to different, more stringent concerns or regulations. So, while the earlier law has clearly been clarified or supplemented in directions that would require certain specific steps of separation, little else has changed. To this point, therefore, there is still no evidence of systematic separation of dishes, at least not in the ideal Jewish household imagined by rabbinic authorities.

EARLY MODERN DEVELOPMENTS

When we turn to the early modern period, we are confronted with confusing and even conflicting evidence. On the one hand, some rabbinic compositions suggest that little has changed from the past. But other rabbinic testimonies indicate that community practice, if not the actual letter of the law, has developed significant stringencies. And the voices of lay Jews [former Jews] describe a popular reality that, at least in certain locales, conforms closely to the "traditional" kitchen practices known among later Jews. Let us consider these various bodies of evidence carefully.

Rabbi Joseph Caro, a renowned Sephardic authority living in Safed, codified Jewish practice in its infinite detail. In his *Shulhan Arukh* (the relevant section of this document was published in 1564), Caro recorded a series of opinions that either repeat those of his predecessors or modestly extend them to newly specified scenarios. So, for example, like Aderet, Caro forbids cutting cheese with a knife that is customarily used to cut meat (*Yoreh Deah*, 89, 4). In the same passage, he also forbids eating cheese on a cloth that has already been used for meat. But he explicitly permits one to keep jugs used for milk and meat together in the same cabinet (*Yoreh Deah* 95, 6). And he even rules that "plates used for meat that were washed in a kettle used for milk, in water hot enough to scald one's hand, even if they had both been used [for meat and dairy] on the same day, it is permitted." (*Yoreh Deah* 95, 3). So, on the one hand, the law continues to express an active fear for the actual combination of meat and dairy food products. And it is true that at least some utensils take on the name of the category of food for which they have been used. But, on the other hand, Caro explicitly does not require (or imagine) the division of a kitchen into meat and dairy territories, and he permits mixing of a sort that would horrify a modern observant Jew. In the law as Caro knows it, and in the communities his opinions reflect, it would appear that little has changed in the conduct of a Jewish kitchen.

Yet, at the same time, R. Moses Isserles' (1530-1572) glosses on Caro's rulings suggest that Jewish practices in Poland and Germany, at least, have begun to shift. In response to ruling after ruling, Isserles dissents; practice as he knows it is more restrictive. So, commenting on Caro's restrictions regarding knives, Isserles adds "all of Israel [all Jews] have already made it their custom to have two knives, and to mark one of them so that it will have a sign, and they are accustomed to marking the one used for dairy, and one should not change the custom of Israel" (*Yoreh Deah* 89, 4). Concerning Caro's permission to keep different categories of vessels together in the same cabinet, he avers that "there are those who are more stringent in this, and it is better to be more cautious in a place where it is unnecessary [to mix them]." The same impulse is reflected in an adjacent comment, where Isserles praises those who keep separate salt dishes for dairy and meat (*Yoreh Deah* 95, 7). In the same connection, Rabbi Shlomo Luria (1510-1574, quoted in *Turei Zahav* on the same ruling) proclaims that it is the established custom of Jews in Germanic lands to have such separate dishes for salt.

In another connection, Isserles reports:

There are those who are stringent with the cover [of a pot], saying that, even if it was not used on the same day it is treated as though it were used on the same day [as we have seen, a vessel not used on the same day was traditionally treated far more leniently], and this is the accepted practice in certain places, and this is my practice because of established custom, though it is a stringency without reason" (*Yoreh Deah* 93, 3).

Of course, if pot covers retain the quality of what was cooked in the pot even for days after the cooking, it will be necessary to maintain a separation between "meat" and "dairy" covers in a more permanent and scrupulous way (though there will still be ways that the meat or dairy quality of the cover could be removed). Even with regard to the question of washing vessels, where Caro permits vessels used for either meat or dairy to be washed together promiscuously, Isserles supports the custom of permitting this only if one category of vessel was not actually used on the same day (*Yoreh Deah* 95, 3). Thus, if the vessels were used on the same day, they would have to be washed separately.

Collectively, these reports of increasing stringency in mid-sixteenth century Ashkenazic practice can be understood as pointing toward an outcome that will be realized in the complete separation of meat and dairy dishes, utensils, etc. Surely, several of the quoted testimonies indicate that, in the awareness of these authorities, separation is already practiced in certain details. But, despite its testimony to significant developments in customs relating to separation, this material still does not provide evidence of a comprehensive, systematic separation. In fact, in his comment insisting upon stricter cautions in washing dishes, Isserles makes it clear that practice as he would regulate it is still far from the familiar separations of later centuries:

> [What I have said] refers specifically to [washing dishes together in] a boiling kettle [a kettle that was placed directly on the fire to boil the water], but if they were washed one after the other, or even together in a vessel that had not been on the fire, it is all permitted... and if he poured boiling water, which is neither of meat nor of milk [it had not been boiled in pots used the same day for meat or milk], upon utensils of meat and milk together— and even if fat/grease is on them—it is permitted (*Yoreh Deah* 95, 3).

Each of these rulings has its technical reason, based upon principles articulated in earlier sources. But it suffices for us to notice that, even in this more stringent environment, vessels used for meat and those used for milk may be thrown together with relative ease. It is not even clear whether Isserles' category associations are meant as permanent designations (that is, whether vessels or utensils in general belong to the category of meat or that of dairy) or whether they simply refer to recent usage. In light of the recorded regulations, it would still be relatively easy to use the same pot or utensil one day for meat and several days later for dairy. In fact, the only items that have explicitly been permanently assigned to milk and meat categories are knives and salt dishes.

But there is another body of evidence, written in German, suggesting that, already by the early sixteenth century, popular Jewish practice in German lands was far more stringent than rabbinic authorities would insist, or even than they report. The earliest evidence of this development is found in the work of a Jewish convert to Christianity, Antonius Margaritha. Margaritha, son of the chief rabbi of Regensburg, converted to Christianity in 1522 in the small Bavarian town of Wasserburg. In

1530, he published a book titled *Der gantz Jüdisch Glaub* [The Entire Jewish Faith], with the aim of exposing the purported anti-Christian content of Jewish law and practice.[3] This work is a remarkable record of contemporary Jewish practice, sometimes distorted and polemical, but, for all that, often quite matter-of-fact. It provides in its details witness to customs unmentioned in the record of rabbinic authorities of the same period. In his chapter on "Their food and vessels, and also how they slaughter and de-vein their livestock," Margaritha reports that "the Jews use two kinds of vessels, one for meat and the other for milk. Therefore, they have two kinds of pots, bowls, spoons, platters and knives." Margaritha's list is a comprehensive one of the sorts of cooking, serving, and eating vessels likely to be found in the home of his day: pots for cooking, bowls and spoons for soups and stews, platters for serving, and knives for multiple purposes. Of equal importance, his list represents a specification of his general rule, that is, that Jews use different vessels for meat and milk.

It is difficult to read this report as saying anything other than that Jews separate their "kitchens," whatever they may look like, into dairy and meat categories. This separation includes everything they cook with, everything they serve with, and everything they eat with. It may or may not include actual sections of the kitchen itself, but on the whole this matters little, for the principle speaks even more eloquently than do the details. Extrapolating from Margaritha, it is not difficult to understand that, however the technologies of food preparation and eating would change, they would become subject to the principle of separation enunciated here. If this principle does not yet define the actual map of the kitchen, at some point in the future it surely would. We see here, in other words, the birth of the modern Jewish kitchen, and this at the very beginning of modernity itself.

By the eighteenth century, testimony to the comprehensive separation of everything pertaining to food in the Jewish household is unambiguous. One M. Marcus, writing in London about *The Ceremonies of the Present Jews* (1728, 1729), reports that Jews have one "set of Dishes, Plates, Knives, and forks for meat, and another for Butter, Milk, and Cheese" (p. 4). A quarter of a century later in Germany, Carl Anton, who converted to Christianity in 1748, writes about these same matters, leaving no room for doubt concerning the practice of separation in the Jewish home. In the eleventh chapter of Anton's *Kurzer Entwurf* (published at Branschweig in 1754), he writes that "every Jew must have double plates, from the least to the greatest." He adds that, "in order to be really careful, they mark either the meat dishes with the word *basar*, meat, or the milk plates with the word *chalebh*, milk." Finally, he reports that some wealthy Jews, to avoid problems that might be caused by their cooks, build two separate kitchens, one for meat and the other for dairy (pp. 92-93).

Notably, the material evidence reinforces the literary record in at least one crucial respect. The Jewish Museum in New York has in its collection 20 plates, mostly of pewter, that have the Hebrew words for milk or meat on them. Of these, only one has a distinct inscription date: 1777/1778. But the style of the lettering helps date some of the others, eight of which were apparently produced in the eighteenth century.

Thus, the separation that typifies the kitchen of the observant Jew in modernity is already practiced, in significant respects, in German-Jewish homes of the early-to-mid sixteenth century, and it is well established by at least the middle of the eighteenth century. Ironically, however, if one examines the rabbinic documentation alone, one finds little evidence of such comprehensive separation. In fact, reading the rabbinic rulings, one is left with the impression that in general little has changed for centuries and that stringencies in force are pious extensions of the law controlled by local custom. As we saw, this is true not only of Caro's delineation of the requirements of halacha, but even of Isserles' reports, which include practices that go beyond the basic demands of the system. It is also true of later rabbinic compositions. As far as I have been able to find, it is only when we turn to latter-day codifications that the permanent, systematic separation of dishes—or something like it—finds explicit mention.

Rabbi Abraham Danzig, in his *Hokhmat Adam* (first published Vilna, 1814), comments: "One must, in any case, fix a usage [either meat or dairy] for a pot" [48, 4)]. To be sure, his ruling is restricted to pots, but at least he is clear about the need to assign pots to a category. A more comprehensive statement is found, finally, in the *Arukh HaShulchan* of Rabbi Yehiel Halevi Epstein (1829-1908; the relevant sections of this work were first published in Warsaw, 1894-1898). Epstein writes:

> And the custom has already spread that in all houses where there is cooking [are kitchens?] there is a plank set aside for placing [upon it] meat pots and a plank set aside for placing

[upon it] dairy pots, and for all things of dairy and meat there are special utensils, and Jews are holy and they are very stringent with themselves in this (*Yoreh Deah* 88, 11).

Further on, he adds:

Small and big dishes in the house, of meat alone and of dairy alone, should be made of two [different] kinds, for recognition, that they not be confused. And the same [should be true] for spoons and forks and the same for all utensils—or they should make markings on those of dairy—and thus have all of Israel made their custom (*Yoreh Deah* 89, 16).

I am not confident that a statement such as these will not be found in a more obscure rabbinic source of a slightly earlier period. But the discovery of such a statement would do little to change the phenomenon we have already observed: rabbinic formulations of law and practice pertaining to the separation of Jewish kitchens into "meat" and "dairy" lag well behind the popular practice. Why is this the case? We might surmise that the popular stringencies reported in the writings of Margaritha, Marcus, and Anton (as well as others, not reviewed here) were as yet unknown to the rabbinic writers. Perhaps they were not yet practiced in the communities in which these authorities lived. This is highly unlikely, however, first because the record documents the practice of separation in at least Germany, Switzerland, and England during these centuries—a significant geographical range—and, second, because the Jewish culture of Poland was related to and influenced by that of Germany. It is nearly impossible to imagine, therefore, that Jews separated their dishes in a permanent and comprehensive way in Germany, but not in Isserles' Poland.

It is far more likely that this lag is a product of the conservatism of rabbinic writings, a conservatism that has ironic consequences when it comes to popular stringencies such as these. Broadly speaking, rabbinic codifiers tend to repeat, in identical or similar words, the formulations of the sources from which they draw. The best example of this, in the present case, is Maimonides' codification, which is virtually identical to its Talmudic source and gives little hint that the law has been elaborated and extended. The same is true, though in different measure, for each subsequent generation of halachic writings, which articulates its claim to traditional authority by incorporating the formulations of its predecessors. So if prior codes spoke of separating knives or pots, rather than all kitchenware, subsequent codes will tend to employ the same language, even if in practice all kitchenware is being separated in a permanent and comprehensive manner. Indeed, this conservatism has what are apparently lenient consequences because, if these writings "err" in any direction, it is in the direction of what was rather than what has come to be; that is, in the direction of what halacha actually requires rather than what popular custom has come to expect.

Even Epstein, whose formulation reports and praises the most stringent developments, does admit the difference between the two. He is unambiguous in describing the practice of comprehensive separation as a custom [*minhag*]. By employing this term, he admits that it is not demanded by the halacha or the letter of the law. He further speaks of at least the first custom (separate counters) as a relatively recent one, and in both cases his language suggests that separation is a popular development, one assumed by "Israel," for he offers no literary source for the practices he reports. Finally, the rhetoric of the statement—"Jews are holy and they are very stringent with themselves in this"—shows that, despite Epstein's obvious support of the practice, he is aware that it goes beyond what the halacha would require. Why, after all, employ such hyperbole if the practice being praised can be taken for granted? If the practice were well grounded in the sources, a simple declarative sentence, in the normal style of such halachic writing, would have sufficed. Epstein applauds the fact that Jews, as he knows them, are stringent with themselves in these matters. Evidently other Jews, in earlier generations and places, saw no need for such stringencies.

So the practice of separating meat and dairy dishes (and pots and counters and cabinets) has developed significantly from its talmudic roots. From simple directives demanding caution with recently used pots or dishes, the law has developed to a point that it literally determines the map of the observant Jewish kitchen, requiring at least separate cabinets for the abundance of meat or dairy cookware, serving and eating utensils, and, in the case of the wealthy, separate sinks or even separate kitchens. Having traced the path of this development, the challenge remains for us to explain, as best we can, why?—Why did a few, simple regulations, laid down in the Talmud to keep the tastes of meat and dairy separate, develop into a comprehensive system that, in its fullest formulation, has come to represent the kitchen of the observant Jew, and even Jewish observance itself?

THE TECHNOLOGIES OF EATING: A HISTORY

Part of the answer to these questions will be found in the history of what we might call the technologies of eating. People in earlier centuries ate in very different ways, employing different utensils than we or, as often, no utensils at all. In the early Middle Ages, eating forks had yet to be invented, and hands were often used for transporting solid foods to the mouth. According to Islamic norms, food was taken from a common tray with one's fingers.[4] In Provence, knives were kept for personal use, and they were for both cutting and spearing foods. Collective dishes—typically wood or bronze trays or deep platters— were used to serve all present at a meal, and only bowls might be used by individual diners.[5] Since soups were the common food for the masses in medieval Europe, spoons and ladles were also essential utensils.

Forks were unknown before the eleventh century, and there is rare evidence of them for centuries thereafter. To perform the function now served by forks, people would use either their hands or, as commonly, knives, whose points were handy for impaling foods and bringing them to the mouth. As late as the early seventeenth century, in Italy forks were used for carving, not eating. But evidence suggests that their use did spread during this century, and by the late eighteenth century, French etiquette manuals require full settings of silverware, including forks. Still, as late as the beginning of the twentieth century, bourgeois people in Vienna were still carrying cakes to their mouths with knives, showing that old habits die hard and relatively more recent practices must struggle to win complete acceptance.[6]

As far as plates are concerned, a similar trajectory of development may be sketched. As described above, in earlier centuries in North Africa, the only "plates" were platters or trays, intended to serve the assembled diners collectively. Trenchers of wood or bread were more common, the former used, again, for common service. Metal flat plates are found in Italy in the early sixteenth century, but hard plates for individual use do not become more common until the seventeenth century. In the seventeenth through eighteenth centuries, the bourgeoisie employed silver plates, while the aristocracy preferred ceramic plates. Still, such plates were not generally accepted, in France at least, until the nineteenth century. The Jewish Museum plates mentioned above reflect this history almost exactly. The earliest plates in that collection, all of pewter, are from the eighteenth century, and the ceramic plates are all from the nineteenth or twentieth century. This history indicates how crucial the question of class is in considering these developments. If the wealthier classes were using plates, common folk were still forced to rely on old technologies, at least until the mass production of inexpensive plates. As is the case with forks, common use of plates is a genuinely modern phenomenon.

These realities have an obvious impact on the eating regulations of Jews in the Middle Ages. As we have seen, in their writings rabbinic authorities of these centuries focus time and again on the same utensils: knives, pots, bowls, and spoons. Not once is there a mention of a fork, and plates (used for serving, not individual eating) are rarely discussed. Of course, the subjects of rabbinic deliberation reflect exactly the realities we have described. Knives were the most important utensil, used for cooking, serving, and eating. Pots were the central and essential means by which foods were prepared. Bowls were used for both serving and eating, as soups and stews formed one of the foundations of the common diet, and spoons, therefore, were essential eating utensils. In any given household, all of these would have been present in relatively small numbers (a couple of pots would serve for a family, individuals kept their own knives), so the sorts of sets that typify modern kitchens would have been unavailable. Simply put, sets of dishes were not separated during these centuries, at least in part because there were no sets of dishes to separate.

In fact, rabbinic authorities were aware of changes in the technologies of eating and commented on how such changes would affect Jewish eating regulations. Responding to a questioner who asks about the need to change tablecloths between meat and dairy meals, R. David b. Solomon ibn Abi Zimra (1479-1573, the Radbaz) refers to an opinion of the Rashba that supports such a requirement. But he then adds: "The words of the master applied only when they placed the meat and the cheese [directly] on the cloth, for there is then a concern that they might get stuck on one another, but it is our practice to bring all foods to the table in bowls, so even if there are meat droppings on the cloth, they [=the different foods] will never touch one another." (Radbaz, *Responsa*, pt. 2, n. 721). So the Radbaz recognizes that eating customs have changed and understands that such changes will demand different precautions in practice. He recalls a reality in which food was placed directly on the table and when individuals used the same tablecloth to clean their hands between foods. But in his day, food is kept in bowls—not placed directly on the table—and small cloths (napkins) are distributed to diners to wipe their hands (he adds this observation below in the same comment). In his opinion, this change should lead to greater leniency with respect to the separation of cloths. But as we look forward, to the centuries in which flat plates and full sets of cutlery become more and more common, the same sensibility might well demand more systematic separations of the vessels that actually contain and manipulate food. When dishes become common, they will be separated. When forks join knives and spoons at each setting, they too will be separated. "Separate dishes" is at least in part the halachic Jewish response to a new reality.

However, as commented earlier, while it is true that such separation is not surprising, neither is it natural or necessary. There is more to this story than the history of how foods were brought from the pot to the mouth.

To begin with, there is not a single, linear history of how foods were consumed, and the ancient reality in Palestine, viewed in juxtaposition with the sparse leniency of the earliest rabbinic laws, shows that later separations were not an inevitable outcome of primary rabbinic intentions. Excavations at Qumran, providing evidence of the practice of at least one community in the late second Temple period, uncovered a large storage room filled with hundreds of serving and eating vessels. Crucially, vessels for serving and those for eating were stored separately, and there was a far larger quantity of the latter than of the former. Moreover, these eating vessels were simple pottery, clearly manufactured for common use. Together, the quantity and simplicity of these vessels suggest that they were intended for use by individuals during their meals. Included in this large stash were cups, bowls, and flat plates with raised rims. Personal dishes, not only those for communal serving, and plates, not only bowls, characterized the eating technologies of the community at Qumran.[7]

The discoveries at the Bar-Kokhba caves, reflecting early second-century practice, similarly reveal that personal plates were at least sometimes employed for eating in ancient Palestine. Though the number of dishes found at the site is small, their purpose is relatively unambiguous. Four complete dishes were found in a basket belonging to a woman named Babatha, thus indicating that they were for personal use. Two are shallow plates, the other two are bowls. All are of a size appropriate for use by an individual, and all are made of unfinished wood, an inexpensive material. Other plates of a similar nature (either whole or in fragments) were discovered in the same caves, and all suggest that Jews and others in Roman Palestine used individual dishes for taking their meals.[8] It is inconceivable that the rabbis would have known a different reality.

Yet, in the Mishnah the rabbis never once mention the need to keep personal plates separate if they have been used for milk or meat. Nor is such a reference, in their name, found anywhere in the talmudic literature. That they did not enunciate such a requirement is not due to the absence of a reality to which it might apply; rather, they did not demand the separation of dishes because they did not imagine such separation to be necessary.

Even in the limited context of later centuries, the expansions we have seen cannot be considered natural outcomes of developing principles. To recognize that the practices of observant Jews might have developed in other directions, we should consider the following rulings, by Caro and Isserles, pertaining to the washing of dishes:

> (Caro) Dishes of meat that were washed in a dairy kettle, in water hot enough to scald the hand, even if both of them had been used on the same day, it is permitted, for it is [a case of] the secondary transmission of a permitted taste.
>
> (Isserles) And there are those who prohibit... unless one of the vessels had not been used on the same day... and this is our practice, and one should not differ. But this is specifically when they were washed together in a vessel in which the water had been boiled, but if they were washed one after the other, or even together in a vessel in which the water had not been boiled, it is all permitted [and] if he poured boiling water which is neither of meat nor of milk [=it had not been boiled is a vessel used for one of those substances on the same day] upon vessels of meat and milk together, even when grease is on them, it is all permitted (*Shulhan Arukh, Yoreh Deah* 95, 3).

These regulations describe the realities of dishwashing long before the invention of the modern dishwasher, when dishes and the like were washed in large kettles or basins of hot water. But even at a remove from this reality, it is easy to appreciate how relatively lenient (relative to modern observant practice) these rulings are. It is fair to say that virtually all contemporary Orthodox Jews—and certainly those who have not studied the halakhic sources in detail—would stand aghast at these rulings. Following them to their most natural conclusion, they would permit the separate washing of both meat and dairy dishes in a single dishwasher. Yet few observant contemporary Jews would even consider such a practice. To be sure, there are real concerns that might lead to a more restrictive practice.[9] But it is clear that the major authorities of the sixteenth century did not deem such concerns to be prohibitive. Accounting for all possible concerns or potential problems is itself a phenomenon worthy of attention and interpretation. If the system developed in more stringent directions, separating the dishes rather than letting them be, we must seek to understand why.

THE STRINGENCIES OF THE PIOUS

In fact, the practice of maintaining separate dishes may be seen as a part of a more prevalent tendency in latter-century Jewish practice to choose the more stringent route in regulations pertaining to eating and, I think it fair to say, in many other matters as well. The testimony of authorities writing on the eating laws leaves no doubt that eating regulations were becoming steadily more restrictive in the sixteenth century and that popular practice was still more stringent than the rabbis report. Significantly, these stringencies clustered particularly in the Jewish communities of Germany and Poland, and more in the latter than the former. The concentration of reports found in the comments of Isserles testifies unambiguously to this reality.

The forces behind this development emerge from the historical conditions affecting these communities in the early modern period. The key to understanding the relevant dynamics is found in the comment of R. Shlomo Luria, who, while commenting on the amount of time one must wait after eating meat before eating dairy, distinguished between the practices of "those who are not children of Torah" and those who are (see *Yam shel shlomo* to Ḥul. 8, #9). The question is, what is the meaning of this distinction?

Luria and Isserles lived in a world of emergent modernity. Poland in their day was a mostly hospitable place for Jews. They flourished economically and had ample opportunity to take advantage of the spirit of enlightenment that had spread northward from renaissance Italy. Jews often enjoyed close relationships—economic and social—with their non-Jewish neighbors, and the practice of many was surely forced to bend before the demands of these relationships. The evidence of such bending is widespread and unambiguous.[10] From the perspective of the rabbinic authorities, at least, contemporary Jewry was divided between the pious and the less-than-pious. Means of distinguishing the latter from the former were crucial, and developments in eating practice—such as the amount of time one waits between meat and dairy—served this purpose well.

Separating the dishes, like separating one's consumption of meat and dairy, could serve the same purpose, creating a profound symbolic and pragmatic boundary between more and less pious Jews. Significantly, in his condemnation of another stringent rule, Luria reveals his keen understanding that such customs will inevitably serve to divide one group from another. Speaking of the eating of meat after cheese, a practice permitted by the Talmud, Luria condemns the custom of those who nevertheless refuse to do so as "sectarian" [*minut*]. By refusing to do what is permitted, they "separate themselves" from the community, creating divisions between Jew and Jew. This is undeniably true. But we must not fail to recognize that such stringencies and differential practices do more than merely divide; at the same time they reflect and reinforce such divisions. There is a dynamic relationship between the practice and the social grouping, according to which divisions lead to different customs and different customs strengthen and multiply social divisions. This is as true of keeping separate dishes as it is of the other stringent regulations noted above.

The practice of separating dishes transformed the kitchen of the pious Jew into a comprehensive symbol of his or her piety. Separating the dishes into meat and dairy sets, he at the same time separated himself, the more pious Jew, from another, less pious one. By marking his plates, some for meat and some for milk, he marked himself off from his neighbor who did not (yet) observe this custom. As had often been true in the prior centuries, once again the eating regulations would be enlisted to distinguish one sort of Jew from another. Both symbolizing and effectuating the separation of the more observant from the less observant, this practice would constitute a powerful bulwark against an encroaching modernity.

WOMEN AND DISHES

Still one more factor may have been instrumental in the development of the practice of keeping separate sets of dishes and cooking ware. The kitchen was (and is), from the perspective of the developing "normative" tradition, a rather odd, because hybrid, realm. It was the primary arena for the acting out of complex rabbinic food regulations. However, the rabbis were not actually the authorities in the kitchen, at least not on a regular basis. Rather, the kitchen was a place for the exercise of popular authority and local expertise.[11] With the rarest exception, the authority in most Jewish—as non-Jewish—kitchens was the woman of the household. It was she (and/or her servants) who prepared the foods and it was she, therefore, who negotiated and adjudicated questions and problems relating to kashrut. This fact had significant ramifications for Jewish practice.

Most Jewish women during these centuries in Europe were not learned, and they were surely unschooled in the technical details of the laws of separating dairy and meat. What they knew, they knew mostly from experience: from watching their mothers' conduct in their kitchens when they were girls. From the model of the prior generation, they knew, more or less, what must be done in any given circumstance. But while they generally knew the "what," they often did not know the "why," at least not as a rabbi would. And this ignorance had its consequences. What would a woman do when things were mixed in her kitchen in ways she did not know how to fix? The safe choice, for a pious woman, would always be to take the more stringent path. To avoid such problems, the same woman would take precautions, establishing more restrictive standards to assure that difficulties would not arise. Not being able to rely upon the technical rabbinic principles that would allow more lenient solutions, she would build in protections that would help her avoid what, in her kitchen, run according to her standards, would lead to unacceptable loss—loss of time, of food (which had to be discarded), and of resources (plates that would have to be replaced, etc.).

An anonymous but reliable source has shared with me the following story: When he, the son of a famous rabbi, was young, his mother took a trip away from home, leaving him and his father in charge of the home and kitchen for the first time. When his mother returned a couple of weeks later, she was horrified by what had become of her kitchen and immediately accused her husband, the rabbi, of *"treifing"* it up. Of course, he had done nothing of the sort. He had merely conducted himself in the kitchen according to what rabbinic sources would require. This, however, was not good enough for her. As ultimate authority in the kitchen, she had established her own standards, and these standards required steps that would not have been found in the formal written rules.

When common people, doing their best to protect the kashrut of their kitchens, make the rules, these rules will inevitably be more stringent than the letter of the law would require. This would particularly be so in a setting such as early modern Ashkenaz, where a pious woman might wish to display her own piety in contrast to what she judges to be the lesser piety of her neighbor. We should not be surprised, then, that when women had to decide what to do with their modern kitchens in the modern world, they decided in favor of a complete and systematic separation. Through this separation, they reminded themselves, their families, and their neighbors who they were and to what community they belonged.

NOTES

[1] *Function and Design in the Talmudic Period* (2nd ed.; Tel Aviv: Haaretz Museum, 1979) 62-71.

[2] S. Goitein, *A Mediterranean Society*,(vol. 4; Berkeley: U. of California Press, 1967-88), 252.

[3] E. Carlebach, *Divided Souls* (New Haven: Yale University.Press, 2001), 55-56, 180-81.

[4] B. Rosenberger, "Arab Cuisine and its Contribution to European Culture," in Flandrin and Montanari, eds., *Food: A Culinary History from Antiquity to the Present* (New York: Columbia University Press, 1999), 208.

[5] Miguel-Ángel Motis Dolader, "Mediterranean Jewish Diet and Traditions in the Middle Ages," in Flandrin and Montanari, *Food: A Culinary History*, 233.

[6] For the history recounted in this paragraph, see Margaret Visser, *The Rituals of Dinner* (New York and London: Penguin Books, 1991), 184-213.

[7] *Function and Design*, 14-15.

[8] Y. Yadin, *Discoveries from the Days of Bar Kokhba in the Cave of Letters* (Hebrew) (Jerusalem: 1963), 132-35 and plates 39-40.

[9] See Binyomin Forst, *The Laws of Kashrus* (New York: Mesorah Publications, 1993), 258-62.

[10] Many examples will be found in Edward Aaron Fram, *Jewish Law and Social and Economic Realities in 16th and 17th Century Poland* (Ph.D. diss., Columbia University, 1991). See particularly 55-57, 101, 116-17 and 225.

[11] See the essay in this volume, Ruth Abusch-Magder, "Kathrut: Women as Gatekeepers of Jewish Identity," in *Food and Judaism* (Studies in Jewish Civilization 15; Omaha: Creighton University Press, 2004).

The Blessing in the Belly:
Mystical Satiation in Medieval Kabbalah

Joel Hecker

In his *Major Trends in Jewish Mysticism*, Gershom Scholem cites Ps 78:25, "Taste and see that the Lord is good," as signifying the quintessence of the mystical experience. As Scholem explains, mysticism is the longing of the finite individual to cross the chasm that divides him from the Divine Infinite.[1] To be able to taste that the Lord is good is to experience, bodily, the nature of divinity.[2] Moving down the alimentary canal, we read in Ps 40:9, "To do what pleases You, my God, is my desire; Your Torah is in my inward parts [*mei'ai*]."[3] Other biblical evidence and surrounding Near Eastern literature associates the term *mei'ai* with the liver, heart, and womb, each of which is connected with emotions. The biblical trope of the Torah in one's "inward parts" is surely not meant by the author to be taken literally, but rather intends that the poet's being is permeated with a fullness of devotion to God and His teaching.[4] The Hebrew word *mei'ai*, translated as heart in Christian Bibles, would have been translated by the thirteenth century Jewish mystics as "inward parts" but also as "belly." A verse declaring "Your Torah is in my belly" signifies an internalization of the Torah that goes beyond affiliation, loyalty, and behavior. It touches upon the bodily transformation of the individual as a living expression of the Torah, having literally ingested Torah and feeling fully satiated as a result.

This paper will focus on "the blessing in the belly," a trope from the *Zohar*, the Kabbalah's central and canonical text.[5] I will show that passages in the *Zohar* indicate the somatic nature of the mystical experience such that Torah, and even Divinity itself, are known through eating, digestion, and repletion. Through the study of instances of gustatory blessing and mystical satiation, we shall discover a range of meanings for this phenomenon; these include enhanced hermeneutical abilities, psychosomatic unity, mystical virility, and sociological

257

commentary. While the *Zohar* will be the primary text under consideration, I will also cite kabbalistic texts from other Castilian works of the late thirteenth to early fourteenth centuries, such as Moshe de Leon's *Sefer ha-Rimmon*, and Joseph of Hamadan's *Sefer Ta'amei ha-Mizvot*. Reaching beyond the question of mystical eating, I will illustrate the variety of experiences of embodiment that are suggested by these kabbalistic texts as part of the larger project of sketching out the history of the human body.[6]

Before proceeding headlong into a discussion of the phenomenology of the mystical meal, some of the basics of the kabbalistic system bear repeating.[7] Building upon a neo-Platonic foundation, the kabbalists understand God to confer life and blessing onto the world through the mediation of ten gradations, called *sefirot*. As light and holiness proceed downward, they become increasingly muted, reflecting the distance they have traveled from divinity while at the same time enabling reception and access. Were God to be known in His most ineffable form, humans would be destroyed by the intensity of the experience. Furthermore, much of kabbalistic activity entails the practice of theurgy, literally "working upon God."

The Kabbalah teaches that through Torah study, prayer, and the performance of the commandments, one effects unions between the different *sefirot*, inducing cosmic harmony. In order to engage in theurgic praxis in the performance of these ritual norms, one has to direct one's attention to one *sefirah* or another. A secondary benefit of successful theurgy is that one can draw down blessing from the *sefirot* with which one is interacting. When eating ritual foods, one of the aims of the mystical adept in his theurgic practice is to attain a "blessing in the belly." When the kabbalists sat down to dine, they would theurgically invoke divine overflow from above and prompt its downward flow upon the individual's table, the bread upon it, and ultimately into the diner's belly. I will be examining the "blessing in the belly" as miraculous satiation, an instance of mystical encounter. While some cases of somatization may be understood metaphorically, frequently the biblical text is interpreted in a "hyper-literal" manner and is suggestive of an embodied spirituality wherein one's viscera are the site of the mystical encounter.[8] The kabbalists ascribe physical attributes to spiritual experiences because that is the way they experienced them. In a discussion of mystical visionary ascents, Elliot Wolfson writes, "The soul undergoes kinesthetic and tactile experiences in the course of its ascent and ultimately enjoys a tangible sense of delight in the moment of the visual encounter with the divine."[9]

Hebrew Scriptures include several tales of miraculous satiation. In Exod 6:18 we read about the manna: "When they measured it by the omer, he who had gathered much had no excess, and he who had gathered little had no deficiency: they had gathered as much as they needed to eat." While the miracle of the manna's sufficiency might have occurred during delivery and collection providing, perhaps, a proto-Marxian parable, the story of Elijah and the widow of Zarephath in 1 Kgs suggests a transformation of the foodstuff itself. The woman laments that she has:

> nothing but a handful of flour in a jar and a little oil in a jug. "I am just gathering a couple of sticks, so that I can go home and prepare it for me and my son; we shall eat it and then we shall die." "Don't be afraid," said Elijah to her. "Go and do as you have said; but first make me a small cake from what you have there, and bring it out to me; then make some for yourself and your son. For thus said the Lord, the God of Israel: 'The jar of flour shall not give out and the jug of oil shall not fail until the day that the Lord sends rain upon the ground.'" She went and did as Elijah had spoken, and she and he and her household had food for a long time. The jar of flour did not give out, nor did the jug of oil fail, just as the Lord had spoken through Elijah (1 Kgs 17:12-16).

Elijah's disciple Elisha performs similar wondrous feats. As Scripture relates:

> A man came from Baa-shalishah and he brought the man of God some bread of the first reaping—twenty loaves of barley bread, and some fresh grain in his sack. And [Elisha] said, "Give it to the people and let them eat." His attendant replied, "How can I set this before a hundred men?" But he said, "Give it to the people and let them eat" (2 Kgs 4:42-44).[10]

In the promise of God's grace described in these legends, the *Zohar* finds a route to mystical satiation in which the stories are unmoored from their historical confines. In the kabbalists' imaginative recreation of these miraculous repasts, the satisfaction of bodily needs did not suffice as evidence of the mystical adhesion; the mystical initiates described further marvels that accompanied the mystical satiation.

HERMENEUTICAL ABILITIES

One dramatic homily recounts the miraculous experiences enjoyed by the Israelites when they would consume the heavenly manna:

> All of the faithful went out and gathered [the manna] and blessed the holy name over it.[11] The manna emitted fragrances of all of the aromas of the Garden, for it was drawn from there and descended below.[12] Any taste that a person wanted he would find in it[13] and [he] would bless the supernal King. He would then receive blessing in his belly [*mitbarekh be-mei'oi*] and would look and know above, seeing supernal wisdom, and for this reason they were called "a knowing generation." These are the faithful and the Torah was given to them to look into and to know its ways.[14] What is written about those who are not amongst the faithful? "The people would go about and gather it" (Num 11:8). What is the meaning of "go about" [*shatu*]? They were taken to folly [*shetuta*] because they were not among the faithful. What is written about them? "[They would] grind it between millstones or pound it in a mortar" (Num 11:8). Who went to all this trouble? Those who were not among the faithful. Similarly those who do not believe in the Holy One, blessed be He, are unable to look in His paths and they have to trouble themselves everyday for food, day and night—lest they not have bread. What causes this to befall them? It is because they are not of the faithful (*Zohar* 2:62b-63a).

This rich passage bears the confluence of several different themes. After gathering the manna, the "faithful,"—mystics—would experience its fragrance and its taste, and then they would recite a blessing after eating it. The individual would receive a blessing in his stomach, following which he would look above, seeing supernal wisdom.[15] The recitation of the blessing below, particularly after eating the manna, appears to be instrumental in inducing the reception of divine blessing from above.[16]

Most striking is that the descending blessing resides in the person's body. In many passages the *Zohar* treats the body as inhabited by the soul; in contrast, here the body itself partakes of the spirituality, yielding an experience of psychosomatic unity.[17] By psychosomatic unity, I mean an experience in which a feeling that one would normally associate with the spiritual component of a person is vividly associated with his or her physical nature.[18] This type of experience, then, is far from a "flight from physicality" or "escape into mysticism," but is rather more like a lived appreciation of "the possibilities provided by fleshliness."[19] The very experience of mystical repletion appears to originate from the fullness that one enjoys following a hearty meal. If so, the kabbalists' metaphor of choice—satiation—is none other than the literal experience itself. In other words, mystical plenitude is an extension of physical plenitude, the latter being a translation of the physical experience into a mystical, that is psychosomatic, experience. In the context of the Jewish tradition—commandments to bless God in advance of a meal, after eating and reaching satiation, as well as the multitude of biblical promises of bounty that God vouchsafes to Israel—this mystical translation has a potent valence.

The passage above regarding manna indicates that the consumption of the idealized food confers insight into divine matters. A parallel may be drawn to the embodied experience of circumcision as analyzed by Wolfson, in which the mark of the covenant [*brit milah*] is the locus of the mystical experience for the kabbalists.[20] Wolfson writes:

> By means of circumcision, one is opened up in such a way that God may be revealed; the physical opening engenders a space in which the theophany occurs…. In the *Zohar*, however, circumcision is not only a prerequisite for the vision of God, but the place of circumcision, the phallus, is itself the locus of such a vision: one sees God from the circumcised flesh or, put differently, from the semiological seal of the covenant imprinted on that flesh.

As with circumcision, in which wisdom is attained somatically, in this instance wisdom is acquired through eating.[21] The eating paradigm can be distinguished from that of the circumcision paradigm in that with eating there is a body technique that can be employed to induce the experience; eating, moreover, is a practical, daily, physical activity and the experience arises from the use of this daily activity as a technique.

The skill most prized among the kabbalists was hermeneutical and it should not surprise the reader that the mystics ascribed collateral benefits to the unique nourishment of the biblical stories; specifically, mystical insight and enhanced hermeneutical abilities. The similarity of eating manna to the hermeneutical project is borne out by the fact that as the Israelites looked into the Torah (or discerned the flavors in the manna), they would receive blessing in the belly. In the course of penetrating the Torah, itself an expression of divinity, divinity in turn penetrates the kabbalist. Joseph of Hamadan writes in a similar vein: "When a person chews he opens his mouth; thus whoever eats the manna opens his heart and his mouth in the account of the chariot."[22] Those who are unfamiliar with or, more likely, not wholly appreciative of the kabbalistic approach[23] were doomed to "wander about," unable to enter into the mystical knowledge promised to the faithful. They fail to realize that there is a mode of assimilating knowledge of the Torah that is immediate and effortless, an entry into an open door as opposed to the travails of wandering and the drudgery of grinding. Grinding refers to the intellectual or philosophical study of Torah, a frequent target of zoharic Kabbalah's polemics.[24]

In the Jewish mystical literature of the thirteenth century this is a familiar dispute. A battle for the hearts and minds of the learned classes was a major point of contention between the kabbalists and those who were following in the tradition of Maimonides. Kabbalists excoriated the rationalism of unnamed figures and their refusal to recognize the mystical depths of the Torah. In *Sefer ha-Rimmon*, Moshe de Leon launches a two-pronged attack against those who have internalized the rationalistic approach:

> I have seen men who used to occupy themselves with Torah and the teachings of the rabbis, may their memory be for a blessing, day and night; and they used to serve the Omnipresent [*ha-maqom*] with a full heart as is appropriate. And then one day scholars of Greek wisdom came to confront the Lord, and Satan too came among them, leading them to leave the Source of Living Waters. They occupied themselves with those books [of Greek wisdom] and their minds were drawn after them until they left the teachings of the Torah and the commandments and cast them aside.[25] In their misguided understanding they considered the teachings of the rabbis to be falsehood. "There was no sound and none who responded,"[26] for they were distant as a result of the Greeks and their supporters. There was no spirit of God within them; they were transformed into other men, casting aspersions on their former selves and fine behaviors according to which they had conducted themselves in the past. They mocked and cast aspersions upon the teachings of [the rabbis], may their memory be for a blessing. . . . I have also seen them during the holiday of Sukkot standing in their place in the synagogue watching the servants of God circling the

Torah scrolls in the ark with their *lulavim* [palm branches] and they were laughing and casting aspersions upon them. They said that they were fools, lacking in understanding, while they themselves had neither *lulav* nor *etrog* [citron]. They contended, "Did not the Torah say that this use [of *lulav* and *etrog*] was on account of the verse 'And you shall rejoice before the Lord your God seven days (Exod 23:40)?' You think that these [four] species will cause us to rejoice? Vessels of silver and gold and [valuable] garments will cause us to rejoice and delight." And they said, "You who think that we must bless the Lord—He needs this? It is all folly." Until *tefillin* would no longer be seen on their heads and when people asked them for the reason they would say, "Is not the idea of *tefillin* none other than that which is written in Scripture, 'And as a reminder on your forehead (Exod 13:9)?' Since there is no better memorial than for us to remember our Creator verbally several times a day, that is a memorial that is better and more fitting.[27]

The rationalists were accused of mercenary motives and antinomian behavior in their more philosophical approach to the Torah and God's will. When the author of the *Zohar* criticizes those who forage needlessly for the manna, he refers to those who must look beyond the holy confines of the Torah for sustenance. Mystical intention must be brought to the eating event, since eating manna is not a mechanical, or innocent, action. This modality ensures that only the faithful participate in the true rewards of the blessing and the food. The *Zohar* is emphatic in its repetition that it was only the faithful who were able to gain the divine insight and blessing that came with the manna; others had to struggle to find it and then grind it in preparation for eating.[28]

Interestingly, the activity of grinding has different valences in the *Zohar* depending upon the agent doing the grinding and upon the realm in which it is being performed. If the grinding is being done within the sefirotic realm, it is considered to be a necessary part of the process of causing the procession of divine flow, or it is sometimes considered a necessary part of eating;29 if, however, grinding is being done by one who is not a "member of the faithful," it is disparaged and compared to the denigrated pilpulistic [*pilpul*, unnecessarily tedious analysis] study of Torah, an activity of those who deny the mystical meaning to the law (see, for example, *Zohar* 2:62b-63a). As with all other activities in the zoharic worldview, there are holy ways of doing an action and demonic ways of doing that same action.

From the perspective of the *Zohar*'s symbolic hermeneutics, actions do not have a fixed value, positive or negative. Usually, the binary distinction is determined by the intention of the action's agent; in this instance, the grinders are cursed with their task. This ambivalence towards work indicates the extent to which the interpretation of food preparation is not an independent protocol but rather one that is driven largely by exegesis. Thus, when grinding is referred to in a rabbinic text as an activity performed in the heavens, it adopts a holy visage; when it is performed by non-believers, the activity itself is deplored. The holy/ demonic code, as determined by the approbation or lack thereof from canonical texts, is the primary determinant of the ontology (holy or demonic) of a given subject. The economy of the struggle for food serves as a basis for distinction between the kabbalists and their opponents (or even those who are merely unlettered in kabbalistic lore).[30] It evinces a reflection upon the biblical verse in Genesis regarding Adam's curse of working by the sweat of his brow more than a personal reflection upon the exigencies of earning a living for oneself and one's family.[31] Thus, the economic theme deals with the mystical and soteriological achievement of overcoming the effects of Adam's curse. The curse here follows from a hermeneutical error, leading to economic misfortune. The foolish fail to comprehend that, unlike normal foodstuffs that require manual labor of grinding in order to render it edible, the manna is ingested effortlessly.[32]

The *Zohar* is emphatic in its repetition that it was only the faithful who were able to gain the divine insight and blessing that came with the manna; others had to struggle to find it and then grind it in preparation for eating. Adam's curse—that he must gain bread with the sweat of his brow, that it will be hard to earn a living—thus plays a role in distinguishing between the enlightened and the obtuse. Adam's curse has perennial currency, and the concern with economics that we saw in the example above is adduced in the Kabbalah of Baḥya ben Asher, Torah commentator and kabbalist of late thirteenth and early fourteenth century Spain.[33]

INDUCED SATIETY AND PSYCHOSOMATIC UNITY
In contrast to the somewhat materialist nature of this approach, the *Zohar* avers that the meaning of Scripture's saying that Mephiboshet

would always eat at King David's table[34] is that he did not have to pursue other economic avenues to take care of his material needs; that is, he would be able to rely on providential care (*Zohar* 2:153a). In this instance, the *Zohar* turns to a classical, rabbinic approach, contending that the problem of economics is resolved through faith. The nature of the mystical satiation adopts different garbs: one, as discussed above, occurs within the belly of the consumer; the second occurs in terms of the daily search for food, rendered facile for the faithful and arduous for those of improper faith.

Elsewhere the *Zohar* treats satiety by spiritualizing it:

Rabbi Ḥiyya began, saying, "When you have eaten and been sated you shall bless the Lord your God (Deut 8:10)."[35] Is it the case that unless one has eaten to satiety and filled his stomach that he should not bless the Holy One, blessed be He? [If that is so,] to what [amount of food] do we apply the verse "When you have eaten and been sated you shall bless [the Lord your God]?" Rather, even if a person eats only an olive's-volume of bread [*ke-zayit*] and his "intention" is upon it, and he has considered it (that morsel) to be the essence of his meal, he is deemed "sated."[36] This is as it is written, "You open your hand and feed every creature as it wills [*razon*] (Ps 145:16)." It is not written "every creature," rather [it is written, "every creature"] "as it wills." That intention [*razon*] which he directs to that food is called "satiety" even if one has nothing more than a small olive's-worth before him. He has directed the "intention of satiety" to it. Therefore, [it is written,] "and feed every creature as it wills." It is written "as it wills" and not ["feed every creature] its food." For this reason it is written "and you will bless," in actuality [*vadai*],[37] and a person is obligated to bless the Holy One, blessed be He, in order to give pleasure above (*Zohar* 2:153a-b).

In contrast to Scripture's injunction to recite Grace upon satiation, Jewish law requires that one recite Grace after the intake of an olive's-volume of bread [*ke-zayit*]. Responding to the contradiction between holy writ and norm, the author of the homily contends that the blessing will follow either satiety or a contemplation-induced satiety. Because Scripture specifies satiety, satiety there must be. The term "satiety," then, serves as a technical term, not necessarily referring to a physical experience. Physical satiation is actually irrelevant: according to the

Zohar's hermeneutic, in this instance "satiety" is a cipher signifying fulfillment of normative halacha accompanied by the appropriate mystical intention and does not necessarily refer to a literal physical state at all. The body serves as a trigger—one must eat in order to incur the obligation of Grace; thus, the term "satiety" of the verse refers to a particular kind of contemplation rather than a physical experience. The *Zohar* refers to an induced satiation, a somatized feeling of mystical fullness in which the contemplative application of *kavannah* [proper intention] to one's meal results in both a unitive mystical experience and a physical sensation of saturation that is consequent upon that experience.[38]

Capitalizing on the gap between halacha and the simple meaning of the biblical verse,[39] the author of the *Zohar* has made contemplation the central aim of the practice through his understanding of the verse "and feed every creature as it wills." What one "wills," in terms of satiety, is a state of contemplation. The *Zohar* concludes, saying that one has an obligation to bless in order to give pleasure above; while this is not speaking overtly about physical pleasure, especially since it is referring to the divine realm, it does return the reader's attention to factors of sensual experience and pleasure. The Kabbalah's ubiquitous mirroring of the human and sefirotic realms suggests that the joy given to the Divine at the end of the passage is subsequent to the mystic's own sensual experience. "Satiety" thus acts as both a technical term and reference to a felt experience, but one that is induced by contemplation, rather than one produced by a meal.

Joseph of Hamadan offers a similar rendition of satiation from a *ke-zayit* in his teaching about the face-bread [*leḥem ha-panim*]:

> To set forth bread and frankincense before the Lord on each Sabbath, as it is said, "And on the table you shall set the *leḥem ha-panim* [literally, bread of the face] before me always." The essence of this commandment has already been stated by our masters, may their memory be for a blessing, with regard to the *leḥem ha-panim*: Why is it called *leḥem ha-panim*? Because each and every side has a face (*panim*) and since it is expressive of the face (*panim*) in its totality40 it is called *leḥem ha-panim*. The Holy One, blessed be He, caused blessing to descend there. When the priests would eat of the *leḥem ha-panim*, they would be satiated [even if] they would eat only a *ke-zayit*, since "there the Lord ordained blessing, everlasting life" (Ps 133:3)—[the

esoteric meaning is that] the priests were nourished from that place because the blessing would descend there and [they would attain] everlasting life.[41]

In this example, the *ke-zayit* also serves as a marker, not of physical satiation or psychosomatic plenitude, but rather of soteriological fulfillment: upon eating this meager portion of bread, one gains "blessing and everlasting life."

This example shows the priests attaining physical nourishment and the physical experience of satiety through eating a different idealized food. Thus, as opposed to the zoharic examples in which there is often a strong spiritual or mystical component to the satiety, here the spirituality is also strongly materialist. It can be inferred that the kabbalist cum "priest" gains the physical experience of satiety through a meager portion of bread. This passage addresses the economics question treated above: if one can eat food that has been blessed by God, one can survive on considerably less than a normal person. Joseph of Hamadan makes clear that the point of eating is nourishment, not pleasure or even divine wisdom: his portrayal of the idealized food is of a substance that has been energized so that its functionality has been enhanced. In this instance, mundane needs drive the mystical endeavor. Also different is the fact that the body is not being treated instrumentally in this instance; rather it is the redemption gained through eating blessed bread that concerns this kabbalist.

A passage in Moses de Leon's *Sefer ha-Rimmon*, also dealing with mystical satiety, simultaneously adopts two differing attitudes towards the body:

> A person who recites the Grace after eating gives power to the attribute of *Tov* [Goodness] which is the attribute that receives from *Ḥesed*.[42] The appearance of this known attribute that receives food is satiated, totally filled with goodness. The lighting and sparking of the brilliant light is good and satiating, without causing harm. In any event, when he recites the Grace after he has been sated, his blessing is a good blessing [*berakhah tovah*], as it is said, "For then we had plenty to eat, we were *tovim* [good ones] (Jer 44:17)."[43] Therefore it is incumbent upon each person to bless his Creator . . . as it is written, "When you have eaten and been sated you shall bless the Lord (Deut 8:10)." For this reason they [the rabbis] have said, may their memory be a blessing, in the tractate *Berakhot*[44] regarding the mystery

of that which it says, "The Lord show favor unto you45 and
grant you peace!" (Num 6:26): the ministering angels said
before the Holy One, blessed be He, "Master of the universe, is
it not written in your Torah '[For the Lord your God is God
supreme and Lord supreme] who shows no favor and takes no
bribe (Deut 10:17)?' How can you show favor to Israel?!" He
said to them, "How could I not show favor to Israel? I have
written in my Torah, 'When you have eaten and been sated you
shall bless . . .' and they eat only an olive's-worth and bless
before Me." In any event, when a person is sated or appears
sated with regard to his food he should bless his master. This
causes the ascent of favor above and increases the attribute of
Goodness [*Tov*] (*Sefer ha-Rimmon*, 104-105).

The conclusion of this section follows the same line of thought as that
of the *Zohar*: whether one is actually sated or has only eaten an olive's-
worth, he should recite the Grace. Thus, satiety bears significance as a
sign of the normative requirement for the blessing; blessing is incumbent
upon the individual as a mark of piety, at a stage that precedes satiation.
It thus marks the religious intention that one should have in turning to
God. Moreover, this foodless satiation is an example of the *Zohar*'s
representation of the human body that is *not* a body; that is, an instance
in which the mystical experience entails transcendence of the body's
normal limits.[46]

At the beginning of this passage, however, the embodied experience
of satiety results in a blessing of superior quality. While it might be
suggested that de Leon intends that the resultant feeling of comfort
and joy will give one greater ability to bless with the desired *kavvanah*,
there is no such suggestion here.[47] Further, the use of terms in both the
human and divine realms strongly anchors the experience in the physical.
When a person recites the Grace, he draws blessing from the *sefirah* of
Ḥesed, causing it to flow onto the *sefirah* of Yesod, identified by the
cognomen *tov*. Yesod, referring to the phallus of the divine anthropos, is
said to be sated with food. Consequent upon its satiation, Yesod provides
nourishment to the feminine *Malkhut*. Similarly, those reciting the Grace
following their own satiation are said to be *tovim* [good ones] and affiliate
themselves with the *sefirah* Yesod. The kabbalist bodily expresses his
satiety in terms of sexual potency; in the anagogic relationship between
human and Divine, both gain sexual potency as a result of consuming
food. The Deity and the kabbalist are both full and sexually puissant.

Satiety now has the additional meaning of virility, and this potency expresses itself theurgically in the quality of the blessing directed towards the Divine.

Rather than considering the human being as a binary combination of body and soul that is irreparably divided against itself until the time of redemption through the soul's transcendence of its material habit, the *Zohar* conceptualizes the human being, ideally, as a creature whose mystically-energized body itself contributes to the blessing that he gives to the divine realm. The body eclipses its normal alienation from the spiritual, becoming assimilated to the divine flow: a different kind of body has emerged—one of psychosomatic unity, in which body is assimilated to soul and soul with the supernal.[48] This ideal yields a construction of the individual as an en-souled body in which the exclusive primacy of the soul has faded.

In the same passage, de Leon considers two different constructions of the body: one that focuses on the spiritual and the other presenting an alternative of unity of spirit and body. I contend that the transformation of the physical body evidenced here is one of the chief spiritual goals of zoharic Kabbalah. This is, in fact, the force of the biblical proof text: "For then we had plenty to eat, we were good ones [*tovim*]." In the eating the mystic becomes an actual manifestation of that *sefirah* from which he benefits. The experience described here is one of psychosomatic fullness in which both body and soul respond to their receipt of an external overflow with an overflow of their own, proceeding upwards.[49]

EATING, THEURGY, AND PHALLIC POTENCY

The bivalence of the body noted above can be seen in the *Zohar*'s treatment of physical pleasure derived from eating and drinking. When the verse from the book of Ruth says, "Boaz ate and drank and his heart was joyful [*va-yitav libo*] (Ruth 3:7)," the *Zohar*, drawing on a rabbinic teaching, interprets Boaz's good mood to mean that he recited the Grace after the Meal.[50] While in the biblical context Boaz's pleasure both results from his meal and foreshadows the upcoming intercourse with Ruth, the *Zohar* says that this blessing was directed to the place called *lev*, that is, the *Shekhinah* (*Zohar Ḥadash* Ruth 86c).[51]

As we saw above, the term *tovim* had a technical meaning referring to those who had recited the Grace after the Meal. The *Zohar*'s interpretative approach is here steered by its own idiosyncratic understanding of the terms. The term *tovim* has a phallic valence. Boaz, too, is associated with the *sefirah Yesod*, the male potency on the divine Anthropos.[52] Moreover, the phrase *va-yitav libo*, referring to his recital of the Grace after the Meal, takes on phallic significance as well through the extension of the kabbalistic code. Boaz's joy, *va-yitav libo*, builds on the same root *tov* that played a sexual role above. The *Zohar's* chain of associations conflates the joy from food, the recital of *birkat ha-mazon* [Grace after the Meal], and the act of sexual union with the *Shekhinah*, which Boaz achieves through the intercourse with Ruth, the repast that follows his meal. From this vantage point, even the eating and drinking itself may be understood to be metaphorical for the sexual moment.[53] Eating becomes part of the broader kabbalistic discourse about sex, which in itself has to do with the broader discourse of mystical union and the overcoming of polarities.

One additional characteristic of this passage that deserves attention is the causal link of eating and praise of God. It appears that the blessing or praising of God is understood to be the automatic response of eating. How does the consumption of material food contribute to an overflow from the individual upwards to God? Neither the *Zohar* nor contemporaneous kabbalistic literature provides an adequate description of the process, a practice that gains devoted attention in the sixteenth century Kabbalah of Zfat and especially in the eighteenth century in Eastern European Jewish mysticism.54

SATIETY FROM *RAZON* VERSUS REAL FOOD: SOCIOLOGICAL REVERBERATIONS

The notion that satiety can be achieved with a morsel and a bit of *kavvanah* is placed in a sociological framework in a section of text that distinguishes between different grades of satiety: that of the rich man, of the poor man, and, finally, of all people:

> In all, three kinds of food are described here. "[The eyes of all look to You expectantly] and you give them their food when it is due (Ps 145:15)." This is the food of the wealthy to whom an abundance of food is given at the appropriate time [*be'ito*]— that is, one [type of food].[55] The second [kind of food] is, as it is written, "and favorably [*razon*] sate all creatures (Ps 145:16)." This is the food of the poor who are sated with favor [*razon*] and not with an abundance of food.[56] The third is, as it is written, "You open Your hand [and favorably [*razon*] sate all

creatures] (Ps 145:16)." This is the power of that place through which favor and satiation emerge for all when He opens His hand (*Zohar* 3:226a).

This passage invokes the question of the sympathy, even identification, that the kabbalists had for the poor. Anger towards the moneyed class is sprinkled liberally in the *Raya Mehemna* and the *Tiqqunei ha-Zohar*, the latter strata of the *Zohar*. [57] In the *Zohar* itself, though, the poor represent the lowly and humble, are associated with the *Shekhinah*, and, as such, are worthy models for the kabbalists. There are two possible approaches that one can adopt with regard to the similarity of the poor to the kabbalists, both of whom are able to subsist on *razon*, through reading each in light of the other. The kabbalists may be poor themselves and through kabbalistic concentration are able to defeat their hunger.

This last passage would then have to be understood as one of the polemical pieces in the *Zohar* that critique the upper classes—the latter attend to their material needs while the poor kabbalists are concerned with spiritual ends. Alternatively, the poor, by virtue of their misfortune, inexorably attain a spiritual grade that is superior to that of their more affluent counterparts. The *Zohar* claims, similarly, that King David is able to transform himself into a poor person through contemplation, citing Ps 102:1 as proof: "A prayer of the lowly man when he is faint and pours forth his plea before the Lord."[58]

This transformative capacity is valued because God is said to be more attentive to the petitions of the lowly; in this instance, that attentiveness could be the promise of real food yet-to-come or it could be the satiation granted by *razon* alone. The closing sentence of the passage ("This is the power of that place through which favor and satiation emerge for all when He opens His hand") suggests the latter: ultimately, all creatures will be sated with God's favor as strength is given to *Malkhut* [that place], which then disseminates favor and satisfaction to all. Further, the poor are nourished from the *Keter*, the highest of the *sefirot*, while the wealthy receive their abundant food from the relatively lowly *Yesod* and *Shekhinah*. In this nexus of the material, spiritual, and economic spheres, the entire populace is not promised the boon of wealth and comfort; rather, the superior advantages normally conferred upon the poor will ideally be given to all creatures. Here again, satiety is spiritualized, drawing on the material metaphor only to deny it.[59]

The kabbalists, in identifying with the poor, meld their experience with that which they project onto the poor. Their own superlative experiences interact imaginatively with the presumably quite different experiences of the pious poor. Further, this body-technique of experiencing satiation with minimal provisions underscores and harmonizes well with the ascetic inclinations of the kabbalists.[60] In this manner, their mystical experience is wedded to their ethical program: not only should one not eat too much, but, in fact, in constraint the practicing kabbalist will experience a *real* physical satiation, a far cry from the clearly metaphorical satiety that one acquires through spiritual activities such as Torah study.[61] The consequence of this is that inasmuch as the "experience" of satiety can be attained through a somatized spiritual event and this event corresponds to the experience of the impoverished, there is a dialectic of opposites that constitutes the existing consuming body. The idealized body is determined in the dialogue with the actual body, a body that knows hunger full well. Arthur Frank effectively characterizes this insight of Michel Feher's by suggesting that "Feher's most important idea may be the emphasis on the body being perpetually reconstituted in processes which are each hermeneutic: the body's interior to its exterior, the relation of male to female, of body to state, and so forth. In these oppositions, neither term is fixed, but each mutually constitutes the other. The body is process, a hermeneutic recursion of oppositions which are themselves in perpetual reconstitution."[62]

CONCLUSION: EATING, IMAGINATION, HERMENEUTICS

In the foregoing discussion we have considered the phenomenon of mystical satiation as related in zoharic Kabbalah. It is by now a truism that our experiences of food are always colored by our preconceptions, cultural dispositions, and ritualizations associated with eating. For the mystics, longing for ecstasy in every bite, eating is a complex interplay of textual readings, consumption of food, and the imagination's new conceptualization of the activity of eating. In the film, *Like Water for Chocolate*, cooking is transformative for the diners, with the emotion of the cook being magically invested in the food; grief, joy, and passion are all transferred from food-preparer to food-consumer.[63] While the kabbalists do not describe the actual preparation of food, their preparation for eating elicits profound experience. Their preconceptions about eating and study, food and nourishment, all play a role in producing satisfaction on a range of physiological and psychological levels. In the end, what distinguishes the Jewish mystics from other Jewish eaters is the pursuit of the miraculous within the mundane, the inclination towards transcendence within the tidbit.

NOTES

[1] Gershom Scholem, *Major Trends in Jewish Mysticism* (New York: Schocken, 1941), 4.

[2] Scholem himself suggests a more spiritualized understanding of the verse by the kabbalists.

[3] Unless otherwise noted all Biblical translations are from *TANAKH: A New Translation of The Holy Scriptures According to the Traditional Hebrew Text* (Philadelphia: The Jewish Publication Society, 1985).

[4] For instances that extend the metaphor, see *Pesikta de-Rav Kahana, 'Aser te'aser* (vol. 1; ed. Mandelbaum; New York: Jewish Theological Seminary, 1961), 167; *Midrash Tanhuma* (Warsaw) *Re'eh* 17; *Midrash Tanhuma* (Buber) *Re'eh* 12; Maimonides, *Guide of the Perplexed* I 46. For an approach that is clearly more literally somatic, see Tosafot on *b. Ket* 104a s.v. *lo neheneiti* citing a midrash: "Before a person prays that the Torah should enter his body he should pray that delicacies do not enter his body." I have been unable to locate the source of this midrash. For the Torah residing in one's body serving an apotropaic function, see *b. Sanh.* 106b.

[5] Given that the *Zohar* refers to the notion of something holy being contained in one's inward parts in a number of passages, it is surprising that it never cites this verse (Ps 40:9). See, e.g., *Zohar* 1:32b; 2:3a, 167b, 197b; 3:141b (*Idra Rabba*), 296a (*Idra Zuta*); *Midrash ha-Ne'elam* 87b.

[6] This essay is part of a larger study: Joel Hecker, *Mystical Bodies, Mystical Meals: Eating and Embodiment in Medieval Kabbalah* (Detroit: Wayne State University Press), 2005.

[7] For an introduction to the literature of the *Zohar*, its authorship, and the doctrine of the *sefirot* and practice in relationship to them, see Arthur Green, *A Guide to the Zohar*, (Stanford: Stanford University Press, 2004).

[8] Daniel C. Matt, "Introduction," in *Zohar: The Book of Enlightenment* (Ramsey: Paulist Press, 1983), 31.

[9] Elliot R. Wolfson, "Forms of Visionary Ascent as Ecstatic Experience in the Zoharic Literature," *Gershom Scholem's Major Trends in Jewish Mysticism: 50 Years Later*, eds. Joseph Dan and Peter Schäfer (Tübingen: J.C.B. Mohr, 1993), 222-23. See also *Zohar* 1:88b (*Sitrei Torah*), which refers to the "delight of Torah in his inward parts" [*hamidu de'oraita be-mei'oi*]. Describing the resurrection of the dead, the *Zohar* gives assurance that people will regain the Torah that they had had in their original incarnation and that once again it will reside in their innards.

[10]This last story is echoed in the Gospel renditions of Jesus feeding the five thousand with a handful of loaves and fishes. See Matt 14:15-21, Mk 6:35-44, Luke 9:12-17, John 6:1-15. For discussion of these passages and their relation to the marvelous satiation provided by manna, see Peder Borgen, *Bread from Heaven: An Exegetical Study of the Concept of Manna in the Gospel of John and the Writings of Philo* (Leiden: Brill, 1965). See *Targum Tehillim* 78:25.

[11]Moses Cordovero, the sixteenth century kabbalist, suggests that "the blessing of the holy name" refers to the reciting of the blessing, '*ha-moẓi leḥem min ha'areẓ*' [Who brings forth bread from the earth], and that this blessing had the effect of drawing the aroma of the Garden of Eden into the manna. Moses Cordovero, *Or Yaqar* (vol. 8; Jerusalem: Ahuzat Israel, 1976), 77-78.

[12]In the *Zohar*, the Garden is generally a cognomen for the *Shekhinah*; thus, this passage indicates that the manna has come from this gradation within the Godhead.

[13]*b. Yoma* 75a. It could be argued that the *Zohar*'s direct adoption of an existing rabbinic source does not reflect personal experience. However, the kabbalistic practice of pneumatic engagement with the text militates against such reserve. See the discussion in the present author's article, Joel Hecker, "Eating Gestures and the Ritualized Body in Medieval Jewish Mysticism," *History of Religions* 40:2, 2000, 128. Caroline Walker Bynum has noted that the medieval feast was more an aesthetic and social event than a gastronomic one, being visually astounding in terms of illusions devised. Ordinary food was often an illusion so it was not surprising that bread, meaning the Eucharist, should adopt various tastes. See Caroline Walker Bynum, *Holy Feast and Holy Fast: The Religious Significance of Food to Medieval Women* (Berkeley: University of California Press, 1987), 60. Could it be that the Jews had similar feasts with visual and sensual surprises that made the rabbinic statement about the multi-flavored manna more readily acceptable? This possibility must remain in the realm of conjecture.

[14]See *Tanḥuma* (Warsaw) *Beshalaḥ* 20.

[15]On synesthesia in zoharic Kabbalah, see Elliot R. Wolfson, *Through a Speculum That Shines: Visionary Experience and Imagination in Medieval Jewish Mysticism* (Princeton: Princeton University Press, 1994), 287-88, 345-46.

[16]See *Zohar* 3:287b, in which the kabbalist raises his hands during prayer and thus receives illumination. In that instance the kabbalist induces the descent of the divine efflux as preparation for the revelation of esoterica.

[17]In textual situations such as the one that I am discussing here, the soul is not only body-like inasmuch as it is anthropomorphic; it is, indeed, the spiritual counterpart to the body and all of its limbs, so that an experience felt in the body is also *felt* in that part of the soul which resides in that part of the body.

[18]The theme of psychosomatic unity is one that has been used both in the philosophical literature regarding the problem of mind/body and inside/outside as well as in scholarship treating the history of the body. See for example, Mark Johnson, *The Body in the Mind: The Bodily Basis of Meaning, Imagination, and Reason* (Chicago: University of Chicago Press, 1987); Caroline Walker Bynum, *The Resurrection of the Body in Western Christianity, 200-1336* (New York, 1995); Michel Feher, ed., *Fragments for*

a History of the Human Body (New York: Zone Books, 1989), 14-15. Bynum writes that the medieval preachers assumed a person to be a psychosomatic unity and so understood unusual body events to be expressions of the soul and that the body was a means of access to the Divine. See Caroline Walker Bynum, "The Female Body and Religious Practice in the Later Middle Ages," in Feher, *Fragments*, 196. On the theoretical level, both Maurice Merleau-Ponty and Pierre Bourdieu have sought, in different ways, to overcome the body-soul dichotomy in their respective delineations of the self. For a valuable analysis comparing these two theorists' approaches, see Thomas J. Csordas, "Embodiment as a Paradigm for Anthropology," *Ethos* 18:1 (1990): 5-47.

[19]Bynum, *Holy Feast and Holy Fast*, 6, 246-56. Bynum argues that because the flesh was associated with the feminine, somatic expressions characterize women's spirituality. Bynum, "The Female Body and Religious Practice," 196. While this may explain some of the body-soul phenomena in the *Zohar*, what I am calling 'psychosomatic experiences' are often not explicitly addressing the body-soul polarity.

[20]Wolfson shows how circumcision is correlated with textual interpretation, theurgy, and the ability to see the *Shekhinah*, involving an erotic union with Her. Elliot R. Wolfson, "Circumcision, Vision of God, and Textual Interpretation: From Midrashic Trope to Mystical Symbol," *History of Religions* 27, 1987, 205-06.

[21]In the writings of Baḥya ben Asher we find considerable attention given to the idea that food will prepare one for supernal wisdom. See, for example, Baḥya ben Asher, *Shulḥan shel Arba* in *Kitve Rabbenu Baḥya* (ed. C. Chavel; Jerusalem: Mossad ha-Rav Kook, 1970), 457-8, 461, 493, 501-510; *ibid., Kad ha-Kemaḥ*, 186. See also *Zohar* 3:296a: "Knowledge is established in the belly."

[22] Joseph of Hamadan, "*Sefer Toledot Ha-Adam*," in *Sefer Ha-Malkhut* (Casablanca: Imprimerie Raẓon, 1930), 72b. This is a rare treatment of chewing in Castilian Kabbalah.

[23]Scholem, *Major Trends in Jewish Mysticism*, 180, 211; Tishby, *The Wisdom of the Zohar*, 1431-32.

[24]See, for example, *Zohar* 3:272a.

[25]See Neh 9:26.

[26]I Kgs 18:29.

[27]*Sefer ha-Rimmon*, mss. British Museum 107b-108a from the text cited in Scholem, *Major Trends in Jewish Mysticism*, 397-98 n. 154.

[28]For the common formulation that the manna is ground for the righteous in the heaven called *Shehaqim*, see *Ḥagigah* 12b; *Zohar* 3:26a and other zoharic sources in Margaliot n. 2; Yosef Giqatilla, *Sha'arei Orah*, 155-156; *Sha'arei Ẓedeq*, 16b. For other sources regarding the grinding of manna for the righteous in the world to come, see *Zohar* 3:292b (*Idra Zuta*); 3:236a; *Sefer ha-Rimmon*, 190, 404, *Seder Gan Eden*, in *Beit ha-Midrash*, 139; *Sod Eser Sefirot Belimah*, mss. a, 379-380; mss. b, 380; *Sefer Shushan 'Edut*, 338, 360. One Talmudic statement says that various groups had to travel different distances to gather the manna, contingent upon their spiritual status. *b. Yoma* 75a.

[29] See, for example, *Zohar* 3:246a *Raya Mehemna*.

[30] See also *Tiqqunei ha-Zohar* 3 140b.

[31] See Baḥya ben Asher's *Shulḥan shel Arba*, 457-9, 493 for repeated emphasis on this aspect of the curse and on the simplified economics of gathering manna. One rabbinic tradition emphasizes the difficulty encountered by God in attempting to provide sufficient food for humanity; see *Pesaḥ.* 118a. Further, there is praise for R. Ḥanina, who sustained himself week to week on a small portion of carob (*b. Ber.* 17b).

[32] The question of the correct hermeneutic as a point of distinction between the kabbalists and the non-kabbalists as presented in zoharic literature is one that has considerably exercised modern scholars of the Kabbalah. See Gershom Scholem, "The Meaning of the Torah in Jewish Mysticism," in *On the Kabbalah and Its Symbolism* (reprint 1965; trans. R. Manheim; New York: Schocken, 1960), 68-70; Tishby, *The Wisdom of the Zohar*, 1090-1101.

[33] See Baḥya ben Asher's *Shulḥan shel Arba*, 457-59, 493 for repeated emphasis on this aspect of the curse and on the simplified economics of gathering manna. There is a rabbinic tradition that emphasizes the difficulty for God to find food for humanity; see *Pesaḥ.* 118a. Further, there is praise for R. Ḥanina who sustained himself week to week on a small portion of carob (*b. Ber.* 17b).

[34] 2 Sam 9:7.

[35] The word *u-verakhta*, in the biblical text, can mean either "you *will* give thanks" or "you *shall* give thanks." The first suggests that in response to the abundance that the Israelites would find in their new land their natural response will be to bless God. This approach is found in Nahmanides' initial, *peshat* interpretation of the verse. The latter, suggesting that it is a commandment to bless God following a meal, is the normative understanding of the rabbis. See *b. Ber.* 21a. The JPS Bible translation offers "When you have eaten your fill, give thanks…"; See Jeffrey H. Tigay, *The JPS Torah Commentary: Deuteronomy* (Philadelphia: The Jewish Publication Society, 1996), 94-95.

[36] See *b. Ber.* 20b; *b. Yoma* 79b. On the nature of mystical intention in Jewish mysticism of Provence and Spain see Gershom Scholem, "The Concept of *Kavvanah* in the Early Kabbalah," in *Studies in Jewish Thought: An Anthology of German Jewish Scholarship* (ed. A. Jospe; trans. N. J. Jacobs; Detroit: Wayne State University Press, 1981). For Scholem, the term *kavvanah*, as used by the early kabbalists, refers to a voluntaristic, meditative contemplation that leads to *unio mystica* with the *sefirot*. In the later kabbalists, '*kavvanah*' takes on a magical meaning as well in terms of eliciting benefit for personal needs.

[37] The hermeneutical function of the terms *vadai* and *mamash*, each meaning roughly "in actuality" is to indicate the convergence of the signifying symbol and the mystical entity it signifies, the *peshat* and the *sod* [esoteric meaning]. For a discussion of this hermeneutical trope, see Matt, "'New-Ancient Words,'" 203-204; Elliot R. Wolfson, "Beautiful Maiden Without Eyes: *Peshat* and *Sod* in Zoharic Hermeneutics," in *The Midrashic Imagination: Jewish Exegesis, Thought, and History* (ed. M. Fishbane; Albany: State University of New York Press, 1993) 175-78, 199 n.140.

[38]There is one explicit statement in the *Zohar* saying that the physical, human body can be nourished with "spiritual food": "The portion of the body is fortunate because it can be nourished by the food of the soul" (*Zohar* 2:61b-62a).

[39]It would, of course, be unusual to be sated by an olive's-worth of bread.

[40] Literally, "it is all faces" [*kulo panim*].

[41] Joseph of Hamadan, *A Critical Edition of the* Sefer Taamey Ha-Miẓwoth (*'Book of Reasons of the Commandments) Attributed to Isaac Ibn Farḥi* (ed. M. Meier; New York: Brandeis University Press, 1974), 114.

[42] *Tov* is a cognmen for *Yesod*, the *sefirah* representing the phallus of the divine anthropos.

[43]The text cites the Scriptural verse with some minor deviation.

[44]*b. Ber.* 20b.

[45] Usually translated as "lift up His countenance to you," I have translated to reveal the play on words between the two passages: *yissa panav*, literally, "lift up His face" and *lo yissa fanav*, "will not lift up His face."

[46]Another bold example of fantastic bodies is the vision of the kabbalists with trees growing out of their heads (*Zohar* 3:203a). Regarding the body that is not a body, see Jean Vernant-Pierre, "Dim Body, Dazzling Body," in *Fragments for a History of the Human Body* (New York: Zone Books, 1989), 18-48.

[47] See *Sefer ha-Rimmon*, 210 where there is a causal link of eating and the praise of God. The poor person responds automatically—giving praise is the natural response to eating.

[48]The Talmud commentaries of Rashi suggest similar notions of magical satiation and psychosomatic unity. In one passage (*b. Sanh.* 65b, *s.v. 'igla tilta*), two rabbis create a partially grown calf as a regular activity on Friday afternoons. Rashi says that they were sated by this calf, notwithstanding its small size. When an opinion in the Talmud suggests that one gains an extra soul on the Sabbath, Rashi says that this means that "one's heart has greater capacity for rest and joy and is open to calmness. He will be able to eat and drink and his soul will be undisturbed." (*b. Beizah* 16a s.v. *neshamah yeteirah*). In a parallel passage he says, "His mind has greater capacity for eating and drinking" (*b. Ta'anit* 27b s.v. *neshamah yeteirah*). For another instance in Rashi of preternatural satiation see his commentary on Lev 26:6 s.v. *ve-akhaltem* where he also refers to a curse in the belly. Regarding Rashi's relationship to esoteric thought, see Ephraim Kanarfogel, *"Peering Through the Lattices": Mystical, Magical, and Pietistic Dimensions in the Tosafist Period* (Detroit: Wayne State University Press, 2000), 144-53.

[49]Consider the suggestive statement in *b. Bava Batra* 12b: "Before a person eats and drinks he has two hearts; after he eats and drinks he has only one heart." Though the rabbinic author may not be dealing with the strict dichotomy of body and soul assumed doctrinally by the kabbalists, the ability to appease the evil inclination and thus bring harmony between it and the good inclination suggests an understanding close to the psychosomatic unity that I have been suggesting in the zoharic literature.

See Daniel Boyarin, *Carnal Israel: Reading Sex in Talmudic Culture* (Berkeley: University of California Press: 1993), 61-76.

[50]See *m. Ruth Rab.* 5:15.

[51]See also *Zohar Hadash Ruth* 45c, 87c; *Zohar* 2:207b, 218a.

[52]*Zohar* 2:218a.

[53]See Elliot R. Wolfson, "Crossing Gender Boundaries in Kabbalistic Ritual and Myth," 95, 210 n.84.

[54]See Louis Jacobs, "Eating as an Act of Worship in Hasidic Thought," in *Studies in Jewish Religious and Intellectual History: Presented to Alexander Altmann* (ed. R. Loewe and S. Stein; Tuscaloosa: University of Alabama Press, 1979), 157-66; see also the article in this volume, Alan Nadler, "Holy Kugel! The Sanctification of East European Jewish Ethnic Foods at the Hasidic Tisch," in *Food and Judaism* (vol. 15; Studies in Jewish Civilization; ed. L. J. Greenspoon, et al.; Omaha: Creighton University Press, 2005).

[55]The term *be'ito* refers to the *Shekhinah*. See *Zohar* 3:58a.

[56]Unlike other passages that indicate that food comes from *Tif'eret*, here food is said to be coming from the *sefirah* of *Keter* as indicated by the cognomen *Razon*. See *Zohar* 2:62a; Tishby, *Wisdom of the Zohar*, 962.

[57]Scholem notes that the *Zohar* uses the same term for the poor as it does for the mystics themselves, *bnei heikhla de-malka*; see *Major Trends in Jewish Mysticism*, 234. See Tishby, *The Wisdom of the Zohar*, 1438-47. Yitzhak Baer argued that there was a valorization of poverty in the thought of the *Ra'aya Mehemna* and *Zohar*. J.F. Baer, "The Historical Background of the *Raya Mehemna*," *Zion* 5:1 (1939): 10-27. Both Scholem and Tishby are critical of Baer's thesis that the *Raya Mehemna* and the *Tiqqunei Zohar* glorify poverty as a religious value under the influence of the Franciscans in whose environs they lived. Tishby draws a distinction between "holy poverty" and the "holy poor," only the latter of which are lauded. He considers the option that the righteous are equated with the poor, suggesting that the author and his class of scholars were indeed not well patronized. The matter remains unresolved.

[58]*Zohar* 1:168a.

[59]Cf. *Zohar* 3:226a. This passage analyzed above, however, is another example of the *Zohar's* multifarious method of solving problems: harmonization of disparate entities and hierarchical privileging are both operative. There are, then, dual ideals with regard to satiety: one physical and one spiritual. Etan Fishbane has recently demonstrated how Moshe de Leon, in his *Sefer Shekel ha-Kodesh*, is similarly comfortable with a range of approaches to textual problems

[60]The ascetic orientation arises at least partly from the neo-Platonic grounding of the Kabbalah. Body/soul binaries often lead to negative representations of the body and to sharp curtailment of the enjoyment of physical activities. While this asceticism is most often discussed with regard to sexual relations, it finds expression with regard to eating and other activities as well. The attitude of the Castilian kabbalists towards sex has been debated by Idel and Wolfson. Idel reads the *Iggeret ha-Kodesh*, a kabbalistic manual for sexual relations, and regards it, justifiably, as being favorably disposed

towards the physical activity of sex itself. Wolfson, in contrast, stresses the kabbalists' adoration of the *Shekhinah*, and their valorization of their status as eunuchs through the course of the week. Elliot R. Wolfson, "Eunuchs Who Keep the Sabbath: Becoming Male and the Ascetic Ideal in Thirteenth-Century Jewish Mysticism," in *Becoming Male in the Middle Ages* (ed. J. J. Cohen and B. Wheeler; New York: Garland, 1997), 151-85.

[61] See *Zohar* 1:88b *Sitrei Torah*.

[62] Arthur W. Frank, "For a Sociology of the Body: An Analytical Review," in *The Body: Social Process and Cultural Theory* (ed. M. Featherstone, et al.; London: Sage, 1991), 47. See Michel Feher, "Introduction," in *Fragments*, 10-17.

[63] Alfone Arau, *Like Water for Chocolate*, Mexico, 1992.

Food of the Book or Food of Israel?
Israelite and Jewish Food Laws
in the Muslim Exegesis of Quran 3:93

Brannon Wheeler

INTRODUCTION

Although scholars have commented on the proximity and possible overlap of Islamic and Jewish food laws, little has been said about how the recognition of these shared concepts are viewed by Muslim and Jewish scholars.[1] The Quran itself comments on what are taken to be Israelite and Jewish food laws, and Muslim exegesis on these verses contains lengthy explanations of how and why Islamic food laws compare with those attributed to the Israelites and Jews. In fact, Muslim exegesis focuses on the Israelite food laws, still observed by the Jews in the time of the prophet Muhammad, as restrictions repealed by the revelation of the Quran. Just as Christian scholars used Jewish observance of certain food laws (along with circumcision and keeping the Sabbath) as indicators of the Jews' bondage to the law, Muslim exegetes argued that certain Israelite and Jewish food laws were imposed upon the Israelites (and unnecessarily followed by the Jews), along with the rest of the laws in the Torah, as a punishment for their sins.

The following pages examine select Muslim exegesis of certain Israelite food laws mentioned in the Quran, especially the understanding of how Muslim practice is distinguished from Judaism by acknowledging the circumstances of the imposition and subsequent abrogation of these laws. This article concentrates on the exegesis of Quran 3:93 and related verses to show how Muslim scholars recognized both the dependence of the Quran on the Bible and the supersession of the Bible by the Quran. It also shows how Israelite food laws were used by Muslim scholars to demarcate an exegetical image of the Jews in the time of the prophet Muhammad, an image that could demonstrate the status of the Bible as revealed but non-authoritative.

281

Q 3:93 AND ITS EXEGESIS

In the exegesis of Q 3:93, Muslim exegetes state that God made certain foods prohibited to the Israelites in the Torah because of their disobedience:

> Q 3:93: All food was allowed for the Israelites except that which
> Israel prohibited himself before the revelation of the Torah. Say:
> Bring the Torah and recite from it if you are truthful.

Muslim exegetes link this verse to the revelation of other verses (i.e., Q 4:18, 4:160, and 6:146) and to the claims of the Jews living in the time of the prophet Muhammad that these food prohibitions did not originate with Israel/Jacob but went back to the time of Abraham and Noah.[2] Muslim exegetes further maintain that the verse is connected to the Jewish attempt to hide references to the prophet Muhammad that were originally found in the text of the Torah.

Q 3:93 does not make explicit the reason for the addition of food prohibited in the Torah nor does it identify the food said to have been prohibited by Jacob. Two separate explanations are given by Muslim exegetes for the reason and the food prohibited, linked to different verses in the Torah. One explanation is that the food prohibited by Jacob was sinews, relating Q 3:93 to Gen 32:33. Ibn Kathir states that Jacob was afflicted with sciatica that would keep him awake all night, so he made a vow to God that if God cured him he would never again eat sinews, nor would his sons following him.[3] Other exegetes mention a report given on the authority of Ibn ʿAbbas that Jacob prohibited the eating of sinews because of his sciatica, and Qatadah states that the food prohibited by Jacob before the revelation of the Torah was sinews.[4]

Genesis 32:33

Genesis 32:33 also makes reference to the prohibition against eating sinews or the sciatic nerve, and it is noteworthy that these exegetical reports do not claim that such an interpretation of Q 3:93 originates with the prophet Muhammad or information derived from him. Note also that in Gen 32:33 Jacob seems not to be responsible for the prohibition of eating sinews though such a link is made explicit in the Muslim exegesis. According to Qurtubi, the reason for Jacob's prohibition of eating sinews is linked to his being attacked and injured by an angel:

> Jacob was returning from Harran, heading toward Jerusalem,
> at the time he was fleeing from his brother Esau. He was a
> strong man, and on the way he met an angel, and Jacob thought

that he was a robber, so he wrestled with him. The angel injured Jacob's thigh and then ascended into the sky. Jacob looked at it and his sciatic sinew was inflamed. In consequence of this, there was great pain. He could not sleep the night from the pain, and he passed the night screaming. So Jacob swore that if God cured him he would not eat sinews, and would not eat food in which there were sinews. He prohibited it himself. Following him, his children removed the sinews from meat.[5]

According to Qurtubi, the angel attacked Jacob only because he had not fulfilled an earlier vow he had made with God:

The reason for the angel injuring Jacob was that Jacob had vowed that if God gave him twelve sons and he reached Jerusalem safely, that he would sacrifice the last of his sons. This was an exemption from his vow.[6]

Such an interpretation retains the tradition of a vow linked with Jacob's prohibition of sinews, but here it is Jacob's not keeping his vow that leads to the injury that causes Jacob to prohibit sinews.

This interpretation parallels closely the account of Jacob's fight with the angel (or God) in Genesis 32. Gen 28:20-22 describes the vow Jacob makes with God to give to him a tithe of everything God gives him, on the condition that God return him safely to his father. This tithe is not a revealed requirement but an obligation that Jacob makes incumbent upon himself with his vow. Although Jacob acquires livestock and sons through the intervention of God in Genesis 29-32, there is no indication in Genesis that he makes a tithe of these possessions to God.

Rabbinic exegesis of Gen 32:23-33 also states that Jacob was attacked by God because Jacob had not fulfilled the vow he made in Gen. 28:20-22. The *Pirqe de Rabbi Eliezer* narrates how the angel stops Jacob and demands that he tithe his livestock and sons before attacking him.[7] *Targum Yerushalmi* on Gen 32:25 also states that the angel reminded Jacob of his vow before attacking.[8] In another account in the *Pirqe Rabbi Eliezer*, Jacob agrees to tithe his livestock but not his sons because he excluded the firstborn sons of the four mothers and counted only eight sons.[9] This corresponds to both Gen 32:15-22 and 33:1-11 in which Jacob does not make a tithe to God when he crosses the river and returns safely to his father but instead makes a tithe to his brother Esau, whom he calls "his lord" (Gen 32:19). *Tanhuma* and *Gen. Rab.* on Gen 32:21 stress that Jacob is giving to Esau what he should be tithing to God; Ramban states that Jacob had only given the tithe to Esau as an appeasement, thus demonstrating that Jacob did not trust God's promise to protect him from his brother.[10] This is made explicit in *Pirqe R. El.* 37, which states that at this time God reversed the promise made to Jacob in Gen 25:33, so that Esau would rule over Jacob until the end of the world.[11]

Rabbinic exegesis also maintains that the Israelites prohibited the eating of sinews because they were the cause of Jacob's injury, and Rashi also states that the prohibition of sinews was as a commemoration of Jacob's injury.[12] Quoting Jer 51:30 and Gen 41:51, the tractate *Ḥullin* links the injury received by Jacob with the fulfillment of his vow.[13] As reported by Qurtubi, rabbinic exegesis states that Jacob is injured by God because he does not fulfill a self-imposed vow and that it is his injury that leads to the eventual prohibition against eating sinews. Thus, Jacob brings the prohibition of sinews upon himself and the Israelites as a punishment for not fulfilling his vow.

Genesis 9:3

Muslim exegetes also link Q 3:93 with Genesis 9:3, by stating that the food prohibited by Jacob was camel meat and milk. In his exegesis of Q 3:93, Tabari mentions this interpretation:

> A group of Jews came to the Apostle of God and said: "Oh Abu al-Qasim, tell us what food Israel prohibited for himself before the revelation of the Torah." The apostle of God said: "I entreat you by the one who revealed the Torah to Moses, do you know that Israel-Jacob was very sick for a long time, so he made a vow to God that if God would cure him from this disease then he would prohibit his favorite food and drink. His favorite food was the meat of camel and his favorite drink was camel's milk."
> The Jews said: "By God, yes."[14]

Note that this interpretation, unlike those identifying the prohibited food as sinews, claims that it was the prophet Muhammad who said the prohibited food was camel meat and milk when he was challenged by the Jews.

That a particular verse was revealed in response to the objections of the Jews to the authority of the prophet Muhammad is well known in the exegesis of Quran verses relating to the Torah and the stories of the Israelites.[15] In this case, however, the revelation of Q 3:93 seems to come first, and it is to the revelation of this verse and its implications that the Jews are supposed to have objected. The Jews ask the prophet

Muhammad to tell them what food is meant by Q 3:93 after its revelation, but they do not accept his answer, which is not reported by Muslim exegetes to have been obtained through revelation.

Although Tabari's account does not mention the wrestling between Jacob and the angel, Qurtubi does relate two reports that make further connections. In his collection of *hadith* reports, Tirmidhi narrates a story in which the Jews ask the prophet Muhammad what Jacob forbade himself, to which the prophet Muhammad responds that Jacob used to live as a nomad and found that only camel meat and milk would relieve his sciatica, so Jacob prohibited camel meat and milk as a vow for God to relieve him of the sciatica.[16] Qurtubi also relates that Jacob renounced camel meat and milk as part of a vow that God would cure him of his sciatica. By linking Q 3:93 and the "good things" prohibited for the Jews mentioned Q 4:160, Qurtubi further emphasizes that Jacob's prohibition of camel meat and milk was due to his disobedience of God in not fulfilling his vow.

Abu al-Hasan al-Wahidi, in his book detailing the circumstances in which certain Quran verses were revealed, states that Q 3:93 was revealed because the Jews objected to the prophet Muhammad's claim that he was following the religion of Abraham:

> This [Q 3:93] was revealed when the Prophet said that he was following the religion of Abraham. The Jews objected: "how can this be when you eat the flesh of camels and drink their milk?" The Prophet said: "this was lawful for Abraham, and is also lawful for us." The Jews said: "everything we now consider unlawful was unlawful for both Noah and Abraham, and has thus come down to us." Then God revealed this verse [Q 3:93].[17]

With this interpretation, al-Wahidi relates the revelation of Q 3:93 to a claim of the Jews that the food prohibition followed by Jacob was one that was originally introduced by Noah and followed later by Abraham. Thus, in al-Wahidi's account, the Jews deny that Jacob prohibited camel meat and milk, but in the accounts of Tabari and Ibn Kathir the Jews affirm that Jacob did prohibit camel meat and milk. Here the emphasis is shifted away from Gen 32 and towards the food prohibitions associated with Noah in Gen 9:3.

According to Fakhr al-Din al-Razi, the Jews' claim that their current food prohibitions go back to the time of Noah is related to the mention of the Torah in the second part of Q 3:93. The Jews objected to the prophet Muhammad's claim that he followed the religion of Abraham because he ate camel meat and milk, which Abraham is not supposed to have consumed, following the prohibition of these things by Noah. Q 3:93 affirms that this food was allowed to Abraham, Ishmael, Isaac, and Jacob until Jacob prohibited it upon himself. The challenge for the Jews to produce the Torah is thus understood as a challenge for the Jews to show that there is a verse in the Torah in which camel meat and its milk was forbidden to Abraham.[18] Fakhr al-Din al-Razi thus concludes that the absence of any such verse in the Torah demonstrates the truth of Q 3:93 and the authority of the prophet Muhammad.

If the food prohibited by Jacob is understood to be sinews, then Gen 32:33 would confirm Q 3:93 that Jacob prohibited for himself food before the revelation of the Torah. If, however, the challenge to produce the Torah is only that the Jews could show evidence that there were any food prohibitions before Jacob, then the Jews could have cited Genesis 9:3-4 from the time of Noah. Genesis 9:3-4 mentions the food laws given to Noah and thus could be used to invalidate Q 3:93, that there were no food prohibitions before the time of Jacob. Such a reference is well known in rabbinic exegesis in the discussion of the so-called "Noahide laws" given to Noah and incumbent upon all of his descendants. The seven laws revealed to Noah are mentioned in the Babylonian Talmud:

> Our Rabbis taught: seven precepts were the sons of Noah commanded: social laws, to refrain from blasphemy, idolatry, adultery, bloodshed, robbery, and eating flesh cut from a living animal. R. Hanania b. Gamaliel said: also not to partake of the blood drawn from a living animal.[19]

The rabbis considered these precepts to be revealed law, to which would be added only the three additional precepts of keeping the Sabbath, honoring parents, and the social laws revealed to the Israelites at Marah.

By identifying the food prohibited in Q 3:93 as camel meat and milk, Muslim exegesis precludes the use of Gen 9:3-4 against Q 3:93. Instead, the absence of a verse prohibiting camel meat and milk before the revelation of the Torah becomes a critique of the rabbinic claim that the laws of the Torah were in effect before the time of Moses. Fakhr al-Din al-Razi makes such a linkage explicit:

> A number of proofs for the prophethood of Muhammad were indicated by this. The first is that the Jews were unable to deny this issue of abrogation. Second, their lies became apparent

because they attributed things to the Torah which were not in it and denied things from it which were in it. Third, the Apostle was an illiterate man who could not read nor write and was thus prevented from knowing these heavenly secrets from the sciences of the Torah except by information from heaven.[20]

The idea that the Jews attempted to hide or deny the existence of Gen 9:3, because it would appear to confirm Q 3:93, corresponds closely to the implication of other verses referring to the difference between Muslim and Israelite or Jewish food prohibitions such as Q 6:145 and Q 5:3.

The rabbis themselves recognized the difficulty with the concept that the food laws of the Torah were in effect before the time of Moses. Genesis 7:2 and Gen 8:20 both seem to indicate that the food laws concerning clean and unclean animals were known to Noah. Rashi recognizes this, but goes on to conclude that Noah did not know the Torah. It was only that God ordered Noah to take seven clean animals in Gen 7:2 so that an offering could be made of them in Gen 8:20.[21] *Midrash Rabbah* on Gen. 8:20 explains that Noah only knew which animals to sacrifice because God had commanded him to bring extra ones of certain species; if Noah knew the Torah, then why did he make a sacrifice from the animals forbidden by the Torah as offerings?[22] Other rabbinic sources mention that Noah did not actually perform the sacrifice mentioned in Gen. 8:20 and that knowledge of the Torah skipped Noah and went directly from Enoch to Shem.[23] The seven Noahide precepts were given to Noah because God decided that all of the Torah was too much to impose upon Noah after the flood.[24]

The Muslim exegetical claim that it was camel meat and milk referred to in Q 3:93 is consistent with Jewish and Christian understandings of Gen. 9:3 as a relaxing of the earlier food prohibitions imposed upon Adam in Gen 3:18-19. According to *m. Rab.* on Gen 9:3, Adam was allowed to eat only the foliage of plants, but not meat.[25] The reference to the "good things" forbidden in Q 4:160 is paralleled by Adam's punishment: he was forbidden good foods that had been permitted him before.[26] Genesis 3:18-19 lists the food laws given to Adam as punishment for his eating from the forbidden tree in Eden, laws that are seen as a substitute for Adam's earlier access to the Tree of Life.[27] Just as Jacob's breaking of his vow results in the prohibition of sinews or camel meat and milk, so Adam's sin of eating from the forbidden tree in Eden results in food prohibitions. After Gen 9:3 there are no additional food prohibitions until those associated with Jacob in Gen 32:33.

Following Jacob, the next food prohibitions come when the Torah is revealed to Moses, which, according to Muslim exegesis, is imposed as a punishment for the Israelites' disobedience.

FURTHER CONSIDERATIONS

Muslim exegetes recognized the close relationship of the Quran and Bible, and debated how the Quran and its status as law were related to the revealed but non-canonical status of the Bible. One of the issues central to this debate is the Muslim claim that the Jews removed from the Torah references to the prophet Muhammad. There are various accounts in which Jewish converts to Islam attest to the existence of such references in earlier copies of the Torah.[28] Some Muslim exegesis, such as that on Q 2:79, maintains that the Jews in the time of the prophet Muhammad altered the text of the Torah to eliminate the name of Muhammad.[29] Other exegesis explains that God recalled part of the Torah from the Israelites as punishment for their disobedience.[30] Such accounts are of special significance to the development of Islamic legal theories concerning how the Quran supersedes the Torah and other earlier revealed texts.

Many of these theories regarding the relative authority of the Quran and Torah are relevant to the Muslim exegesis of verses, such as Q 3:93, that are understood in the context of a conflict between the prophet Muhammad and the Jews of his time. The well-known issue of the so-called "stoning verse"—removed from the text of the Quran, but shown by the prophet Muhammad to be present in the Torah despite the objections of the Jews—is closely related to claims that the Jews also obfuscated references to Muhammad in the Torah.[31] In the case of the stoning verse, Ibn al-Jawzi explains that the Jews were not hiding the fact that the punishment of stoning existed in the Torah, but rather that the Torah had the same verses in it and thus confirmed the Quran.[32] As is the case with Q 3:93, Muslim exegesis maintains that the Torah and the traditions of the Jews themselves demonstrate the veracity and authority of the prophet Muhammad.

Whether or not the contexts associated with the exegesis of Q 3:93 represent historical encounters between the prophet Muhammad and the Jews of his time, they do reflect an exegetical dialogue about the status of the Quran in relation to the Torah. That the challenge to produce the Quran was a means to verify Q 3:93, and the authority of the prophet Muhammad's interpretation of this verse, demonstrates some of the ways Muslim exegesis defined the relationship between the Quran and Torah. The identification of the prohibited food with sinews and camel allowed Muslim exegetes to link Q 3:93 not only with Gen. 32:33 and Gen. 9:3, but also with Jewish and Christian exegetical traditions regarding these biblical passages.

By relating Q 3:93 to different verses from Genesis, Muslims exegesis is able to emphasize different aspects of how the Quran is designed to supercede the Torah. Relating Q 3:93 to Gen 32:33 stresses that the food prohibitions followed by the Israelites and Jews originated not as divine revelation, but as a result of Jacob's vow, and ultimately his disobedience. The link to Gen 9:3 highlights God's imposition of more restrictive food laws upon the Israelites on account of their disobedience. The existence of the Torah is thus integral to the Muslim exegesis of Q 3:93, both as evidence of the prophet Muhammad's authority and as proof that God imposed special laws upon the Israelites as punishment.

Muslim exegesis insists that the Israelites instituted their own laws and then attributed these laws to divine revelation. Tabari relates this conclusion to his interpretation of Q 3:93:

> By this [Q 3:93] God meant that he had not prohibited any food, before the revelation of the Torah, to the Israelites—the Israelites being the descendents of Jacob son of Isaac son of Abraham the friend of God. Rather, all of this was allowed for them except what Jacob had prohibited to himself. His descendents prohibited it, introducing a customary practice [*istinana*] on the authority of their father Jacob without God's prohibiting this to them by inspiration, revelation, nor from the word of his prophet to them, before the revelation of the Torah.[33]

According to Tabari, what the context of Q 3:93 demonstrates is that the Jews made a false claim in saying that their food prohibitions go back to a time before Jacob and that they were of divine origin. Tabari underlines that it was the descendents of Jacob who introduced the practice and then attributed it to Jacob without his consent:

> Others say: there was nothing from that [food] prohibited for them nor did God prohibit it in the Torah, but it is something they prohibited themselves following their father. Then they attributed its prohibition to God. Thereby they lied about God in attributing this to him. God said to our prophet Muhammad:

"Say to them Muhammad: if you are truthful, bring the Torah
and recite so that we will see whether this is in it or not."[34]
Tabari further concludes that the reason the Jews were challenged to
produce the Torah was so that they would be forced to admit that the
Torah and their own interpretations of it demonstrated the same point
as Q 3:93.

The implication of this interpretation is that the food prohibitions
followed by the Israelites and the Jews were first introduced by the
Israelites themselves and only later confirmed in the revelation of the
Torah to Moses as a punishment:

The Jews said: "We only prohibit that which Israel prohibited
himself, and Israel prohibited sinews for he was afflicted with
sciatica, afflicting him in the night but leaving him in the
morning. Therefore he swore that if God cured him from it he
would not eat sinews ever again." Subsequently, God prohibited
it for the Jews. Then he said: "Say: bring the Torah and recite it
if you are truthful"; this was not prohibited upon you except
by your own injustice. Likewise the word of God: "on account
of the injustice of those who are Jews we prohibited for them
good things which were allowed for them" [Q 4:160].

God prohibited for the Israelites in the Torah that which
Israel had prohibited himself, on account of their rebellion
against themselves and their injustice to the Torah. Say
Muhammad: "Jews, come and deny that this is in the Torah,
recite it if you are truthful, that God did not prohibit this for
you in the Torah, but that you prohibited it on the basis of
Israel's prohibition of it on himself."[35]

Ibn Kathir sees Q 3:93 as reference to one of many examples from the
Torah demonstrating that God did impose different laws at different
times and that the Torah imposed prohibitions not in effect before its
revelation:

God showed that abrogation [*naskh*], the occurrence of which
they denied, was possible and had taken place. God had written
in their book, the Torah, that when Noah left the ark God
permitted for him to eat from all the animals of the earth. Then
after that, Israel forbid himself the meat of camel and its milk,
and his sons followed him in this. The Torah came forbidding
this and other things in addition to this.

God allowed Adam to marry his sons to his daughters, and then this was prohibited after that. To take a concubine as a wife was permitted in the revealed law [*shariʾah*] of Abraham, as Abraham did with Hagar when he took her as a concubine along with Sarah. God made this likewise prohibited in the Torah for the Jews. Likewise, marriage to two sisters at the same time was allowed just as Jacob did marrying two sisters. Then God prohibited this for the Jews in the Torah.

All of this was written for them in the Torah which they have. This is precisely abrogation. Of a similar nature is what God legislated for Jesus in his allowing some of what was forbidden in the Torah. Why did the Jews not follow him but instead lied about him and opposed him? Of a similar nature is that which God sent with the prophet Muhammad from the religion of the upright and straight path, the community of Abraham. Why did they not believe?[36]

For Ibn Kathir, the dispute behind Q 3:93 was the Jews' refusal to admit that abrogation did occur in the Torah and that the prophet Muhammad's use of such abrogation is merely a return to the original covenant made with Abraham, a covenant that had been displaced by the Torah, which was revealed specifically and only to the Israelites as a punishment.

This attitude toward abrogation and supercession corresponds also with some early Christian views of the Old Testament. Romans 4 states that the Mosaic law of the Torah is applicable only to the Israelites, while following the religion of Abraham is for all of his descendants including the Gentiles. Galatians 3 refers to the Torah as a curse, temporarily suspending the promise made to Abraham in Gen. 17:4-8.[37] Some Christian exegesis, such as the *Epistle of Barnabas*, takes the implication of such passages to be that the Torah was revealed as a punishment for the Israelites, specifically for their worship of the golden calf.[38] Christian exegesis also focuses on the revelation of food prohibitions in the Old Testament, with special emphasis on Gen 9:3.[39] The rabbis also recognized the significance of the golden calf episode and its implications for the Israelites' reception of the promises made to Abraham.[40]

According to the Muslim exegesis of Q 3:93, the revelation of the Torah entails specific consequences for the Israelites and the Jews who follow after them. By linking Q 3:93 to other verses referring to food

prohibitions such as Q 4:160, Muslim exegetes emphasize that the
Torah reminds Jews that the Israelites were prohibiting good things,
which should otherwise be enjoyed, as a punishment. The revelation of
the Torah is also a revocation of the covenant made with Abraham. The
Israelites forfeited their claim to the promise made to Abraham and
instead received stricter laws to remind them of their sinful disobedience.
With the revelation of the Quran, the prophet Muhammad offers to
Jews a chance to renounce the disobedience of the Israelites and return
to the original covenant with Abraham. For this reason, the Quran and
Islamic law is to abrogate all previous revelations:

> God states that he wrote for them the prohibition of this in the
> Torah, but God abrogated all of this with the law [*shari'ah*] of
> the prophet Muhammad. He caused to be allowed for them
> what used to be forbidden for them as a punishment by means
> of hardening their burden with great prohibitions. The
> prohibition ceases with the prophet Muhammad and his
> community. Incumbent upon all of creation is the religion of
> Islam, what it allows, what it prohibits, what it commands,
> and what it forbids.[41]

The claim here is not that the Quran supercedes the Torah by
implementing a new revelation, but rather that the Quran revives the
original revelation that was temporarily suspended with the Torah because
of the sins of the Israelites.[42]

To allow the Quran to be identified with the Torah would have
several consequences for the authority of the emerging classical law
schools. By developing reasons to doubt the soundness of the extant
text of the Torah and the methods or motives of the Jews in their
interpretation of it, ninth and tenth century scholarship was able to
maintain the privileged position of the Quran. Provided such reasons,
it would be possible to retain and explain the passages in the Quran
that seem to link and conflate the prophet Muhammad and Moses or
the Quran and the Torah. The practice of the prophet Muhammad had
been defined as the necessary and most authoritative interpretation of
the text of the revelation. The Quran, whatever its precise relationship
to earlier revealed books, was defined as the most clear revelation of
God's principles, relatively unaffected by faulty textual transmission,
and guaranteed by the evidence of the prophet's practice as interpreted
by the classical schools of law. Defined in this way as a source of Islamic
law and the legal authority of the schools, the Quran and its status as

"canon" had to be distinguished from other revealed but no longer authoritative books.

NOTES

[1] For an exception to this, see Michael Cook, "Early Islamic Dietary Law," *Jerusalem Studies in Arabic and Islam* 7 (1986). Also see the useful comments in M. Cook, *Commanding Right and Forbidding Wrong in Islamic Thought* (Cambridge: Cambridge University Press, 2000). Specific instances of the recognition and/or attribution of food laws shared by Jews and Muslims are discussed in Steven Wasserstrom, *Between Muslim and Jew: The Problem of Symbiosis under Early Islam* (Princeton: Princeton University Press, 1995), especially 102-103. The commonality is recognized by Emory C. Bogle, *Islam: Origin and Belief* (Austin: University of Texas Press, 1998), but the conclusion that the "numerous Qur'anic references to food merely state that Muslims should follow the law of the Jews," 39, is blatantly incorrect.

[2] al-Zamakhshari, *al-Kashshaf 'an haqa'iq ghawamid al-tanzil wa 'uyun al-aqawil ri wujuh al-ta'wil* (Beirut: Dar al-Kutub al-'Ilmiyah, 1415), 1:377, s.v. Q 3:93-94.

[3] Ibn Kathir, *Tafsir al-Qur'an al-'azim* (Beirut: Dar al-Jil, n.d.), 1:361, s.v. Q 3:93.

[4] al-Tabari, 3:350-351, s.v. Q 3:93. This account is also found in al-Razi, s.v. Q 3:93.

[5] al-Qurtubi, *al-Jami' li-ahkam al-Qur'an* (Beirut: Dar Ihya' al-Turath al-'Arabi, 1405), 4:134-134, s.v. Q 3:93. See Mahmoud Ayoub, *The Qur'an and its Interpreters: the House of 'Imran* (Albany: SUNY, 1992), 252.

[6] al-Qurtubi, 4:135, s.v. Q 3:93. See Ayoub, *The Qur'an and its Interpreters*, 2:252.

[7] Hereafter, all biblical and talmudic texts will be referred to by title and chapter according to the usage of the Society of Biblical Literature *Handbook of Style*, P. Alexander et al., eds. (Peabody: Hendrickson, 1999).

[8] Citations from the Jerusalem Talmud are taken from the *Miqra'ot Gedalot*.

[9] *Pirqe R. El.* 37. See Gerald Friedlander, trans., *Midrash Pirke de Rabbi Eliezer* (4th ed.; London, 1916; New York: Sepher-Hermon, 1981), 284.

[10] A similar theme is reflected in some of the accounts which, building on the mention that Jacob was afraid of his older brother, state that the angel attacked Jacob in order to help prepare him for his encounter with Esau. See Abkir in *Yal* 1:132 and *Ephr* 1:181. Other accounts mention that the blessing that Jacob demanded of the angel was a confirmation of his birthright over Esau. See the *Zohar* 3:45 and *Tanh* 1:127.

[11] A similar stress upon Jacob's mistake and God's modification of his promise is found in *Gen. Rab.* 76:2-3, 11 on Gen 32:21. Also see Gerson D. Cohen, "Esau as a Symbol in Early Medieval Thought," in *Studies in the Variety of rabbinic Culture* (Philadelphia: Jewish Publication Society, 1991), 243-69.

[12] See, for example, *Sefer ha-Zohar* 1:203; Midrash ha-Gadol 1:513-524; Da'at, Hadar, and Pa'aneah on Gen 32:33. *Gen. Rab.* on Gen 32:33 (78:6) states that although God permitted the eating of sinews, the Israelites prohibited them anyhow. Linked to Gen 32:33, this act of piety seems to be a commemoration of Jacob's injury.

[13]See Rashi on Gen 32:33. Also see "Gid ha-Nashe" in *Hidushe rabenu Yitzhaq br Abraham 'al halakhot ha-Rif me-Msekhet Ḥullin* (Jerusalem).

[14]al-Tabari, 3:352, s.v. Q 3:93. See Ayyoub, *The Qur'an and its Interpreters*, 251.

[15]For an overview of this genre of explanation, see Jalal al-Din al-Sayuti, *al-Itiqan fi 'ulum al-Qur'an* (ed. M. D. al-Bugha; Damascus: Dar Ibn Kathir, 1416), ch. 9; Badr al-Din al-Zarkashi, *al-Burhan fi 'ulum al-Qur'an* (ed. Y. 'Abd al-Rahman al-Mar'ashli et al.; Beirut: Dar al-Ma'arifah, 1415), ch. 1, (note the many bibliographic references on 115-16).

[16]al-Qurtubi, 4:134, S.V. Q 3:93.

[17]al-Wahidi, *Asbab al-nuzul* (Beirut: al-Maktabah al-Thaqafiyah, 1410), 61, s.v. Q 3:93. This is also found in Ayoub, *The Qur'an and its Interpreters*, 250, s.v. Q 3:93. A similar account is found in Fakhr al-Din al-Razi, *Mafatih al-ghayb* (Beirut: Dar al-Kutub al-'Ilmiyah, 1411), 8:120, s.v. Q 3:93.

[18]Fakhr al-Din al-Razi, 8:120, s.v. Q 3:93. Also see Ayoub, *The Qur'an and Its Interpreters*, 2:253-254.

[19]*b. Sanh.*, 56b.

[20]Fakhr al-Din al-Razi, 8:120, s.v. Q 3:93. See Ayoub, *The Qur'an and its Interpreters*, 2:253-254.

[21]Note that Rashi seems to suggest that Noah was commanded to take seven clean animals, three pairs and one extra, not seven pairs of clean animals. The odd clean animal was the one to be sacrificed after the subsiding of the Flood. See Minhas Yehudah, Sifre Ha-Hamim and Bi'r Yitzhaq on Gen 7:2. Compare with *Gen. Rab.* 7:2 (34:9) and *Tanḥ.* Vay-yakhel 6.

[22]See *Gen. Rab.* 8:20 (34:9) and Levush Ha-Orah.

[23]See *Sefer ha-Zohar*, "Noah 29." Also see the account in *Tanḥ. Noah* 9. Note the account in al-Razi in his exegesis of Q 3:9 that the Jews claimed that the prohibition of camel had been in effect since the time of Adam (8:119-120). See Ayoub, *The Qur'an and its Interpreters*, 2:253-254.

[24]See *Sefer ha-Zohar*, "Noah 29" and compare *Tanḥ. Noah* 9. Also see *m. Tanḥ.* Buber 2:127. See also *m. Rab.* 26:1 and 34:5; *Pirqe R. El.* 23, and Gen 8:20 and 22:9 in Yerushalmi; Ginzberg, 1:165-66.

[25]Also see Origen's homily on Gen (1:17) where he states that to Adam God permitted the eating of vegetables and fruits but eating meat is only later allowed after the covenant made with Noah. See Ronald E. Heine, trans., *Origen: Homilies on Genesis and Exodus* (Washington: The Catholic University of America Press), 69-70. A similar interpretation is given by Philo. See Ralph Marcus, trans., *Philo: Questions and Answers on Genesis* (Cambridge: Harvard University Press, 1953), 2:57 on Gen 9:3, 143. See also the article in this volume, Gary A. Rendsberg, "The Vegetarian Ideal in the Bible," in *Food and Judaism* (vol. 15; Studies in Jewish Civilization; ed L. J. Greenspoon et al.; Omaha: Creighton University, 2005).

[26]See *Avot R. Nathan* 42, 116-117 on the prohibition of good foods and the substitution of agriculture for the fruits in the Garden of Eden.

[27]In *m. ha-Gadol* on Gen 3:24 it is said that the Torah replaces the Tree of Life for Adam as punishment for his sin. In his interpretation of Gen 3:24, Philo states that Adam could always look back to the Garden and remember his expulsion. See Marcus, *Philo*, on Gen 3:24 (1:57). Also see the excursus in Gen 3:24 in Yerushalmi.

[28]See, for example, the *hadith* taken from Ibn Sa'd, 7:309-310. Versions of this can be found in Ibn Hajar, *Tahdhib al-tahdhib*, s.v. A large number of the traditions relating to the life of Ka'b can be found listed in Sezgin, 1:304-305. There is a discussion of this and other versions of Ka'b's conversion in M. Pearlmann, "Another Ka'b al-Ahbar story," *Jewish Quarterly Review* 45 (1954): 48-58. For a longer, but dated study of Ka'b, see Israel Wolfensohn, *Ka'b al-Ahbar und seine Stellung im Hadi• und in der islamischen Legendenliteratur,* Dissertation at Johann Wolfgang Goethe-University of Frankfurt (Gelnhausen: F.W. Kalbfleisch, 1933).

[29]See, for example, al-Tabari, *Jami' al-bayan fi tafsir al-Qur'an,* s.v. Q 2:79.

[30]This sort of argument can be found in al-Jassas, *Ahkam al-Qur'an* (Hyderabad: Dar al-Khulafah, 1335), 2:398-399. There is a brief discussion of this point in John Wansbrough, *Quranic studies* (Oxford: Oxford University Press, 1977), 190-192.

[31]On this issue, see Brannon Wheeler, "The 'New Torah': Some Early Islamic Views of the Quran and other Revealed Books." *Graeco-Arabica* 7-8 (1999-2000): 371-604.

[32]This is discussed in Wansbrough, 195.

[33]al-Tabari, *Jami' al-bayan fi tafsir al-Qur'an* (Beirut: Dar al-Kutub al-'Ilmiyah, 1412), 3:348, s.v. Q 3:93.

[34]al-Tabari, 3:348, s.v. Q 3:93.

[35]al-Tabari, 3:348, s.v. Q 3:93.

[36]Ibn Kathir, 1:361, s.v. Q 3:93. See Ayoub, *The Qur'an and Its Interpreters,* 2:251-252.

[37]For an overview of these ideas, see James Kugel and Rowan Greer, *Early biblical Interpretation* (Philadelphia: Westminster, 1986), 126-54, esp. 142-45.

[38]On the views of Barnabas, see Pierre Prigent, *Les testimonia le Chréstianisme primitif: Épître de Barnabé i-xvi et ses sources* (Paris: Études bibliques, 1961); L.W. Barnard, *Studies in the Apostolic Fathers and their Background* (Oxford: Balckwell, 1966), ch. 9; K. Wengst, *Tradition und Theologie des Barnabasbriefes* (Berlin: Walter de Gruyter, 1971). For an overview of the golden calf episode in the biblical context, see G.W. Coats, *Rebellion in the Wilderness* (Nashville: Abingdon, 1968) and I. Lewy, "The Story of the Golden Calf Reanalyzed," *Vetus Testamentum* 9 (1959): 318-22.

[39]See *Dialogue with Trypho,* 46. A similar argument is made for the practice of keeping the Sabbath, 29; Justin Martyr, *Dialogue with Trypho,* 20 in *Saint Justin Martyr* (trans. T. B. Falls; New York: Christian Heritage), 178; Aphrahat, *Demonstration* 15 in Jacob Neusner, trans., *Aphrahat and Judaism: the Christian-Jewish Argument in Fourth-Century Iran* (Leiden: E.J. Brill, 1971), ch. 5, 53-54; Tertullian, *Against the Jews,* 1:6-7, *Corpus Christianorum* 2, 1340. For a brief discussion of this remark, see Pier Cesare Bori, *The Golden Calf and the Origins of the Anti-Jewish Controversy* (trans. D. Ward; Atlanta: Scholars, 1990), 15. On Tertullian's views of the Torah, see C. Aziza, *Tertullien et le judaïsme* (Paris: Les Belles Lettres, 1977).

[40]See *Antiquities*, 3:95-101; Thackeray 360-365. See Bori, *Golden Calf*, 13.

[41]Ibn al-'Arabi, 2:296, s.v. Q 6:146.

[42]Ibn Hazm states that the Islamic Shariah applies to all people, Muslim and non-Muslim alike. See his *al-Ahkam fi usul al-ahkam* (Beirut: Dar al-Kutub al-'Ilmiyah, n.d.), Chapter 30, 2:103-114. Note, however, especially as evinced in the legal exegesis surrounding Q 5:41-45, that Ibn Hazm's claim is not without some disagreement. Hanafi scholars, for example, allow Jews and Christians to treat wine and pigs as property. Abu Hanifah and Muhammad al-Shaybani also allow Jews, Christians and Magians to regulate themselves in marriage according to their own laws. See Abu Bakr al-Jassas, *Ahkam al-Qur'an* (Beirut: Dar al-Kitab al-'Arabi, n.d.), 2:234-237, s.v. Q 5:42. For further discussion of the application of marriage laws, see al-Tahawi, *Sharh ma'ani al-athar*, 4:143.

Meals as Midrash:
A Survey of Ancient Meals
in Jewish Studies Scholarship

Jonathan D. Brumberg-Kraus

At my synagogue in Providence, Rhode Island, there is a sort of folk wisdom, remembered especially around Purim, that all Jewish holidays can be reduced to one succinct explanation: "They tried to get us, God rescued us, let's eat!" We are a religion that solemnly prays ancient recipes or menus to mark each Sabbath or new moon. "Gastronomic Judaism" is the catchphrase among contemporary sociologists of Judaism to explain a modern secular form of Jewish identity. Perhaps even more than the covenant at Mt. Sinai, blintzes and bagels make many of us "members of the tribe." Some say that the holiday observed by more Jews than any other is Passover—and it is the one more than any other that centers on a big meal. Meals play such a central role in Jews and Judaism that to understand them is perhaps the most direct route to understanding the core values of Jews and Jewish tradition. This assumption, and the experiences behind it, shapes any discussion of meals and Judaism.

Therefore, it will not be enough to limit this survey to a synchronic analysis of what Jewish studies tell us about meals in the Greco-Roman period, the main focus of this essay. A significant number of Jewish approaches to meals are diachronic; in other words, how were the meal practices in question a reworking of earlier biblical and Jewish traditions, and into what were they transformed subsequently? The answer to this question is that meals themselves become midrash, a commentary or exposition on biblical texts. Midrash is, perhaps, the fundamental mode of expressing or exploring the Jewish worldview, if there is such a thing. Sometimes midrash is explicit, as when ritualized words or other table talk are linked to the eating to make a point: table blessings, the Haggadah narrative at the Passover Seder, or any "words of Torah spoken over the table." At other times it is implicit, subconscious.

In place of the long destroyed Temple altar, every Jewish table became a substitute *mikdash me'at* [little Temple], a microcosm of Jewish experience. Jews intuitively seem to gravitate to meals as ritual strategies to link themselves to and to differentiate themselves from past history, present neighbors, and future hopes or fears. Every Jewish meal, or at least any self-consciously Jewish meal, however broadly one defines "Jewish," is, in a sense, a feast of history. On some subconscious level, it is always a statement about history and within history.

Therefore, I will survey "Ancient Meals and Jewish Studies" so as to try to do justice both to my sense of the diachronic dimension of meals in Judaism and Jewish studies and to the specifics of meals in the Greco-Roman period. As I see it, Jewish studies have contributed certain key ideas to the understanding of meals in the Greco-Roman world, summarized in the following eight theses:

1. The Pharisees were a table fellowship group.
2. The Passover Seder was a symposium.
3. Jewish meal rituals replaced the biblical Temple sacrifices.
4. Jewish meal rituals combine food and table talk.
5. Distinguishing between fit and unfit foods is a crucial component of Jewish meals.
6. Meals establish Jewish identity; they function to differentiate competing Jewish groups from one another and between Jews and Gentiles.
7. Jewish meal practices tend to be less ascetic than Christian and other Greco-Roman philosophical groups.
8. There is a tension between vegetarianism and meat eating in Jewish meals.

Most of these ideas are generally accepted both within Jewish studies and in cognate fields. Some, such as "the Pharisees were a table fellowship group" and "the Passover Seder was a symposium," are more controversial. And two of these theses, that "Jewish meal rituals combine food and table talk" and that "there is a tension between vegetarianism and meat eating in Jewish meals," are probably too new to the discussion to have generated either universal assent or controversy. It is certainly fair to say that this list represents my idiosyncrasies and biases. Nevertheless, based on my observation of the field, I think that I am not reading too much into the scholarship. Indeed, these eight theses might provide some useful guideposts to navigate more broadly the rich and varied territory of meals in Jewish studies.

THE PHARISEES WERE A TABLE FELLOWSHIP GROUP

The impact of Jacob Neusner's thesis in *From Politics to Piety: The Emergence of Pharisaic Judaism*, that the Pharisees were a table fellowship group, has been profound and widespread in New Testament and Jewish studies.[1] Baruch Bokser, whose book on *The Origins of the Passover Seder* has in its own right contributed much to the discussion of meals in Jewish studies, assumes Neusner's position on the Pharisees and thus nicely summarizes it as follows:

The activities of the Pharisees apparently were centered on a table fellowship. Meals enabled them to express their piety and belief that God's presence was not limited to the temple, but could be experienced in one's home. Therefore, the Pharisees taught that people should prepare and eat a regular meal as priests prepare and eat consecrated food.[2]

In my view, their procedures for acquiring food and maintaining households or other spaces fit for such gatherings were strategies to influence non-Pharisees to "convert" to Pharisaism.[3] Also following Neusner, New Testament scholar Gerd Theissen argues that these practices were a programmatic "intensification of Jewish norms," which distinguished the Pharisees from other Jewish renewal movements in first century Palestine.[4] Similarly, Marcus Borg says that the earliest Christian traditions about Jesus and his followers understood the Pharisees as a "holiness movement" actively competing against the "mercy movement" of Jesus.[5] The Pharisees' characteristic behavior of eating tithed, ordinary food in a state of ritual purity had special, symbolic importance in the competition for followers among various Jewish renewal movements of the first century.[6] Neusner's discussion of the Pharisees as a table fellowship group is complemented by the earlier studies of rabbinic traditions about *haverim, ne'emanim* [Torah-literate Jews], and their antithesis, the *ammei ha-aretz* [illiterate Jews].[7] The *havurot*, whom many scholars identify with the Pharisees, distinguished their full members [*haverim*] from initiates or novices [*ne'emanim*] and from non-members [*ammei ha-aretz*] on the basis of the food-tithing and purity rules for eating that they did or did not take on themselves.[8] The *havurot* were probably responsible for the "Blessing of Invitation" [*birkat ha-zimmun*],[9] a call-response prayer formula introducing the recitation of a grace after the meal, and were probably the group from which the rabbinic Passover Seder itself emerged.[10] Many scholars identify these rabbinic *haverim* and *ne'emanim* with the Pharisees of the New Testament, and the "tax collectors and sinners" with the *ammei ha-aretz*, although some demur.[11] Finally, the *havurot* of the Second Temple period, whether Pharisaic, Essene, or groups like Philo's Therapeutae, with their communal lists of rules and their communal meals, were analogous to other Greco-Roman voluntary associations (funereal clubs, professional guilds, religious associations, etc.); they were basically Jewish versions of these Hellenistic private clubs in which members typically assembled for communal meals.[12] It is significant that rabbinic Judaism of the Mishnah and Talmud looks back to the Pharisees; that is, a table fellowship group, as the founders of its new religious program. Even though Torah study rather than eating becomes the central focus of rabbinic Judaism, the Pharisees' legacy is quite apparent in the continued emphasis on meals as the ritual means to realize their ideals, specifically, in institutions like table blessings, the Passover Seder, *derekh eretz* [rules for meal etiquette], not to mention kashrut. Thus, it is still the case that wherever "three have eaten at one table and have spoken over it words of the Torah, it is as if they had eaten from the table of God" (*m. Avot* 3:3).

THE PASSOVER SEDER WAS A SYMPOSIUM

A second major contribution of Jewish studies to meals in the Greco-Roman world is idea that the Passover Seder was a Greco-Roman symposium. This thesis has opened two especially fruitful lines of inquiry: the relationship between Jewish and Hellenistic culture and the relationship between actual meal practices and literary texts about them.[13] Sigfried Stein noted that many of the features of the Passover Seder, such as the four questions, the emphasis on reclining, the convention of talking about the food on the table or other topics related to the meal practices, games and word play, and a hymn at the end [*Hallel*], have parallels in Greco-Roman symposium literature.[14] The two most important subsequent book length treatments of the Passover Seder, Baruch Bokser's *Origins of the Seder* and Joseph Tabory's *Pesaḥ Dorot* [The Passover Ritual through the Generations], come down on different sides of Stein's thesis.[15] Bokser says the Passover Seder is not a symposium; Tabory says it is, as do I.[16] The issue at stake in this controversy is an old one: was Judaism influenced by Hellenism? Thus, though Bokser concedes that participation in wider Hellenistic culture was a factor "shaping [the] Passover Seder and the formation of early rabbinic Judaism in general," he cannot accept Stein's argument that "symposium literature 'gave the *impetus*'…to the form of the Passover Seder as it stands before us."[17] Rather, according to Bokser, the internal Jewish historical crisis of the loss of the Temple in Jerusalem shaped the form of the rabbinic Seder.[18] Bokser, in an approach typical of much modern Jewish critical scholarship, insists on the decisive impact of internal, autonomous Jewish factors on Jewish religious texts rather than external Hellenistic cultural influences.

However, I see no reason why symposium conventions and the loss of the Temple in 70 CE could not both be decisive factors shaping the form of the early rabbinic Seder.[19] In any case, I think that the thesis that the Passover Seder is a symposium has done much to advance more sophisticated understandings of the profound interaction between biblical/Jewish and Greco-Roman cultural conventions for meals. In addition, the thesis has led to a deeper exploration of the relationship between meal rituals and texts about or otherwise related to them.[20] Some studies of the Passover Seder as a symposium seem to confuse the symposium as a performed ritual with symposium texts that are literary representations of meals.[21] Thus, they miss the important point that literary representations of Jewish meals according to symposium literary conventions are themselves significant interpretations and transformations of experienced rituals into conceptual ideals. The Passover Seder in chapter ten of *m. Pesaḥim* is a literary idealization of Jewish meal practices according to early rabbinic values, just as the wide variety of Socratic, encyclopedic, and satirical literary symposia, as well as sympotic lists of meal rules and stylized meal scenes imbedded in fictional narratives, are idealizations of other extra-textual Greco-Roman meal practices.[22] The literary representation of symposia according to the conventions of the genre and sub-genres turns actual meal settings and practices into objects of intellectual reflection, to be contrasted with one another, to be preferred or rejected, or simply to demonstrate that proponents of the various schools represented at banquets do or do not practice what they preach.[23]

Tabory and I offer broad sketches of the historical development of the literary genres of symposia in order to situate the Passover Seder within them. Tabory does this to suggest that development of the Passover Haggadah, from a Midrash on Deut 26:5-8: "My father was a wandering Aramean…" to the lengthy rite in *m. Pesaḥ.* 10 prescribing the explanation of the foods at the table, parallels the literary development of Greco-Roman symposia. Tabory says Greco-Roman symposia developed from a first stage of Socratic symposia that focus on the dramatic intellectual dialogues between the meal participants, to second and third stages of symposia that describe the food.[24] Remarkably, though, Tabory claims that only with Athenaeus, c. 200 C.E., (stage three) had "the sympotic literature…developed into a literary *genre rather than descriptions of actual symposia.*" In contrast, I treat all the examples of symposium literature as different literary genres and sub-genres, in order to identify the Passover Seder in *m. Pesaḥ.* 10 as a specific sub-genre of symposium literature. It is a "list of meal rules" loosely imbedded in rabbinic "dialogues," analogous at least in form to the list of banquet rules imbedded in Lucian's comic dialogue *Saturnalia.*[25] Moreover, I stress that the Passover Seder form represents a conscious and intentional choice of one symposium literary form over other available ones because it was the right medium for the ideological message the rabbis wanted to convey—instead of its being the inevitable result of symposium literature's linear historical development, as Tabory seems to imply.

In short, the sympotic features and form of the Passover Seder were not incidental accretions or unconscious developments. The symposium literary tradition provided the composers of *m. Pesaḥ.* 10 (as well as their ideological rivals) with a wide range of options from which to choose to idealize their characteristic communal meals. Their choices were intentional and were recognized as such—at the very least to distinguish their way as preferable to others. It is a symposium convention itself to assert or imply that "we conduct ourselves at the table in enlightened and decorous ways, while our rivals don't," or, as *m. Pesaḥ* 10 puts it, "After the Passover offering, one does not end with *afikomen* [*epikomion*, or after-dinner revelry], that is, like everybody else besides us does!"[26] Bokser's, Tabory's, and my discussion of the Passover Seder (as well as that of other Jewish studies scholars) also emphasizes the points that Jewish meal rituals replace the Temple sacrifices, link eating and table-talk, and differentiate Jewish groups from one another and from non-Jews. However, because their significance for understanding Jewish meals goes far beyond the Passover Seder, I will treat each of these points in their own right.

JEWISH MEAL RITUALS REPLACED THE BIBLICAL TEMPLE SACRIFICES

The thesis that Jewish meal rituals replaced the biblical Temple sacrifices is widely recognized and accepted, but nevertheless can still be further nuanced. Certainly, the important studies of Neusner on the Pharisees and Bokser on the Passover Seder stress this point. However, this thesis raises almost as many questions as it answers. First, how does one account for the fact that Jewish groups like the Pharisees, Essenes, Jewish Christians, and Greek-speaking Egyptian Jews were apparently conducting meals as alternatives to the Temple sacrifices even before the destruction of the Temple in 70 CE?[27] Secondly, why are meals per se preferred as an alternative to the Temple sacrifices? After all, it is a commonplace in early rabbinic, Qumran, or early Christian literature that prayer replaces sacrifices, or study of the sacrifices replaces sacrifice, or Jesus is the new sacrifice.[28]

The study of rabbinic transformations of biblical cultic language is particularly instructive in this regard.[29] On the one hand we have statements like:

"This is the *torah* of the burnt offering ['*olah*], the grain offering [*minhah*], the sin offering [*hattat*], the guilt offering ['*asham*], etc." Whoever *engages in the study* of the Torah portion on '*olah* is as if he sacrificed an '*olah,* the portion on *minhah,* as if he sacrificed a *minhah,* the portion on *hattat,* as if he sacrificed a *hattat.*[30]

This is from *b. Men.* 110; similarly, in *m. Pesah* 10: "Rabban Gamaliel said, 'Whoever did not *say* these three things on Passover did not fulfill his obligation: *pesah, matzah,* and *merorim.*'" This suggests that it is enough to study or simply talk about sacrificial foods. On the other hand, *m. Avot* 3:3 states that Torah study at ordinary meals makes them like priestly sacrifices, and meals without Torah talk are like sacrilege:

R. Simeon said, "Three who have eaten at one table and have not said words of Torah over it, it is as if they have eaten from sacrifices of the dead [*mi-zivhei metim*]....But if three have eaten at one table and have spoken over it words of Torah, it as if they have eaten from the table of God, as it is written (Ezek 41:22), 'And he told me: This is the table that stands before the Lord.'"

Are the Pharisees or rabbis claiming that their meals, blessings, and study of the sacrifices stand in stead of the sacrifices, or do they claim that the blessings themselves are like the sacrifices? As I have stated elsewhere, whereas the Bible advocates "[the] *torot* of the priests and their sacrifices, not the master/disciple relationship...as the basis of Israelite cultural identity," rabbinic interpretations of this matter differ, casting them "almost entirely in the language and institutions of their own rabbinic concerns, namely the master/disciple relationship."[31] Further, "the written priestly *torot* of Leviticus require rabbinic Oral Torah for clarification, specification, and application, and it is enough to study the priestly *torot* rather than do them."[32]

By playing down the actual eating of the food and emphasizing substitute actions, the rabbis compare themselves to priests, primarily to assert that they have replaced the priests. On the other hand, later medieval kabbalistic traditions revive the sacrificial language and restore the theurgic priestly dimension to the meal rituals of rabbinic scholars, so that their eating as well as their study has a theurgic world-regenerating function.[33] This historical development of the use of biblical cultic language is especially apparent in changing interpretations of meat eating in the verse, "this is the torah of beast and fowl" in its biblical context and in rabbinic and medieval kabbalistic literature.[34]

The dominant attitudes toward meat eating at these key stages reflect the development of more basic patterns in the history of Jewish religion. The term "torah" had the dual meaning of teaching and practice. It was both the lore priests taught each other and other Israelites and the sacrificial and purification rituals the priests—and the Israelites, as a "kingdom of priests"—were themselves to perform. Thus, "the torah of beast and fowl" in Lev 11:46 reflected the original dual connotation of Torah. It was both a doctrine (about animal meat fit or unfit to eat) that the priests were to teach the Israelites and prescribed dietary rituals to be performed (on the one hand, to differentiate Israelites from non-Israelites, priests from non-priests; on the other hand, to maintain God's presence among them). Later rabbinic tradition tended to separate these roles, stressing the value of teaching and studying priestly lore over its performance in sacrificial rites. The rabbinic sages kept the metaphor of priesthood to sacralize their status, but redefined its qualifications: learned expertise in rabbinic Oral and Written Torah rather than the hereditary birthright of the priesthood.

In this view, meat eating becomes a privilege denied to those who are ignorant of the Torah. However, Kabbalah tended to recombine these roles, reviving the language of the sacrificial system to emphasize the equal value of study (of the "secrets of the Torah") and ritual performance.[35] Kabbalah couched its theory of transmigration of souls in the language of sacrifices, so that meat eating becomes an opportunity for the "enlightened ones" to unite their esoteric knowledge with actual ritual performance of eating in a single, cosmos-regenerating action.[36] Here is another important instance in which looking at Jewish meals outside the period of late Greco-Roman antiquity is helpful for determining what is distinctive about them during this period. Finally, a common thread in the discussion of Jewish meal rituals as replacements for the biblical sacrifices is the frequent and self-consciously intentional presence of words at or about the table that make it a "Jewish" table; for example, blessings, psalms, "words of Torah," "engagement in the study of sacrifices," and explanations of the foods.

JEWISH MEAL RITUALS COMBINE FOOD AND TABLE TALK

Words at the Jewish meal, even apart from the particular foods eaten, are one of the main features that distinguish Jewish meals as Jewish. We've already seen how the words prescribed for the Passover Seder— the telling of the story and especially the words explaining the symbolism of the food (the Passover lamb, the matzoh, and the bitter herb [*maror*]) are important. After all, were one to use different words—for example, that the Passover lamb or the matzo at the table is the body of Christ and the wine his blood—it would naturally give the meal a completely different character, that of a Christian liturgical ritual. Words at the table, whether the Passover table or the table for other Jewish meals, such as blessings over the food or *divrei torah* [words of Torah], have an important ritual function in linking the particular actions of eating to the general or a certain sectarian Jewish myth. When one says in Hebrew, "Blessed are You YHWH our God, King of the Universe, who creates the fruit of the vine" or "who commanded us concerning [the washing of] the hands" or "who brings forth bread from the earth," or "Blessed is YHWH our God from whose table we have eaten," one is affirming the fundamental Jewish myths that the YHWH created the world at the beginning of time, that the food and drink served on the table are more or less the direct result of that creation *in illo tempore*, that the God whom we directly address as "You" has personally commanded us (presumably from Mt. Sinai) to wash our hands, and that it is indeed from His food that we have eaten [*she-akhalnu mi shelo*, as if we were like the priests].[37]

If we were Qumran sectarians, we would allude to the messianic array of the myriads of the armies of God joining our small group, at least in our apocalyptic imagination, when we recite our distinctive grace after the meal.[38] If we were Jewish Christians, "every time [we would] eat this bread and drink this cup [we would] proclaim the death of the Lord until he comes."[39] Thus, I fundamentally disagree with Neusner when he claims that Pharisaic and Qumran Essenic table fellowship, despite its liturgical components, did not constitute "intense ritual meal[s]... [their] eating was not a ritualized occasion," and thus was decisively different from their early Christian counterparts.[40] On the contrary, the words at the Jewish meals are among the most important components for transforming the ordinary activities of eating into ritualized occasions.[41] Rituals are "modes of paying attention." The words that introduce, conclude, or otherwise comment on an action—whether during the performance of rituals or as glosses on written accounts of them—all call attention to ordinary activities; that is, "ritualize" otherwise unconsciously habitual or accidental actions.[42] Indeed, it is not surprising that the Second Temple period proponents of Jewish meals found Hellenistic symposium conventions so amenable. Perhaps the most characteristic symposium literary convention is the use of *faits divers*, incidental events or props, especially those naturally found at the dinner table, as pretexts for playfully learned discussions.

While this is fairly self-evident for Jewish table blessings and the Passover rite prescribed in *m. Pesaḥ.* 10, the ritualization of Torah study at the table, *divrei ha-torah al shulḥan* [words of Torah about the table/ over the table], is another striking development in the rabbinic meal. Ze'ev Gries, in his study of a relatively modern Jewish literary genre, *sifrei hanhagot* [popular manuals of ethics and ritual practices], discusses earlier precedents for this type of literature in the interpretations of *m. Avot* 3:3. The rabbinic and medieval classical Jewish tradition turns this from a description to a prescription: one ought to speak words of Torah over the table.[43] This prescription is then taken in two directions. One may recite the grace after meals [*birkat ha-mazon*], which includes quotations and allusions to Torah and suffices to fulfill this obligation. Otherwise, one is literally required to engage in a give-and-take discussion of Torah verses over the table, in addition to the required blessings.[44]

At least one medieval rabbi, Rabbenu Bahya ben Asher, goes a step further to advocate that one must "speak words of Torah about the table" over the table, playing on the double meaning of the preposition "*al*" in the original rabbinic quotation from *m. Avot* 3:3.[45] "Rabbenu Bahya creates new rituals by having people say or concentrate on specific scriptural metaphors at the specific time they are gathered together for communal meals."[46] This in effect turns the meals themselves into performances of the scriptural metaphors: this table over which students of the sages are presently discussing scriptural passages and eating their meal is indeed "the table which is before YHWH" (Ez 41:22); it is at this table here and now that the elite of the children of Israel "have envisioned God while eating and drinking"[47] (Exod 24:11).[48] Jewish meals become an occasion to "ritualize metaphors," the canonical metaphors of Scripture.[49] Though this example from a thirteenth century kabbalistic ethical manual is from a much different place and time than the Greco-Roman world that is our focus, one can see a very similar phenomenon earlier in the rabbinic Seder, when the Mishnah prescribes that one eats the symbolic foods, matzo and *maror*, over which certain scriptural verses have been recited. It is as if one is eating both the Scripture and the food that "carries" it. In this, the meal becomes a sort of experiential Midrash on the scriptural verses, a way of making ancient texts real and relevant to one's contemporary experience.

DISTINGUISHING BETWEEN FIT AND UNFIT FOODS IS A CRUCIAL COMPONENT OF JEWISH MEALS

There is no question that Mary Douglas' theory, emphasizing the importance of distinctions between animals prohibited and permitted for food and Israelite abhorrence of anomalous mixtures, has had a profound impact on the dietary laws in Jewish studies.[50] Even though scholars such as Jacob Milgrom and Baruch Levine disagree with Douglas on matters of detail and emphasis, they still recognize that the command to "be holy" has something to do with distinguishing between fit and unfit foods. In their view, other principles of distinction are operative besides the abhorrence of animals whose mode of locomotion isn't consistent with the division of nature that is their main habitat (specifically, birds that can't fly, sea animals that crawl rather than swim, or rabbits that hop rather walk on the ground like cattle and sheep).

Thus, Levine argues that animals that eat other animals tend to be prohibited. And Milgrom suggests that the distinction between clean and unclean animals is but one of several important ethical principles behind the dietary rules, such as the avoidance of the lifeblood of animals and the prohibition of the cruelty of cooking an animal in its mother's milk; indeed, for him the prohibition of the life blood, the "*dam* which is the *nefesh*," seems to be the most important ethical principle. Why post-biblical Judaism chose to emphasize the separation of milk and meat products when eating or preparing them, when it did, and the way it did still seem to be open questions.[51] To a certain extent, Douglas' implication that there is a systemic Jewish abhorrence for mixing species [*kelaim*] probably has something to do with the intensified emphasis on separating milk and meat foods, but this does not really address the ideological significance of the rabbinic innovations regarding the separation of milk and meat in their particular historical and cultural contexts.

MEALS ESTABLISH JEWISH IDENTITY; THEY FUNCTION TO DIFFERENTIATE COMPETING JEWISH GROUPS FROM ONE ANOTHER AND BETWEEN JEWS AND GENTILES

The consensus of contemporary Jewish scholarship, as reflected in the recent commentaries on Leviticus by Baruch Levine and Jacob Milgrom, is that the main purpose of the Torah's dietary laws is to distinguish Israelites from non-Israelites. Thus, as Levine says: "Underlying all the dietary regulations is a broad social objective: maintaining a distance between the Israelites and their neighbors."[52] Similarly, in the conclusion to his discussion of Mary Douglas' theory of animals prohibited and permitted for food, Milgrom notes the insight of the founders of Christianity:

> To end once and for all the notion that God had covenanted
> himself with a certain people who would keep itself apart from
> all the other nations. And it is these distinguishing criteria, the
> dietary laws (and circumcision), that were done away with.
> Christianity's intuition was correct: Israel's restrictive diet is a
> daily reminder to be apart from the nations.[53]

On the other hand, Milgrom observes that the most basic ethical foundation of the dietary system, the prohibition of blood, is intended to be universally applicable: "In effect, Israelite and non-Israelite are equated. Jew and non-Jew are bound by a single prohibition, to abstain from blood."[54] Certainly this seems to be the view of James' Jewish Christian faction at the Apostolic Council in Acts 15:20, 29.

Secondarily, meals became an important means for intra-Jewish group distinctions, especially in the Second Temple period. Jewish sectarian movements in the Greco-Roman period distinguished themselves from one another by means of their distinctive meal practices.[55] Also, diet served to distinguish different classes of Jews from one another; for example, priests from ordinary Israelites in the biblical period, *talmidei-hakhamim* from *ammei ha-aretz* [Torah scholars from Jews who didn't engage in Torah study] in the rabbinic period, kabbalists who understand the esoteric mystery of the biblical sacrifices and eating from Jews who didn't in the medieval period.[56]

JEWISH MEAL PRACTICES TEND TO BE LESS ASCETIC THAN CHRISTIAN AND OTHER GRECO-ROMAN PHILOSOPHICAL GROUPS

This theme raises two questions: one regarding definitions of asceticism and the other, the role of scriptural conceptions of "sacrifice." First, are Jewish dietary rules, as self-conscious restrictions of all possible edible things to only those that are "clean," tithed, dedicated or not dedicated to priests, correctly slaughtered, and properly preceded and followed by blessings, and the like, per se forms of asceticism? Or must they be integrated with a dualistic philosophical perspective that dichotomizes "material" versus "spiritual" to be "ascetic"? Secondly, to what extent do the biblical priestly traditions of sacrifice shape the mythic function of this sort of "domestic asceticism"; in other words, make it "less" ascetic? I think there is an "ascetical tension" in medieval kabbalistic interpretations of eating that is inseparably connected to a theurgical understanding of sacrifice as "cosmos regeneration."

Just as the biblical priests acted as sort of "surrogate stomachs" for God—consuming the bounty of the earth on the altar fires so as to send its essence back up to the Creator as "a pleasing fragrance" [*reakh nikhoakh*]—so some thirteenth century kabbalists, such as Rabbi Bahya ben Asher, transferred this same role (by way of rabbinic and mystical interpretations of the Temple sacrificial system) to the Torah scholar and his table. The metaphor of the biblical sacrifices, in which elite Jewish eaters must consume food to send it back up to God, seems to push one to eat, rather than to abstain from eating, if one is to give God His due. An empty oven cannot cook. This idea of eating is later developed in Hasidic thought as one of the principle means of "*avodah be-gashmiyut*" [service of God through the physical body].[57]

In addition, the joy one is supposed to experience from celebrating the festivals commanded by God is specifically associated with the eating of meat and the drinking of wine, although, as the Talmud puts it, "when the Temple existed there was no rejoicing except with meat...but now that the Temple no longer exists, there is no rejoicing except with wine."[58] Is this asceticism? We may compare this to the ecstatic rejoicing of Therapeutae at their meatless and wine-less meals that Philo praises in his treatise *On the Contemplative Life*. Is the absence of sacrificial language, plus Philo's philosophical preference for Platonic mind-body dualism, what makes this description of a Jewish meal diverge from what seems to be the general non-ascetic tendency of Jewish meals?

THERE IS A TENSION BETWEEN VEGETARIANISM AND MEAT EATING IN JEWISH MEALS

Finally, Jewish scholarship is calling increasing attention to the tension between vegetarianism and meat eating in Jewish meals. It has become a commonplace to recognize that the Bible originally prescribed a vegetarian diet: "See I have given you every plant yielding seed...to everything that has the breath of life I have given every green plant for food" (Gen 1:29-30).

Later, after the flood God concedes to humanity the permission to eat meat: "Every moving thing that lives shall be food for you; and just as I gave you the green plants, I give you everything" (Gen 9:3), provided that they observe the prohibition against eating blood (so, Gen 9:4: "You must not however eat flesh with its life-blood in it"). Both Levine and Milgrom emphasize that the blood prohibition in Leviticus' dietary laws are reminders that meat eating is a departure from the original Edenic vegetarian ideal.[59] In his chapter in this volume, Gary Rendsburg suggests that the Bible sets forth this ideal in three stages.[60] In a related chapter in this volume, I present classic post-biblical Jewish arguments both for meat eating and for vegetarianism, concluding that that the positions coexist in tension with one another in Jewish tradition.[61] I also think that meat eating plays an important role in reinforcing hierarchal social roles in Jewish society (rational, imaginative humans over brute animals, men over women, Torah scholars over those unschooled in Torah, and ethnic/kinship ties over ties based on shared faith or shared charismatic experiences).[62] In other words, Jewish groups bound by blood eat meat together; early Christian groups desiring to break down ethnic barriers between Jews and Gentiles did so at a communion meal of wine and bread. Shared meat was conspicuously absent.

SUGGESTIONS FOR FURTHER RESEARCH

Having set out these eight theses about meals in Jewish Studies, I can see more clearly what is missing. I suggest three directions for further study. First, it's clear that I've omitted discussion of certain genres of literature connected with meals that should not be neglected for a full picture. The *Derekh Eretz* literature, so-called minor tractates of the Talmud like *Derekh Eretz Rabba* and *Derekh Eretz Zuta*, though probably written down in the period of the Babylonian Amoraim, contain much material on meal etiquette that is strikingly similar in form to the lists of rules for Hellenistic associations.[63]

Another promising area would be stories about meals, meal scenes, or *chriae* with meal settings imbedded in talmudic narratives or legal discussions. Finally, there is an extensive critical discussion of "medicine in the Talmud" that is full of material about nutritional and dietary practices, but which is rarely mentioned in any of the Jewish studies scholarship on meals.[64]

A second major lacuna in my survey is the topic of Jewish meals and gender. Two questions are particularly important in this regard. First, are Jewish meals gendered? Obviously, yes, but a lot of work still needs to be done to spell out exactly how gender roles play a part in ancient Jewish meals.[65] Study of gender roles in Jewish meals needs to carefully lay out the different activities involved in a Jewish meal: production of food, acquisition of food, preparation of food, and consumption, as Ruth Abusch-Magder argued in her chapter for this volume.[66] The second main question that must be addressed is: are Jewish critical studies of meals themselves gendered?

This brings me to my third desideratum: we need to see more studies that self-consciously integrate texts, practice, and realia of meals. Two studies of medieval food practices set the standard for this sort of integration of textual, anthropological, and sociological analysis: Caroline Walker Bynum's *Holy Feast, Holy Fast* and Ivan Marcus's *The Rituals of Childhood.*[67]

I would add one more desideratum as sort of a postscript. Post-biblical research on Jewish meals is not well represented in recent important general (European) cultural histories of food (e.g., Jean-Louis Flandrin and Massimo Montanari's *Food: A Culinary History from Antiquity to the Present* and Montanari's *Culture of Food*) or vegetarianism (e.g., Colin Spencer's *The Heretic's Feast: A History of Vegetarianism*).[68] Therefore, I think it is important that we communicate the results of our research not only to our colleagues in Jewish and religious studies, but also to the scholars in the increasingly prominent and popular discipline of Food Studies. Unless we do, we will continue to have an incomplete view of "the big picture" of the cultural histories of food.

ACKNOWLEDGMENTS

This paper was originally written for the inaugural panel discussion session of the Consultation on Meals in the Greco-Roman World at the Society of Biblical Literature Annual Meeting in Toronto, November 2002, and printed here with the permission of Dennis Smith, one of the co-chairs of the Consultation. I would also like to thank my research assistant, Jacklyn Schmitt, for her invaluable assistance with this project.

NOTES

1 Jacob Neusner, *From Politics to Piety: The Emergence of Pharisaic Judaism* (New York: KTAV, 1979). Important studies influenced by this thesis, are, for example, Martin Jaffee, *Early Judaism* (Upper Saddle River: Prentice Hall, 1997) 79-82; Baruch Bokser, *The Origins of the Seder: The Passover Rite and Early Rabbinic Judaism* (Berkeley: University of California, 1984) 7,11; Anthony J. Saldarini, *Pharisees, Scribes, And Sadducees In Palestinian Society: A Sociological Approach* (Grand Rapids: Eerdmans/ Dove, 2001); Marcus Borg, *Conflict, Holiness, and Politics in the Teaching of Jesus* (Lewiston: Mellen, 1984) 307, 139-140; and E. P. Sanders, *Jewish Law from Jesus to the Mishnah* (London: SCM/Trinity, 1990) 167, though Sanders claims to disagree with Neusner. However, it seems that all Sanders is saying is that Pharisees were interested in purity, but they were not exceptional among other Jews for being so (245, cf. 242).

² Bokser, *Origins of the Seder*, 11.

³ Jonathan Brumberg-Kraus, "Were the Pharisees a Conversionist Sect? Table Fellowship as a Strategy of Conversion," 6 November 2002 (online: <http:// acunix.wheatonma.edu/jkraus/articles/Pharisees.htm>).

⁴ Gerd Theissen, *The Sociology of Early Palestinian Christianity* (Philadelphia: Fortress, 1978), 77-99.

⁵ Borg, *Conflict*, 73-143.

⁶ *Ibid.*, 93ff.

⁷ Saul Lieberman, "The Discipline of the So-Called Dead Sea Manual of Discipline," *JBL* 71 (1952): 199-206; Joseph Heineman, "Birkat Ha-Zimmun and Havurah Meals," *JJS* (1962): 23-29; Aharon Oppenheimer, *The 'Am Ha-Aretz: A Study In The Social History Of The Jewish People In The Hellenistic-Roman Period* (Leiden: Brill, 1977).

[8] Lieberman, "The Discipline of the So-Called Dead Sea Manual," 199-206. Among the relevant texts are *m. Dem.* 2:2-3[but not R. Judah's description of *haver* in 2:3]; 4:2; 6:9; *t.Dem.*2:15-24; 3:1-9; also *m. Tohar.*7:4; 8:5; *m. Git.*5:9.

[9] Joseph Heinemann, "Birkat Ha-Zimmun and Havurah Meals," 23-29. See *m. Ber.* 7:1, when three or more people (even a table server or a Samaritan) have eaten together "*demai*-produce, or First Tithe [*ma'aser rishon*] from which the Heave-offering [*terumato*] had been taken, or Second Tithe [*ma'aser sheni*] or dedicated produce [*hekdesh*] that had been redeemed," one of them is required to "invite [*le-zamen*]" the others to recite *Birkat ha-Zimmun.*

[10] Joseph Tabory, *Pesah Dorot: Perakim Be-toldot Layl Ha-Seder* (Tel Aviv: Hakibbutz Hameuchad, 1996) 50-51.

[11] I identify the *haverim* and *ne'emanim* with the Pharisees in Brumberg-Karus, "Were the Pharisees a Conversionist Sect?" but Saldarini, *Pharisees, Scribes, and Sadducees*, 216-20 and Shaye J.D. Cohen, *From the Maccabees to the Mishnah* (Philadelphia: Westminster, 1989) 158, both question that identification.

[12] B. Dombrowski, "'Yahad' in 1QS and '*to koinon*': An Instance of Early Greek and Jewish Synthesis," *HTR* 59 (1966): 293-307. M. Delcor, "Repas Cultuéls Esséniens et Thérapeutes, Thiases et Haburoth," *RQ* 6 (1968): 401-425.

[13] Henry A. Fischel, ed., *Essays in Greco-Roman and Related Talmudic Literature* (selected with a prolegomenon by [the editor]; New York: KTAV, 1976. Siegfried Stein's seminal article "The Influence of Symposium Literature on the Literary Form of the *Pesah* Haggadah," though originally published in the *Journal of Jewish Studies* in 1966, became widely known in Jewish studies circles through its inclusion in Fischel's volume, a collection of essays specifically intended to break down the excessive dichotomization of "Judaism vs. Hellenism" characteristic of much previous Jewish scholarship

[14] Stein, "Influence of Symposium Literature."

[15] Bokser, *Origins of the Seder,* 50ff; Tabory, *Pesah Dorot,* 367-77; and for his argument in English, see Joseph Tabory, "Towards a History of the Paschal Meal," in *Passover and Easter: Origin and History to Modern Times* (vol. 5; *Two Liturgical Traditions*; ed. P. Bradshaw and L. Hoffman; Notre Dame: Notre Dame University Press, 1999) 62-80.

[16] Jonathan Brumberg-Kraus, *Memorable Meals: Symposia in Luke's Gospel, The Rabbinic Seder and the Greco-Roman Literary Tradition* (Notre Dame: University of Notre Dame Press, forthcoming), 10-13.

[17] Bokser, *Origins of the Seder*, 12, 52-53.

[18] *Ibid.*, 12.

[19] Brumberg-Kraus, *Memorable Meals*, 12-13, 17.

[20] Jonathan Brumberg-Kraus, "'Not by Bread Alone...' Food and Drink in the Rabbinic Seder and in the Last Supper," special issue of *Semeia 86: Food and Drink in the Hebrew Bible and the New Testament* (ed. A. Brenner and J. W. van Henten; 1999): 154-79 and Brumberg-Kraus, *Memorable Meals.*

[21] See, for example, Stein, " The Influence of Symposium Literature" (even though he says that he is examining the Passover Haggadah as an example of the genre of symposium literature); Gordon J. Bahr, "The Seder of Passover." *NovT* 12 (1970): 181-202; and Gillian Feeley-Harnik, *The Lord's Table: Eucharist and Passover in Early Christianity* (Philadelphia: University of Pennsylvania, 1981).

[22] Brumberg-Kraus, *Memorable Meals*, 70-110.

[23] *Ibid.*, 109-10.

[24] Specifically, stage two is Plutarch's "Convivial Questions" and the Roman satirical symposia; stage 3 comprises the encyclopedic symposium of Athenaeus' *Deipnosophistae*. See Tabory, "Towards a History of the Paschal Meal," 65-69.

[25] Brumberg-Kraus, *Memorable Meals*, 45-46.

[26] Other examples can be found in the description of meals in Philo's *On the Contemplative Life,* and Clement of Alexandria's *Paidagogus*, which Bokser, *Origins of the Seder*, 56-57, 65-66, cites, without recognizing their conventional nature. See also Athenaeus, *Deipnosophistae*, Book V:177.

[27] See especially Baruch Bokser, *Philo's Description of Jewish Practices.* (Center for Hermeneutical Studies in Hellenistic and Modern Culture; *Protocol of the Thirtieth Colloquy*; Berkeley, 1977); Bosker, *Origins of the Seder*, 4-8, 14-28.

[28] See Elisabeth Schussler-Fiorenza, "Cultic Language in Qumran and the New Testament," *CBQ* 18 (1976):159-77.

[29] See, for example, Baruch Bokser, "Ma'al and Blessings over Food: Rabbinic Transformations of Cultic Terminology and Alternative Forms of Piety," *JBL* 100 (1981):557-74; Jonathan Brumberg-Kraus, "Meat-Eating and Jewish Identity: Ritualization of the Priestly 'Torah of Beast and Fowl' [Lev 11:46] in Rabbinic Judaism and in Medieval Kabbalah," *Association for Jewish Studies Review*, 24/2 (1999): 227-62.

[30] *b. Men.* 110.

[31] Jaffee, "Rabbinic Ontology," 6.

[32] Brumberg-Kraus, "Meat-Eating and Jewish Identity," 249-50.

[33] *Ibid.*, 257.

[34] *Ibid.*, 227-62. See also the article in this volume, Joel Hecker, "The Blessing in the Belly: Mystical Satiation in Medieval Kabbalah," in *Food and Judaism* (vol. 15; Studies in Jewish Civilization; ed. L. J. Greenspoon, et al.,; Omaha: Creighton University Press, 2005).

[35] See especially Joel Hecker, "Eating Gestures And The Ritualized Body In Medieval Jewish Mysticism," *History of Religions* 40/2 (2000): 125-52; Hecker, *Each Man Ate an Angel's Meal: Eating and Embodiment in the Zohar* (Ann Arbor: UMI, 1996).

[36] Brumberg-Kraus, "Meat-Eating and Jewish Identity," 256-57.

[37] Brumberg-Kraus, "Were the Pharisees a Conversionist Sect?" 20.

[38] 1 *QS* 6:3-7; 1 *QSa* 2:17-18. See Brumberg-Kraus, "Were the Pharisees a Conversionist Sect?", 20, n. 70.

[39] 1 Cor 11:26.

[40] Neusner, *From Politic to Piety*, 89.

[41] As I have argued in Brumberg-Kraus, "Were the Pharisees a Conversionist Sect?" 20:

> The religious function of many rabbinic blessings, and *Birkat ha-Zimmun* in particular, is to invoke the presence of God for otherwise ordinary human activities: eating, smelling, seeing, recovery from sickness, marriage, etc. Blessings that allude to what God created in the beginning ("...who creates the fruit of the vine") or how God sits on his throne in heaven with his heavenly entourage put the natural human activities of convivial eating and drinking in a supernatural, mythic context. Blessings are abbreviated myths, ritual shorthand to evoke the longer biblical myths of creation, revelation, and redemption — of the past, present, and future kingdom of God.

[42] B. Bokser, "Ritualizing the Seder," *JAAR* 56 (1988):445; compare J. Z. Smith, "The Bare Facts of Ritual," *HR* 20 (1980): 113-115 and Brumberg-Kraus, "'Not by Bread Alone,'" 69.

[43] Zeev Gries, *Sifrut ha-hanhagot: toldoteha u-mekomah be-haye haside R. Yisra'el Ba'al Shem-Tov* (Tel Aviv: Mosad Bialik, 1989), 18-22.

[44] Gries, *Sifrut ha-hanhagot*, 21-22.

[45] R. Bahya ben Asher, *Shulhan Shel Arba*, (ed. C. Chavel), 474; Jonathan Brumberg-Kraus, "The Ritualization of Scripture in Rabbenu Bahya ben Asher's Eating Manual *Shulhan Shel Arba*'," *Proceedings of the Thirteenth World Congress of Jewish Studies* (Jerusalem: Hebrew University/Magnes Press, forthcoming), 3.

[46] Brumberg-Kraus, "The Ritualization of Scripture," 3.

[47] *Ibid.*, 4-5.

[48] R. Bahya b. Asher, *Shulhan Shel Arba*, 492-3; Brumberg-Kraus, "The Ritualization of Scripture," 10.

[49] Ivan Marcus uses the term "ritualization of metaphors" to interpret medieval Northern European Jewish eating rituals in his book, *The Rituals of Childhood* (New Haven: Yale University Press, 1996) see especially 5-7.

[50] Mary Douglas, "The Abominations of Leviticus," *Purity and Danger* (London: Routledge, 1966); "Deciphering a Meal," in *Food and Culture: A Reader* (ed. C. Counihan and P. Van Esterik; New York: Routledge, 1997), 36-54.

[51] See the article in this volume, David Kraemer, "Separating the Dishes," in *Food and Judaism*.

[52] Baruch A. Levine, "Excursus 2: The Meaning of the Dietary Laws," *The JPS Torah Commentary: Leviticus* (Philadelphia: Jewish Publication Society, 1989), 244.

[53] Jacob Milgrom, *Leviticus 1-16* (The Anchor Bible; New York: Doubleday, 1991), 726.

[54] Milgrom, *Leviticus*, 713.

[55] Gillian Feeley-Harnik, *The Lord's Table: Eucharist and Passover in Early Christianity* (Philadelphia: University of Pennsylvania, 1981), 91-96; see also Theissen, *The Sociology of Early Palestinian Christianity* and Borg, *Conflict, Holiness, and Politics*.

[56] See Brumberg-Kraus, "Meat-Eating and Jewish Identity," which traces the biblical antecedents and post-biblical interpretations of the rabbinic baraita: "Rabbi said, it is

forbidden for an *am ha-aretz* to eat meat—as it is written, 'This is the torah of beast and fowl' (Lev 11:46)—for all who engage in Torah—it is permitted to eat the flesh of beast and fowl. But for all who do not engage in Torah, it is not permitted to eat beast and fowl." (*b. Pesaḥ.* 49b)

[57] Louis Jacobs, "Eating as an Act of Worship in Hasidic Thought," *Studies in Jewish Religious and Intellectual History: In Honour of Alexander Altmann on the Occasion of His Seventieth Birthday* (ed. S. Stein and R. Loewe; London: Institute of Jewish Studies, 1977). See also the article in this volume, Alan Nadler, "Holy Kugel! The Sanctification of East European Jewish Ethnic Foods at the Hasidic Tisch," in *Food and Judaism*.

[58] *b. Pesaḥ.* 109a.

[59] For example, Lev 17:14: "For the life of all flesh—its blood is its life. Therefore I say to the Israelite people: You shall not partake of the blood of any flesh, for the life of all flesh is its blood. Anyone who partakes of it shall be cut off."

[60] See the chapter in this volume, Gary Rendsberg, "The Vegetarian Ideal in the Bible," in *Food and Judaism*.

[61] See the chapter in this volume, Jonathan Brumberg-Kraus, "Does God Care What We Eat?" in *Food and Judaism*.

[62] Brumberg-Kraus, "Meat-Eating and Jewish Identity," 259-62; "Not by Bread Alone,"172-177.

[63] Daniel Sperber, A *Commentary On Derech Erez Zuta* (Ramat-Gan, Israel: Bar-Ilan University Press, 1990) 9; *Masekhet Derekh Erets Zuta* (Jerusalem: Tsur-Ot, 1982.

[64] For example, *Julius Preuss' Biblical And Talmudic Medicine* (trans. and ed. F. Rosner; New York: Sanhedrin Press, 1978; Fred Rosner, *Medicine In The Bible And The Talmud: Selections From Classical Jewish Sources* (New York: KTAV House, 1977); Irene and Walter Jacob, eds., *The Healing Past: Pharmaceuticals In The Biblical And Rabbinic World* (Leiden; New York: E.J. Brill, 1993). See also John Cooper, *Eat And Be Satisfied: A Social History Of Jewish Food* (Northvale, N.J.: Jason Aronson, 1993; David Kraemer, *Reading The Rabbis: The Talmud As Literature* (New York: Oxford University Press, 1996); Jeffrey L. Rubenstein, *Talmudic Stories: Narrative Art, Composition, And Culture* (Baltimore: The Johns Hopkins University Press, 1999).

[65] Athalya Brenner, "The Food of Love: Gendered Food and Food Imagery in the Song of Songs," *Semeia 86: Food and Drink in the Hebrew Bible and the New Testament* (ed. by Athalya Brenner and Jan Willem van Henten; 1999) 101-112. Nancy Jay, *Throughout Your Generations Forever: Sacrifice, Religion, and Paternity* (Chicago: University of Chicago Press, 1992). See Brumberg-Kraus, "Meat-Eating and Jewish Identity," 259ff- and Jay, *Throughout Your Generations Forever,* xxiii. See also *Nashim* 5: *Feeding an Identity: Gender, Food, and Survival* (ed. Norma Baumel Joseph; Fall 2002).

[66] See the article in this volume, Ruth Abusch-Magder, "Kashrut: Women as Gatekeepers of Jewish Identity" in *Food and Judaism*.

[67] Caroline Walker Bynum, *Holy Feast and Holy Fast: The Religious Significance of Food to Medieval Women* (Berkeley: University of California Press, 1987); Ivan G. Marcus, *The Rituals of Childhood* (New Haven: Yale University Press, 1996).
[68] Jean-Louis Flandrin and Massimo Montanari, eds., *Food: A Culinary History from Antiquity to the Present* (trans. Clarissa Botsford, et al. ; New York: Columbia University Press, 1999); Massimo Montanari, *The Culture of Food* (trans. Carl Ipsen; Oxford: Blackwell, 1994); Colin Spencer, *The Heretic's Feast: A History of Vegetarianism* (Hanover: University Press of New England, 1995).

The Vegetarian Ideal
in the Bible

Gary A. Rendsburg

The first thing one learns in almost any Introduction to the Bible course offered on college campuses today is that Genesis begins with not one, but two, stories of creation. These two narratives, we are taught, offer two greatly differing accounts of the creation of the world. In the first story (Gen 1:1-2:4a), which proceeds day-by-day over the course of seven days, God first creates elements of the cosmos, the living things in the order of vegetation, the animal kingdom, and, finally, humans. The method of creation is by fiat: God says simply "let something happen" and it happens. The creation of humans includes both man and woman—male and female—at one and the same time.

In the second story (Gen 2:4b-3), a very different view is presented. There is no attempt at a time frame; items such as the sun, the moon, and the stars are not mentioned; the order of creation is first, man, then vegetation, then animals, and, finally, woman; the method of creation is by physical means, as indicated by the words "formed," "planted," and "built," all predicated of God; and, unlike the first story, man and woman are not created at the same time, but rather Adam is created first and only later is Eve fashioned out of Adam's side (the Hebrew is traditionally understood as "rib," but more likely means "side").

In addition, the name by which God is called in these two accounts is different. In the first story the deity is referred to as Elohim = "God"; in the second story the name used is the compound form YHWH-Elohim = "LORD God." Those scholars who engage in traditional source criticism ascribe the first of these stories to the priestly source, or P, and the second of these stories to the Yahwist source, or J. I will not proceed further along the lines of the documentary hypothesis, mentioning it only in passing as an important element of modern biblical scholarship— not immediately relevant to our discussion of food, except, perhaps, as food for thought.[1]

In my attempt to work with these two accounts as two pieces of a literary whole, I am struck by the fact that the two accounts present totally different perspectives of the one singular creation. The perspectives may be termed, respectively, the cosmocentric view and the anthropocentric view. In the first one, we see the entire cosmos created, thus the references to light, expanse, dry land, seas, sun, moon, stars, and so forth; we also can understand the use of creation by fiat, characteristic of an awesome and majestic God. In the second account, we see only the view from earth, and thus we can understand the author's use of more basic methods of creation, such as God's forming man from the clay, in the manner in which a potter forms a vessel, or God's planting the Garden of Eden, in a style no different than a backyard gardener planting his or her own garden.

The text even provides a valuable clue for the reader to recognize this crucial difference of perspective. The first story is introduced by the phrase, "when God began to create heaven and earth" (traditionally rendered in English as "In the beginning God created the heaven and the earth"). Note the order of the two main items: "heaven" and "earth" (Gen 1:1; see also Gen 2:4a). The second story, by contrast, is introduced by the expression "on the day that LORD God made earth and heaven"; note the changed order, "earth and heaven" in this verse (Gen 2:4b).[2]

Pamela Reis shares a similar approach to the one that I am taking here, although she took this understanding of these chapters one step further. Reis contends that we should read the beginning of Genesis in the same way that we view the classic Japanese film *Rashomon*, directed by Akira Kurosawa.[3] The brilliance of the film lies in Kurosawa's allowing different characters to tell the same story, each from his or her perspective. Similarly, with the Torah we should read the narrative as a literary whole, though we recognize that two different viewpoints underlie the two stories.

Where does this leave us? As the title of my talk adumbrates, there is no meat to my topic. Yet, as the two creation stories differ in so many ways, their singular vision is truly extraordinary: the two accounts share only one major theme in common—the vegetarian ideal.

In both stories, God creates a world characterized by vegetarianism. In the first account, we read, "And God said [to the human couple], 'Behold I give to you all the vegetation that sprouts seed which is upon the face of all the earth, and every tree in which the fruit of the tree sprouts seed, for you it shall be as food'" (Gen 1:29). God then continues,

"'And to all the animals of the earth and to all the birds of the sky and to all that creeps on the earth, in which there is a living life, [I give] all the green vegetation for food'" (Gen 1:30). Not only are the humans created as vegetarians, but the entire animal kingdom is, too. We humans, of course, can live as vegetarians, and a large portion of the animal kingdom is herbivorous. At the same time, however, the ancient Israelites obviously knew that many species of animals were not simply omnivores but rather carnivores. Species like the lion, the leopard, and the bear, among the land animals, and species like the eagle, the vulture, and the owl, among birds, are all mentioned in the Bible; they are native to the land of Israel, and they are all meat eaters. Never mind, says the idealistic author of Gen 1: at the time of creation God established a purely harmonious world, one characterized by vegetarianism.

The vegetarian ideal is somewhat less explicit in the second creation story, but it is present there nonetheless. After creating man, God planted a garden in Eden and then placed man in the garden to till it and to keep it. We next read, "And the LORD God commanded man saying, 'From every tree of the garden you indeed may eat'" (Gen 2:16). The passage continues with the famous prohibition forbidding man from eating from the tree of knowledge, for which the general command, to eat of the other trees, serves as background. While there is clearly something quite specific intended here, I would still read the command to eat of the trees of the garden, without any other mention of eating in this chapter, as implying a vegetarian world in this second creation story as well. Further confirmation for this view appears in the next chapter, which focuses on the hard work required in the cultivation of crops (Gen 3:17-19), with the explicit statement, "and you shall eat of the vegetation of the field" (Gen 3:18).[4]

Two stories with major, and in fact irreconcilable, differences have one thing in common: God commands a vegetarian lifestyle for humans in both stories (God also commands it explicitly for the animal kingdom in the first story and probably implicitly in the second story). The vegetarian ideal in these two stories is, I submit, like the dagger in *Rashomon*. Each of the four storytellers in the film has a different tale to tell, but they all agree on one detail, the presence of the dagger. The bandit, the woman, the dead man (who speaks in the film through a medium), and the woodcutter each tells his or her own tale, each, as in the biblical narratives, with contradictory information, but Kurosawa ensures that our attention is turned each time to the special dagger that plays a central role in each character's version. In like manner, the biblical author ensures that our ears focus on the food that humans are to eat. In fact, in contrast to the usual economical writing style employed by the biblical prose writers, there is a certain verbosity in the description of the vegetarianism inherent at creation, especially in the first account. Let me cite those words once more: "And God said, 'Behold I give to you all the vegetation that sprouts seed which is upon the face of all the earth, and every tree in which the fruit of the tree sprouts seed, for you it shall be as food. And to all the animals of the earth and to all the birds of the sky and to all that creeps on the earth, in which there is a living life, [I give] all the green vegetation for food'" (Gen 1:29-30). This is by far God's longest speech in the first creation story. It is as if a movie camera focuses for a moment on this aspect of the narrative.[5]

If the world is established in a vegetarian mode, what happens? As narrated in Genesis, humans are unable to live up to the ideals that God established at creation. Even God's first command, the relatively simple prohibition not to eat from the tree of knowledge, is too much to follow. Then we read of the world's first murder, the fratricide of Abel by Cain (Gen 4). Next we read of the lascivious relationships conducted by the "sons of God" and the "daughters of man" (Gen 6), acts accepted in the world of ancient Near Eastern mythology, but ones which the Bible presents as the epitome of worldly depravity. These transgressions lead God to destroy the world that he has created, with Noah and his family and the pairs of animals Noah gathers as sole survivors of the flood.

After the flood, we have a fresh beginning. In Gen 9, God repeats many of the same words that he expressed to the first human couple in Gen 1 to Noah and his sons, including such expressions as "be fertile and multiply and fill the earth" (Gen 9:1; compare Gen 1:28). But there is a major difference now. God realizes that man cannot live up to the ideals established at creation, so a different set of rules is now presented. Among these rules is the permission to eat meat: "every creature which lives, to you shall be for food, as with the green vegetation, I give to you everything" (Gen 9:3). To which is attached one important proviso: "however, flesh with its life-blood in it, you shall not eat" (Gen 9:4). In the Torah's grand narrative, accordingly, the consumption of meat is a compromise, a divine acceptance of human inability to adhere to the utopia established at creation.

It is important here to add a word on this passage from Gen 9. Meat is now permitted, but as this verse indicates and as we shall see further below, especially in connection with the dietary laws distinctive to the people of Israel, wanton consumption of meat is not permitted. Eating meat is a compromise, requiring the killing of an animal. It violates the vegetarian ideal established is Gen 1 and 2. Therefore, humans cannot eat blood, the essential ingredient of life in all living creatures. The Torah is stating very clearly that one may take the life of an animal if necessary, but must not consume its life-essence. The reader of the Torah is reminded that eating meat compromises the Torah's utopian *Weltanschauung*.

We now turn our attention to the most detailed presentation of kashrut in the Bible, Lev 11. Numerous scholars have attempted to determine the reasons behind the dietary laws in the Torah. The key questions are: Why are these specific animals considered kosher? And why are other specific animals deemed not kosher? Further, is there any system which coheres throughout that would make the dietary laws explicable? In the many attempts to answer these questions, two approaches rise above the rest. The first is the approach of Mary Douglas.[6]

In her anthropological field work in the Congo in the 1960s, Douglas noted that many primitive[7] societies have complex dietary laws. As an example, Douglas presented the evidence of the Bushmen, first studied by Louis Fourie in the 1920s, later used by Claude Lévi-Strauss in the development of his theory of totemism.[8] Among the Bushmen, the various parts of an animal killed in the hunt are divided up among the various elements of the society. Women may never eat the liver. The wife of the man who killed the animal can eat only the superficial covering of meat and fat surrounding the hindquarters and the entrails. Young boys eat only the abdominal wall, the kidneys, the genitals, and the udder. The man who actually killed the animal can eat only the ribs and the shoulder blade from one side of the animal. The tribal chief and his family are treated to a thick steak from each quarter and a cutlet taken from each side. Arbitrary as these rules may seem to the modern reader, there are credible reasons for some of these divisions. Since the liver, with its high blood content, would spoil before it was brought back to camp, this organ was eaten on the spot by the men; therefore women never had the opportunity to eat the liver. The presentation of the animal's genitals to the young boys has obvious connections.

For the other parts of the animal divided up among the other elements of the society, there are presumably also reasons, even if we cannot deduce them so readily. In truth, however, a search for the origin of each distribution is unnecessary, for such a "logical" search overlooks the essential meaning of the rules surrounding food. As Lévi-Strauss maintains, it is crucial to recognize that the classification of the animal's anatomy serves as a schematization of social categories. That is to say, the Bushmen have projected their own social structure onto the animal. As we view the practice described above, it is not important that we understand why food is distributed in the way it is. It is only important to know that the distinctions exist. The practice reflects the Bushmen's self-understanding of organizational and governing principles for their society. In short, the animal killed by the Bushmen hunter represents the Bushmen people, the individual sections corresponding, in some way, to the people themselves, with part A allocated to society segment X, part B to society segment Y, and so on.

Those societies are not alone in their natural urge to organize the world around them. We in the modern world have taken the art of taxonomy to new heights with our ever-expanding world of knowledge. In the field of linguistics, for example, the world's languages are divided along various lines. Historical linguistics classifies them genetically: English is an Indo-European language, Hebrew is Semitic, Chinese belongs to the Sino-Tibetan family, and so on. Typological linguistics divides the world's languages into three groups: inflecting, agglutinating, and isolating, depending on how the language expresses tense, plurality, and other grammatical issues. Syntactic analysis allows for still another system, depending on the order of the subject, verb, and object in the sentence: English is an SVO language, Japanese is an SOV language, and Welsh is a VSO language, to cite one example from each of the most common types. Chemists, biologists, and other scientists have similar ways of carving up their worlds. In fact, such worlds are ever-changing. When I learned the periodic table, the six gases at the far right of the chart were called the inert gases, my children have learned them as the noble gases, and chemists are more likely to refer to them as Group 18.[9] But it is not just the knowledge explosion of the twentieth century which has allowed us this ability to classify. It is a natural desire among humans to classify and organize the world around us. In this way I would explain the remarkable lexical lists of the ancient Akkadian scribes, cataloguing in great number different birds, different trees, the names of various gods, and so on.

To return to ancient Israel, the Torah begins, as we noted earlier, with a creation story presenting an orderly world, including the subdivisions of the animal kingdom. Leviticus 11 continues that system, but it goes a step further. This chapter of the Torah dislikes animals that are, to use Mary Douglas's terminology, "out-of-place"; that is, they do not quite fit the classification system.[10] The three major domesticated animals—cattle, sheep, and goats—have a split hoof and chew the cud; an animal that does not have both of these traits is out-of-place and is therefore considered impure and not to be eaten. Sea creatures should have fins and scales to enable them to swim easily through the water; those marine animals that do not, such as mollusks and crustaceans, are once more out-of-place and thus may not be eaten. Birds are meant to fly and have tiny legs; those that cannot fly, such as the ostrich, or those that have large legs with talons, such as the eagle, or those animals that fly but are not birds at all, such as the bat, are all non-kosher. The non-kosher animals, therefore, are all out-of-place; they thus elicit disgust, much as a modern Westerner would be disgusted to find a pair of shoes, even a clean pair, on the kitchen table or a hairbrush in the living room.[11]

For Douglas, it is not important that goats are kosher and pigs are not: it is important only that there are distinctions, that the people of Israel saw the one as in-place and the other as out-of-place. To my mind and in line with a study by Walter Houston, the defining criterion for why the cloven-hoofed ruminants are in-place, while the pig is out-of-place, has to do with Israel's pastoral origins, where sheep, goats, and cattle were the animals with which the people lived, to the exclusion of the pig, which neither grazes nor provides humans with milk.[12]

Regardless of the origins of these distinctions, more important for Douglas is the dichotomy itself, representing Israel's worldview: just as only certain species among the entirety of the animal kingdom are deemed suitable for eating, so is Israel among all the peoples of the world deemed suitable as the covenant partner of God. For Douglas, behind the very abstruse details of Israelite dietary laws lies a profound theological message:

> They [the people of Israel] have been singled out for the honour of being consecrated to God, to be his people. The height and depth of this honour is inexpressible. At another level it is a parallel honour for their flocks and herds, the cloven-hoofed ruminants, to be singled out of all animal kinds to be

consecrated to God. This paradigm turns the covenant animals into vassals in relation to the people of Israel, as are the people of Israel the vassals of God.[13]

Jacob Milgrom, who has been in dialogue with Mary Douglas for three decades, is not convinced of her entire argument, but he does accept one major component of it: the idea that the permitted animals serve as a projection of the people of Israel into another realm. Milgrom goes one step further in adapting Douglas's view, and he does so in a most constructive way. The humankind/animal kingdom parallel works at three levels [fig. 1].[14] There are many peoples in the world and there are many animals in the world; in theory all peoples can eat all animals, as the story of Noah in Gen 9 affirms. But a unique people, the people of Israel, can eat only a certain subset of those animals, the ones delineated in Lev 11 as kosher. Furthermore, Milgrom argues that of the kosher animals, only certain among them can be offered as sacrifices. Deer, fish, ducks, chicken, locusts, and other creatures are kosher, but they cannot be sacrificed on the altar. This distinction reflects, not surprisingly, the fact that within the people of Israel there is a specific subset of people who are seen as even more special, unique, set off from the rest of the people, and they are the *kohanim*, the priests, whose sole consumption of meat, according to the book of Leviticus, comes from the sacrificial altar.

There is, however, another approach to the dietary laws worthy of our consideration. This second approach takes note of the important fact that the permitted animals are all herbivores. I have not been able to isolate the scholar with whom this view originates, but here I would mention, among recent authors, Baruch Levine and Ed Greenstein.[15] This approach, moreover, is the one to which I subscribe, though I will, in just a moment, add something new.

Let us first review the basic facts. The land animals are the three domesticated cloven-hoofed ruminants, to which can be added one wild animal, the deer (including the many individual species subsumed in that category, such as the gazelle and the antelope). These mammals are all herbivores. Note again that the pig, the lone outcast among the major farm animals, is an omnivore.

Fish must have fins and scales in order to be eaten, and this description therefore excludes the various scavengers on the river bed or the ocean bed, such as crabs, lobsters, shrimp, and crayfish. Leviticus 11 provides no traits for the permitted birds, but from the list of the twenty forbidden species,[16] including eagles, vultures, owls, and so on, we may conclude, as does the Mishna (*Ḥullin* 3:6), that birds of prey are forbidden, while other birds, such as doves, pigeons, and quail, are permitted. Finally, we may note that four species of locusts are kosher, even though most Jewish communities no longer eat these creatures.

From what I have just described, it is clear that the permitted animals are all herbivores. There are, I admit, some minor exceptions. Clearly the pastoral origins of ancient Israel, which we mentioned earlier, would preclude an intimate familiarity with fish (some permitted fish do eat others) and with fish-eating fowl (such as ducks). And even after the Israelites settled the mountainous spine of the central hill country in the land of Canaan, there still would be little acquaintance with these creatures. Most importantly, the herbivore approach explains the fact that locusts are permitted, for they are the plant devourers par excellence in our ancient sources; note such diverse texts as Exod 10 describing the eighth plague and Joel's use of the locust metaphor to describe the utter destruction wrought against the people of Israel (Joel 1:4).

The bottom line of this argument is this: humans are unable to live up to the vegetarian ideal set forth at creation; God compromises and allows humanity to eat meat.[17] But Israel wishes to adhere to that ideal, even in compromised fashion, and therefore Israel consumes only those animals that themselves have not killed other animals. The prohibition against eating blood, which I mentioned earlier, should also be worked into this equation. We know that other cultures did consume blood; we have specific evidence of this from Ugarit, for example.[18] Israel, however, holds to the ideal of not eating blood; in fact, it is a major component of the laws of the Torah, repeated time and again in Leviticus with echoes throughout the Bible. Accordingly, Israel prohibits not only the eating of blood but also the consumption of those animals that themselves ingest blood, lest Israel consume blood "through the backdoor," as it were. Note that according to my reconstruction here, the vegetarian ideal comes first, and only secondarily were distinguishing characteristics (cloven hoof, rumination, fins, scales, etc.) noted, in somewhat artificial fashion.

Of these two approaches, the Douglas-Milgrom approach on the one hand, and the herbivore model on the other, there would appear to be little common ground. I here propose, however, that the two perspectives can fit together: permitted animals, the vegetarians, can be viewed as a projection of Israel's values onto the realm of the animals.

Israel clearly stressed the vegetarian ideal, and while it could not uphold the ideal, it transfers that ideal onto the animal kingdom, permitting herbivorous animals to be eaten. These animals, I submit, remind the Israelites of who they are or at least of who they should aspire to be in an ideal world.[19]

I admit this schema is not entirely satisfactory, since the Torah itself specifically mentions the camel, the hyrax, and the rabbit, all herbivores, as forbidden animals, as are horses, donkeys, and other animals with which the Israelites were familiar. I would comment only that one must recall, as noted above, the pastoral origins of Israel, in which cattle, sheep, and goats played such a major role. If coincidentally the deer had the same characteristics it might also be considered kosher.[20] But animals that lacked these traits or that had only one of them, even if they be herbivores, were simply excluded. Douglas would for this reason call these excluded animals out-of-place,[21] not appropriate in light of Israel's origins as a pastoral society located on the fringe of the desert.

I have dealt with the distant past—creation—and I have dealt with the present—the reality of the dietary laws from the biblical period until today. But I cannot conclude this essay without dealing with the third epoch of linear time—the future, which in the biblical world view is associated with the eschaton [the term is based on the Greek for "last things"].

The prophets of ancient Israel recognized that they lived in a most difficult period. Isaiah, for example, lived at the time of the Assyrians, the greatest military power the world had ever known and creators of the world's first real empire. He witnessed the Assyrian destruction of the northern kingdom of Israel. In time, these Assyrians would sack dozens of Judean cities as well and besiege Jerusalem for three years, though the city remained inviolate. Isaiah understood these devastations as divine punishments for Israel's and Judah's misdeeds. Yet he never lost hold of the prophetic spirit, which looked to a time in the future when the world would be a better place than it is today. This eschaton is described in Isaiah in various ways. Among the most famous passages is Isa 2 (see also Micah 4), in which people "shall beat their swords into plowshares and their spears into pruning hooks," bringing an end to all warfare, a time when "nation shall not lift up sword against nation, and neither shall they learn war any more" (Isa 2:4 = Mic 4:3).

My favorite description of the eschaton occurs in Isa 11, in which Isaiah portrays harmony not among nations, as in chapter 2, but among animals. The natural enemies, the animals that prey and the animals that are preyed upon, are paired off, as an exemplar of what the world will be like in this period of perfect harmony: "And the wolf will dwell with the sheep, and the leopard will lie down with the kid, and the calf and the young lion and the fatling together, with a young lad leading them. And the cow and the bear shall graze, together their young shall lie down, and the lion shall eat straw like the ox" (Isa 11:6-7). Thus, in Isaiah's portrayal of the future world, the animals return to their vegetarian state, no longer consuming their traditional prey: the lion will have to learn to eat straw like the ox. At this time we all will return to the paradise of creation. Isaiah's worldview can be viewed through the a timeline [fig. 2], with (a) creation at one end, characterized by peace and harmony and vegetarianism; (b) history displayed on the great length of the timeline, characterized by war and violence and meat-eating; and (c) the eschaton at the other end, once more characterized by peace, harmony, and vegetarianism. When Isaiah sought to highlight what the eschaton would be like, he settled upon vegetarianism, just as the author(s) of Gen 1-2 had.

Finally, and perhaps even more remarkably, Isaiah's words were reused about 160 years later by Second Isaiah, an anonymous prophet who lived in exile in Babylon around 540 BCE. The culminating verse in one of the most glorious passages in the entire Bible is found in Isa 65, where the prophet presents his view of a new heaven and a new earth (65:17), a world in which all troubles will be forgotten (65:16). In this new world order, Jerusalem will be a joy, there will be no more weeping and wailing, a hundred-year-old man will be reckoned as one accursed, people will plant vineyards and enjoy the fruit, and they shall be blessed by the LORD (vv. 18-24). And then the final lines: "The wolf and the lamb will graze together, and the lion shall eat straw like the ox . . . they shall not do evil and they shall not destroy in all my holy mountain, says the LORD" (18:25). This crucial passage found both in Isa 11 and in Isa 65, speaks volumes. It epitomizes the vegetarian ideal that permeates the spirit of the Bible and the life of ancient Israel.

ACKNOWLEDGMENTS
I am most grateful to Mary Douglas for her critical reading of an earlier draft of this paper. I alone remain responsible for any deficiencies herein.

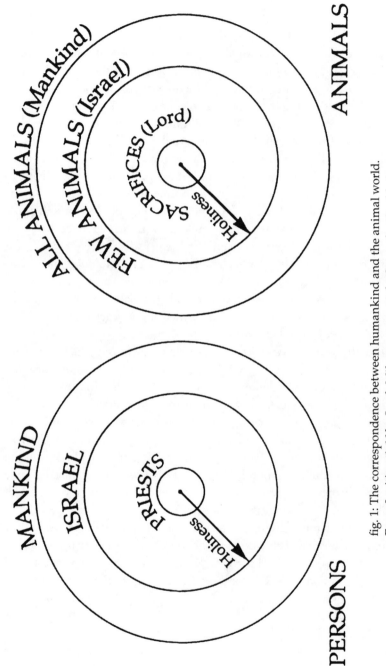

fig. 1: The correspondence between humankind and the animal world. From *Leviticus 1-16* by Jacob Milgrom, copyright © 1991 by Doubleday. Used by permission of Doubleday, a division of Random House, Inc.

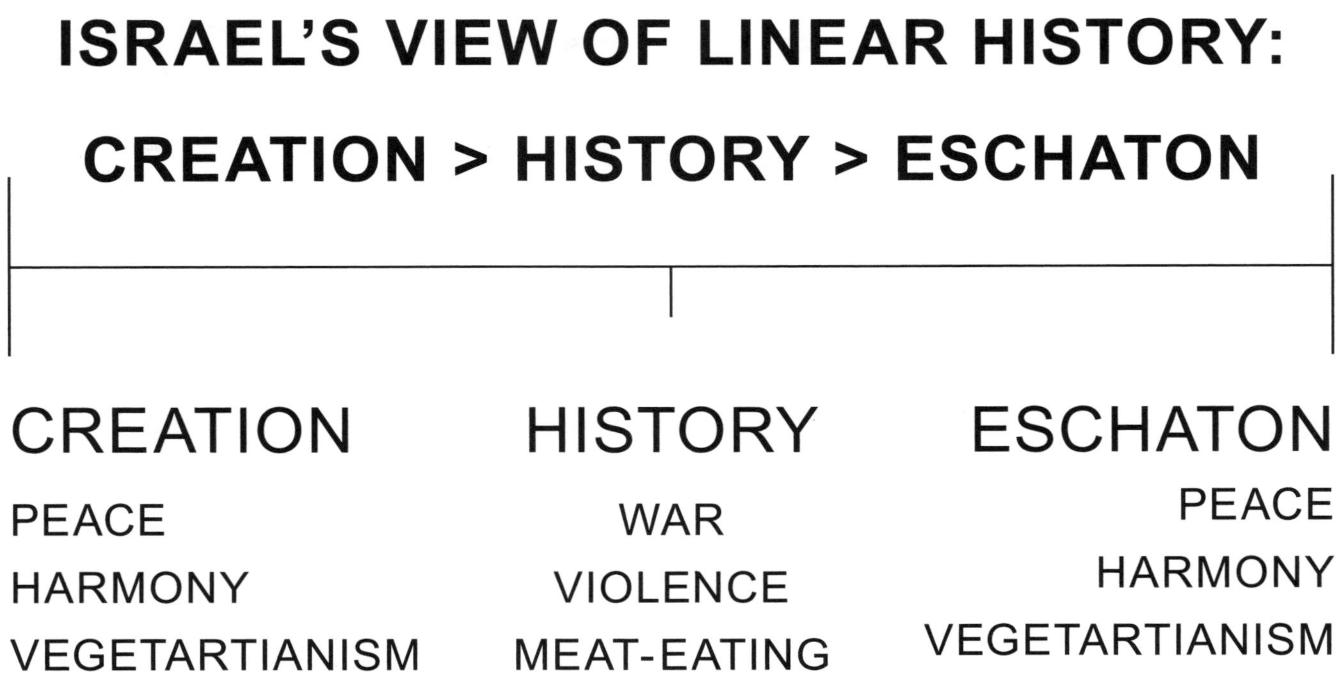

ISRAEL'S VIEW OF LINEAR HISTORY:

CREATION > HISTORY > ESCHATON

CREATION	HISTORY	ESCHATON
PEACE	WAR	PEACE
HARMONY	VIOLENCE	HARMONY
VEGETARTIANISM	MEAT-EATING	VEGETARTIANISM

fig. 2: Israel's view of linear history, as reflected in the Bible.

NOTES

[1] I desist from the JEDP discussion for another reason. I reject the idea that the narratives of the Torah should be divided into smaller parts, much preferring to treat the extended narratives as literary wholes, in line with the work of scholars such as Robert Alter and Meir Sternberg, who have written on the authorial style of the ancient Israelite literati. Naturally, one still must reckon with the many differences between the two creation stories enumerated above, so I do not mean to minimize these differences or to sweep the whole problem under the rug. But simply to ascribe one story to one source and the other story to a second source is a modern evasion, in my view. The community of ancient Israel read these two chapters as one story, and we should, too. See R. Alter, *The Art of Biblical Narrative* (New York: Basic, 1981); and M. Sternberg, *The Poetics of Biblical Narrative* (Bloomington: Indiana University Press, 1985).

[2] Other scholars who have noted the different viewpoints in these two stories include Joseph Soloveitchik and Jonathan Sacks, both of whom worked in a Jewish philosophical mode. See J. Soloveitchik, "The Lonely Man of Faith," *Tradition* 7:2 (1965): 5-67 (reprinted as a monograph: *The Lonely Man of Faith* [New York: Doubleday, 1992]), and J. Sacks, "What is Faith?" a public lecture available at http://www.chiefrabbi.org/faith/faith.html. I am most grateful to my dear friend Jane Slotin for bringing Rabbi Sacks's important essay to my attention.

[3] P. T. Reis, "Genesis as Rashomon," *Bible Review* 17:3 (June 2001): 26-33, 55.

[4] The vegetarianism inherent in Gen 2-3 is treated in detail by H. J. Lundager Jensen, *Den fortærende Ild: Strukturelle anaylser af narrative og rituelle tekster i Det Gamle Testamente* (Aarhus: Aarhus Universitetsforlag, 2000). I am aware of the existence of this volume through the review of Geert Hallbaeck published in *RBL* at <http://www.bookreviews.org/pdf/2716_1916.pdf>.

[5] See the article in this volume, S. Daniel Breslauer, "The Vegetarian Alternative: Biblical Adumbrations, Modern Reverberations, in *Food and Judaism* (Studies in Jewish Civilization 15; ed. L. Greenspoon et al.; Omaha: Creighton University Press, 2004).

[6] Mary Douglas, *Purity and Danger* (London: Routledge and Kegan Paul, 1966). The most recent treatment is in Mary Douglas, *Leviticus as Literature* (Oxford: Oxford University Press, 1999). It is important to note that there are differences between these two works, and that Douglas's approach has evolved over the course of more than three decades. In the following digest of her scholarship, I sometimes refer to her 1966 stance, while at other times I refer to her 1999 position. I do so, with personal apologies to my esteemed colleague, and with the hope that she will understand that in an essay such as this one, especially given its popular presentation, one cannot enter into in-depth arguments at all times, with a detailed treatment of the differences between the two works. Moreover, and most importantly, there are aspects of both treatments which I find convincing and which serve as support for my own position.

[7] My term, not Douglas's.

[8] The original work is L. Fourie, "Preliminary Notes on Certain Customs of the Hei-/om Bushmen," *Journal of the Southwest Africa Scientific Society* 1 (1927) (*non vide*). Lourie's work is cited by Claude Lévi-Strauss, *The Savage Mind* (London: Weidenfeld and Nicolson, 1966), 103. See Douglas, *Leviticus as Literature*, 23-24.

[9] My thanks to my former colleague Roald Hoffman (Cornell University) for confirming the accuracy of my statement here, especially given my woefully poor knowledge of the physical sciences.

[10] Douglas, *Purity and Danger*.

[11] See Douglas, *Purity and Danger*, 36-37; and a personal example reported by Jacob Milgrom, *Leviticus 1-16* (AB 3; New York: Doubleday, 1991), 720.

[12] W. Houston, *Purity and Monotheism: Clean and Unclean Animals in Biblical Law* (JSOTSS 140; Sheffield: Sheffield Academic Press, 1993).

[13] Douglas, *Leviticus as Literature*, 149.

[14] Milgrom, *Leviticus 1-16*, 722.

[15] B. A. Levine, *Leviticus: The JPS Torah Commentary* (Philadelphia: Jewish Publication Society, 1989), 243-48; and E. L. Greenstein, "Dietary Laws," in *Etz Hayim: Torah and Commentary* (ed. D. L. Lieber; New York: The Rabbinical Assembly, 2001), 1460-464, especially 1461-462.

[16] Deuteronomy 14 has a slightly longer list, with 21 different birds enumerated.

[17] See also the article in this volume, Jonathan D. Brumberg-Kraus, "Does God Care What We Eat?" in *Food and Judaism*.

[18] See the description of Anat drinking blood in *KTU* 1.96:4, from which we may conclude, via the doctrine of *imitatio dei*, that worshippers of Anat, i.e., the Canaanites, consumed blood as well. There is some doubt as to whether Anat is the subject of this difficult text, but regardless of this issue, the drinking of blood is clearly described. For a brief treatment and a translation of this text, see M. S. Smith, "*CAT* 1.96," in *Ugaritic Narrative Poetry* (SBL Writings from the Ancient World Series; ed. S. B. Parker; n.pl.: Society of Biblical Literature, 1997), 224-28.

[19] If one wished to follow this line of thinking a bit further, one might suggest that those animals which may be sacrificed, as indicated by the innermost concentric circle of the diagram (sheep, goats, cattle, and pigeons), are truly vegetarian. Within the middle concentric circle one finds those animals which are primarily vegetarian, but which on occasion also eat other creatures (I refer here to fish, ducks, etc., as per the above). I am not ready to pursue this line of reasoning, but I raise the point should the reader wish to consider it further. The diet of the three ruminants does not require comment, but since the diet of the pigeon is less well-known, I add the following: it consists primarily of seeds and berries; see W. J. Beecher, "Pigeon," in *Encyclopaedia Britannica* (Chicago: Encyclopaedia Britannica, 1964), 17.920.

[20] As in other languages of the world, so in Hebrew, there is some crossover between words for "deer" and words for either "sheep" or "goat." Note *'ayyal* [gazelle] and *'ayil* [ram]. The reason for such confusion is clear, since the horns of these animals often are quite similar. More than once I have had a student who has visited Ein Gedi tell me

that he or she thought the ibex easily visible at this location were deer, though in reality the ibex is a wild mountain goat.

[21] Thus Douglas, *Purity and Danger*; less so Douglas, *Leviticus as Literature*.

Food Fight: The Americanization of Kashrut in Twentieth-Century America

Jenna Weissman Joselit

In the annals of American Jewish history, July 11, 1883, is a day that lives in infamy. On that balmy summer night, hundreds of bedecked and bejeweled American Jews gathered together at Highland House, one of Cincinnati's most elegant establishments, to celebrate the ordination of America's very first graduating class of Reform rabbis. Spirits ran high as guests made their way into the glittering banqueting hall, eagerly anticipating a lavish meal. No sooner did they take their seats than two of the guests, themselves rabbis, hastily rose from the table and rushed from the room, creating "terrific excitement" in the process.[1] Expecting a "cosher" meal, they found instead a parade of unkosher foodstuffs, the customary bill of fare at princely dinners like this one: clams on the half shell, soft shell crabs, and frog's legs.[2] "No regard [was] paid to our dietary laws," reported an indignant Henrietta Szold, who, using the pen name of Sulamith, was in town and at the banquet to cover the festivities for the *Jewish Messenger*. "Would it do violence to the palate or the feelings of the majority to eat food prepared according to the laws of Moses?"[3] While Szold and several other kosher attendees remained at the table, choosing simply to refrain from eating rather than kick up a fuss, their abstinence made their shellfish-consuming tablemates uncomfortable, even hostile. "[We were] stared at as if we were mummies or fossil remains" and reminded that "this is the nineteenth century," she recalled hotly.[4]

In the days that followed, some pointed an accusatory finger at the Committee on Arrangements, a group of well-heeled Cincinnati Jews, charging it with a severe breach of etiquette. "It would be wanting in breeding and hospitality for a host to place before a guest such viands as he knows are disliked, how much greater then the insult for Jews to offer to Jews, to ministers, a banquet...where articles of food positively forbidden were at the table," related a gentleman who styled himself "Old Fogy."[5] Still others blamed the caterer. He was hired to prepare a kosher meal, related the *American Israelite*, hoping to absolve the Jews of Cinncinati, who were known for their hospitality, from blame. "We do not know why he diversified his menu with multipeds and bivalves."[6]

No matter where culpability lay, the event quickly became known as the "*trefa* banquet," underscoring the growing divide between those who kept kosher and those who did not. [7] As far as most of the guests at the banquet were concerned, kashrut, that elaborate chain of food-based rituals, had become a useless anachronism, an age-old practice entirely devoid of meaning. Insisting that the "mosaic ceremonial system," of which kashrut was an integral part, "speaks to us...in a religious language not our own," Reform Jews banished it from the table. Judaism, they maintained, was not a matter of cuisine but of conscience.[8] As the *American Israelite* put it categorically, in the wake of July 11th, "the American Hebrew's religion centres not in kitchen and stomach."[9]

The deliberate, purposeful disentangling of the dietary laws from definitions of Judaism and, with it, the jettisoning of kashrut from American Jewish daily life reflected a broad-based process of sweeping religious reconfiguration known simply as Reform or, more elaborately, as the "de-orientalization" of Judaism. By whatever name, this process affected everything from liturgical behavior and the calendar to the life cycle and its rites of passage. Anything that seemed to smack of oriental practice—head coverings, separate seating in the synagogue sanctuary, mourning practices, even bar mitzvah—was let go by Reform Jews determined to demonstrate that they were "Occidentals in every respect."[10] Nothing, however, epitomized the now-anathemized orientalism of traditional, rabbinic Judaism more than kashrut. Of this, Kaufman Kohler, one of Reform Judaism's leading theologians, declared in 1907, kashrut laws "are dead and buried for us and no power in the world can resuscitate them."[11]

Kohler's words seemed prophetic as a steadily growing number of American Jews from the tail end of the nineteenth century through the 1940s seemed to honor kashrut exclusively in the breach. "The question of kashruth today is a mooted one," acknowledged Mrs. Jesse Bienenfeld, a synagogue sisterhood leader, in 1939. "So many of us disregard the Jewish dietary laws yet we have no personal misgivings on that account nor do we seem to have our status as Jews questioned, nor our membership in the Jewish community challenged."[12] Their consciences untroubled, growing numbers of American Jews abandoned kashrut, their decision fueled more by pragmatism or even indifference than by ideology. In the New World, acting on what Rabbi Maurice Harris called the "freedom to observe and the freedom to neglect," many American Jews found it simply easier not to observe the "dietary injunctions." [13] And so, little by little, in households across the country, kashrut's importance diminished with the passage of time and the passing of one's more religious relatives.

And yet, there is another dimension to this story, a kind of counter-narrative, that focuses on the efforts of those American Jews who not only continued to keep kosher but who explained their retention of and affinity for this hoary practice in avowedly modern, twentieth century terms. Feeling increasingly at ease in pre-war America, a loosely bound coalition of rabbis, educators, and sisterhood women sought to make a case for the ongoing relevance of the dietary laws. To those no longer able or willing to take matters simply on faith, they argued that "kashruth need not be a burdensome affair. The substance of kashruth needs only to be made available in terms that are understandable." [14] To that end, proponents of the dietary laws drew on modern values and forms of expression—science, consumer culture, and sentimentality—to plead their virtues. Their efforts at reinterpretation suggest that far from being inimical to religious ritual, modernity could actually make room for and embrace it. Or, to put it another way, the modernization of kashrut enabled its adherents to showcase not just Judaism, but America too.

THE SEARCHLIGHT OF SCIENCE

When it came to demonstrating the viability of kashrut, its champions made sure to harness science to their cause. Through exhibitions and publications, they stressed the rational underpinnings of the ancient dietary laws. Take, for instance, the International Hygiene Exhibition of 1911. Held in Dresden, Germany, it was designed to bring before the professional world and the general public the "mighty acquisitions of modern hygiene." [15] Hundreds of public health workers, doctors, and scientists from the continent mingled with the local citizenry eager to spread—and receive—the gospel of "hygienic enlightenment." [16] "Our generation is in a hygienic mood," observed the event's organizers. "Man longs for an intensified feeling of good health and demands hygienic instruction." [17]

Mindful of the growing popularity of exhibitions and attentive to their effectiveness as a mode of both entertainment and education, the organizers of the 1911 exhibition celebrated artifacts at the expense of texts. "We wish the exhibition to appeal directly and forcibly to the eye," they explained, insisting on the use of "plastic objects," as well as on models, photographs, and drawings in place of documents, which were used sparingly.[18] Their hope was that the "attentive and intelligent visitor," when faced with a dazzling array of images—a "bad well" and a "very bad well," models of Babylonian drains, a display of pointy Prussian military hats, snug fitting bowlers and sleep top hats to illustrate the "heating and cooling" properties of headgear—would leave the exhibition "impressed with the wonderful complexity of the body and filled with the resolve to preserve this precious gift with care."[19]

The attentive and intelligent visitor also left with a great deal of information about the hygienic practices of the Jews. Two galleries in the International Hygiene Exhibition, known as the "Jewish section," were given over to a display of Jewish ritual matters.[20] In one area, visitors gazed at a table set for the Sabbath, replete with challah, candlesticks and a kiddush cup; in another, they encountered a display of knives ("real masterpieces of art"), some of which were used for circumcision and others for *shehitah* [ritually acceptable slaughter of animals]. A maquette of a bloodless heart of a ritually slaughtered animal rounded out the scene. A Torah, purportedly a thousand years old, was also on hand, from which visitors learned that Moses was himself a "great sanitarian." Lest they missed the point, visitors had another opportunity to learn more about Jewish ritual practice by observing the walls of the gallery, where they could find Hebrew and German translations from the Bible writ large, highlighting the Bible's "hygienic legislation."

Through it all, Judaism was portrayed favorably, as an ancient religion based on "scientifically justifiable principles."[21] The Sabbath tableau, for instance, demonstrated Judaism's sensitivity to body and soul. Its accompanying text panel allowed how this display, "apart from its interesting and folklore aspects, stands as an expression of the social thinking of an ancient people who made it a law to have rest on the seventh day of the week."[22] Kashrut, for its part, also came in for considerable approbation. Science, declared the exhibition, had proven that the "dietary laws of the Jews conform to the dietary as well as the sanitary laws of today; they have received the unanimous sanction of the medical profession and every unbiased sanitarian."[23]

What rendered the International Hygiene Exhibition's take on Judaism so arresting was not its novelty; after all, its line of thinking could be traced back to Maimonides. What rendered the International Hygiene Exhibition's take on Judaism so arresting was the authority on which it now rested—science rather than halacha—and its context, an international gathering of scientists or what contemporaries called a "parliament for health" rather than a rabbinic tribunal or a synagogue gathering.[24] Here, for all to see in 1911 Dresden, was tangible, visible proof that Judaism was actually a sensible religion: orderly, rational, systematic, and presentable. More remarkable still was that this exhibition of Jewish hygienic artifacts and practices took place at a time when anti-Jewish prejudice had received a new lease on life with the medicalization of anti-Semitism. Racializing various maladies from a stuffed nose and flat feet to syphilis as singularly Jewish ailments, medical men in Germany and Austria now insisted that distinctive ritual practices such as circumcision or kashrut had contributed to their etiology. In an era during which doubts about the physical assimilability of the Jews had come dramatically to the fore once again, the International Hygiene Exhibition's "Jewish section" served as a graceful, effective, and public rebuttal.[25]

Little wonder that these proceedings were followed closely on this side of the Atlantic. For one thing, Jewish newspapers such as the *American Hebrew*, a periodical usually not given to covering scientific matters, proudly carried news of the exhibition. For another, the exhibition also generated a number of related monographs, of which Noah Aronstam's 1912 text, "The Dietary Laws from a Scientific Standpoint," ranks perhaps among the most influential. In crisp, no-nonsense prose, Aronstam, a Detroit physician who specialized in what he liked to call "sociologic studies of a medico-legal nature," drew on the very latest findings in evolutionary zoology to prove that kashrut made scientific sense. Kosher animals and fish, he maintained with a great show of data, were not only easier to digest, they were also of "greater nutritive value than the scale-less inhabitants of the Neptunian kingdom" and stood higher on the food chain than those critters outlawed by the Bible.[26] When subjected to the "searchlight of science," concluded the good doctor, there was every reason to believe that the dietary laws were "in accordance with the doctrines of modern sanitation." When subjected to the searchlight of science, the Bible was without question the "pioneer of the sanitary sciences of today."[27] For those determined to establish the legitimacy of the dietary laws, what better proof could there be than that?

SHELF LIFE

In the years that followed, the conflation of kashrut with health cleared an even larger place for itself on the shelves of the neighborhood grocery store as leading American food manufacturers produced and distributed dozens and eventually hundreds of ritually supervised foodstuffs: from baked beans and white bread to gefilte fish, "hygienic matzoh," and beef fry, a kosher meat product that tasted and smelled just like bacon. By the interwar years, kashrut had become a big business. Thanks, in part, to the efforts of self-styled Jewish market consultants such as the New York based firm of Joseph Jacobs, the nation's industrial giants— General Foods, Procter & Gamble, and Heinz 57 Varieties, among them—became keenly aware of the existence and potential of the kosher market.

To persuade Heinz and others of the economic and cultural viability of the kosher consumer, Jacobs drew on both the claims of ancient history and those of contemporary sociology. Among the Jews, he explained in one of the many promotional pamphlets he produced to make Judaism understandable—and profitable—to corporate America, the battle "against disease and contagion is as old as Passover itself. To argue whether the Hebrews primarily regarded cleanliness as part of godliness, or whether they made it part of godliness to lend the campaign greater popular appeal, is as futile as to argue whether a chicken produced the first egg or an egg the first chicken."[28] Concern for the body, he intimated, had always been an intrinsic Jewish value.

It remained a modern one, according to Jacobs. Invoking the very latest market research, he pointed to recent surveys showing that American Jews were wonderful consumers. For starters, they bought more pharmaceutical products per capita than any other segment of New York's population. What is more, Jewish women purchased far more cosmetics than other women. Even though "women have always been women," the market consultant added, warming to his topic, Jewish women were "culturally prepared by traditions for a realistic appreciation of the value of cosmetics."[29] Much the same could be said of their appetite for food or what one authority called the Jews' "unusual recipe-consciousness." [30] Whether purchasing cosmetics or Crisco shortening (for which, claimed its manufacturers in a characteristic show of advertising bravado, the "Hebrew Race has been waiting for 4000 years"), Jewish consumers of both sexes responded enthusiastically to the mass production of kosher food products and the reassuring advertising copy promoting it. [31]

To ensure consumer loyalty while also allaying concerns about germs, canned kosher goods and packaged matzos routinely invoked the shibboleths of quality, sanitation, and cleanliness. "You may assure yourself against disappointment" promised Horowitz Bros. & Margareten, "by looking and asking for the package with the Red Shield of David inscribed therein." Their products were, they claimed, "kosher in the true sense of the word and leave nothing to be desired in quality or in cleanliness." [32] In no time at all, mass-produced kosher food came to connote healthy food produced in cheery, "sunflooded" factories and under the most rigorously hygienic conditions. [33] In language reminiscent of the International Hygiene Exhibition or, for that matter, the American domestic science movement (whose rhetoric likened the kitchen to a laboratory), matzo manufacturers were especially quick to extol the virtues of their "scientific baking." "We have raised the kneading and baking of matzoh from haphazard, careless, hit-or-miss to a science," crowed Horowitz & Margareten. "The temperature of the oven to the exact degree and the time of the baking in seconds as well as the thickness of the matzoh in fractions of an inch, are all noted. We bake by carefully computed formulae," the company further boasted, making the production of matzo seem much more like a high school science experiment than a millennial religious tradition. [34]

By taking the mystery out of matzo, America's food manufacturers also took the mystery out of kashrut and, by extension, those who practiced it, normalizing both. No longer was kashrut (or its adepts, for that matter) regarded as outmoded or outlandish. The Jewish dietary laws, explained General Foods in 1934, "may appear bizarre, some even fantastic, but one fact must be stressed...they are universally premised upon sound reason....Superstition, irrational belief, and narrow-mindedness have no place in Jewish observance." [35] Thanks to corporate America, kosher food had become as American as, well, apple pie. [36]

MAGIC CHARM

Despite the weight of science and the aroma of beef fry, another group
of latter-day kashrut champions preferred to leaven their arguments on
its behalf with emotion. From their perch in the kitchen and their
position as members of the synagogue sisterhood, growing numbers of
middle-class American Jewish women, for their part, increasingly moved
beyond the claims of science and hygiene to press those of sentimentality
instead. By their lights, kashrut was far "more than a matter of health
and sanitation." It was, they said, a "state of mind."[37] Invoking the
sanctity of motherhood, tradition, and history, proudly modern Jewish
women sentimentalized the dietary laws. The best way to preserve and
transmit them to the next generation, they felt, was "by the beautiful
expedient of surrounding food with the halo of religious associations
and with...magic charm."[38]

Kosher cookbooks and manuals on how to be Jewish in modern
America, many of them the handiwork of the synagogue sisterhood,
avidly promoted the sentimentalist approach to kashrut. Some went
further still, aestheticizing the practice and aligning it with bourgeois
norms of acceptability. A case in point is the *Jewish Home Beautiful*,
arguably one of American Jewry's most popular publications, having
gone though twelve editions in less than twenty years since its publication
in 1941. "Living as a Jewess," proclaimed the text, "is more than a
matter of faith, knowledge or observance. To live as a Jewess, a woman
must have something of the artist in her." [39] Kashrut, then, became the
implied medium and Jewish cuisine the means by which the talent,
artistry, and modern sensibility of contemporary Jewish women—
especially those aspiring to the middle class—could be unveiled.
Aesthetizing the practice of kashrut, and with it, the celebration of
Jewish holidays, *Jewish Home Beautiful* and other publications like it
promoted the notion that Judaism could more than hold its own in
loveliness, tastefulness, and contemporaneity.

Where others might view the dietary laws as needlessly expensive,
socially restrictive, and gastronomically inferior, the inhabitants of *Jewish
Home Beautiful* cheerfully sang its praises. "There's no need for a young
Jewish bride to feel sorry for herself or to envy her friends who don't
observe kashruth," Miriam Isaacs and Trude Weiss Rosmarin, authors
of *What Every Jewish Woman Should Know: The Intelligent Jewish Woman's
Guide to Jewish Life*, reassured their readers in 1941. "In culinary
perfection and variety, the kosher kitchen can well hold its own."[40] Or,

as another champion of the dietary laws ringingly put it: "In a Jewish home, a perfectly prepared meal, daintily served, is not enough. It may satisfy the physical desires and the esthetic sense but to be perfect, it must be kosher."[41] When seen from this perspective, kashrut, class, and charm were all of a piece.

In the end, however, whether seeking perfection, scientific legitimacy, or just a good meal, those who kept kosher remained a minority of the population. On the cusp of World War II, the overwhelming majority of American Jewry resisted arguments for kashrut; at best they consumed kosher food only on the holidays, prompting sociologist Herbert Gans to note that the commercialization of kashrut enabled the "prodigals [to] restore some kosher items to their menus without pain and effort...and [to feel] they are once again following tradition."[42] True enough. And yet, in their own way, those American Jews who continued to keep kosher did enjoy a certain measure of success. For one thing, they succeeded in taking an ancient and seemingly intractable ritual and adapting it to modern life, demonstrating in the process that ritual observance did not have to stand in the way of feeling at home in America. For another, they succeeded in standing on its head a powerful, multi-layered critique of Judaism as an antiquated, impoverished, and lackluster phenomenon. Recasting the dietary injunctions in alternately scientific, consumerist, or aesthetic terms, kashrut's devotees provided a contemporary and resolutely upbeat imperative for continuing and sustaining the practice. Perhaps Rose Goldstein, a kosher keeping housewife of the 1950s, put it best. In an article published in *Outlook*, a Jewish woman's magazine, she reminded latter-day readers of an eternal truth, a truth that transcends galleries, factories, and exhibitions, a truth that transcends science and sentiment, health and aesthetics. In the final analysis, Goldstein observed, a "balanced Jewish diet involves more than food. It calls for the intake and transmission of the heart of Judaism, the everyday spiritual values."[43]

NOTES

[1]David Philipson, *My Life as an American Jew: An Autobiography* (Cincinnati: John G. Kidd & Son, 1941), 23.
[2]The Unconventional, "Cincinnati Conventionalities" *American Hebrew*, July 10, 1883: 111; "The Jewish Press on That Trefa Banquet," *American Hebrew*, August 4, 1883: 151.

[3]Sulamith, "The Cincinnati Convention," *Jewish Messenger*, July 28, 1883: 6.

[4]*Ibid.*

[5]"Correspondence," *American Hebrew*, July 20, 1883: 114.

[6]"The *American Israelite*, quoted in "The Jewish Press on That Trefa Banquet," *American Hebrew*, August 4, 1883: 151.

[7]See, for example, "The Trefa Jewish Banquet: Letter of Sabato Morais to the Editor," *American Hebrew*, July 20, 1883: 114.

[8]Kaufman Kohler, "The Origin and Function of Ceremony in Reform Judaism," in *Central Conference of American Rabbis Year Book* [hereafter *CCAR Year Book*] (vol. 17; 1907), 210.

[9]The *American Israelite*, quoted in "The Jewish Press on That Trefa Banquet," *American Hebrew*, August 4, 1883: 151.

[10]Kohler, "The Origin and Function of Ceremony," 208.

[11]Kohler, "The Origin and Function of Ceremony," 210.

[12]Mrs. Jesse Bienenfeld, "Observance of Jewish Dietary Laws," *Outlook* 9:3 (March 1939): 7.

[13]Rabbi Maurice Harris, "The Dangers of Emancipation," *CCAR Year Book* (vol. 4; 1893), 61. David Macht, "The Scientific Aspects of the Jewish Dietary Laws," in *The Jewish Library* (2nd series; ed. L. Jung; New York, 1930), 219.

[14]"Why the Kosher Cookbook?" *Jewish Examiner Prize Kosher Recipe Book* (ed. "Balebusta"; New York, 1937), iv.

[15]"Programme of the International Hygiene Exhibition," Dresden, 1911, 7.

[16] *Ibid.*, 11.

[17] *Ibid.*, 10.

[18] "Notes for Contributors to the Historical Section of the International Hygiene Exhibition," Dresden, 1911, 2.

[19]"Historical and Popular Exhibition at the International Hygiene Exposition in Dresden," *Scientific American* 105 (August 5, 1911): 120-21.

[20]What follows is drawn from "Our London Correspondent," *Reform Advocate*, May 14, 1910: 576-77; "Jewish Hygiene Exhibition at Dresden," *American Hebrew*, September 8, 1911: 548; Max Grunwald, ed., *Die Hygiene der Juden* (Dresden, 1911).

[21]Noah Aronstram, *The Jewish Dietary Laws from a Scientific Standpoint* (New York: Bloch, 1912), 1.

[22]"Jewish Hygiene Exhibition at Dresden," *American Hebrew*, September 8, 1911, 548.

[23]Quoted in Aronstam, *The Jewish Dietary Laws*, 5.

[24]"Parliament for Health," *Survey* 29 (October 5, 1912): 3-6.

[25]On attempts to rationalize circumcision as well as kashrut, see John Efron, *Medicine and the German Jews* (New Haven: Yale University Press, 2001), especially Chapter 6, "In Praise of Jewish Ritual," 186-233.

[26]Aronstam, *The Jewish Dietary Laws*, 14.

[27]*Ibid.*, 4, 25.

[28]Joseph Jacobs, "Patterns of Health and Hygiene in Jewish Life" (n.d.), 6, 13.

[29]*Ibid.*

[30]Rumford Company, *What Shall I Serve? Famous Recipes for Jewish Housewives* (1931), 2.

[31]*Crisco Recipes for the Jewish Housewife* (Cincinnati, 1933), 82.

[32]"Has Matzoh A Taste?" *Hebrew Standard*, February 20, 1920, 7; "The Case for Horowitz Matzoh," *Hebrew Standard*, March 26, 1920, 7; Advertisement in United Synagogue of America, *Directory of Kosher Hotels, Boarding Houses and Restaurants* (New York, 1919), 8.

[33]I. Rokeach & Sons, *The Rokeach Recipe Book* (New York, 1933), n.p.

[34]"Has Matzoh a Taste?" 7.

[35]General Foods Corporation, *Customs and Traditions of Israel* (New York, 1934), 3.

[36] See the article in this volume, Joan Nathan, "A Social History of Jewish Food in America," in *Food and Judaism* (vol. 15; Studies in Jewish Civilization; ed. L. J. Greenspoon et al.; Omaha: Creighton University Press, 2005).

[37]*Jewish Examiner Prize Kosher Recipe Book*, iii.

[38]Betty D. Greenberg and Althea O. Silverman, *The Jewish Home Beautiful* (New York: Women's League of the United Synagogue of America, 1945), 88.

[39]Greenberg and Silverman, *Jewish Home Beautiful*, 13.

[40]Miriam Isaacs and Trude Weiss Rosmarin, *What Every Jewish Woman Should Know: A Guide for Jewish Women* (New York: The Jewish Book Club, 1941), 73.

[41]Deborah Melamed, *The Three Pillars of Wisdom* (New York: Women's League of the United Synagogue of America, 1927), 41.

[42]Herbert Gans, "American Jewry: Present and Future," *Commentary* 21:5 (May 1956): 429.

[43]Rose B. Goldstein, "A Balanced Jewish Diet," *Outlook* 27:4 (May 1957): 26.